SOCIAL BEHAVIOR

A Program for Self-instruction

SOCIAL BEHAVIOR

A Program for Self-instruction

Vernon H. Edmonds
Florida State University, Tallahassee

Donald E. Allen
University of South Florida, Tampa

Donald L. Lantz
University of South Florida, Tampa

Herschel E. Aseltine
University of South Florida, Tampa

John B. Adams
University of South Florida, Tampa

Leslie F. Malpass, Editor
Virginia Polytechnic Institute, Blacksburg

McGraw-Hill Book Company

New York St. Louis San Francisco
Toronto London Sydney

SOCIAL BEHAVIOR: A program for self-instruction

Library of Congress Catalog Card Number 66–26085

1 2 3 4 5 6 7 8 9 0 HD 7 3 2 1 0 6 9 8 7 6

preface

The primary intent of this book is to provide provocative and stimulating information about man's social behavior. Each major section of the book is concerned with a significant aspect of such behavior.

Since man is a social being, it is well to understand something about the social circumstances and events which are fundamental to his behavior. Consequently, Part 1 introduces major concepts about culture and society in general and about social stratification in American society in particular. Material from cultural anthropology, sociology, and social psychology is used to demonstrate how these social phenomena influence both groups and individuals. Criteria for distinguishing the major social classes are provided, so the reader can identify his own behavior and that of others according to this classification system. He is warned, however, that "all generalizations are false"—including this one.

Since man learns principally from interaction with others, the second part of the book presents material about social learning and social control. Behavioral and social scientists have formulated principles by which learning processes common to man and other animals can be explained and have found that application of these principles can be used effectively to modify behavior. On the other hand, there are some forms of learning that seem to be used primarily, if not exclusively, by man himself. Some basic principles of learning have been presented already in the companion volume to this program, *Human Behavior: A Program for Self-instruction* (New York: McGraw-Hill Book Company).

Because, in part, some users of this text will not have access to that volume and also because there is a somewhat different emphasis given to learning theory in this volume, an Appendix has been added which includes these basic principles of learning. The reader who is not familiar with learning theory should read the Appendix prior to reading Part 2.

The first unit in Part 2 deals with uniquely human learning processes, and emphasizes the role of symbols in learning, notably, the utilization of language. The second unit presents a unique and comprehensive picture of the broad topic of social control of behavior—the types of control men use and problems that are raised thereby. Knowledge of both social learning and social control is necessary if one is to appreciate fully the complexities of human behavior and develop ways for predicting and handling it effectively.

Among the most important molders of behavior in our society are the family, the school, and the church. The influence of these social institutions is analyzed in Part 3. Somewhat more attention is given to the family than to the other two institutions, in part because the family seems to be more basic and pervasive in its influence but also because of the wealth of empirical studies dealing with the family. The family, the school, and the church are representative of a larger number of social institutions, such as business associations, labor unions, and political institutions, which are not included here because of the major emphasis of the book and space limitations.

In the same way, mental illness, minority groups, and methods are presented in this text as merely representative of significant social problems. Each of these is presented in Part 4. When one realizes that people with psychiatric disabilities occupy more than one-half of all the hospital beds in the United States and that a significant proportion of all patients seen by most general medical practitioners suffer more from distress arising from psychological than physiological sources, it is easy to see why mental illness is considered one of the most pressing social problems in our society. As well, the prevalence of alcoholism, drug addiction, and mental retardation, and our relatively ineffective means for coping with such problems, suggests that a student of social science should be aware of the factors that operate in their development and potential control. Similarly, the deepening involvement of all segments of our society in the implications of the civil and moral rights of minority groups almost demands that this topic be included in a book such as this.

This self-instructional program, then, avails the reader of a description of significant social processes, institutions, and problems. Studies and firsthand observation document generalizations about social behavior. Some concepts are new, and some traditional data from the social sciences are treated in a unique manner. All the material has been carefully evaluated and organized to permit systematic study of man's social behavior. It is this latter emphasis which provides the unifying principle for the book as a whole.

Leslie F. Malpass

use of the book

This self-instructional program has been developed primarily for use in undergraduate college courses in the social and behavioral sciences. It is a companion volume to *Human Behavior: A Program for Self-instruction,* also published by McGraw-Hill. These books may be used as the primary textbooks for interdisciplinary courses or as supplementary textbooks in psychology, sociology, or education courses. In particular, *Social Behavior* may be used for introductory sociology or educational sociology courses.

If this book, in whole or in part, is used as a supplement to other conventional textbooks, it should not be used as a workbook. That is, the self-instructional material should be introduced *before,* not after, related material in a prose-type text. The nature of programmed learning indicates that the student will be better prepared to further his knowledge from other sources by reading this program first.

Thus, in presenting studies and concepts about social behavior in a programmed format, this book should enable the reader to learn related material from other textbooks more easily and effectively. It should also promote stimulating discussion about the nature of social science and about the fascinating topic of behavior itself.

The main sections of the program have been prepared so that they can be studied independently or in an order different from that given in the book. For example, Part 3 can be read without essential reliance on any of the other sections. Also, if it is preferred, the units dealing with social problems can be read prior to those dealing with social stratification. This feature maximizes flexibility of usefulness without destruction to the orderly presentation of topics which has been arranged. If used in its entirely, the prose introductions to each major section of the book serve as conceptual bridges from one area of study to the next. Thus, they facilitate the use of the book as the major reading resource in a sequential course of study.

Programmed Instruction in the Book

The contents of each unit in the program are developed along familiar lines, for the most part. The presentation of the major content material, however, is in the form of sentences or short paragraphs called "information frames," although introductions and summaries for each section are in prose style. Each of these frames has an important word or phrase missing, or else the reader is required to make a choice among alternative responses or to answer a direct question.

In the information frames, missing words are indicated by blank lines like this: ______. Missing phrases (four words or more) are indicated by +++++. You should have no difficulty in understanding the type of response which is required in each information frame. Furthermore, if you study the frames carefully, you will find that you will make very few errors. We strongly recommend that you write your responses to the information frames on a piece of paper. You will find it easy to "fudge" if you do not write the answer, and you will thereby lose much of the advantage of the programmed format.

In the left margin of each page is a column of answers. In order to obtain best results from the program, you should cover the column of answers with the mask provided when you begin each page. As you complete each information frame and write down your answer, lower the mask so that you can check your response with the answer. The requirements of giving an active response to each unit of information and then getting immediate information about the correctness of your answer are unique and significant differences between programmed instruction and conventional study procedures.

The frames given below illustrate the format used in the program. They serve to introduce you to the technique of programmed instruction.

1 In order to use this book correctly, you should cover the responses in the left-hand margin. Cover them now. Each frame in this program presents some information which requires a(n) ______ from you.

response (answer)

written

2 Do not uncover the answer which corresponds to this information frame until after you have ________ your response on a piece of paper.

phrase

3 A missing word is signified by a blank line. A required phrase of four or more words is indicated by five +++++'s. When you encounter +++++, you know that a ________ is necessary for the correct response.

answer (response)

frame

4 When your response is different from that given in the answer, check to see if your ________ is a reasonable synonym. If it is not, correct your response before going on to the next information ________.

principles

5 Programmed instruction is based on empirically derived principles of learning. There are several basic components of programmed instruction based on these ________ of learning.

programmed

6 Effective study is promoted by (*a*) the sequential presentation of information (*b*) in small units, each of which (*c*) requires an active response from the reader, with said responses (*d*) being confirmed or corrected immediately. The preceding sentence is a description of the basic components of ________ instruction.

If you cannot, reread frame 6 carefully.

7 Can you give the basic components of an effective program of self-instruction? +++++

As you read through the program, you will come upon bibliographical references in the information frames; they will be given in parentheses, usually including the name of an author and the date of his publication. A list of these references, given at the end of each unit, provides extended discussions of specific points made in the program.

At the end of each unit you will also find a self-review quiz with answers for each quiz given at the end of the book. These self-review quizzes have been prepared so that they cover the major points made in the unit and should be taken as often as desirable for study purposes. They should not only help you to review the material, but should also provide an index of how well you understand the material.

Review

Once you have completed a programmed unit, a quick and thorough review can be made by following these suggestions:

1. Reread the introductory paragraphs.
2. Reread the summary paragraphs for the subsections and for the entire unit.
3. Check the answers within the unit. If you cannot spontaneously associate a given response with a concept or bit of information, read the corresponding information frame.
4. Complete the self-review quiz. If you cannot answer an item correctly, go back to the program and study the relevant information frames again. You will find it advantageous to do this immediately.

By following these procedures, your retention of the material in a unit should increase significantly. Comprehension, not speed, is the *sine qua non* of learning. By reviewing carefully, you will find that both your retention and your comprehension will be facilitated.

Using Study Time Effectively

In using study time effectively, self-pacing is much more important than most people realize. Like any other textbook, this program will permit you to progress at your own rate. Research with this program indicates that some people take much longer than others to complete a given part. There will also be some variation in your own pace from unit to unit. It is wise, therefore, to find a study pace that is most appropriate for the time you have available. Do not try to crowd too much into one study period.

Most of the units consist of approximately two hundred frames which are subdivided into several subsections, each with a topical heading. A majority of college students who used a prior edition of this program found that they could study effectively from sixty to one hundred frames in thirty to seventy minutes. Consequently, an entire unit should take from about one hour to a little more than two hours to complete.

Most people find they cannot concentrate on programmed material for more than thirty to forty minutes at a time (and some people cannot do so for that long). It is recommended, therefore, that you do not try to complete any given unit in one study period. Rather, divide the unit into convenient sections for study periods of twenty to forty minutes each. If you review each preceding section before beginning the next one, you will probably remember better both the old and the new material. In turn, this procedure should make review of each complete unit much easier for you and thus enable you to use your study time most effectively.

Related Textbooks

A cross-reference to some textbooks in related areas is provided on the inside front cover of this book. Included are representative texts used for courses in introductory sociology, introductory anthropology, social psychology, and social foundations of education. The units in this program and the cross-listed chapters from these books cannot be used interchangeably, of course. The information in this book supplements and provides a different means of studying related material.

The numbers under each of the books in the table refer to the chapters associated with the topical units in this book. The full bibliographical references are given below:

Sociology

Broom, L. and P. Selznick, *Sociology* (3rd ed), New York: Harper & Row, 1963.

Green, A. W., *Sociology* (4th ed), New York: McGraw-Hill, 1963.

Horton, P. B. and C. C. Hunt, *Sociology,* New York: McGraw-Hill, 1964.

Ogburn, W. F. and M. F. Nimkoff, *Sociology* (3rd ed), Boston: Houghton, Mifflin, 1958.

Anthropology

Beals, R. L. and H. Hoijer, *Introduction to Anthropology,* New York: Macmillan, 1959.

Goldschmidt, W., *Exploring the Ways of Mankind,* New York: Holt, Rinehart and Winston, 1960.

Social Psychology

Krech, D., R. S. Crutchfield, and E. L. Ballachey, *The Individual in Society: A Textbook of Social Psychology,* New York: McGraw-Hill, 1962.

Newcomb, T. M., R. H. Turner, and P. E. Converse, *Social Psychology*, New York: Holt, Rinehart and Winston, 1965.

Shibutani, T., *Society and Personality*, Englewood Cliffs, N.J.: Prentice-Hall, 1960.

Social Foundations of Education

Cox, P. W. and B. E. Mercer, *Education in Democracy: The Social Foundations of Education*, New York: McGraw-Hill, 1961.

Kollenbach, W. W. and H. M. Hodges, Jr. (eds.), *Education and Society*, Columbus, Ohio: Charles E. Merrill, 1963.

Acknowledgments

The authors are indebted to students in various behavioral and social science courses at the University of South Florida, Florida State University, Southern Illinois University, Bucknell University, and the University of Tennessee. By responding to this and earlier versions of the program, they enabled this final revision. By making observations about programming style and content, they increased the quality of our effort.

Gratitude is also expressed for the able assistance given by teaching colleagues at these universities. Their keen analyses of the problems involved in translating traditional prose style into teaching frames were invaluable. Without their help, and the forebearance of our wives, children, and secretaries, it would have been impossible to produce this novel and, hopefully, stimulating contribution to social science.

contents

I

culture, society, and social stratification

A comprehensive understanding of man's social behavior would not be possible without a corollary understanding of the social milieu in which he operates. In its broadest sense, this milieu consists of his culture—the myriad of objects, events, institutions, arts, and skills which influence him directly and indirectly. At the same time, the human society of which he is a part must be considered. The study of culture and society is the special province of anthropology. Consequently, the first unit of this part is written by a cultural anthropologist, Dr. John B. Adams. He overviews in broad perspective some of the concepts about symbols and language, but goes beyond them to examine major components of culture from a biocultural point of view.

The second unit deals specifically with correlates of behavior which are influenced by the social stratum to which one belongs. Dr. Vernon H. Edmonds develops the thesis that social stratification is a determinant of behavior and cites many interesting studies to reinforce his point of view. Occupational prestige is of particular significance in European countries as well as in the United States.

Social mobility is an important corollary to social stratification. Whether a person is able to move up the social ladder depends to a great extent on the social class into which he is born, the opportunities available to him for vertical social mobility, and the effort he makes to exploit these opportunities. As you will see, studies cited in Unit 3 suggest that such mobility is not so open and free to all as popular legends and sayings would have us believe.

culture and society

JOHN B. ADAMS

1

Although, as a social science, anthropology is concerned with the study of man, it does not usually amount to that. For various reasons, some practical, some theoretical, some historical, anthropologists have confined most of their attention to a few aspects of the study of man. One of the most important of these is his culture. Anthropologically speaking, culture refers to the arts, skills, instruments, objects, and institutions of a group or society which distinguishes it from another group or society. In brief, it refers to shared ideas or shared behaviors. In this sense, it means more than "to refine by education," or some such other common definition.

Anthropologists sometimes like to examine "total" cultures. Hence, they have often turned their attention to so-called "primitive" or "folk" societies which are small enough, isolated enough, homogeneous enough, and self-contained enough to study as independent entities. Concepts of "ecological system," "social structure," "value system," or "pattern," derived from small communities are not often applicable to larger, more interdependent societies.

Nevertheless, anthropology has done valuable service in discovering the origins of man and his culture, in describing the development of these, and, especially, in describing the relationships between man, his culture, and his physical environment at least at the simple level where these relationships are vital.

This unit does not pretend to cover all the major areas of anthropology, but it does introduce the reader to some of the most significant aspects of culture and society.

Anthropological Approaches to the Study of Man: Some Definitions

1 The word "anthropology" (Greek *anthropos*—"man"—plus *logos*—"study") means the ________ ________ ________.

study of man

2 Anthropology is a natural science. It is also a social science. That part of anthropology concerned with the physical nature of man is a ________ science.

natural

3 When concerned with the works of man as a member of society, anthropology is a ________ science.

social

4 Culture includes all the works of man and all learned behavior characteristic of members of a society that is not biologically inherited. The anthropologist who is interested in the works of man is, by definition, interested in ________.

culture

5 An anthropologist interested in culture is called a ________ anthropologist.

cultural

6 Archaeologists are another type of anthropologist. They study extinct cultures or past phases of living. Men who scientifically study Aztec, ancient Egyptian, or ancient Oriental cultures are called ________.

archaeologists

7 Another branch of anthropology is ethnography. It is a descriptive discipline. Data collection and fact finding about mankind are the main pursuits of ________.

ethnography

8 Ethnologists are scientists who are concerned with the distribution of culture. If the ethnographer is interested not so much in describing individual cultures but in the development of and the distribution of culture traits in a large culture area, he is called an ________.

ethnologist

9 Like the ethnographer and ethnologist, the social anthropologist is interested in ________; but his major interest is in deriving scientific generalizations from specific data about human relationships. This latter interest he shares with the sociologist.

culture

10 In the broadest sense, social anthropology and sociology are closely related, for both concern themselves with human relationships. Their historical developments have been slightly different and their methods and techniques may vary. Sociology tends to devote itself to segments of Western society, whereas social ________ is more apt to deal with whole societies.

anthropology

11 The scientific study of language is an important branch of cultural anthropology. Linguistics is the term used to designate the study of ________.

language

12 That branch of anthropology concerned primarily with the study of language is called ________.

linguistics

REVIEW: *An anthropologist who specializes in the study of culture is called a cultural anthropologist. One who specializes in extinct cultures is termed an archaeologist. Data collection about the distribution of men and their cultures is the prime concern of the ethnologist and ethnographer; the linguist is interested principally in the study of language.*

Aspects of Culture and Society

13 As concepts, "society" and "culture" must not be confused. Society may exist without ________.

culture

14 In nonhuman societies, social interaction is largely the product of unconditioned responses. However, even conditioned ________ are largely the result of individual experience that can be communicated only through direct interaction.

responses

15 Many anthropologists define culture almost entirely in terms of shared ideas or conventional understandings. They refer to the behavior and the artifacts that are more or less determined by them as manifestations of ________.

culture

Ultimately, every society is composed of an aggregate of individuals. But Linton (1936) indicates that society is more than merely such an aggregate.

Two fundamental processes seem to transform an aggregate of individuals into a society. One is the adaptive behavior of individuals; the other is the development of group consciousness.

16 Let's review Linton's ideas about society. First, individuals ________ their behavior to others in the group. Second, Linton claims that society develops a feeling of unity with, and of belonging to, the society, i.e., a feeling of ________ ________.

adapt

group consciousness

17 Adaptive behavior depends in part on ideal patterns of interaction, and group consciousness depends upon shared values, ideas, and conditioned emotional responses. Hence, both processes are part of the ________ of society.

culture

18 The ideal patterns of interaction between members of a group or society are seldom planned intentionally. Rather they come into existence +++++ over a long period of time.

by trial and error
gradually

19 Members of a group teach these ________ ________ to new members.

ideal patterns

20 Thus such patterns persist through time, but they also change, though often less rapidly than the actual behavior of the members of a ________.

group (society)

21 Hence, one can seldom equate ________ ________ with actual behavior.

ideal patterns

22 Ideal patterns and shared behavior are two basic *concepts* of culture (Linton, 1936). One cannot assume that what an anthropologist is *told* by an informant is what actually happens. That is, neither ideal patterns nor ________ ________ necessarily represent reality.

shared ideas

23 We may conclude, then, that any concept of culture which sees behavior and artifacts only as "manifestations" of culture, or which sees culture as either only (*a*) ________ ________ or (*b*) ________ ________, is likely to be unrealistic.

(*a*) ideal patterns
(*b*) shared ideas

24 Race, physical environment, or the movements of the heavens are noncultural phenomena. Thus it would also be ________ to decide that culture is caused by these factors.

unrealistic

25 But noncultural factors such as physical environment greatly influence culture. To put it another way, culture is largely affected by the physical ________, such as the part of the country one lives in, the street on which one's home is situated, and even the home itself.

environment

26 Culture is also made possible by man's unique physical and psychological characteristics. His erect stance, which frees the hands for manipulative purposes, his unusually large brain, his flexible digits and remarkable hand-eye coordination are examples of man's unique ________ characteristics.

physical

psychological

27 Also important are the judgment, foresight, memory, and reasoning which are typical of man's behavior. These exemplify ______ characteristics which make culture possible.

REVIEW: *Society and culture are not the same, although the terms are often interchanged for convenience. "Society" refers to an aggregate of individuals; "culture" refers to their common attributes.*

Symbols, Language, and Culture

symbols

28 Man's unique ability to form and use symbols is another characteristic which makes culture possible, because a complex cultural pattern could not be transmitted from generation to generation without ______.

Signs and symbols convey meaning. The study of meaning is shared by many disciplines, such as psychology, philosophy, and anthropology. For example, Langer (1957) writes: "The interpretation of signs is the basis of unusual intelligence. Animals presumably do not distinguish between natural signs and artificial or fortuitous signs; but they use both kinds to guide their activities. We do the same thing all day long. We answer bells, watch the clock, obey warning signals, follow arrows, take off the kettle when it whistles, close the windows when we hear thunder. The logical basis of these interpretations, the mere correlation of trivial events with important ones, is really very simple and common."

sign

29 A sign stands for something. Many things can be denoted by a single ______, e.g., the ring of a bell.

signs

30 Hence it is easy to make mistakes in using ______.

symbols

31 Many animals use signs, but man is the only one who uses ______.

functions (uses)

32 A symbol stands for a concept of something. Logically, then, the difference between sign meaning and symbol meaning is that signs and symbols have different ______.

33 Culture depends on symbols. Indeed, culture, in the sense that it is a system of shared ideas, is a system of ________.

symbols

34 The commonest symbol system for the communication of shared ideas is ________.

language

35 It must not be supposed, however, that language has only a utilitarian function. What is communicated in poetry, for example, usually is not particularly ________.

utilitarian (useful)

36 There are other kinds of symbols perhaps equally important for culture. Sounds, rhythms, pitch, colors, lines, forms, textures, masses, images can be combined in different ways and combinations that have symbolic ________.

meaning

37 As in the case of poetry, it is almost impossible to interpret the meaning of the arts, myth, and religion from a merely nonsymbolic or ________ point of view.

utilitarian

38 Man is the only animal that makes noise for non-utilitarian purposes. Human infants apparently make noise for the sheer joy of it when they babble. Babbling has no obvious utilitarian ________.

purpose (value)

Langer (1957) writes: "A genuine symbol can most readily originate where some object, sound, or act is provided which has not practical meaning, yet tends to elicit an emotional response, and thus holds one's undivided attention. Certain objects and gestures, appear to have this phenomenological, dissociated character for some apes, as well as for man; sounds have it for man alone."

39 Hence, the sounds that infants make most easily have become verbal ________.

symbols

40 Language was probably not the earliest form of symbolism developed by man. Dance ritual to exemplify feelings of joy, anger, or desire probably developed earlier. Other forms of symbolism such as ________ quite likely originated in ritual dances.

language

41 Rhythmical noises including those made by the human voice (perhaps like the nonsense syllables found in much folk music) probably accompanied primitive ________ ________.

ritual dances

symbols (words)

42 Such sounds, dissociated from the actual occasion, can be used to denote a particular occasion, or what it celebrates. When so used they become ________ for the occasion or event.

dance

43 It is possible that the earliest paintings—rhythmical arrangements of parallel lines or equally rhythmical paintings of animals—were done in the course of a ritual ________.

creation

44 Perhaps some sort of fertility cult was a source of inspiration for this art, and perhaps the act of artistic creation was supposed to encourage biological ________.

symbols

45 At any rate, the rituals and the paintings symbolized the concept of something else, i.e., natural creativity. Hence, they fit our general definition of ________.

religion

46 There are many theories of the origin of religion. Fetishes were probably used earlier than the rituals in which they played key roles and may have originated in dream objects. The development of fetishes and rituals certainly preceded the development of ________.

myth

47 Similarly, myths may have originated in part from dreams which were retold until their merely personal images and meanings were eliminated. It is possible, then, that stories about dreams gave rise to ________.

symbols

48 Different forms of communication have been developed by man to symbolize his feelings and ideas. They include the dance, language, and various art forms. Another important function of ________ is to provide a sense of identity.

symbols

49 By enabling us to gain a systematic impression of the world we live in, ________ help us achieve a sense of identity.

REVIEW: *Most anthropologists have tended to view symbol systems as utilitarian in one way or another—for expressing some basic need for movement or play or to communicate some useful (utilitarian) patterns of behavior. Another important function of our symbol system is to permit us to gain a sense of personal identity.*

Broad Classifications of Culture

50 There are two broad classes of culture: material (tangible) and nonmaterial (intangible). Most of what we know about primitive man has come from analysis of the former, i.e., ________ culture excavated by archaeologists.

material

51 Much material culture is lost to us because it is perishable. Wooden artifacts are examples of ________ ________ that rarely survives the ages.

material culture

52 Our understanding of nonmaterial prehistoric culture is usually implied or inferred from recoverable items. Language, beliefs, ideas, customs, and all human knowledge are examples of ________ ________.

nonmaterial culture

53 Each of the two major classes of culture, ________ and ________, is composed of hundreds of elements or traits.

material
nonmaterial

54 The smallest identifiable bit of culture is called a culture element or ________.

trait

55 A knife is a culture trait; so is a fork. A chopstick is a Chinese ________ ________.

culture trait

56 To know that one person eats with knife and fork and that another eats with chopsticks tells us something about the ________ of each.

culture

57 If the individual with chopsticks eats rice three times a day and sits on the floor rather than in a chair, we have three culture ________ in association.

traits

58 A number of closely related traits form a culture complex. This book is part of a culture ________.

complex

59 The book complex is composed of such traits as paper, ink, binding, format, symbols, and even a reader, to mention only a few of hundreds of traits in the ________.

complex

60 A number of complexes in association form a culture pattern. The book complex is associated with the automobile complex, education complex, political complex, and many more to form a distinctive ________ ________.

culture pattern

complexes / traits

61 When we say that a certain group possesses a particular culture we usually mean that the group exhibits a specific collection of cultural patterns that sets it apart from any other group. These patterns are composed of ______, which, in turn, are made up of ______.

REVIEW: *The traits, complexes, and patterns are composed of both major classes of culture, i.e., material and nonmaterial culture.*

Culture, Ritual, and Religion. Variations in religious ritual and belief are reflected in part by the architecture of churches in different societies. The sixteenth-century South American church serves a poor rural community, while the modern Danish cathedral is supported by an urban, sophisticated, prosperous congregation. Each serves to differentiate the cultural group it represents.

62 Any group of people, no matter how small or primitive, possesses a heritage of cultural traits that number into the tens of thousands. Inasmuch as it is impossible to itemize every single trait, students of culture prefer to work with the larger units of ______ and ______.

complexes / patterns

63 These features, in significant association, help us distinguish the many cultures on earth today. They may be mapped as ______ areas.

culture

64 Area boundaries, however, are not razor-sharp, and wide transition zones normally separate the cores of culture ______.

areas

nonmaterial

65 Notions, attitudes, ideas, beliefs, and knowledge—all items of ______ culture—enable the people of a given culture area to have values and to make value judgments.

The value system of a people decides for them whether a thing is "good" or "bad," "valuable" or "worthless." By means of value judgments, people give significance to their natural (physical) environment. Some people consider a forest a useless and undesirable feature of the landscape. Others consider it of inestimable value.

value

66 People will not use timber from forests to build wooden houses if their ______ system is opposed to the idea.

REVIEW: *The above shows a relationship between wooden houses and ideas, or between the two major classes of culture, material and nonmaterial.*

traits

67 The superb mind of man has enabled him to concoct an infinite variety of cultural elements, or ______.

man's (human)

68 By studying tangible traits we can often make a close approximation of the intangibles contained in ______ behavior.

biological

69 Man has even modified the biological behavioral patterns that are quite similar to those of the higher primates. In most cases, we find that culture greatly modifies ______ behavior.

biological / culture

70 Digesting food is a biological trait, and man, as well as every other animal, must digest food. But culture often forces human beings into rigid patterns—setting eating times, foods, techniques, and etiquette. This is an example of the modification of a ______ drive by ______.

biological

71 Thousands of culture traits impinge on our ______ urges. This is true for every culture on the face of the earth. You might stop and think of a few examples for yourself.

surviving

72 Culture is worldwide, and is exclusively human. Every society has a "minimally satisfactory" culture in the sense that it enables its members to survive. Thus, if the minimal culture is inadequate, the group will find difficulty in ______. (For example, subcategories of food, clothing, and shelter—all related to survival. You can list hundreds.)

human

73 All the traits, complexes, and patterns tend to aid man in his struggle to endure on earth. Without culture he might have survived as an animal but not as a ______ animal.

culture

74 Apes are living proof that primates can maintain themselves with no culture, or at least with an absolute minimum of culture (see Washburn, 1960). Man *could* exist much like the other higher primates without ______.

REVIEW: *If man suddenly lost the ability to transmit his culture to future generations, man as we know him could not survive; his behavior would revert to lower forms of animal behavior. Thus, we can say that without culture there is no human behavior.*

Components of Culture

ideas (beliefs)

75 Many anthropologists agree that there are four components of culture, each dependent upon articulate speech. They are *ideological, sociological, attitudinal,* and *technological.* The first component is ideological, which suggests that this component deals with ______.

speech

76 The communication of ideas and beliefs from one person to another depends on articulate ______.

ideological

77 A belief that seven years of bad luck will follow the breaking of a mirror illustrates the ________ component of culture.

believe (expect)

78 A dog may be cut by a broken mirror and may ever after avoid mirrors. It associates a physical experience with glass. Other dogs will not make this association without first experiencing the cut. Humans may avoid a broken mirror because they ________ it will cut them if broken.

experience (association)

79 A human belief, then, may require no physical ________.

experience

80 In fact, a belief may be contrary to all sensory experience. A belief among a primitive tribe that the earth turns and the sun is fixed is actually contrary to sensory ________.

ideological

81 An association of beliefs may compose a philosophy. Human philosophies are a part of the ________ component of culture.

beliefs (ideas)

82 By this definition, then, a philosophy is a collection of ________. (This is admittedly a restricted definition and merely serves to make a point.)

believed

83 It is perhaps well, if not completely necessary, to point out that something is not necessarily true because it is ________.

ideological

84 Truth, as such, may have little to do with the ________ component of culture.

REVIEW: *The component of culture that consists of all beliefs, true or false, is the ideological component.*

society (sociology)

85 Culture also contains a sociological component, which suggests that this component deals with ________.

sociological

86 Rules, laws, institutions, and customs constitute the second, or ________, component of culture.

response

87 Some behavior may be taught with no verbal communication. One teaches a lower animal by primary reinforcers (such as food or pain) or by gestures. Such learning has been explained in terms of association between stimuli and ________.

communication

88 A child may be taught to eat at a certain hour simply by withholding food at all other times; but a human cannot distinguish a cousin from an uncle or grasp the symbolism of Sunday worship without adequate verbal ______.

sociological

89 Verbal communication (either oral or written) in turn implies interaction between two or more people. This is included in the ______ component of culture.

REVIEW: *The rules, laws, institutions, customs, and communications that regulate the social behavior of men are included under the sociological component of culture.*

learned

90 Attitudes (sentiments) constitute the third component of culture. As with the ideological and sociological sectors they must be ______.

attitudinal

91 A dislike of snakes, a fear of growing old, and attitudes toward sex are examples of the ______ component of culture.

REVIEW: *The three components of culture presented so far are the ideological, sociological, and attitudinal components.*

cultural

92 The fourth component of culture is technology, which greatly affects and is affected by the first three ______ components.

physical (external)

93 Technology includes all ways of maintaining human life, such as food production and protection. To some extent, this component involves adjustment to the external world. By the external world we mean the ______ environment.

technological

94 It is perfectly obvious that human behavior is directly affected by the ______ component of culture.

behavior

95 The acquisition of the bow and arrow, the horse, or iron tools by primitive peoples had a profound influence upon the social ______ of the recipients.

technological

96 If social organization is partially determined by technologies, then social change will follow ________ change.

behavior

97 The philosophy and behavior of a people vary as technology varies. Thus, rapid transport and communication have quite clearly altered American ________ in the past fifty years.

philosophy

98 Simple, primitive farmers do not share the same ________ with large-scale, mechanized, capitalist agriculturalists.

technology

99 Primitive philosophies, which depend on magic and superstition, flourish when there is a low order of technology. By its nature, ________ encourages rational thought rather than reliance on superstition.

magic / superstition

100 When technology is advanced to a point where nature can be understood and often controlled, there is little reason to rely on ________ and ________.

technology

101 Quite clearly, there is a relationship between the level of ________ and human behavior.

biological

102 A prime function of culture is to make life secure for the individual and to ensure that the species will be perpetuated. No subhuman animals have culture in the sense of our use of the term. They do sustain themselves through ________ behavior, of course.

cultural

103 In a real sense, humans perpetuate their kind by means of ________ as well as biological mechanisms.

culture

104 In addition to his biological characteristics, man has another mechanism to make his life enduring. This mechanism is ________.

technological

105 Man relates to nature through tools, food production techniques, clothing, dwellings, and utensils. These are all parts of the ________ component of culture.

ideological / sociological
attitudinal

106 In order to produce and use the technological devices of culture, human beings must make use of the other three aspects of culture, i.e., the ________, ________, and ________ components.

REVIEW: *In order to sustain life, then, culture serves to relate man to his physical environment. Man is related to his natural surroundings by means of the four components of culture. These are the ideological, sociological, attitudinal, and technological components.*

Recreational Pursuits Demonstrate Components of Culture. These scenes from a baseball game in the United States and a Spanish bullfight combine the major components of culture described in the text. The symbolism of the bullfight illustrates ideological aspects of Spanish culture, and both recreational forms are related to sociological, attitudinal, and technological aspects of the people who support and participate in these activities.

The Biocultural Viewpoint

107 It is perfectly obvious that man must deal with the external world. But culture also serves man's nonmaterial or spiritual needs by exploiting resources of the internal world. Hence, pride, courage, inspiration, confidence, hope of success, sense of worth, and comfort are examples of ________ needs.

nonmaterial (spiritual)

108 "Man does not live by bread alone" is another way of saying that man has ________ needs that are served by culture. Culture helps to relate man's two basic "worlds," the material and nonmaterial.

nonmaterial (spiritual)

109 The term "bioculture" suggests a relationship between ________ and ________.

biology (life) / culture

110 Nonbiological, or psychological, needs are as real to man as biological needs. Both types of needs must be served if man is to survive. It is the function of ________ to serve those needs.

culture

111 Man created culture and he is necessary for its continued existence. One would expect culture to be influenced by man's ________ nature.

biological

112 Biologically influenced cultural behavior and its converse, culturally influenced biological behavior, might be termed ________ behavior.

biocultural

113 Playing the piano, eating food, and waving goodbye are illustrations of ________ behavior.

biocultural

114 The symbolism for each of the above actions is cultural, but each is also solidly linked with man's ________ makeup.

biological

115 There seems to be a generic relationship between man and culture. The term "bioculture" expresses this ________ relationship.

generic

116 Though there is clearly a relationship between culture and human biology, i.e., a ________ relationship, there is no proof of a specific relationship between culture and any group of people.

generic

117 That is, a specific relationship would exist if your physical type disposed you to eat with a knife and fork rather than with chopsticks. The mere use of any eating utensil with the hands is a generic relationship; the disposition for a particular utensil illustrates a ________ relationship.

specific

118 Despite many physical types within the human species, man is a fairly constant biological creature in the sense that his temperature, his circulatory and digestive systems, and his other biological systems and processes are highly similar from group to group. Human culture, however, is quite ________.

variable (changing)

119 There is no proof that a particular "temperament" is inherited; but if there is such a thing as "Irish temper" or "Latin emotion," it illustrates the specific relationship between a particular people and a particular ________. That is, these examples of temperament would represent biocultural characteristics.

culture

120 The relationship between football as a game and the ability of a player to throw a pass illustrates ________ behavior.

biocultural

121 The biological aspect of a pass as a play in a football game requires a rotating arm, prehensile (grasping) digits, an opposable thumb, and binocular, stereoscopic vision. The general ability to throw, as a part of the game, represents the ________ relationship between culture and biology.

generic

122 Only people in certain cultures play football, but all people have the biological capacity for playing football. This illustrates the constancy of human biology and the ________ of human culture.

variability (differences)

123 Not everyone farms, but all people are biologically capable of such a technology. Different modes of food production reflect ________ in culture.

differences (variations, etc.)

124 Within the same culture, however, people may produce food in different ways, especially if they are strongly influenced by the ________ environment.

physical

125 We may recall that one of the functions of culture is to relate man to man; another is to relate man to his ________ ________.

physical environment

physical environment

126 We have been dealing here with three discrete classes of phenomena that may be separated for logical analysis but which in actuality are interlinked. The three classes are culture, biology (body), and ________ ________.

biology / culture
culture / physical environment

127 "Biocultural" suggests the relationship of ________ and ________. "Culturo-environmental" suggests the relationship of ________ and the ________ ________.

REVIEW: *Interrelationships and influences do not imply lack of choice. Man may and does make choices, and often they are illogical ones. But any choices he makes will be within the limits permitted by his culture, his biology, and his physical environment.*

Culture Participation

knowledge (familiarity, etc.)

128 No one can be familiar with every element of his particular culture. All of us, however, function quite well without complete ________ of our society.

understand (comprehend)

129 Even the simplest culture is too complicated for any one individual to fully ________.

elements
understand

130 We do not understand many cultural ________. For example, many of us do not understand how a neon tube or gasoline engine works. There are many others which we ________, although we may never be able to use or express them in action.

use

131 That is, knowledge or understanding of a cultural item does not necessarily mean that it will be put to use. Participation in culture means that our knowledge of a cultural situation is put to ________.

participates

132 When a woman dresses in accordance with the rules of the culture, she ________ in culture.

participate

133 A man may know all the female articles of clothing and the rules for their wearing, but he does not express this knowledge by action and therefore does not actively ________ in this aspect of culture.

subculture

134 It is possible, however, for a man to wear female clothing and thus to participate in a certain ________.

135 Most people will never orbit the earth, although many already know something of that segment of culture which deals with astronauts, NASA, missiles, capsules, and so on. It is apparent that one cannot ______ in all parts of his own ______.

participate
culture

136 There are many aspects of American culture that you have never heard of and never will. You obviously cannot participate in these. Participation is limited to a ______ of the culture with which you are familiar.

part (aspect, etc.)

Levels of Cultural Participation

137 Linton (1936) recognizes three levels of cultural participation. These are *Universals, Specialties,* and *Alternatives.* Action and ideas common to all normal adults *within a given society* are called "Universals." In the United States the wearing of clothing would be an example of a ______.

Universal

138 Some exceptions are permitted within Linton's scheme. Nudists may exist in a clothes-wearing society; even they wear clothes in public places. Within their own small subculture, however, nudity would be a cultural ______.

Universal

139 We see that a culture element may be a Universal in one culture and absent in another. Universals include a particular language, clothing style, dwellings, and social behavioral patterns. Some of these are not universal throughout the United States, and this fact suggests that our counry includes more than one ______ within its national boundaries.

culture

140 A Specialty is unlike a Universal in that it is not shared by the total population. Those culture elements which are *shared only by members of certain socially recognized categories of people within a society* are called ______.

Specialties

141 The practice of medicine, carpentry, or law represents participation in ______ within our culture.

Specialties

142 Although the skill (usually manual or technical) of a Specialty is confined to a small group within any culture, the benefits that come from the specialist are shared by the entire ______.

culture (society, population)

143 Not everyone can be a movie or television star or an astronaut, but everyone in the culture may share in any ________ arising from each.

benefit

144 Most members of a society have a good idea of what the end products of most ________ will be.

Specialties

145 Specialties appear in all societies and result from the necessity for a division of labor. Since basic divisions of labor are typically related to sex and age, in this instance, then, they are illustrations of ________.

Specialties

REVIEW: *Two levels of culture participation are defined by culture elements termed Universals and Specialties. Give examples of each. If you cannot, refer to frames 137 and 140.*

146 Alternatives make up the third level of cultural participation. Cultural traits *shared by certain individuals* but not Universal (common to all of society) or Specialty (common to all of a socially recognized group) are called ________.

Alternatives

147 When we wish to travel we may choose from several transportation ________ (bicycle, auto, plane, etc.).

Alternatives

148 Advanced, complex, and highly technical cultures like our own include countless thousands of Alternatives. On the other hand, there are very few Alternatives in primitive ________.

cultures (societies)

REVIEW: *The three components of culture studied so far are Universals, Specialties, and Alternatives.*

149 There is a fourth category of actions and ideas that lie beyond culture; that is, they are not shared. Individual Peculiarities technically are not cultural because they are not ________.

shared

150 Unless an action or idea is ________ there can be no participation.

shared

Cultural Universals, Specialties, and Alternatives. Dress and play are Universals, but their forms are demonstrated as Specialties and Alternatives. The three poorly dressed Mexican peasant children, who hold iguanas they captured to sell, have no choice in the clothing they wear. The Mexican city boy dressed as a folk-hero demonstrates that his family can afford to provide special clothing for his play.

151 Usually Individual Peculiarities are not transmitted. If they are, only a few individuals receive them and the traits soon drop out of the cultural stream. If a trait is accepted by the culture or a segment of the culture, it cannot be classified as an ________ ________.

Individual Peculiarity

152 Every person in every culture (modern or primitive) possesses certain Individual Peculiarities. In fact, every discovery and invention by an individual may be classed as an ________ ________ in the beginning.

Individual Peculiarity

153 Since every original idea begins as a noncultural (nonshared) Individual Peculiarity, we must be careful not to condemn every minority idea. Not only is the minority often right, but a minority of one may have discovered a new truth. Often an Individual Peculiarity may be culturally desirable while something shared by everyone, i.e., a ________, is culturally undesirable.

Universal

Specialty

154 If an Individual Peculiarity is accepted by a segment of a socially recognized group it becomes a ________.

Alternatives

155 Many Specialties and Alternatives differ from one another and lack cultural stability. The "Twist" and "Rock and Roll" illustrate what we mean by differences among ________.

stability

156 The older trait, "Rock and Roll," is threatened (at this writing) by the newer "Twist." When there are many Alternatives (as with dances) some will inevitably disappear. This illustrates the lack of ________ that occurs among Alternatives.

Specialties / Universal

157 Only a few Alternatives advance to the next level to become ________. Fewer still reach the top, or ________ level.

REVIEW: *The four major components of culture described by Linton are Universals, Specialties, Alternatives, and Individual Peculiarities. You should be able to give examples of each.*

SUMMARY

Anthropology is, by definition, the study of man. The field incorporates several specialties which analyze, respectively, man's customs, rituals, and material products (cultural anthropology), his remote and recent past (archaeology and physical anthropology), his characteristic ethnic groupings (ethnology), and his language patterns (linguistics). This unit emphasizes findings from cultural anthropology.

Culture can be classified according to nonmaterial and material objects. The former include attitudes, customs, and values which represent and motivate behavior. The latter include all types of man-made tangible objects, from axes to automobiles. This dichotomous classification can be broken down further to include four major components of culture—the ideological, sociological, attitudinal, and technological. Each of these components serves to relate man to his environment. The biocultural point of view emphasizes this integration of man and culture.

Finally, a useful way of analyzing culture is in terms of participation by its members. Thus, Universals are aspects of the culture respected or utilized by practically all members; Specialties are those used by only some groups.

Alternatives consist of things or behaviors available to most members but participated in by some, or used consecutively with other aspects of the culture over time. Individual Peculiarities refer to unique material objects or events; usually they are not transmitted, and if they are, only a few members receive them.

Anthropology, then, provides useful tools for understanding man's social behavior, the groups to which he belongs, the interests he develops, and the ways he devises to meet his material and nonmaterial needs.

SELF–REVIEW QUIZ

1 Anthropology literally means "the study of man." As such, in part it is a ________ science; in part, a ________ science.

2 Culture includes which of the following:

a. all characteristics that are derived from man's evolution and development

b. man's implements, skills, biological capacities, language, and housing

c. all of man's arts, skills, communication, transportation, and inherited capacities

d. all the learned behavior and products of man's efforts that are not biologically endowed

3 Learned attributes are to culture as aggregate of individuals is to ________.

4 A sign stands for something; a ________ stands for the concept of something.

5 The development of fetishes and rituals almost certainly preceded the development of ________.

6–8 Match the items 6 through 8 with the two broad classes of culture:

a. tangible (material)
b. intangible (nonmaterial)

6. Ashanti language
7. fashions in dress
8. this book

9 Culture is exclusively human; lower forms of animal life have no culture. Can man exist without culture?

10 There are three main components of culture in addition to technology. What are they? Can you give examples of each?

11 Not everyone fishes but virtually everyone is capable of this technology. Different modes of fishing represent variations within or among ________.

12 The biocultural point of view emphasizes interrelationships between man's biology, his culture, and his ________ ________.

13 Linton (1936) recognized three levels of culture participation. Supply the technical term ascribed to each of the definitions given below:

a. Actions and ideas shared by all normal adults in a given society.

b. Culture elements shared only by certain groups or categories of people within a society.

c. Culture traits shared by only particular people.

REFERENCES

Bournouw, V.: *Culture and Personality*, Dorsey Press, Homewood, Ill., 1964.

Eliot, T. S.: *Notes towards the Definition of Culture*, Harcourt, Brace & World, Inc., New York, 1949.

Goldschmidt, W. (ed.): *Exploring the Ways of Mankind*, Holt, Rinehart and Winston, Inc., New York, 1960.

Kluckhohn, C.: *Culture and Behavior: Collected Essays*, The Free Press of Glencoe, New York, 1960.

Langer, S.: *Philosophy in a New Key: A Study in the Symbolism of Reason, Rite, and Art*, 3d ed., Harvard University Press, Cambridge, Mass., 1957.

Linton, R.: *The Study of Man: An Introduction*, Appleton-Century-Crofts, Inc., New York, 1936.

Montagn, A.: *Education and Human Relations*, Grove Press, Inc., New York, 1958.

Sahlins, M. D.: "The Origins of Society," *Scientific American*, 203:78–87, 1960.

Washburn, S. L.: "Tools and Human Evolution," *Scientific American*, 203:62–77, 1960.

Washburn, S. L., B. C. Joy, and J. B. Lancaster: "Field Studies of Old World Monkeys and Apes," *Science*, 150:1541–1547, 1965.

White, L. A.: *The Science of Culture: A Study of Man and Civilization*, Farrar, Strauss, & Cudahy, Inc., New York, 1949.

social stratification

VERNON H. EDMONDS

One of the distinctive characteristics of human society is that people who are included within some social statuses are respected more and shown more deference than people who are included in other statuses. Although it is logically possible to have a society organized in terms of status and role without having differences of social standing, it seems probable that no such society has ever existed. The extent of social stratification within societies is highly variable; however, the United States, like all large complex societies, is so highly stratified that virtually all aspects of life are significantly affected by the stratification system. In this and the next unit we shall examine the characteristics of these strata, their sources, and their effects.

Major Criteria

top
bottom

1 "Stratification" refers to "a layer arrangement of things." As a minimum there must be a ______ and a ______ layer. There may or may not be intermediate layers.

power

2 In human societies such layers consist of differences of power, wealth, or prestige. Which of these types of stratification definitely occurs among both human and infrahuman species? ______.

power

3 Under certain conditions, chickens develop a definite pecking order. Usually one hen pecks all the others and is pecked by none. Another hen usually exists that is pecked by all the others and pecks none (Allee, 1938). This is an example of stratification in terms of ______.

wealth

4 If the food supply is quite limited, then such differences of power result in differences in the possession and consumption of food. In a rather broad sense, these hens can be thought of as stratified in terms of ________ as well as power.

power

5 In certain species of animals, such as baboons and elks, severe competition over mates results in the collection of harems which a male possesses as long as he can defeat his challengers. Such males are obviously differentiated in terms of ________.

wealth

6 Since some of the males possess much more of a commodity (namely, female mates) than others, the males are also stratified in terms of ________ in a rather broad and loose sense of the term.

prestige

7 "Prestige" refers to "the degree of honor or respect most people have for a known person or group." Although the "pecking orders" of sororities have striking resemblances to the pecking orders of hens, the sorority pecking orders are surely based much more upon ________ than are the hen pecking orders.

sorority

8 Although the deference order is very similar in both cases, it is never based upon who can hit the hardest in the ________ groups.

prestige

9 In short, stratification in terms of power is frequently found in nonhuman groups. When the members of animal groups are engaged in competition for something limited in supply, there is some stratification in terms of wealth in a rather broad and loose sense of this term. On the other hand, stratification in terms of ________ is probably exclusively a human characteristic.

prestige

10 "Social class" has been defined as "two or more orders of people who are believed to be, and are accordingly ranked by members of the community, in socially superior and inferior positions" (Warner and Lunt, 1941). Social class is thus synonymous with stratification in terms of ________.

Correlation

In order to understand the sources and consequences of social class, one must have at least a rudimentary knowl-

edge of the concepts of correlation and causation and be capable of making simple inferences from correlation coefficients.

A correlation is an index of the degree and direction of a relationship between variables. Correlations may be either positive or negative.

11 A correlation is said to be positive if the two variables increase or decrease in the same direction. In other words, a correlation is positive if, as one variable increases, the other variable also ________.

increases

12 As the amount of food a person consumes increases, his weight increases. Consequently, the correlation between weight and food consumption is ________.

positive

13 A correlation is said to be negative when the correlated variables change in opposite directions. A correlation is negative if an increase in one variable coincides with a ________ in the other.

decrease

14 As the amount of food consumed at any given time increases, the intensity of the hunger drive decreases. The correlation between food consumption and the hunger drive is ________.

negative

15 A correlation is said to be neutral when an increase in one variable is not associated with any change in the other variable. A neutral correlation is really ________ correlation at all.

no

16 As the height of women increases, the intelligence of their husbands remains constant. The correlation between height of women and the intelligence of their husbands is therefore ________.

neutral (zero, absent)

17 Positive correlations are sometimes referred to as "direct" correlations. There is a positive, or ________, correlation between a person's intelligence and the number of years he lives.

direct

18 This means that as intelligence increases, longevity (or life span) ________.

increases

19 Negative correlations are sometimes referred to as "inverse" correlations. There is a negative, or ________, correlation between family income and fertility (Winch, McGinnis, and Barringer, 1962).

inverse

20 This means that as family income increases, the number of children per married couple ______.

decreases

21 Just as length is measured by such numbered units as feet and inches, the direction and magnitude of a correlation is ______ by a correlation coefficient.

measured

22 A plus sign (+) before a number indicates the presence of a positive correlation. The correlation coefficient between a family's wealth and social standing in most communities is probably about +.75. This means that an increase in family wealth coincides with an ______ in social standing.

increase

23 A negative sign (−) before a number indicates the presence of a negative correlation. The average correlation coefficient for income and rate of admission to mental hospitals in United States urban areas is probably about −.75. This means that an increase in income coincides with a ______ in mental hospital admission rates.

decrease

24 The plus sign is frequently omitted from a positive correlation coefficient; however, the minus sign is never omitted from a negative correlation coefficient. A correlation coefficient of .75 necessarily means that the two variables are ______ correlated.

positively

25 The highest positive correlation is designated by a coefficient of +1.00. This means that a given increase in one variable coincides with a definite and predictable ______ in the other variable.

increase

26 If the correlation coefficient were computed for the following fictional table, would it be a +1.00?

No

Food consumed per day, lb	*Weight, lb*
.5	100
1.0	110
1.5	120
2.0	120
2.5	140
3.0	150

27 In order for the correlation to be +1.00, the person who consumes 2 pounds of food per day would have to weigh ______ pounds.

130

28 If the person who ate 2 pounds of food per day weighed 130 pounds, could one predict exactly how much a person would weigh by knowing the amount of food consumed? ________.

Yes

29 A correlation coefficient of -1.00 means that a given increase in one variable coincides with a definite and predictable ________ in the other variable.

decrease

30 A correlation coefficient of -1.00 is therefore the ________ negative correlation coefficient that one can obtain.

highest

31 If a correlation coefficient were computed for the following set of fictional data, would it be -1.00? ________.

Yes

Weight of executives' wives, lb	*No. of executive flirtations with secretaries per week*
80	5
90	4
100	3
110	2
120	1
130	0

32 The percentage of variation in one variable that is "determined" by variation in the other variable is obtained by squaring the correlation coefficient.[1] In the foregoing fictional illustration, what percentage of the variation in frequency of flirting with secretary is determined by weight of wife? ________.

100 ($-1.00 \times -1.00 = 1.0000 = 100$ percent)

33 The correlation coefficients between scholastic aptitude measures and grade point average in college average about $+.45$. What percentage of the variation in grade point average is determined by scholastic aptitude? ________.

20 ($+.45 \times +.45 = .2025 = 20.25$ percent)

[1] Variation in one variable can be determined by variation in the other variable in either a logical-mathematical or causal sense. The causal relationship must always be inferred from information in addition to that given in the correlation coefficient. Causal relationships are assumed here for illustrative purposes. Whether the assumptions are correct is not important at this point.

56 ($-.75 \times -.75 = .5625 = 56.25$ percent)

34 In one study (Clark, 1953), the coefficient of correlation between average incomes for given occupations and the rate of admission to mental hospitals as psychotics was −.75. Occupational income "determines" about ________ percent of the variation of "insanity" rates.

Correlation and Causation

cause

35 Perhaps the simplest definition of "cause" consists of equating the term with "the antecedent of an invariant sequence." If X is always followed by Y, then X is said to be the ________ of Y.

cause

36 If frustration is always followed by hostility, then frustration is, by this definition, appropriately called the ________ of hostility.

sequence

37 In the primitive or commonsense notion of "cause," an element of vaguely conceived "force" or "compulsion" is added to the mere occurrence of a ________.

does not

38 The invariant sequence definition of cause (does/does not) correspond to the primitive or commonsense definition of cause.

cause

39 A stone falling into a pool of water is always followed by waves. The plunge of the stone would be labeled the ________ of waves by people operating with the commonsense notion of cause.

sequence

40 Likewise, with the commonsense notion of cause, a cue stick striking a billiard ball would be thought of as the cause of the ball's movement. In this case, as in the preceding one, one only *observes* a ________ but not the "compelling force" entailed in the primitive concept of cause.

compelling forces

41 Hence, one of the basic difficulties of utilizing the primitive or commonsense notion of cause is that the element of ________ ________ is not detectable by sensory means.[2]

cannot

42 Definitions (can/cannot) be true or false. However, different definitions have different logical consequences.

[2] This becomes especially apparent when one deals with the physics of light or magnetism or, for that matter, with many of the aspects of human behavior.

detectable (ascertainable, etc.)

43 The antecedent of an invariant sequence is used as the reference of cause in this and the next unit. This definition is preferred because the compelling force reference of the commonsense notion of cause is not ________ by any kind of observation.

No[3]

44 If one rubs a standard wooden match across a solid surface, the head of it usually, but not always, bursts into flame. Is rubbing the match against the solid surface the cause of the flame? ________.

No[4]

45 If one puts a nickel into the coin slot of a gum delivery machine and pulls the appropriate knob, a package of gum usually, but not always, falls into the receptacle. Is this a cause-and-effect relationship? ________.

In order to discover a more invariant relationship in the "match-rubbing → flame" sequence, we would have to note other conditions present when the flame occurs and absent when it does not occur. With enough observation, we would discover a number of conditions that are normally, but not always, present, such as dry surface, rough surface, dry match, etc. We might arrive, then, at some highly qualified statement which would look something like this: "If one rubs a dry match against a dry, rough, solid surface with pressure X, distance Y, and speed Z, then the match will burst into flame."

Yes[5]

46 Could we now have an invariant sequence that could fit our definition of cause? ________.

invariant

47 It should be apparent that very few sequences we discover are going to be ________.

[3] Most people would certainly say "Yes." However, since the sequence is not invariable it would not, in a strict sense, qualify as a cause-and-effect relationship by the first definition.

[4] Again, one would normally say "Yes." Again, the sequence is not invariable, so it does not, strictly speaking, qualify as a cause-and-effect relationship by the first definition.

[5] There might, of course, be failures of the sequence owing to the absence of events that are so constant as to normally escape our detection. Some matches might have changed sufficiently in chemical content to make them uninflammable; temperatures might fall sufficiently below those used in establishing the sequence to prevent its recurring, etc.

cause

48 However, this surely does not mean that such sequences as we have mentioned have no causal relationship. What we have usually discovered when we carelessly labeled something the cause of something else is that it would be more accurate to label it one of the more important parts of the ________ of the event.

parts (components)

49 That particular part or component is important because it is much more variable than other ________ which may remain so constant as to escape our attention or even our ability to discover them.

invariant

50 These relatively constant conditions of the occurrence of an event are frequently referred to as "underlying conditions." If these conditions were completely constant and always present, we would find it easy to discover ________ sequences.

variable

51 These underlying conditions make the pursuit of invariant sequences troublesome because they are both numerous for many sequences and occasionally absent from, or ________ within, the antecedent conditions.

parts (components, etc.)

52 Strictly speaking, we are thus practically forced to deal not with the cause of an event, but rather with ________ of the cause.

underlying conditions

53 Our formulations of causal propositions, consequently, are usually of this form: "If X_1, X_2, X_3, and X_4 occur, then Y very probably will occur." In making this statement, we almost always ignore some of the ________ ________ that are so constant as to escape our attention or concern.

variation

54 It frequently happens that a variation of an event is always followed by a ________ of another event.

occur

55 In such cases, events vary rather than merely ________ as is sometimes the case.

correlation

56 If we measured the direction and the magnitude of covarying event classes, we would have a positive or negative ________ coefficient.

If two event classes (A and B) are known to be correlated, there are four generic causal possibilities:

1. *A is the cause or a part of the cause of B or contains within itself the cause or a part of the cause of B.*

2. *B is the cause or a part of the cause of A or contains within itself the cause or a part of the cause of A.*
3. *A and B are the cause or a part of the cause or contain within themselves the cause or a part of the cause of each other.*
4. *Some other event(s) is/are the cause or a part of the cause of A and B.*

57 It is sometimes maintained that there is another possibility, namely, no causal relationship between the variables. Is this a logical possibility? ________.

No[6]

58 Consider the alleged fifth alternative, namely, that two classes of events can be correlated but not causally related. This would imply that certain changes in event class A could always be followed by certain changes in event class B and still not be ________ related in any way.

causally

59 The "chance" alternative in such a situation is logically impossible unless cause is used in its ________ sense where some element of compelling force is inferred.

primitive

60 The antecedent event class of any invariant sequence is, by definition, the ________ of the following event class whether the concomitance involves variation or mere occurrence of the events.

cause

61 If we combine our definitions with the assumption that all variations are preceded by variations and that sampling error is not involved, then a correlation implies some type of ________ relationship.

causal

62 One frequently hears that correlation coefficients tell one nothing about causation. Is this true? ________.

No[7]

63 A number of studies have disclosed a high negative correlation between psychoses rates and social class. Letting C stand for "social class," P stand for "psychoses rates," → stand for "is the cause or a part of the cause of," and X stand for "some other event(s)," we can diagram the logical causal possibilities. (Do this yourself.)

(1) C → P
(2) P → C
(3) C ⇄ P
(4) X → C and P

[6] If one is using "cause" to refer to a temporal sequence and one is dealing with event classes of a population, the answer is "No."

If one is using "cause" in its primitive sense or dealing with two specific and unique events, then the answer is "Yes."

[7] If one is dealing with a correlation coefficient, event classes, rather than the concomitance of two specific and unique events, are necessarily involved. Ignoring gross sampling errors, which may be involved but can usually be detected and eliminated, there are no more than four generic logical causal possibilities. Furthermore, additional information frequently and substantially reduces this number.

You should have crossed out options 2 and 3.

64 It is known that a person's social class is determined before he develops or does not develop a psychosis (Hollingshead and Redlich, 1958). (See response 63. Cross out the logical causal possibilities that are eliminated by this information.)

1 and 4[8]

65 Only two logical causal possibilities remain. What are they? ________. (See response 63.)

A special hypothesis, related to the fourth alternative, is that people who are so constituted by hereditary or environmental traits as to make them upwardly mobile also possess hereditary or environmental traits that make them relatively resistant to the development of a psychosis. From one study (Myers and Roberts, 1959) there can be little question that psychotic patients are much more prone to status striving and are actually much more upwardly mobile than their nonpatient siblings.

disconfirms

66 This fact ________ the hypothesis that upwardly mobile people are especially free of psychotic tendencies.

disconfirms

67 Sometimes the special hypothesis, related to option 4, is that hereditary qualities which increase chances for upward mobility also reduce the chances for developing psychotic behavior. The same fact, namely, that upwardly mobile persons have a higher psychosis rate than their nonmobile siblings, ________ this hypothesis.

one

68 We can now tentatively cross out option number 4, which leaves us with ________ generic logical causal possibility out of the original four.

(1) $I \rightarrow C$
(2) $C \rightarrow I$
(3) $I \rightleftarrows C$
(4) $X \rightarrow I$ and C

69 In another study (Mayer and Hoult, 1955), a high inverse correlation was obtained between family income (I) and Korean War casualty rates (C). Without considering any information that would constitute evidence for reducing the logical causal possibilities, diagram the logical causal possibilities of the correlation per se.

2 / 3

70 We know, of course, that the family's income was ascertained before the men entered the armed services. Consequently, options ________ and ________ can be crossed out, leaving us with two logical causal possibilities.

[8] Either certain conditions more prevalent in lower-class life are the cause or a part of the cause of psychoses, or some unknown variables are the cause or a part of the cause of both social class and psychoses.

71 To the author's knowledge, there is no information that would enable one to rule out either of the two remaining logical causal possibilities. However, if one uses quite a bit of indirect factual information, the most plausible hypothesis appears to be that family income is highly correlated with certain occupational aptitudes and achievements that, if utilized in the Armed Forces, would place persons in positions of differential risk of life. If so, then family income could largely determine occupational aptitudes and achievements and indirectly chances of being killed. Which option is symbolized by this contingency?
1 ________.

72 Where the person who subsequently enters the Armed Forces has established independent residence, it seems likely that the education and training needed for his occupation determine both the family income and his chance of being killed by virtue of affecting his placement in high- or low-risk military positions. This, of course, is
4 option number ________.

73 In any case, correlation coefficients do tell one something
four thing about causation. There are at most ________ generic logical causal possibilities.

74 If a temporal separation of the correlated event classes can be ascertained, the number of logical causal
two possibilities can be further reduced to ________.

75 It also frequently happens that additional information will reduce the logical causal possibilities to only
one ________.

Social Class Determinants

76 From studies of many different societies, it would seem that an elaborate division of labor, or more appropriately, *occupational specialization,* is the one thing that is always present in an elaborately stratified society
occupational special- and always absent from societies with little stratification.
ization This indicates that ________ ________ is both a necessary and sufficient condition of the development of social classes.

77 In other words, the organization of society in terms
occupational of ________ statuses and roles seems to be the cause of social stratification along the dimension of prestige.

occupation

78 This would suggest that a person's social class, if he is an adult male, is largely determined by his ________.

family

79 If the prestige of the family head is transferred to the whole family, as it is in communities where family affiliation is widely known, the basic unit of stratification is the ________ group.[9]

occupation

80 The social class of children and housewives is, to a very substantial extent, determined directly by their family membership and indirectly by the ________ of the family head.

In a number of studies made by Warner and associates (1949), a presumably valid measure of the social standing of families, as determined by evaluation of them by a representative sample of the community in which they lived, was correlated with such variables as income, source of income, prestige of the family head's occupation, house type, and type of dwelling. The presumably valid measure of social class correlated more highly with occupational prestige of the family head than with any other measured variable.

most

81 This indicates that occupation of the family head is the ________ important determinant of social class in America.

81

82 In a number of studies, the correlation coefficients between occupational rank of the family head and the social rank of the family averaged about +.90. Assuming that occupation of the family head is the independent variable, about ________ percent of the variation in social class of families is determined by the occupational prestige variations of family heads.

wealth
60 (59.29 to be exact)[10]

83 In one study a combined index of total wealth was correlated with a measure of social status and a coefficient of +.77 was obtained (Lenski, 1952). It would seem that, in this community, variations in total ________ determined about ________ per cent of the variation in prestige of families.

[9] For illustrations and evidence of this phenomenon, see, especially, A. B. Hollingshead, *Elmtown's Youth,* John Wiley & Sons, Inc., New York, 1949.

[10] In this and in subsequent computations of variance relationships rounded-off figures will be used. If the reader gets within a few percentage points, this is accurate enough.

84 A number of other studies have yielded correlation coefficients ranging from about +.60 to about +.80 between measures of wealth and measures of family prestige. It seems that the amount of variance of family social standing accounted for by variations in family wealth is little less than ______ percent and little more than ______ percent.

36
64

85 The average of these coefficients between family wealth and family prestige seems to be fairly close to +.70. Making a rough statistical estimate, we find that the amount of variation in social class in the United States that is apparently determined by variations in wealth is about ______ percent.

50

86 In another study "judged class" was correlated with education of the family head and a rather complicated measure of the prestige of residential areas in New Haven, Connecticut (Hollingshead and Redlich, 1958). The coefficients were, respectively, .78 and .69. Assuming judged class to be a valid measure of social class and the dependent variable in this correlation, about ______ percent of its variance is determined by education of the family head and about ______ percent by the family's place of residence.

60

47

87 If one combines the presumably determining influences of both *residence* and *education,* ______ 100 percent of the variance of social class is accounted for.

over (more than)

88 This is a common result of combining correlation coefficients. It means that the independent variables, in this case, residence and education, are ______ with each other in addition to being correlated with the dependent variable, in this case, judged class.

correlated

89 The impact of one independent variable upon a dependent variable while the other independent variables are held constant can be approximately determined by a statistical procedure known as "partial correlation." Since learning this procedure is beyond the limits of this unit, you should avoid trying to make a meaningful combination of correlated ______ ______ insofar as the percentage of variance of the dependent variable is concerned.

independent variables

REVIEW: *From these studies, one can conclude that occupational prestige of the family head is the most impor-*

tant determinant of a family's social standing in a community.

Occupational Prestige

prestige

90 Education of the family head and wealth possessed by the family are apparently of about equal importance. Both are apparently less important than the ________ of the family head's occupation.

dependent

91 These generalizations concerning the sources of family prestige in the United States assume that: (*a*) the samples studied are representative of the American population, (*b*) the sources of prestige in the communities studied are similar to the sources of prestige in other American communities, and (*c*) family prestige is the (dependent/independent) variable.

social class

92 Since the prestige of the occupation of the family head is the most important direct determinant of a family's social class, knowledge of the determinants of occupational prestige will provide us with knowledge of the indirect determinants of a family's ________ ________.

indirect determinant

93 If, for example, the amount of education or training for entrance into an occupation is highly correlated with occupational prestige, then the amount of education or training required for entrance into an occupation is probably an important ________ ________ of the social class position of the family head and, consequently, of the family.

correlate

94 The determinants of occupational prestige should be those occupational characteristics which ________ highest with occupational prestige.

correlated

95 Table 1 contains a summary of four studies in which ratings of occupations in terms of certain characteristics are ________ with prestige ratings of the same occupations.

cause

96 It is, of course, possible for something to be highly correlated with occupational prestige and still not be a part of the ________ of occupational prestige.

correlated

97 Nonetheless, it is still true that *if* something is an important source of occupational prestige, then it must be moderately or highly ________ with occupational prestige.

Table 1. Comparison of Occupational Prestige-trait Correlations of Four Studies

Occupational trait	*Osgood and Stagner*	*Attneave*	*Baudler*	*Garbin and Bates*
Intrinsic nature of the work:				
Dealing more with people than with things		.64		.49
Honorable and morally good work				.75
Interesting and challenging work	.99			.90
Service to humanity an essential			.60	.59
Work calls for originality and initiative		.93		.87
Intellectual and training requirements:				
Education required				.83
Education and training required		.95	.86	
Intelligence required	.96			.90
Scarcity of personnel who can do the job				.90
Training required				.84
Individual independence in the work situation:				
Being one's own boss		.70	.65	.57
Free time on the job				.15
The working conditions:				
Clean work			.46	.51
Flexible working hours			.50	.44
Safe work				.35
Interpersonal relations:				
Having an influence over others			.90	.86
Regarded as desirable to associate with			.96	.84
Responsibility to supervise others		.82		.79
Rewards of the work:				
Income	.97	.94	.85	.78
Opportunities for advancement		.84		.71
Security	.79		.22	.79

SOURCE: A. P. Garbin and F. L. Bates, "Occupational Prestige: An Empirical Study of Its Correlates," *Social Forces*, 40:135, December, 1961. Used by permission.

work / interesting
challenging

98 In the study by Osgood and Stagner (1941), the occupational characteristic most highly correlated with occupational prestige involves the intrinsic nature of one's ________ and specifically consists of how ________ and ________ one's work is.

intellectual and training requirements
education / training

99 In the study by Attneave (1951), the occupational characteristic most highly correlated with occupational prestige involves +++++ and consists, more specifically, of the amount of ________ and ________ required for entrance into the occupation.

interpersonal relations
desirable to associate with

100 In the study by Baudler (1956), the occupational characteristic most highly correlated with occupational prestige involves ________ ________, and specifically consists of the extent that people in given occupations are considered +++++.

interesting / challenging / intelligence
scarcity

101 In the study by Garbin and Bates (1961), the occupational characteristics that correlated highest with occupational prestige are the extent to which the work is ________ and ________, the amount of ________ the work apparently requires, and the ________ of personnel who can do the job.

REVIEW: *If one picks the five most important determinants of occupational prestige that are indicated by two or more studies and contraindicated by none, these variables are interesting and challenging work, originality and initiative called for, education and training required, intelligence required, and having an influence over others.*

94

102 It is commonly thought that the average income of the different occupations is the most important determinant of occupational prestige. Notice that average income for the occupations studied accounts for about ________ percent of the variance of occupational prestige in the 1941 study (Osgood and Stagner).

88
72
61

103 In the 1951 study (Attneave) the occupational prestige variance accounted for by income is ________ percent, but in the 1956 study (Baudler) this variance figure is reduced to ________ percent, and falls still further to ________ percent in the 1961 study (Garbin and Bates).

prestige

104 Assuming that the samples and methods of study are comparable, the average income of an occupation is rapidly becoming a relatively poor index of occupational ________.

disconfirmed

105 The hypothesis that occupational prestige is primarily determined by the amount of money people in the different occupations earn is rather strongly ________ by the data.

electrician / bookkeeper / janitor

106 Further information on the relationship between occupational prestige and income is provided in Table 2. Notice that the rank orders of occupational prestige and income coincide exactly or almost exactly for the three occupations of ________, ________, and ________.

Table 2. Prestige Ratings and Median Wage or Salary Income of 24 Selected Occupations

	Prestige rating		*Median wage or salary income in 1949*	
Occupation	*Score*	*Rank*	*Dollars*	*Rank*
College professor	89	1	4168	4
Minister	87	2	2319	20
Chemist	86	3	4004	5
Civil engineer	84	4	4453	2
Artist who paints pictures	83	5	3500	7
Public school teacher	78	6	3353	12
Farm owner and operator	76	7	4598	1
Electrician	73	8.5	3453	8
Trained machinist	73	8.5	3300	13
Bookkeeper	68	10.5	3370	10
Insurance agent	68	10.5	3566	6
Policeman	67	12.5	3164	14
Railroad conductor	67	12.5	4266	3
Mail carrier	66	14	3381	9
Carpenter	65	15	2483	17
Plumber	63	16	3360	11
Garage mechanic	62	17	2879	16
Barber	59	18	2172	21
Streetcar motorman	58	19	3079	15
Lumberjack	53	20	1140	24
Taxi driver	49	21	2482	18
Clothes presser in laundry	46	22	2476	19
Bartender	44	23.5	2049	22
Janitor	44	23.5	1843	23

SOURCE: W. F. Ogburn and M. F. Nimkoff, *Sociology*, 3d ed., Houghton Mifflin Company, Boston, 1958, p. 174. Used by permission.

second
twentieth

107 The occupation of minister, though ranking ______ in terms of occupational prestige, ranks ______ in terms of median salary.

prestige

108 There are only ten occupations which are within 2 rank order points of each other with respect to median income and ______ rating.

70 (If you missed this, reread frame 32.)

109 What is most important for our present purpose is that the rank order correlation coefficient between occupational prestige and income is +.56. This means that about _______ percent of the variation in occupational prestige is accounted for by variables other than income.

Attneave

110 Since the data used in this table are for the year of 1949, the result is most inconsistent with that obtained by _______ (Table 1 and frame 103).

real (actual, etc.)

111 The discrepancy may be due, partly or completely, to the fact that Attneave (1951) used estimates of income, whereas Ogburn and Nimkoff (1958) used _______ income data.

cannot

112 In any case, the results of studies which correlate occupational prestige and income are sufficiently variable that one (can/cannot) conclude that income is the most important determinant of occupational prestige.

REVIEW: *The results of the studies in which family prestige and family wealth were correlated would further confirm (or support) the hypothesis that variables other than income are of equal or greater importance for determining occupational prestige.*

Social Perception of Social Class Order

small

113 If we measured the height of a large number of people and then lined them up in order of height we would find that the difference between any two adjacent people would be very _______ or entirely absent.

Still, if we asked people at random to label other people's heights we would very probably find them labeled in terms of about six categories running from very tall to very short. The point is that people categorize variables in their thought and language even if the variable referred to is continuous, i.e., varying in terms of a smooth, almost limitless number of differences.

categories (classes)

114 There is substantial evidence that social class, like height, weight, intelligence, etc., is a continuous variable and not a discrete variation of prestige _______ (Cuber and Kenkel, 1954).

(*a*) the way people's minds work

115 Still, when people classify others according to their social position in a community, they typically use about five categories (Hollingshead, 1949; Kahl, 1961). This comparatively small number of categories is, however, a function of [select one] (*a*) the way people's minds work or (*b*) the categorical nature of social class. ________.

classes (categories)

116 Since social class, by definition, refers to the social ranking given to members of a community, it is appropriate to refer to social ________ rather than to social class continua even though the classes are imposed upon phenomena that are continuous in their objective variations.

lower lowers

117 The literature abounds with social class references in terms of a five- or sixfold typology. When words are used to designate these classes the highest class is typically referred to as "upper class" if a fivefold typology, and "upper-upper class" if a sixfold typology. Below this class are the "upper middles," the "lower middles," the "upper lowers," and finally the ________ ________.

Such terminology is, of course, virtually limited to social scientists. Some of the most common labels as well as perspectives of the class structure are given in Figure 1.

social class

118 It is apparent from a study of label usage that many linguistic labels of social classes depend as much upon the ________ ________ of the people using the term as upon the social class of the people referred to.

conceived (perceived, viewed, etc.)

119 This study confirms the hypothesis that social class is ________ differently by the different classes.

more

120 There are apparently more common labels for those at the top and the bottom of community stratification than for those in between. This indicates that membership in the upper-upper and lower-lower classes in American communities is ________ clear-cut than is membership in the intermediate classes.

confirmed (indicated to be true, etc.)

121 This hypothesis is ________ by the fact that scores on the three index variables of occupation, education, and residence were substantially more homogeneous at the upper and lower end of the scales in a New Haven, Connecticut, study (Hollingshead and Redlich, 1958).

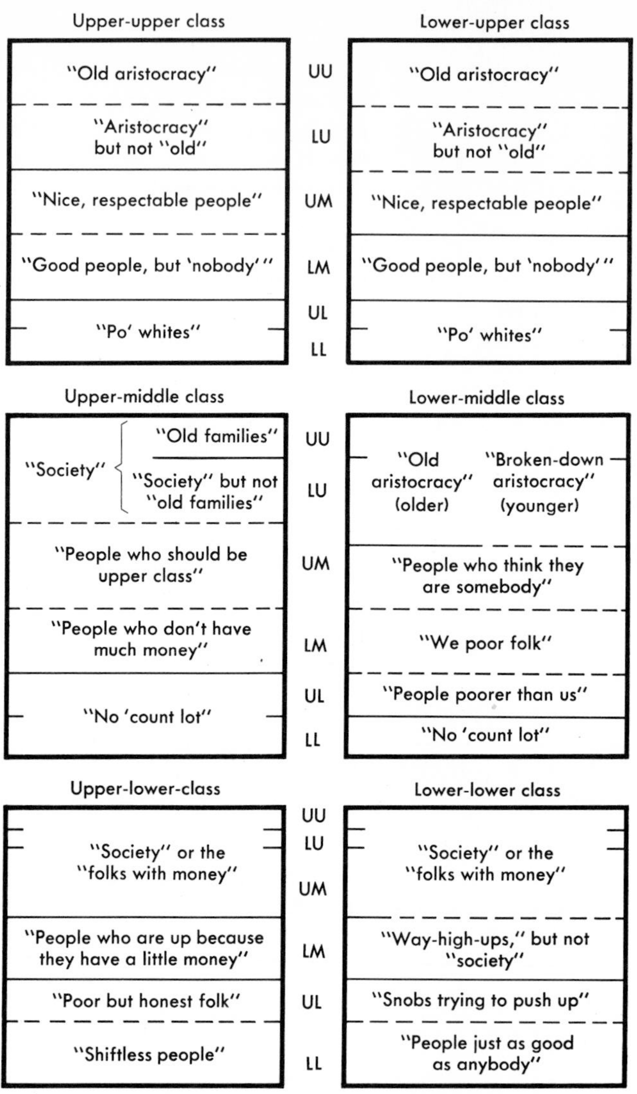

Figure 1. Social perspectives of different social classes in a Deep South community. SOURCE: Allison Davis and B. B. Gardner, *Deep South: A Social-Anthropological Study of Caste and Class,* The University of Chicago Press, Chicago, 1941, p. 65. Used by permission.

lineage

122 Although social class placement at all levels is based largely upon variables relating to occupation, education, residence, and wealth, membership in the upper-upper class necessitates additional variables of "lineage" and "breeding." When a person says, "Family background, who you are—these are the things that count," he is referring to the variable of ________."

breeding

123 When a person says, "They are fine, respected people, but their tastes are really quite common," he is referring to the variable of ________.

Box 1 contains a rather concise summary of the more salient characteristics of the different classes in New Haven, Connecticut. In the class typology used in Box 1, class I is approximately equivalent to upper class, class II to upper-middle class, class III to lower-middle class, class IV to the upper-lower class, and class V to lower-lower class.

Box 1. Essential Characteristics of the Different Social Classes

CLASS I. *This stratum contains approximately 3 per cent of the Greater New Haven population and it is composed of wealthy families whose heads are leaders in the community's business and professional pursuits. Its members live in those areas of the community generally regarded as the best. The adults are college graduates, many with professional training, who have gone to well-known private institutions. These people occupy positions of high social prestige. Almost all gentile families in this group are listed in the New Haven Social Directory, although few Jewish families are so listed.*

CLASS II. *Adults in class II are almost all college graduates. The males occupy high managerial positions or are engaged in the lesser ranking professions. These families, who comprise 9 per cent of the community's population, are relatively well-to-do, but there is no substantial inherited or acquired wealth. Its members live in the better residential areas. About one-half of these families belong to lesser ranking clubs, but only 5 per cent are listed in the New Haven Social Directory.*

CLASS III. *The 21 per cent of the community's population in this stratum includes the vast majority of small proprietors, white collar office and sales workers, and a considerable number of skilled manual workers. Adults are predominantly high school graduates but a considerable percentage have attended business school and small colleges for a year or two. They live in good residential areas. Less than 5 per cent belong to private clubs and few are included in the New Haven Social Directory. Their social life tends to be concentrated in the family, the church, and the lodge.*

CLASS IV. *This stratum consists predominantly of semi-skilled factory workers. Its adult members have at least finished the elementary grades, but the older people have not completed high school. However, adults under 35 years of age have generally graduated from high school. Its members comprise 49 per cent of the community's households and their residences are scattered over wide areas. Social life is centered in the family, the neighborhood, the union, and public places.*

CLASS V. *Occupationally, class V adults are overwhelmingly semi-skilled factory workers and unskilled laborers. Educationally, most adults have not completed the elementary grades. These families, comprising 18 per cent of the population, are concentrated in the tenement and cold-water flats of New Haven. Only a small minority belong to organized community institutions. Their social life takes place in the family flat, on the street, or in a neighborhood social agency.*

SOURCE: Jerome K. Myers and Bertram H. Roberts, *Family and Class Dynamics in Mental Illness*, John Wiley & Sons, Inc., New York, 1959, pp. 25–26. Used by permission.

Although our portrait of social classes in the United States is still quite rudimentary, some hypothetical cases will probably be instructive at this point.

lower-lower

124 Richard L.[11] lives in the tenement district. His neighbors and friends spend their leisure time in warm weather playing cards on the front steps and stickball in the street. Richard is almost certainly a member of the ________-________ class.

upper-upper

125 The Adams family and their servants leave for their summer home in Newport in June and return to the city shortly after Labor Day. The Adams family is rather definitely ________-________ class.

upper-upper

126 Gilbert and his brother attended private schools. They have now enrolled at Harvard, the fourth generation of their family to do so. Gilbert is almost certainly ________-________ class.

[11] All names used in this section are fictitious.

127 Mrs. Fairbanks comments on the Armstrong family by saying, "They are not really old New Haveners; they first settled Saybrook in the 1640s, but the family did not move to New Haven until 1772." Mrs. Fairbanks is almost certainly a member of the ________-________ class.

upper-upper

128 Opal W. is the daughter of a sawmill hand. She lives in a small, painted frame house with her family. She completed the tenth grade and works as a clerk in a department store. Opal is apparently a member of the ________-________ class.

upper-lower

129 Durwood K. was the son of a Southern sharecropper; however, he was successful in school and eventually earned a Ph.D. degree. He is now a member of the faculty of a state university where he earns $12,000 a year. He has moved from a ________-________-class position to an ________-________-class position.

lower-lower
upper-middle

130 Mrs. Hickman does not have enough money to own an automobile and she wears worn, old-fashioned clothes. Her home is ramshackle and unpainted. She is very probably a member of the community's ________-________ class.

lower-lower

131 A distinction is usually made between personal esteem and social class. "Personal esteem" refers to "a person's general social standing." Personality characteristics are to personal esteem as social positions are to ________ ________.

social class

132 Mr. Armstrong is chairman of a department at a state university. Although he is known as an autocratic chairman by his colleagues, he makes about $20,000 per year and lives in an exclusive residential area. Mr. Armstrong has little personal esteem among his colleagues. Nonetheless, his social standing, or social class, is undoubtedly well above ________.

average

Occupational Prestige Orders in Different Countries

133 The early social scientists usually ascribed social position to either wealth or occupation of family head. Recent statistical studies in the United States indicate that ________ of the family head is rather definitely the more important determinant.

occupation

(1) interesting and challenging work
(2) work calls for originality and initiative
(3) intelligence required
(4) education and training required
(5) having an influence over others
(6) scarcity of personnel who can do the job

134 The most important sources of occupational prestige in the United States are: +++++. (List at least five. See Table 1, page 41, or the Review, page 42, if you were unable to do so.)

positive

135 If other countries have similar occupational prestige orders, then one should obtain high ________ correlation coefficients between occupational prestige rank orders of the United States and the other countries.

low / negative

136 We would conclude that the occupational prestige orders were not similar if the correlation coefficients were either ________ and positive or ________.

similar

137 If such correlation coefficients were either low or negative, we would also have to conclude that the sources of occupational prestige were not ________.

common

138 In other words, either low or negative correlation coefficients between occupational prestige rank orders in these countries would indicate that the sources of occupational prestige in such countries would have little in ________.

similar

139 In this statement an assumption is made that similar occupations in the different countries have ________ relative characteristics, such as the amount of education and training required, etc.

more

140 For example, we must assume that, compared with the training required for public school teachers, a college professor requires ________ training.

same

141 But we need not assume that the ________ level of education and training is required for the occupation of college professor in the different countries.

very probably (Take another look at the important determinants of occupational prestige.)

142 Is the assumption that occupations have about the same relative standing with regard to prestige-determining characteristics a sound one? ________.

Table 3. Correlations between Prestige Scores (or Ranks) Given to Comparable Occupations in Six National Studies

	U.S.S.R.	*Japan*	*Great Britain*	*New Zealand*	*U.S.*	*Germany*
U.S.S.R.		.74	.83	.83	.90	.90
Japan			.92	.91	.93	.93
Great Britain				.97	.94	.97
New Zealand					.97	.96
United States						.96
Av. correlation	.84	.89	.93	.93	.94	.94

SOURCE: A. Inkeles and P. H. Rossi, "National Comparisons of Occupational Prestige," *American Journal of Sociology,* 61:332, 1956. Used by permission.

Great Britain / New Zealand; New Zealand / the United States; Germany / Great Britain

143 The paired countries in Table 3 which have the most similar occupational prestige ranks and, consequently, probably the most common sources of occupational prestige are: ________ ________ and ________ ________; ________ ________ and ________ ________ ________; ________ and ________ ________.

94

144 In each of these paired countries, the sources of occupational prestige in one would account for about ________ percent of the variance of occupational prestige in the other.

Japan / U.S.S.R.

145 The two countries having the least similar sources of occupational prestige are ________ and the ________.

55

146 The sources of occupational prestige in Japan would account for about ________ percent of the variance of occupational prestige in the U.S.S.R.

U.S.S.R.

147 The occupational prestige ranking of the ________ deviates most from the occupational prestige ranks of the other countries.

Japan

148 ________ is also somewhat deviant in this respect from the other countries.

identical (the same)

149 The three Western nations and New Zealand have almost ______ rank orders of occupational prestige.

87

150 On the average about ______ percent of the variance in occupational prestige in these countries is determined by common variables.

No

151 Have the Russian Communists attained their expressed goal of a classless society as the term class is used in this unit? ______.

no

152 If the Russian nation were a classless society, there would be ______ differences in prestige of the different occupations in the U.S.S.R.

.00 (absent)

153 Consequently, the correlation coefficient of occupational prestige orders between Russia and any other nation would be ______.

similar

154 The correlation coefficient of .90 between the prestige of different occupations in the United States and their counterparts in the U.S.S.R. indicates not only that the U.S.S.R. is stratified, but that the stratification is based upon characteristics that are very ______ to those in the United States.

high prestige

155 This means that an occupation which is accorded high prestige in Russia is almost certainly accorded ______ ______ in the United States.

REVIEW: *The hypothesis that industrialized societies have very similar relative occupational prestige classes is confirmed by the data in Table 3. The hypothesis that the sources of occupational prestige in industrialized societies are very similar is also confirmed but with less certainty.*

Social Mobility

d

156 If the social class of a person or a family changes, the change is known as "social" or "vertical" mobility. Which of the following occupational changes would quite definitely involve social or vertical mobility? (See Table 2, page 43.)

a. electrician to trained machinist
b. insurance agent to bookkeeper
c. railroad conductor to policeman
d. lumberjack to college professor

high

157 An "open class system" is "a social structure with a relatively ______ degree of vertical mobility."

low

158 A "closed class system" is "a social structure with a relatively ______ degree of vertical mobility."

social class (social position)

159 When vertical mobility approaches zero, it is virtually impossible for people to change their ______ ______. This phenomenon is called "caste."

determined (fixed)

160 In other words, a person's caste position is "inherited." This means that a person's class is ______ by the class position of the family he is born into.

caste

161 In the United States the social prestige of the two social statuses of Negro and white are largely fixed by the ______ into which one is born.

caste

162 In some parts of the rural South no person classified as a Negro possesses as much prestige as any white person. In such areas one may appropriately speak of a ______ system in relation to the comparative prestige of Negroes and whites.

vertical social mobility

163 In other words, vertical social mobility relative to the two racial statuses is impossible. Of course, ______ ______ ______ can occur within each racial group.

Yes. This is apparently the case in all industrialized nations.

164 Is it possible to have a high degree of social mobility along with a high degree of social inequality? ______.

constant

165 The amount of stratification present in a society is independent of the degree of social mobility, so long as the proportion of the population in each stratum remains ______.

constant

166 Although the proportion of the population occupying each stratum may not remain exactly constant with changes in social mobility, there is little question that it can remain approximately ______.

social inequality (social stratification)

167 Equality of opportunity could not exist in the absence of a high degree of vertical social mobility; however, a high degree of vertical mobility does not substantially lessen ______ ______.

is not

168 The amount of total vertical mobility (is/is not) highly variable for the countries listed in Table 4.

Table 4. Comparative Indices of Upward and Downward Mobility, Nonfarm Populations Only (Percentage Distribution)

Country	*Upward mobility (nonmanual sons of manual fathers)*	*Downward mobility (manual sons of nonmanual fathers)*	*Total vertical mobility (nonfarm population mobile across the line between working and middle class)*
United States	33	26	30
Germany	29	32	31
Sweden	31	24	29
Japan	36	22	27
France	39	20	27
Switzerland	45	13	23

SOURCE: S. M. Lipset and R. Bendix, *Social Mobility in Industrial Society,* University of California Press, Berkeley, Calif., 1959, p. 25. Used by permission.

169 The country with the greatest amount of vertical mobility is ________.

Germany

170 Still, the difference between Germany, with the highest amount of vertical mobility, and ________, with the lowest amount of total vertical mobility, is relatively small.

Switzerland

171 What do all the nations in Table 4 have in common? +++++.

They are all urbanized, industrialized societies.

172 The data in Table 4 indicate that the amount of total vertical mobility in urbanized and industrialized societies is approximately ________.

constant (the same)

173 Although total vertical mobility in these countries is approximately constant, there are considerable variations in the relative amounts of ________ and ________ mobility.

upward / downward

174 We often hear that America is *the* land of opportunity. Do the data in Table 4 confirm this hypothesis? ________.

No

175 The land of greatest opportunity is apparently ________ where ________ percent of sons in nonmanual occupations had fathers in manual occupations.

Switzerland / 45

176 This upward mobility figure is ________ percent higher than the comparable figure for the United States.

12

the United States

177 Furthermore, the second best place to lose social standing is ________ ________ ________.

Germany

178 One is more likely to lose than to gain social standing in ________.

the United States / Sweden

179 One's chances of moving up are about equal to one's chances of moving down in ________ ________ ________ and ________.

disconfirmed

180 "In America there is considerably more mobility than in Europe." This hypothesis is ________ by the data in Table 4.

4

181 In Table 5, the figures are average ratios of the percentage of sons in given occupations, whose fathers were in different occupations, to the percentage of all employed persons in the given occupation. Approximately 4 percent of the total population in this sample were professionals. If the ratio of professional sons of professional fathers to the proportion of total employed population were 1.00, then ________ percent of the sons in professional occupations would have fathers in professional occupations.

professionals

182 Likewise, if the ratio were 1.00, 4 percent of the sons of unskilled workers would also be ________.

Table 5. Average Mobility into Each Occupation, 1910 and 1940

	Average mobility	
Occupation	*1910*	*1940*
Professional	0.81	1.01
Semiprofessional	1.09	1.01
Proprietors, managers, officials	0.94	0.80
Clerical and sales	1.02	0.91
Skilled manual	0.77	0.84
Semiskilled	0.90	0.84
Unskilled	0.64	0.68
Protective service	1.06	0.84
Other services	0.86	0.86
Farming	0.17	0.29
All occupations	0.82	0.81

SOURCE: Natalie Rogoff, "Recent Trends in Urban Occupational Mobility," in Richard Bendix and S. M. Lipset (eds.), *Class, Status, and Power,* The Free Press of Glencoe, New York, 1953, p. 446. Used by permission.

5.25

183 In reality, 21 percent of the sons of professional fathers were professionals. This gives a ratio of _______ between percentage of fathers-in-occupation and percentage of total population-in-occupation with respect to persons in professional occupations.

more

184 This means that professional fathers contributed many _______ professional sons to the population than would have happened if all occupations had contributed equally.

.25 (¼)

185 Less than 1 percent of the sons of unskilled workers entered into professional occupations. The corresponding ratio for this group is less than _______.

4

186 If occupational entrance were unrelated to father's occupation, then _______ percent of the sons of unskilled workers would have been professionals.

1.00

187 This would have given a ratio of _______ between percentage of unskilled workers' sons in professional occupations and percentage of people in professional occupations.

32 percent in each case

188 Thirty-two percent of the sample were skilled laborers. What percentage of the sons of fathers in the following occupations would have to be skilled laborers if complete equality of opportunity existed? _______.

a. professionals
b. proprietors
c. clerks
d. skilled workers
e. unskilled laborers

below

189 The average ratio for a given occupation can be 1.00 even though the ratios for sons of fathers in different occupations are above or _______ 1.00.

stability (immobility, etc.)

190 The ratios in Table 5 are averages of ratios between the percentage of sons of fathers in nine occupational classes and the percentage of the total occupied population in each given occupation. In this tabulation, the percentage ratios of fathers and sons in the same occupations were omitted. Those instances in which father and son are in the same occupational class would be instances of occupational and vertical _______.

mobility

191 Conversely, those instances where father and son are in different occupational classes would be instances of occupational and vertical _______.

vertical occupational mobility

192 Table 5 is thus a table of ________ ________ ________ for the periods of 1910 and 1940.

lower

193 If social mobility in the United States had declined between 1910 and 1940, the overall ratio for intergenerational occupational mobility should be substantially ________ in 1940 than it was in 1910.

lower

194 The intergenerational occupational mobility in 1940 was not significantly ________ than it was in 1910.

disconfirmed

195 The common allegation that social stratification in the United States is becoming more rigid is ________ by the data in Table 5.

constant

196 The data in Table 5 indicate that social mobility in the United States is remaining relatively ________.

leave

197 In both periods there was a marked tendency for sons of farmers and laborers to ________ the occupations of their fathers.

higher (greater, etc.)

198 In both periods there was a rather marked tendency for people to enter occupations with ________ prestige.

occupational prestige

199 In general, then, the American population was being "upgraded" in terms of ________ ________ during both periods.

constant

200 At the same time, total vertical mobility remained approximately ________.

representative

201 All these conclusions logically presuppose that the population of Indianapolis, where the study was made, is ________ of the population of the United States.

REVIEW: *Several other studies dealing with intergenerational mobility in terms of both income and occupation between fathers and sons are consistent with the data in Table 5. They support the hypothesis that social mobility in the United States is remaining constant, and not decreasing.*

SUMMARY

It is customary to think of three major types of stratification of human groups or communities. These are variations in power, prestige, and wealth. Of these three, the variable of prestige has been selected, by common definition, to constitute the reference of the term "social class." The relationship between these variables in urbanized and industrialized societies is only moderately high. Consequently, one cannot extend conclusions derived from the study of any one of these variables to either of the others without, perforce, getting on more shaky ground.

In trying to expand one's understanding of the sources and effects of social class differences, one is compelled to rely largely upon correlation data. This, however, is not so limiting as is sometimes supposed. Where correlation coefficients are established for a population there are four generic logical causal possibilities. Knowledge of a temporal separation of the correlated event classes reduces these logical causal possibilities to two, and further information is frequently available which reduces the logical causal possibilities to one.

With the use of correlation data, it has been rather firmly established that, of all the correlated variables, occupational prestige of the family head is the most important determinant of the social standing of the family and, consequently, of the social standing of its individual members. Wealth, education, where one lives, and what one lives in, are decidedly less important.

In a similar study of the indexes, and presumably the determinants, of occupational prestige, several variables emerge as apparently the most significant. The occupations that are accorded high prestige are conceived of as occupations that are interesting and challenging. They are commonly thought to be filled by people who possess an extraordinary amount of originality, initiative, education, and intelligence. Consequently, the higher the prestige of the job, the fewer the people presumably qualified to fill it. It is to be emphasized that this is what people think about the jobs and the people that fill them. The reality in some cases may be at marked variance with the common impression.

It has been shown that the rank orders of occupational prestige in a number of urbanized and industrialized countries are very similar. It has been inferred from this and other information that social class and many of its correlates are common to all urbanized and industrialized societies.

Although relevant data do not yield a certain conclusion, they do rather definitely indicate that the United States is not the "land of opportunity" that it is commonly alleged to be. Not only is upward mobility less in the

United States than in several other countries, but where mobility between manual and nonmanual occupations is tabulated, people in the United States are almost as likely to be downwardly mobile as upwardly mobile.

From a variety of studies, but especially from a study of intergenerational vertical mobility in Indianapolis, one can reasonably conclude that movement up or down the social scale has not significantly changed in the United States during this century. For, near the turn of the century as well as near the middle of it, there was a fairly marked but equal tendency for men to move into higher prestige occupations.

SELF-REVIEW QUIZ

1–7 Matching. Select the one best logical relationship.

CLASSES

a. upper class
b. upper-middle class
c. lower-middle class
d. upper-lower class
e. lower-lower class

CHARACTERISTICS

1. Though many of them attend state universities, almost all adults in their class are college graduates.
2. This stratum consists predominantly of semiskilled factory workers.
3. Most adults in this stratum have not completed grade school.
4. This stratum includes the vast majority of small proprietors, white-color office workers, and salesmen.
5. Males in this stratum occupy high managerial positions or are engaged in the lesser ranking professions.
6. Social life is centered in the family, the church, or the lodge.
7. Families in this stratum are well-to-do, but there is little inherited or acquired wealth.

8–16 Multiple-choice. Select the one best answer.

Items 8 through 11 are based upon the following episode. Joe Torquemonger jumps into his jalopy, depresses the accelerator twice, turns the ignition switch on, and presses the starter. At this point the engine starts and Joe roars off to school.

8 After many observations under diverse conditions, we would say that an abstract cause-effect symbolization of engine starting as an event class would look something like which of the following:

a. If X_1, X_2, X_3, and X_4 occur, then Y very probably will occur.
b. If X occurs, then Y occurs.
c. If X_1, X_2, X_3, and X_4 are true, then Y is true.
d. If Y_1, then X_1. If Y_2, then X_2. If Y_3, then X_3, etc.

9 Pressing the starter is most accurately designated as:
  a. the cause of the engine starting
  b. an antecedent correlate of the engine starting
  c. a part of the cause of the engine starting
  d. a sufficient condition of the engine starting

10 One could compute a correlation coefficient between:
  a. turn of ignition switch and engine starting
  b. number of accelerator depressions and engine starting
  c. starter pressure and engine starting
  d. accelerator depression and speed

11 The correlation coefficient in the above illustration would be:
  a. high and negative
  b. zero
  c. low and positive
  d. high and positive

12 The single best indicator of the social class of a family is:
  a. the family's self-rating
  b. total wealth of the family
  c. educational attainment of the family head
  d. occupational prestige of the family head

13 The correlation coefficient between occupational prestige and rate of admission to mental hospitals as psychotics was —.83. This indicates that:
  a. about 83 percent of the variance in psychotic admission rates is determined by variations of social class
  b. a significant increase in social class coincides with a significant increase in psychotic admission rates
  c. some aspects of life in the different social classes are important determinants of psychotic behavior
  d. there is no important causal relationship between social class and psychotic behavior

14 Which of the following is true?
  a. If the correlation between A and B is high and positive, then one must be the cause of the other.
  b. If the correlation between A and B is high and negative, then A and B are not causally related.
  c. If A is the cause of B, then the correlation must be high and positive.
  d. If A is the cause of B, then the correlation between A and B must be high, but can be either positive or negative.

15 Which of the following is a comparatively unimportant determinant of occupational prestige?
  a. interesting and challenging work
  b. intelligence required

c. education and training required
d. income

16 Which of the following hypotheses has been disconfirmed?
a. Where societies are composed of social classes, the social structure generally resembles a truncated pyramid.
b. In modern, urban America traditional social classes are nonexistent or imperfectly developed.
c. Mobility does not necessarily lessen inequality.
d. In America there is considerably more mobility than in Europe.

REFERENCES

Allee, W. C.: *The Social Life of Animals,* W. W. Norton & Co., New York, 1938.

Attneave, C. L.: "Occupational Prestige: An Experimental Analysis of Its Correlates," unpublished doctoral dissertation, Stanford University, Stanford, Calif., 1951.

Baudler, George: "A Comparative Study of Fifteen Occupations and Certain Factors of Prestige," cited in L. G. Thomas, *The Occupational Structure and Education,* Prentice-Hall, Inc., Englewood Cliffs, N.J., 1956.

Bierstedt, Robert: *The Social Order,* McGraw-Hill Book Company, New York, 1957.

Clark, R. E.: "Psychoses, Income, and Occupational Prestige," in Richard Bendix and S. M. Lipset, *Class, Status, and Power,* The Free Press of Glencoe, New York, 1953.

Cuber, J. F., and W. F. Kenkel: *Social Stratification in the United States,* Appleton-Century-Crofts, Inc., New York, 1954.

Garbin, A. P., and F. L. Bates: "Occupational Prestige: An Empirical Study of Its Correlates," *Social Forces,* 40: 131–136, December, 1961.

Hollingshead, A. B.: *Elmtown's Youth,* John Wiley & Sons, Inc., New York, 1949.

Hollingshead, A. B., and F. C. Redlich: *Social Class and Mental Illness,* John Wiley & Sons, Inc., New York, 1958.

Inkeles, Alex, and P. H. Rossi: "National Comparisons of Occupational Prestige," *American Journal of Sociology,* 61: 329–339, January, 1956.

Kahl, J. A.: *The American Class Structure,* Holt, Rinehart and Winston, Inc., New York, 1961.

Lenski, G. E.: "American Social Classes: Statistical Strata or Social Groups," *American Journal of Sociology,* 58: 139–144, September, 1952.

Lipset, S. M., and Richard Bendix: *Social Mobility in Industrial Society,* University of California Press, Berkeley, Calif., 1959.

Mayer, A. J., and T. F. Hoult: "Social Stratification and Combat Survival," *Social Forces,* 34:155–159, December, 1955.

Myers, J. K., and B. H. Roberts: *Family and Class Dynamics in Mental Illness,* John Wiley & Sons, Inc., New York, 1959.

Ogburn, W. F., and M. F. Nimkoff: *Sociology,* 3d ed., Houghton Mifflin Company, Boston, 1958.

Osgood, C. E., and Ross Stagner: "Analysis of a Prestige Frame of Reference by a Gradient Technique," *Jour-*

nal of Applied Psychology, 25:275–290, June, 1941.

Rogoff, Natalie: "Recent Trends in Urban Occupational Mobility," in Richard Bendix and S. M. Lipset, *Class, Status, and Power,* The Free Press of Glencoe, New York, 1953.

Warner, W. L., and P. S. Lunt: *The Social Life of a Modern Community,* Yale University Press, New Haven, Conn., 1941.

Warner, W. L., Marchia Meeker, and Kenneth Eells: *Social Class in America,* Science Research Associates, Inc., Chicago, 1949.

West, James: *Plainville, U.S.A.,* Columbia University Press, New York, 1945.

Winch, R. F., Robert McGinnis, and H. R. Barringer: *Selected Studies in Marriage and the Family,* rev. ed., Holt, Rinehart and Winston, Inc., New York, 1962.

3

social class functions

VERNON H. EDMONDS

Social class is important only insofar as it is related to personal and social behavior. This unit describes some of the more significant functions of social class in America, such as religious, political, and economic behavior, and mental and physical illness. Dating and marital patterns, family expenditures, and personal relations are some other areas of social concern that are related to class status. The unit introduces the distinctions between class and caste and points out some of the problems which each raises for our society.

1 "Effect" as this term is normally used means about the same thing as "function" as this latter term is used in this unit. "Effect" is an approximate synonym for ______.

function

2 If Y is said to be a function of X we know that Y (follows/occurs simultaneously/precedes) X. ______.

follows

3 If a variation of X is regularly followed by a variation of Y, then Y is said to be a ______ of X.

function

4 One might just as well use the word "effect" were it not for the implication of "compelling force" in the causal relationship (see the preceding unit). The only difference between "function" as the term is used here and "effect" as this latter term is normally used is that "function" makes no reference to ______ ______.

compelling force

5 An exact synonym for "function" is "dependent variable." If a change in variable X precedes a change in variable Y, then Y is a function of ______.

X

dependent

6 In such a case, Y is the _______ variable and X is the independent variable.

positively

7 Just as "positive" or "direct" factors are terms frequently used in the preceding unit to refer to independent variables that correlate positively with the phenomenon in question, "positive" or "direct" functions will be frequently used in this unit to refer to dependent variables that correlate _______ with the phenomenon in question.

increases

8 To say that church membership is a direct function of social class is to say that as social class increases, the proportion of the population that are church members _______.

church

9 Since class membership precedes church membership, the dependent variable category is _______ membership.

dependent

10 Just as "negative" and "inverse" factors were terms frequently used in the preceding unit to refer to independent variables that correlate positively with the phenomenon in question, "negative" and "inverse" functions will be frequently used in this unit to refer to _______ variables that correlate negatively with the phenomenon in question.

decreases

11 To say that the probability of developing a psychosis is an inverse function of social class is to say that as social class increases, the probability of a person developing a psychosis _______.

social class

12 Since one develops a psychosis long after one's social class is more or less fixed, the independent variable category in the preceding illustration is _______ _______.

Social Class and Religious Behavior

between

13 Stratification of a considerable magnitude is evident both within and _______ the different denominations listed in Table 6.

lower

14 A large number of sects are ranked below the Baptists in class composition. Some of the larger ones are Nazarenes, Jehovah's Witnesses, Seventh Day Adventists, Churches of Christ, Churches of God, and Assemblies of God. The class composition of these sects is almost exclusively _______ class.

Table 6. Class Composition of Religious Bodies, 1945–1946

Denomination	*Percent distribution*		
	Upper class	*Middle class*	*Lower class*
Entire sample	13	31	56
Congregational	24	43	33
Episcopalian	24	34	42
Jewish	22	32	46
Presbyterian	22	40	38
Methodist	13	35	52
Lutheran	11	36	53
Catholic	9	25	66
Baptist	8	24	68

SOURCE: Liston Pope, *The Annals of the American Academy of Political and Social Science,* 256:84–91, 1948. This is based on four nationwide AIPO samples of 3,000 each (total sample size: 12,000). The sample is probably rather representative of the United States population. Class placement, however, is rather arbitrary since cutoff points are rather arbitrary. The rank order of the class distribution in the different bodies seems to be very stable with respect to both time and space in the United States.

Episcopalian and Jewish; Methodist and Lutheran; Catholic and Baptist

15 What three pairs of denominations have almost identical social class distribution? +++++.

Methodist

16 If you wished to take a sample most representative of the United States population with respect to social class, then the ________ Church would be the best single denomination from which to draw the sample.

entire (total)

17 The Methodists are most representative of the United States population with respect to class because the class distribution of the Methodists most closely corresponds to the class distribution of the ________ sample.

Presbyterian
Methodist

18 The largest break in social class composition of the different bodies occurs between the ________ and the ________ denominations.

Congregational / Episcopalian / Jewish / Presbyterian

19 The majority of members are either middle or upper class for the ________, ________, ________, and ________ denominations.

Methodist / Lutheran / Catholic / Baptist

20 The majority are lower class for the ________, ________, ________, and ________ denominations.

social class

21 If you are a member of one of the latter groups, you probably had the impression that the denominational membership was predominantly middle class. This illusion is in part due to the fact that specific congregations are highly differentiated along ________ ________ lines *within* each denomination.

higher

22 Your parents, consciously or unconsciously, have probably encouraged attendance at a particular church within a denomination where the prevailing social class of the congregation is equal to or somewhat ________ than your own.

No. There can be only one "leading congregation."

23 Most Protestant students included in a sample at the University of Washington thought their specific church congregation was "the leading congregation" (socially) in their hometown. Can this be true? ________.

exaggerate

24 Vernon (1960) found that the subjects of his study exaggerated the prestige of their denominations. That is, denominations were rated substantially higher, with respect to social prestige, by their members than by nonmembers. This tends to confirm the hypothesis that subjects ________ the prestige of their denominations.

The tendency to exaggerate the prestige of the groups to which one belongs is sometimes referred to as "self-aggrandizement." Caplow and McGee (1958) made a study of fifty-five different groups. They found that raters overestimated the prestige of their own organization eight times as frequently as they underestimated it, and that net overestimation occurred in every group.

self-aggrandizement

25 Many studies in many societies support Caplow and McGee's research. It would appear that ________-________ is a universal group trait.

prestige

26 Both selective attendance within a stratified denomination and self-aggrandizement prompt people to question the rank order of social ________ of religious bodies included in Table 6.

positively

27 Another way of ascertaining the approximate class differences of denominations is to note the proportion of family heads that have completed a specified number of years of schooling. While educational level of the family head is not a perfect indicator of a family's social class position, it is, nonetheless, a rather close approximation because education of family head, occupational prestige of family head, and social class of family are all highly and (negatively/positively) correlated.[1]

Table 7. Educational Composition of Household Heads by Religious Affiliation, 1955–1956

		Education: highest grade of school completed						
		Elementary school			*High school*		*College*	
Religious preference	*Total*	*0–4 years*	*5–6 years*	*7–8 years*	*1–3 years*	*4 years*	*1–3 years*	*4 years*
Total	100.0	8.9	7.8	24.0	20.2	21.1	9.6	8.4
Episcopal	100.0	2.0	4.2	16.4	10.3	23.2	21.2	22.6
Jewish	100.0	8.3	4.2	13.4	13.2	27.8	10.9	22.3
Presbyterian	100.0	3.2	3.2	17.6	23.6	24.6	14.9	13.0
Other	100.0	23.4	13.6	11.0	11.0	22.4	5.7	12.8
No religion	100.0	10.7	8.7	23.4	20.4	16.9	8.8	11.0
Other Protestant	100.0	6.7	8.7	27.0	18.5	20.5	9.2	9.4
Methodist	100.0	5.3	6.2	20.9	21.5	26.0	11.6	8.6
Lutheran	100.0	5.4	5.2	29.3	22.4	22.4	8.5	7.0
Roman Catholic	100.0	8.0	7.4	25.8	20.6	22.4	8.9	6.8
Baptist	100.0	16.9	11.6	26.0	20.4	14.8	6.1	4.2

SOURCE: Donald J. Bogue, *The Population of the United States,* The Free Press of Glencoe, New York, 1959, p. 701. Used by permission.

Episcopal

28 Persons listing the ______ Church as their preference are clearly the most educated of the groups listed in Table 7.[2]

Jewish

29 Running a close second are those with a preference for the ______ faith.

Presbyterians

30 Somewhat further down in terms of aggregate educational level are the ______.

[1] The product moment correlation coefficient between educational level of the family head and social class of the family is typically about .80.

[2] There are a number of small religious denominations not included in the table in which the educational level is much higher, as, for example, Unitarians, or much lower, as, for example, Jehovah's Witnesses, than any denomination included in the table. It is well to keep this in mind in the following discussion.

educated

31 Both Episcopalians and Jews are much more highly _______ than persons of the other religious affiliations.

Baptists

32 The _______ are clearly the least educated of the denominational groups included in this tabulation.

(e) high and positive[3]

33 If one compares the rank order of the proportion of family heads that are college graduates with the rank order of the proportion who are upper class by the criteria of placement used in Table 6, it is apparent that the correlation is (*a*) high and negative, (*b*) low and negative, (c) absent, (*d*) low and positive, (e) high and positive.

stable (constant)

34 The rank order correlation between the proportion graduating from college and the proportion who are professionals, proprietors, or technicians is perfect save for the relative positions of Lutherans and Baptists (Bogue, 1959). This datum further confirms the hypothesis that the class rank order of the various religious bodies is rather _______ with respect to time.

social class

35 Another manner in which social class and religion are related consists of _______ _______ variations with respect to various dimensions of religiosity.

religiosity

36 Fanaticism, fundamentalism or doctrinal orthodoxy, associational involvement, communal involvement, asceticism, and devotionalism are some of the more important dimensions of _______ (Lenski, 1961; Putney and Middleton, 1961).

fundamentalism

37 "Fundamentalism" is used to refer to "any doctrine of certainty that pertains to the literal passages of a sacred book."[4] "Doctrinal orthodoxy" is a synonym for _______.

Baptists[5]

38 You probably know enough about denominational differences with respect to Christian or Biblical fundamentalism to expect few Congregationalists to be fundamentalists, whereas, at the opposite end of the class continuum, one would expect a vast majority of _______ to be fundamentalists.

[3] The rank order correlation for religious bodies included in both tables is in fact perfect and positive, i.e., +1.00.

[4] Formal definition. Here, as elsewhere, no one is being quoted unless a reference is provided.

[5] In fact, about 99 percent of the Southern Baptists are fundamentalists.

39 Consequently, one would expect social class and Christian doctrinal orthodoxy to correlate highly and ________.

negatively (inversely)

40 Putney and Middleton (1961) reported a correlation of −.13 between measures of socioeconomic status and religious orthodoxy used with a large number of college students from various parts of the country. The correlation is negative, but the magnitude of the correlation in this study is very ________.

low

41 If we assume that the student sample in the Putney and Middleton study is representative of the United States population and that the study validly measured both social class and religious orthodoxy, then we would have to conclude that Congregationalists, as a group, are only a little less orthodox than the two bottom groups in Table 6, namely, ________ and ________.

Baptists / Catholics

42 We might even conclude that Congregational and Episcopalian groups are almost as orthodox, or fundamentalist, as the various ________ -class sects such as Assemblies of God, Jehovah's Witnesses, Churches of Christ, etc.

lower

43 But the following propositions seem to be confirmed beyond any reasonable doubt. One, the aggregate social class composition of the religious denominations listed in the Tables 6 and 7 is very marked and in the order specified (Bogue, 1959; Pope, 1948). Two, Christian doctrinal orthodoxy differs markedly for the denominations listed in Tables 6 and 7 (Glock and Stark, 1965). Three, the social class rank order is exactly, or almost exactly, the inverse of the doctrinal orthodoxy rank order. We are thus forced to conclude that social class and Christian doctrinal orthodoxy are very substantially and ________ correlated insofar as both variables are represented in denominational affiliations.

negatively (inversely)

44 Since one's position on a religious orthodoxy-heterodoxy continuum could hardly determine one's position on the social class continuum, religious orthodoxy is probably an ________ function of social class.

inverse (negative)

confirmation (support)

45 The hypothesis that doctrinal orthodoxy is an inverse function of social class is given further ________ by a Detroit study in which doctrinal orthodoxy among Protestants was found concentrated in working-class groups with comparatively little formal education (Lenski, 1961).[6]

devotionalism

46 Another dimension of religiosity is "devotionalism." Lenski defines devotionalism as "that orientation which emphasizes the importance of private, or personal communion with God" (Lenski, 1961). In Lenski's study subjects who reported praying more than once a day or reported praying only once each day but frequently asked what God would have them do were ranked high with respect to religious ________.

little

47 In Lenski's study, measures of doctrinal orthodoxy and devotionalism correlated only +.23. This means that doctrinal orthodoxy and devotionalism have (little/much) in common.

devotionalism

48 Middle-class respondents reported praying and asking God for guidance more often than working-class respondents. It would seem that the middle classes in Detroit are higher with respect to religious ________ than the lower classes.

middle class

49 Bossard and Boll (1950) report that only the middle-class families included in their sample engaged in regular family prayers in addition to saying grace at mealtime and participating in bedtime prayers for children. Furthermore, they report that only in middle-class families was there a significant proportion of families who observed old-fashioned Sundays in which the whole family engaged in Bible reading and praying. It would appear that devotionalism is concentrated in the ________ ________.

[6] Lenski's operational definitions of the different classes are as follows: "Upper-middle-class respondents are those in families in which the family head was a businessman, a professional man, a clerk, or a salesman, and himself had an income of $8,000 or more in 1957. Those in families whose head was in a similar occupation, but earned less than $8,000, were classified as lower-middle-class.

"Upper-working-class respondents are those in families in which the head was a manual worker or service worker who himself earned at least $5,000 in 1957. Those in families whose head was in a similar occupation, but earned less than $5,000, were classified as lower working class." Gerhard Lenski, *The Religious Factor*, Doubleday & Company, Inc., Garden City, N.Y., 1961, p. 73.

associational involvement

50 Another dimension of religiosity is associational involvement. "Associational involvement," as used here, refers to "the extent of a person's exposure to the activities of a religious congregation." Lenski (1961) used "frequency of attendance at corporate worship services" as a measure of _______ _______.

positive

51 Over one-third of middle-class Protestants in Lenski's sample reported weekly church attendance, whereas about one-fourth of the working-class Protestants reported weekly attendance (Lenski, 1961). It would seem that associational involvement is generally _______ for middle-class persons than for lower-class persons.

Hollingshead and Redlich describe class III[7] as the only class in which adults "take religion seriously; they belong to church, go to it regularly, support it financially and participate in its organizations. In short they are . . . the 'backbone of God's work'" (Hollingshead and Redlich, 1958, p. 101).

associational involvement

52 In the same study class I is said to be the most "unchurched" segment of the population. Though class I's are virtually always nominally affiliated with a denomination, a very large segment of this class is not affiliated with, or active in, a local congregation. It would appear from the data we have examined to this point that both devotionalism and _______ _______ are concentrated in the middle range of the status continuum in the United States population.

associational involvement

53 In the same study class V's[8] are said to rarely attend church or participate in church activities (Hollingshead and Redlich, 1958). It would appear that _______ _______ is comparatively weak at both extremes of the status continuum.[9]

[7] Class III probably corresponds to that segment of a community population that would be labeled lower-middle class by researchers using a sixfold class typology.

[8] Class V is the approximate equivalent of lower-lower class in a sixfold class typology.

[9] Although some have argued that Lazerwitz's data (1961) disconfirm the hypothesis that associational involvement is comparatively weak at both ends of the scale, it should be noted that Lazerwitz's educational occupational classes are insufficiently analyzed, particularly at the upper end of the scales, to have any cogent bearing on the hypothesis.

magnitude (degree, etc.)

54 Lenski (1961) obtained a positive but extremely low correlation between social class and frequency of church attendance among Catholics. Lazerwitz (1961) obtained a high positive correlation between occupational prestige and frequency of reported church attendance for Catholics. The data are consistent with respect to the direction but not with respect to the _______ of the correlation.

negative (inverse)

55 None of the middle-class Jews in Lenski's sample reported weekly attendance at a synagogue or temple, whereas 19 percent of the working-class Jews reported weekly synagogue or temple attendance (Lenski, 1961). From this datum it would appear that associational involvement is a _______ function of social class among Jews.

Lazerwitz's data, however, indicate no significant correlation between occupational prestige level and associational involvement among Jews. Perhaps Detroit Jews are different. Or, perhaps, the Detroit sample is not representative of even the Detroit Jewish population.

communal involvement

56 Another dimension of religious behavior is "communal involvement," defined by Lenski (1961) as "the degree to which the primary-type relations of an individual (i.e., his relations with friends and relatives) are limited to persons of his own group." Those who reported being married to someone of the same religious group and also reported that all or nearly all of their close friends and relatives belonged to the same religious group were scored as high with respect to _______ _______.

There is some evidence that the middle classes are more communally involved than the working classes, but the relationship is still very much of an open question (Lenski, 1961).

ascetic

57 Another dimension of religiosity is asceticism. As used here, "asceticism" refers to "a disapproval of sensory pleasures." When a priest asserts that people should not destroy their "souls" by pursuing "earthly pleasures" he is expressing an _______ value judgment.

Box 1. Asceticism in a Small Town

Sometimes asceticism takes the form of condemning virtually everything that people within a given culture enjoy doing. Note, for example, the following list of things tabooed by a Lutheran minister in this case, but representative of the attitudes of the lower-class Protestant denominations in a small Illinois town:

The Lutheran minister categorically denies his adolescents dancing, cosmetics, curls, permanents, bobbed hair, motion pictures, alcoholic beverages, automobile rides . . . bowling, cards, pool, high school parties. In fact, almost every recreation approved in the non-Lutheran, nonholiness portion of the community comes under the ban. The only sanctioned pleasures are short educational films of religious shrines or foreign missionary work, shown in the church basement, and church-sponsored parties and games (Hollingshead, 1949, pp. 261–262).

inverse (negative)

58 As suggested by the preceding illustration asceticism is a very high ______ function of social class insofar as Protestant denominations are concerned.

ascetic

59 One could include Catholics in this conclusion without differentiating them from Protestants were it not for their comparative lack of concern about drinking, dancing, and gambling (Lenski, 1961). When it comes to sexual matters, Catholics, who are predominantly lower class, are approximately as ______ as lower-class Protestants.[10]

We now come to the question of general attitude toward religion in its institutionalized form. Broadly, we can speak of general approval, disapproval, and indifference. There is some evidence that the attitude of indifference is concentrated in the upper class in America (Bossard and Boll, 1950; Davis, Gardner, and Gardner, 1941; Hollingshead and Redlich, 1958).

lower-middle

60 Something approaching universal approval appears to characterize that segment of the population that is "the backbone of God's work," namely, the ______-______ class.

[10] The effects of "religious devoutness," which for lower-class Protestants and for Catholics generally implies sexual asceticism, is discussed at some length in Kinsey's volume, *Sexual Behavior in the Human Female*, W. B. Saunders Company, Philadelphia, 1953.

The attitudes of the lower classes appear to be polarized in such a way that persons in this segment of the population seem to be either strongly for or strongly against institutionalized religion. Many persons at this level are either zealously evangelistic or strongly antichurch and anticlerical (Davis, Gardner, and Gardner, 1941; Hollingshead and Redlich, 1958).

61 Though the division is not so clear-cut, it would appear that the more superheated forms of religiosity are concentrated in the upper-lower class while the strongest hostility toward institutionalized religion is concentrated in the ________-________ class.

lower-lower

62 Finally, it is probably worth mentioning that denominational membership correlates substantially and positively with social class. The correlation apparently obtains for the entire range of the continuum. Denominational membership is sometimes assumed to be an indication of "religiosity," but as the foregoing data disclose, such an assumption constitutes the greatest of ________.

follies (errors, mistakes, etc.)

We have, thus far, studied eight religious variables insofar as they are related to social class in America. It has been emphasized, first of all, that the social class composition of the various religious denominations in the United States differs very markedly and that the differences are very stable from one region of the country to another and from one period to another. The social class rank order is, of course, given in Tables 6 and 7.

While the available data are not entirely consistent in every respect, they are sufficiently consistent to provide an approximate portrait of the different social classes with respect to religion.

Although the upper classes are more likely to be identified with some denomination than people in the classes below them they appear to be essentially indifferent with respect to institutionalized religion save for observing rites of passage.

It is apparently in the middle classes, particularly the lower-middle class, that religion appears to be most popular. Though they are less doctrinally orthodox and less ascetic in some ways than the more religious segment of the population below them, they are apparently higher in every other dimension of religiosity than those either beneath or above them.

There is a tendency, apparently, for the lower classes to be divided into two diametrically opposed camps with respect to institutionalized religion. They, more than any other class, tend to embrace or reject religion with great vigor. Those who embrace religion usually select a denomination or sect that is literalistic, revivalistic, and ascetic. There is some evidence that the accepters are concentrated in the upper-lower class and the rejecters concentrated in the lower-lower class.

Social Class and Political and Economic Behavior

63 It is highly probable that experiences derived from one's class membership have a much greater impact upon one's economic attitudes than one's economic attitudes have upon one's _______ membership.

class

64 If this is true, then it is highly probable that economic conservatism is a direct _______ of social class.

function

65 Or, in other words, economic liberalism is probably a _______ _______ of social class.

negative (inverse) function

66 In a Detroit study (Lenski, 1961) subjects were asked whether the government was doing too much, too little, or about the right amount with respect to "housing, unemployment, education, and so on." Sixteen percent of the white middle-class Protestants said that the government was doing too much in these areas, whereas only eight percent of the white working-class Protestants took this position. Differences were even greater for other religious and racial groups. The data further _______ the hypothesis that domestic economic liberalism varies inversely with social class.

confirm

67 There are many other studies, all of which are consistent in indicating that domestic economic liberalism, when this is defined as favoring more benefits for the poor, varies _______ with social class.

inversely

68 When, however, one shifts from the domestic to the international scene and measures the proportion favoring foreign aid to poor countries, the direction of this relationship reverses itself (Lenski, 1961). The higher classes are _______ in favor of foreign aid than the lower classes.

more

lower

69 Attitudes toward cooperation with international agencies designed to solve world problems parallel attitudes toward foreign aid. For example, anti-UN sentiment is more prevalent in the ________ classes (Lenski, 1961).

directly

70 "Shouldering international responsibilities" varies ________ with social class.

In the same study, Detroit residents were asked if, in their opinion, the Constitution guaranteed the right of everyone to: (1) "criticize what the President does," (2) "make speeches against religion," (3) "make speeches in favor of Fascism or dictatorship," and (4) "make speeches in favor of Communism." The results are summarized in Table 8.

Table 8. Percentage of Detroiters Expressing Belief That Various Practices Are Protected by the Bill of Rights, by Class and Socio-religious Group

	Percentage believing specified practice protected					
Class: S-r. group	*Criticism of president*	*Attacks on religion*	*Fascist speeches*	*Communist speeches*	*N*	*Mean*
Middle class:						
Wh. Prots	88	65	53	46	117	63
Jews	89	53	47	37	19	57
Wh. Caths	77	52	43	34	92	52
N. Prots	77	54	23	23	13	44
Working class:						
Wh. Prots	69	40	35	33	150	44
Wh. Caths	70	40	32	32	138	44
N. Prots	46	28	30	27	87	33

SOURCE: Gerhard Lenski, *The Religious Factor*, Doubleday & Company, Inc., Garden City, N.Y., 1961, p. 145. Used by permission.

middle-class

71 If we define "liberal" as favoring civil liberties and "conservative" as opposing civil liberties, then it is clear that the most liberal group in Detroit is the white ________-________Protestants.[11]

[11] The exception to this generalization occurs with respect to granting persons freedom to make speeches favoring communism. Here the class differences are negligible except for white Protestants and the difference is not great there. Perhaps the attitude corresponding to the slogan of "freedom for everyone except Communists" has become more or less uniform in the American population.

working-class

72 The most conservative group by a rather wide margin is the Negro ________-________ Protestants.

more

73 In general the middle-class respondents are far ________ liberal with respect to attitudes toward freedom of speech than are their working-class counterparts.

lower (working)

74 Attitudes toward granting minorities equal rights vary in the same direction with respect to social class as do attitudes toward freedom of speech and other civil liberties (Lenski, 1961). One will, therefore, find a larger proportion of staunch segregationists in the ________ classes than in the higher classes.

directly

75 If we define "liberalism" here as favoring equal rights of minorities, then, clearly, liberalism varies ________ with social class.

political / economic

76 Figure 2 shows a definite correlation between occupational class and certain ________ and ________ attitudes.

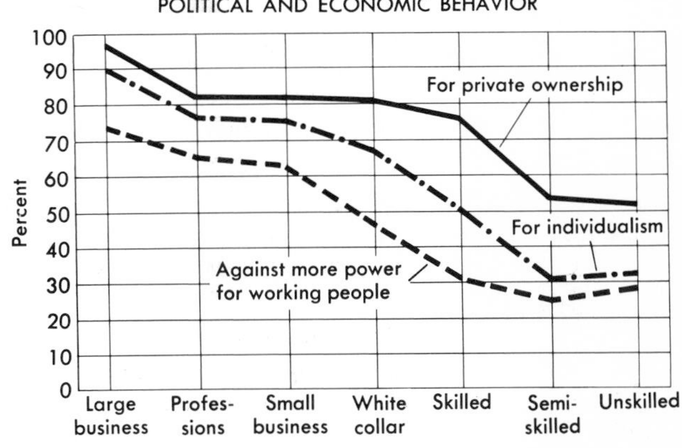

Figure 2. Attitudes of urban occupational groups toward private ownership, individualism, and more power for working people. SOURCE: R. Centers, *The Psychology of the Social Classes*, Princeton University Press, Princeton, N.J., 1949, p. 63. Used by permission.

positive (direct)

77 The proportion that are for individualism was determined by computing the percentage in each occupational group that agreed with the statement: "The most important job for the government is to make it certain that there are good opportunities for each person to get ahead on his own." There is an obvious high and ________ correlation between occupational class and "individualism."

unskilled laborers

78 The only reversal of the positive relationship between occupational prestige and favorable attitude toward individualism occurs in the occupation of semiskilled laborers, in which individualism is slightly less frequent than it is for the occupation of ________ ________.

individualism

79 Being for individualism is equivalent to being opposed to government welfare programs that are designed to assist the economically underprivileged. If attitudes reflect economic self-interest we would expect a high positive correlation between occupational prestige and attitudes favoring ________.

large businessmen

80 If the conservative position with respect to these attitudes is defined as being for private ownership and individualism and against more power for working people, then the most conservative occupational group is the ________ ________.

Yes

81 Likewise, if politico-economic attitudes reflect rational economic self-interest, then the proportion who are for private ownership of property and against more power for working people would vary directly with occupational prestige. Do they? ________.

large business

82 It is probable that representatives of ________ ________ serve as the nation's leaders of economic conservatism on these domestic issues.

semiskilled
unskilled

83 Conversely, economic liberalism on these issues would seem to be most concentrated in the laboring segments of the population, and especially those in ________ and ________ laboring occupations.

dimension (variable)

84 The correlation between social class and liberalism differs with respect to the dimensions of liberalism. It is thus apparent that one cannot describe the higher or lower classes as liberal or conservative without specifying the ________ of liberalism or conservatism.

positive

85 When it comes to religious orthodoxy, attitudes toward aid to foreign countries, granting equal rights to minorities, and attitudes toward civil liberties, liberalism is clearly a ________ function of social standing in American society.

negative (inverse)

86 When, however, it comes to aiding the poor people of this country through any kind of governmental activity, liberalism is clearly a ______ function of social position in American society.

themselves

87 A conspicuous feature of the only form of liberalism which the lower classes possess, namely, pro-welfare sentiment, is that it is geared toward helping (others/themselves).

liberties / foreign
minorities

88 On the other hand, the liberalism of the higher classes seems to have an altruistic component when it comes to attitudes toward civil ______, ______ aid, and attitudes toward granting ______ equal rights.

altruistic

89 When, however, it comes to supporting government programs to help the domestic poor and underprivileged there is little evidence of ______ sentiment in the higher classes except for those in intellectual occupations.

Social Class and Mental Illness

Table 9. Rank Order Coefficients of Correlation Calculated over Seventeen Occupational Groups between Various Psychoses Rates for White-Male First Admissions and the Occupational Factors of Income and Prestige

	Occupational factor	
Type of psychosis	*Income*	*Prestige*
Schizophrenia, all types	−.71	−.81
Manic-depressive psychoses	−.02	.01
Senile psychoses and psychoses with arteriosclerosis	−.57	−.50
Alcoholic psychoses	−.78	−.92
General paralysis	−.75	−.73
Other psychoses	−.53	−.63
All psychoses	−.75	−.83

SOURCE: Robert E. Clark, "Psychoses, Income, and Occupational Prestige," *American Journal of Sociology,* 14:433–440, 1949. Used by permission.

inverse (negative)

90 The data in Table 9 clearly reveal a high ______ correlation between social class and psychoses rates.

psychotic

91 A person is said to have a psychosis when he has undergone a substantial loss of contact with reality. If a person in good health is convinced that his "insides are rotting away"[12] he may be rightly suspected of being ______.

income / prestige

92 Since a person's chances of developing a psychosis do not seem to determine the occupation he enters, it is highly probable that the independent variables in this table are the occupational factors of ______ and ______.

56

93 The occupational factor of income accounts for about ______ percent of the variance of psychoses rates in this sample.

70

94 The occupational factor of prestige accounts for about ______ percent of the variance of psychoses rates.

the one with the highest correlation, i.e., the alcoholic psychosis rate

95 What type of psychosis rate is the best indicator of a person's social class? +++++.

manic-depressive

96 Based on the correlations in Table 9 you might expect to find common factors in all types of psychoses except the type referred to as ______-______ psychosis.

false (spurious, etc.)

97 The hypothesis that the incidence of psychoses is negatively correlated with social class has been rejected by some clinicians who argue that as social class increases wealth increases, and that as wealth increases private care of psychotic patients increases. If the correlation coefficients between the occupational factors of prestige and income, on one hand, and psychosis incidence rates, on the other, were based upon public hospitals alone, then one might well conclude that the correlation coefficients are indeed ______ indicators of the true relationship between social class and psychosis incidence rates.

[12] This is a common delusion of class III (lower-middle-class) schizophrenics (J. K. Meyers and B. H. Roberts, *Family and Class Dynamics in Mental Illness,* John Wiley & Sons, Inc., New York, 1959). It is probably a function of widespread sexual guilt feelings in this class, in which violation of the sexual mores is often described as "rotten," "decadent," etc.

negative (inverse)

98 The correlation data in Table 9 are, however, based upon first-admission records for both private and public psychiatric hospitals in the survey area. When one considers this fact in conjunction with the magnitude of the correlation coefficients and the size of the patient sample (over 12,000) there appears to be a good chance that the true correlation between social class and the incidence of phychoses is high and ______.

false

99 Nonetheless, if psychiatric treatment is an important means of preventing psychoses and if chances of receiving this treatment vary directly with social class, then the high negative correlations could still give a ______ picture of the general relationship between social class and insanity.

lower

100 If the relationship indicated is a spurious one because of a positive relationship between income and preventive treatment, then a correlation between the occupational factor of income and psychoses should be much (higher/lower) if only the ten lowest-paid occupations were included in the computation.

rejected

101 As a matter of record, when such a computation was made, the correlation changed from −.83 for nineteen occupational groups to −.85 for the ten lowest-paid occupational groups (Clark, 1949). This suggests that the "differential preventive-treatment" hypothesis can be ______.

neurotic

102 A "neurotic disorder" is distinguished from a "psychotic disorder" in that in a neurotic disorder the person has not undergone a substantial loss of contact with reality. If, for example, a person exhibits no marked delusions of any kind, but complains of being overburdened by his job, having frequent headaches, being chronically fatigued, and being almost constantly "miserable," and no organic illness can be discovered by physicians, then the person of psychoses is high and ______.

[13] There is very little consensus with respect to a definition of "neurosis." However, there appears to be a general tendency to use the term to refer to a chronic condition of extreme unhappiness in which anxiety is high, constant, and pervasive. There is complete consensus with respect to the exclusion of gross loss of contact with reality from the reference of the term.

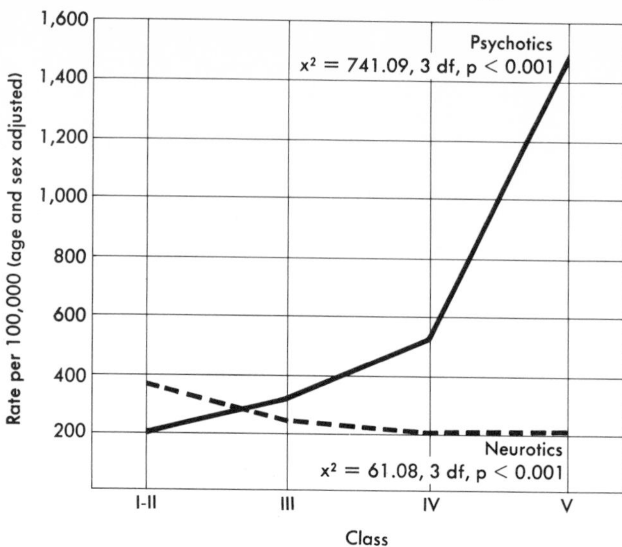

Figure 3. Prevalence of neurotic and psychotic disorders per 100,000 adjusted for age and sex—by class. SOURCE: A. B. Hollingshead and F. C. Redlich, *Social Class and Mental Illness,* John Wiley & Sons, Inc., New York, 1958, p. 230. Used by permission.

103 The social class data in Figure 3 are based upon an index of social position which involves a weighted scoring of measures pertaining to residence, occupation, and education. As one would anticipate from the data presented in the previous unit, occupation received the heaviest weight in the computation of a person's social ________.

position (class, etc.)

104 In Figure 3, social class decreases as the roman numerals increase. The highest class is therefore class ________ and the lowest class is class ________.

I / V

105 The prevalence of neurotic and psychotic disorders for any given class is indicated by the ________ of the lines.

height

106 The magnitudes of the correlations between social class and the two designated types of mental illness are indicated by the ________ of the lines.

slope

107 In Figure 3 the correlation between social class and psychoses rates is high and ________.

negative (inverse)

108 The correlation between neuroses rates and social class is low and ________.

positive (direct)

IV / V

109 The greatest difference in psychoses rates occurs between classes ________ and ________.

7.5

110 If you were selecting people at random from classes I–II and V, your chances of selecting a psychotic from class V would be about ________ times greater for any given one-person selection than your chances of selecting a psychotic from classes I–II.

Yes

111 Are the data in Figure 3 consistent with the data in Table 9? ________.

higher

112 There is some evidence that the probability of receiving treatment or placement in a mental hospital is a positive function of social class (Hollingshead and Redlich, 1958). If such is the case, then the negative relationship between social class and psychoses rates is (higher/lower) than indicated by Table 9 and Figure 3.

lower

113 On the other hand, the rather low positive correlation between social class and prevalence of neuroses is probably somewhat ________ than indicated by Figure 3.

positive (direct)

114 The probability of not being treated for a severe neurosis and hence recorded as a "neurotic" is extremely high for class V in comparison with the other classes. Consequently, the correlation between social class and neuroses rates could well be negative rather than ________.

larger

115 There is a hypothesis known as the "horizontal drift hypothesis" that a substantial number of transient and psychotic or prepsychotic people drift into the lower-class areas of cities. If this hypothesis is true, then one would predict that a significantly ________ proportion of class V schizophrenics would have moved from their place of birth than would have happened for those in classes I–II.

disconfirms

116 In New Haven, 62 percent of the class V schizophrenic patients were born and reared in the same community they resided in when they became known to a psychiatrist or psychologist. The comparable figure for classes I–II was 44 percent. This datum ________ the horizontal drift hypothesis.

downward drift

117 Another hypothesis, known as the "downward drift hypothesis," is that people who become psychotic "drift down" with respect to social class. From a study of previous residences of schizophrenic patients, it was concluded that most of them from both class V and classes I–II had lived in low- and high-prestige areas all their lives (Hollingshead and Redlich, 1958). This datum tends to disconfirm the ________ ________ hypothesis.

disconfirm

118 It should also be noted that, by using the same index of social position, it was ascertained that: (*a*) 91 percent of the schizophrenic patients were in the same class as their parents, (*b*) 1 percent were in a lower class than their parents, and (*c*) over 4 percent were in a higher class than their parents (Hollingshead and Redlich, 1958). These data ________ the downward drift hypothesis at a high level of confidence.

certainty (confidence)

119 Since another excellent scientific study (Farris and Dunham, 1939) indicates that the downward drift hypothesis cannot account for the data, this hypothesis can be rejected, not with complete certainty, but with a very high level of ________.

less

120 Another hypothesis, perhaps best labeled as the "upward drift hypothesis," is that "superior people" have moved and are moving into the higher social class positions. This hypothesis is usually combined with an assumption that certain hereditary qualities which make a person upwardly mobile are combined with hereditary qualities that make him "mentally healthy." Assuming the hypothesis to be true, one would predict that psychotic patients would be ________ upwardly mobile than their brothers and sisters.

disconfirmed

121 In the New Haven study both neurotic and psychotic patients were much more upwardly mobile than their siblings. (Hollingshead and Redlich, 1958; Meyers and Roberts, 1959). The upward drift hypothesis would appear to be ________ by this datum.

mental health

122 Furthermore, almost five times as many psychotics were upwardly mobile as were downwardly mobile. It would appear that upward mobility is more likely to be accompanied by "mental illness" than by ________ ________.

disconfirmed

123 Attempts to explain away the very high inverse correlations obtained between indicators of social class and indicators of psychosis incidence and prevalence rates continue, but it should be noted that the commonly expressed alternatives to the hypothesis that the relationships are genuine have been more or less substantially ________ by the existing data.

social class

124 Since the commonly advanced alternative hypotheses are disconfirmed one might reasonably infer that the prevalence and incidence of psychoses are inverse functions of ________ ________.[14]

more

125 Of course, social class as such is not *the cause* of psychotic behavior. But the correlations do indicate that certain aspects of one's social existence, perhaps the sheer level of frustration, perhaps especially the level of self-disapproval, which converge to produce psychotic behavior are much ________ heavily concentrated at the bottom of the social class continuum.

social classes

126 The correlations between social class and the dimensions of neurotic behavior are much more open to question because the rates of treated neuroses indicated in Figure 3 are probably not proportional to the real rates for the different ________ ________.

increases

127 The reason that the treated rates are probably not proportional to the real rates for the different classes where neuroses are concerned is that receiving treatment for a neurosis, in contrast to receiving treatment (or at least being hospitalized) for a psychosis, is largely contingent upon: (*a*) one's attitude toward psychotherapy, (*b*) one's ability to pay, and (*c*) one's sensitivity to psychological sources of mental and physical difficulties. On all three counts chances of being treated for a neurosis definitely increase as social class ________.

[14] To be sure, the data with respect to the magnitude of the relationship between social class and psychotic incidence (first-admission) rates are not entirely consistent. R. E. Clark ("Psychoses, Income, and Occupational Prestige," *American Journal of Sociology*, 14:433–440, 1949) obtained a very high inverse correlation. A. B. Hollingshead and F. C. Redlich (*Social Class and Mental Illness*, John Wiley & Sons, Inc., New York, 1958) obtained a rather low negative correlation. Hollingshead and Redlich account for the high inverse correlation between social class and prevalence (existing at a given time) rates as the product of a high inverse correlation between social class and length of time spent in the mental hospital.

positive (direct)

128 This is why it would be most naïve to infer that a significant ________ correlation exists between social class and the prevalence of neurotic behavior.

confirmed (supported)

129 One frequently encounters an expression of the belief that happiness is inversely related to social position. The expression usually runs something like this, "Poor people are the happiest people in the world." This hypothesis, while perhaps not directly or definitely verifiable at this time, is certainly not ________ by the preceding data.

The belief that happiness is somehow peculiarly characteristic of the lower classes is perhaps most widespread among white Southerners with respect to the belief concerning the happiness of Negroes. Dollard, when speaking of his observations made in a small town in Mississippi in the thirties, says, "Informant after white informant said that the Negroes are a happy folk, that they never have a worry in the world. Even the troubles they think they have really do not amount to anything" (Dollard, 1957, p. 384).[15]

lower

130 If Negroes were much happier than whites we would expect much ________ rates of psychoses among Negroes.

disconfirmed

131 Psychoses rates for Negroes are in fact much higher (Clark, 1949). The hypothesis that Negroes are a carefree, happy people is substantially ________ by this fact.

more

132 Likewise, if happiness declines as affluence and position increase we would expect that drug addiction and alcoholism rates would correlate positively with social class. The reverse, of course, is true. If happiness varies with social class it is much ________ likely to be a positive than a negative association.

[15] Perhaps the myth of Negro happiness, and particularly the myth of Negro contentment, has been somewhat weakened by widespread Negro riots and demonstrations of the past few years. The myth concerning the happiness and contentment of the poor is, perhaps, as strong as ever. It seems impervious to the accumulation of relevant evidence to the contrary.

Box 2. A Glimpse of Life at the Bottom

HIT-RUN CAR KILLS PENNILESS MIGRANT

By LOUISE CHILDERS
Democrat Correspondent

PERRY—The 42-year-old wife of a migrant worker from Blytheville, Ark., was killed late Saturday when struck by a hit-and-run driver on U.S. 19, three miles south of Salem.

Salem is about 12 miles south of Perry in Taylor County.

The woman, identified as Mrs. L. L. (Inez) Handley, was walking with her husband along the highway headed north. They were apparently trying to make their way back to Arkansas.

According to Sgt. V. C. Amason of the Highway Patrol, the couple had no car and no funds and knowing that no one would pick them up at night, were traveling by foot. They were in the northbound lane and had stopped on the shoulder of the road to read a restaurant sign when the accident occurred.

Handley told Sergeant Amason that he was reading the sign to his wife when he suddenly saw her body "flying in the air and fall at my feet." He said he never saw the car that hit her clearly enough to describe it. She fell about three feet within the shoulder of the road.

Handley said he tried for some time to stop passing motorists without success, but finally one man (unidentified) did contact the Florida Highway Patrol and report that someone was attempting to get help on the side of the road.

Mrs. Handley was taken to the Doctors Memorial Hospital in Perry and pronounced dead on arrival. She suffered a broken neck, according to Dr. John Parker.

According to Handley's report to the Highway Patrol, he and his wife had been working in South Florida, she in a tomato plant and he in field work. He was told he could not work for about 15 weeks because of an arm injury about three weeks ago and they were trying to get back to Arkansas.

When asked where they had planned to spend the night, he said at "some service station." It was between 9:30 and 10 p.m. when the accident occurred. The couple was carrying all their personal possessions in a sack, and had no money with them.

Handley, in great shock, was lodged overnight at the Taylor County Jail and given medical attention. Both Trooper H. D.

Landdell and Sergeant Amason were unable to get much description of the car from the dazed man.

Mrs. Handley's body is now at the J. P. Burns Funeral Home.

SOURCE: Louise Childers, *Tallahassee Democrat,* February 28, 1966. With permission.

There can be little doubt that social class and prevalence rates for psychoses are very highly and inversely related. The same holds true with respect to social class and incidence rates for psychoses, though the relationship is possibly somewhat lower. Many hypotheses have been advanced to explain how the obtained correlations are spurious indicators of the true relationships. All these hypotheses have been substantially disconfirmed.

Since one's position in the class structure is determined in the vast majority of cases prior to the onset of a psychosis, it is eminently plausible to speak of the psychosis rate as a function of social class variations. This, of course, does not mean that social class, per se, is the cause of psychotic behavior, but it does indicate that the social environments conducive to psychotic behavior occur with markedly increasing frequency as social class decreases.

The relationship between social class and treated rates of neuroses is positive but very low. The real correlation between social class and neurotic behavior is open to question. It is my hypothesis, however, that the real correlation is an inverse one. In any event, the treated cases undoubtedly overindicate the real rates, because as social class decreases so does: (1) sensitivity to psychological problems, (2) ability to pay for psychotherapy, and (3) favorable attitudes towards psychotherapy.

The widespread folk belief that Negroes and the lower classes generally are the happiest segment of the population has been examined and rejected in the light of available and relevant data.

Social Class and Physical Illness

133 In Table 10, the independent variable is family income. The dependent variable is ________ ________.

infant mortality

134 From Table 10, one might conclude that if a child is born into a family with a per capita income of $500 or less his chance of dying during the first year of life is almost ________ that of a child born into a family with a per capita income of $850 or more.

double (1.7)

Table 10. Infant Mortality and Income, 973 American Cities, 1939–1940

Per capita income	*Infant deaths per 1,000 live births*
Under $500	63.4
$500–$674	53.7
$675–$849	41.7
$850 and over	37.7

SOURCE: *Public Health Reports,* Federal Security Agency, 1949 (adapted).

negative (inverse)

135 The correlation between family income and infant mortality is high, continuous, and ______.

negative (inverse)

136 In 1935 and 1936, the United States Public Health Service conducted a survey of 740,000 urban and 36,000 rural families (Amidon, 1944). The results showed a marked negative relationship between family income and: (*a*) number of illnesses, (*b*) duration of illnesses, and (*c*) severity of illnesses. Frequency, duration, and severity of illnesses are apparently ______ functions of social class.

negative

137 Figure 4 shows a high ______ relationship between family money income and the proportion of people disabled or limited in their occupation by chronic illness.

decrease

138 Data in Figure 4 indicate that an increase in family income is associated with a ______ in the frequency of severe and disabling injuries and illnesses.

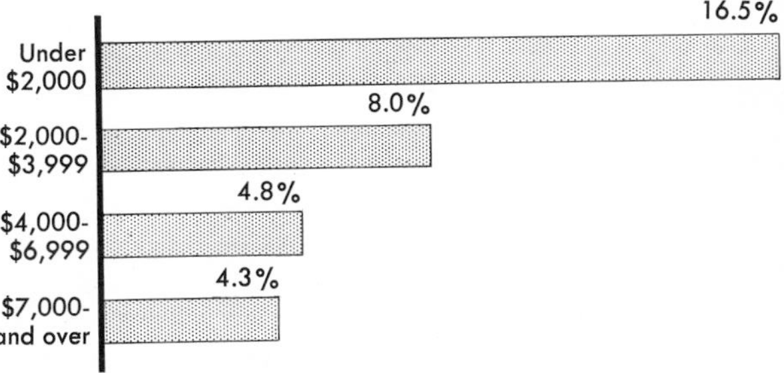

Figure 4. Percentage of persons grouped by family money income who are disabled or whose major activity is limited by chronic ailment, 1958. SOURCE: Conference on Economic Progress, *Poverty and Deprivation in the United States,* Washington, D.C., April, 1962, p. 65.

negative (inverse)

139 If such is the case, then chronic ailments and disabilities are ________ functions of family income.

decrease

140 From Figure 4, one might also infer that an increase in the frequency of chronic ailments and disabling illness would be followed by a ________ in family income.

negative (inverse) function

141 If such is the case, then family income is also a ________ ________ of chronic or disabling illness.

less

142 In 1956 the proportion of persons who saw no physician during the year was three times higher for families with incomes below $1,200 than for those with incomes over $10,000 (Odoroff and Abbe, 1959). Combining this information with that given in Figure 4, we can infer that the more people need medical attention, the ________ likely they are to receive it.

direction

143 It seems highly probable that the (direction/magnitude) of these relationships has not changed since the middle and late 1950s.

magnitude

144 It also seems likely that the ________ of these relationships has not changed substantially since the middle and late 1950s.

death

145 In 1930, life expectancy at birth for those in the lowest of five economic classes in the Chicago area was fifty-two years. It was sixty-five years for those in the highest economic class (Mayer and Hauser, 1953). Economic class was quite literally a matter of life or ________.

decreasing

146 By 1940, these figures had changed to fifty-nine years for the lowest class and sixty-eight years for the highest class. The class differential in terms of life expectancy is apparently ________.

It is thus apparent that the relationship between social class and prevalence, duration, and severity of physical illnesses parallels the correlation between social class and mental illnesses. The causal relationship between social class and physical illnesses is, however, more uncertain. It seems likely that a reciprocal relationship exists here, particularly with respect to family income and disabling physical illnesses.

Chances of receiving any kind of medical treatment for physical illnesses vary directly with social class. Hence here, as in many other areas of life, need is inversely re-

lated to supply. Specifically, the healthier people are, as class groups, the more medical treatment they receive.

Dating and Marriage Patterns

positive

147 Hollingshead (1949) reported the mean number of weekly dates of male adolescents in "Elmtown" for April, 1942, in classes I–II through V as follows: 3.4, 2.8, 2.9, and 1.9. Dating frequency for adolescent males in Elmtown at this time was definitely a (positive/negative) function of social class.

positive (direct)

148 Comparable figures for girls were: 5.2, 3.3, 3.4, and 4.6. Although the relationship between social class and dating frequency for girls was ______, it was rather low and curvilinear.

bottom

149 Girls who dated least were in the middle of the social class order, whereas boys who dated least were at the ______ of the social class order.

higher

150 The frequency of dating for these groups was, in general, a positive function of social class, but the relationship is substantially ______ for males.

boys

151 Lower-class status was a much greater handicap for ______ in Elmtown.

higher

152 In this study, adolescents tended to date within their own class, but when a boy dated outside his class, the odds were 2:1 that the girl was from a lower class. Conversely, when a girl dated someone outside her class, the odds were 2:1 that the boy was from a ______ class.

increases

153 There is some evidence that, as the social class difference of the two persons involved in a date increases, the probability of the date being limited to the relatively temporary gratification of some specific desire also ______ (Hollingshead, 1949).

bargaining

154 These comparatively limited relationships may be of either a bargaining or exploitative nature. "Bargaining" occurs when "the parties to the encounter either explicitly or implicitly agree to provide certain commodities in exchange for other commodities." In Elmtown many of the high school boys directly exchanged money for the sexual favors of the girls who worked for "Polish Paula" (Hollingshead, 1949). This is clearly a ______ relationship.

155 It frequently occurs, however, that one party deliberately misleads the other(s) involved in the relationship. When a person convinces another that some reward is forthcoming when in reality there is no intention of providing this reward, then the relationship becomes ______.

exploitative

156 Many males in the Elmtown study feigned a kind of serious and permanent, or quasi-permanent, interest in girls as a means of securing sexual favors (Hollingshead, 1949). This is clearly an ______ kind of relationship.

exploitative

157 Exploitative relationships, of course, occur between persons who are on the same social level, but the chance of a dating relationship being an exploitative one increases as the class differential between the parties involved ______. This appears to be particularly true of the type of exploitation alluded to in the previous frame (Hollingshead, 1949).

increases

Table 11. Urban Marriages of Urban Males

		Percentage married to women of various occupational strata (as determined by wife's father's occupation)						
Occupational stratum of male	N	*Business executive*	*Profes-sional*	*Small business*	*White collar*	*Skilled manual*	*Semi-skilled manual*	*Unskilled manual*
Business executive	40	15	15	33	13	20	2	2
Professional	44	7	25	30	2	23	13	
Small business	78	3	8	40	8	25	10	6
White collar	88		5	32	23	24	13	3
Skilled manual	81		1	14	9	46	24	6
Semiskilled	85		2	12	8	27	41	10
Unskilled	33			3	12	9	36	40

SOURCE: Adapted from R. Centers, "Marital Selection and Occupational Strata," *American Journal of Sociology*, 54:523, 1949. Used by permission.

158 If we define a "class-endogamous marriage" as one in which a man marries a woman whose father comes from the same or an adjoining occupational class, most men in this study except those in the occupation of ______ ______ contracted class-endogamous marriages. (See Table 11.)

business executive

4 percent (4:100)

159 What were the chances of a business executive marrying a woman whose father was an unskilled or semi-skilled worker? ________.

0

160 What were the chances of an unskilled or semi-skilled worker marrying a woman whose father was a business executive? ________.

37 percent (37:100)

161 What were the chances of a business executive marrying a woman whose father was in the occupational prestige class of white collar or below? ________.

0

162 What were the chances of a man who was in the occupational prestige class of white collar or below marrying the daughter of a business executive? ________.

68

163 The percentage of professional men who married daughters of men in lower occupational strata was ________.

upwardly

164 This means that 68 percent of the women who were wives of professional men were ________ mobile by marriage.

49

165 What percentage of small businessmen married women whose fathers were in lower occupational strata? ________.

11

166 What percentage of small businessmen married daughters of men in higher occupational strata? ________.

more

167 There can be little question that men in this study were much ________ likely than women to marry "down."

easier

168 If women marry "for love," it would seem that many of them find it much ________ to fall in love with men from higher occupational strata.

purchased

169 In many countries wives are purchased directly by their husbands. In the United States many wives are apparently ________ indirectly by their husbands.

Both dating and marriage are highly endogamous with respect to social class; however, when class lines are crossed the male is far more likely to be from the higher class. The result, of course, is that higher-class males have comparatively immense bargaining power in the sex-marriage market in American society because they have access to females throughout the social class continuum. The lower-class females theoretically have the same advantage but to a lesser degree because initiation of dates and marriages are male prerogatives and because males who date very much below their class are frequently aiming primarily at sexual exploitation.

The frequency of dating for boys in American society is probably a high positive function of social class. The relationship between social class and dating frequency for girls is more open to question, but there is some evidence indicating that the highest dating frequencies occur at the top and the bottom of the social class continuum.

Socioeconomic Class and Expenditures

wealthy

170 Nineteen percent of the families in the survey depicted in Figure 5 had annual incomes below $2,000. Two percent had incomes of over $10,000. There were obviously a lot more extremely poor than extremely ______ families in America.[16]

four

171 Although both poor and rich families spend more on food than on anything else, the rich spend over ______ times as much on this "necessity."

eleven
twelve

172 It should be noted that the rich families, making at least five times as much money as the poor families, spent over ______ times as much money on alcohol and over ______ times as much on automobiles.

disconfirmed

173 The hypothesis that poor people spend a very disproportionate amount of their earnings on "liquor and fancy automobiles" is ______ by the data.

because of the high inverse relationship between family income and physical illness discussed previously

174 It is a rather safe assumption that families making less than $2,000 a year need more medical care than those making over $10,000 per year. Why? +++++.

[16] Though incomes vary greatly with the time that the data are collected, any income frequency distribution, past or present, discloses the same fact, i.e., many poor and few wealthy families.

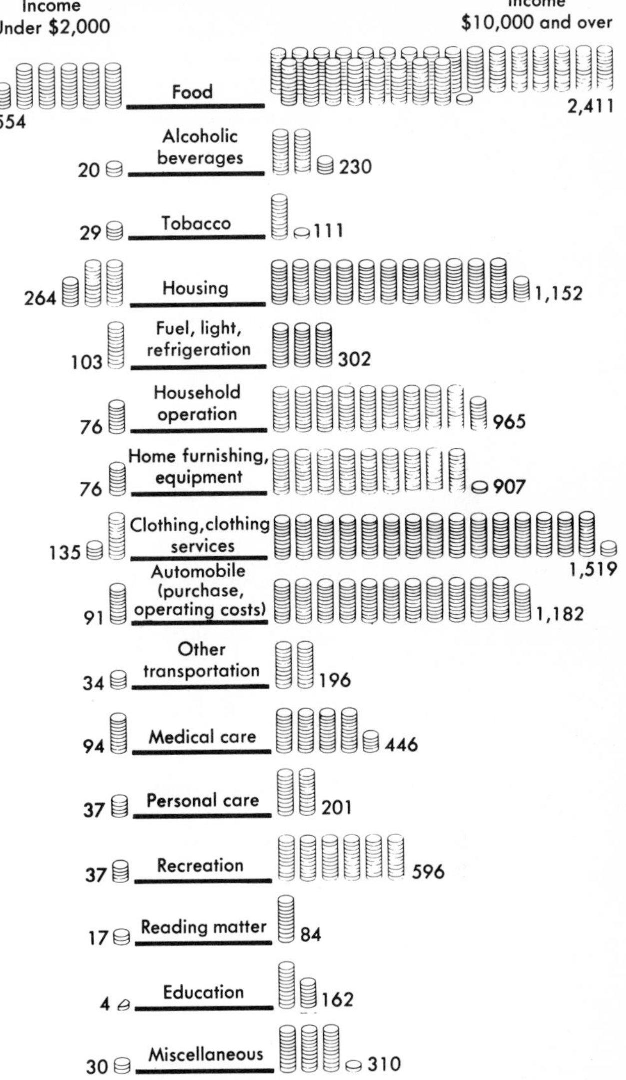

Figure 5. Average annual expenditures for poor and rich families. SOURCE: William F. Ogburn and Meyer F. Nimkoff, *Sociology,* 3d ed., Houghton Mifflin Company, Boston, 1958, p. 168. Used by permission.

four

175 Assuming that people get what they pay for in the area of medical care, the wealthy, who were certainly much healthier, received over ______ times as much medical care as the poor.

$352

176 Poor families probably receive more free medical care. If the poor families received enough free medical care to make up for the difference in the amounts spent, they would have had to average at least ________ worth of free medical care per year per family.

No

177 Is it plausible that family units with incomes below $2,000 per year (19 percent of the United States population) received at least $352 worth of free medical care per year in 1950? ________.

education

178 The greatest proportionate difference in the expenditures of the poor and rich families involves the amount spent on ________.

education

179 The rich spend over forty times as much on education as the poor. This is ironic, because ________ is apparently the most effective avenue to a higher income and social position.

See differences in amounts spent on personal care, clothing, and clothing services (Figure 5).

180 Some studies have shown that children from lower-class families are not nearly so likely to be judged "good looking" by their associates as are the children from upper-class families (e.g., Warner et al., 1949). Do the data in Figure 5 indicate some possible explanation? +++++.

personal / clothing

181 "Good looks" might well be based directly upon the amount of money spent on ________ care, ________, and clothing services.

better looking

182 If medical care and food affect health and health affects good looks, then adequate medical care and food would indirectly make upper-class children ________ ________.

In this section we have compared the expenditures of poor and wealthy families. The United States, like most urbanized and industrialized countries, has always had a lot more of the former than of the latter.

It is probably in no way surprising to discover that comparatively wealthy families spend much more on nonessential commodities. It is perhaps also widely known that vastly larger sums are spent on the essentials of food, clothing, and shelter. But it is not widely recognized that the poor spend much less, both absolutely and proportionately, on alcohol and automobiles. Expenditures on tobacco, though differing greatly with respect to absolute amounts, are proportionately similar for both poor and wealthy families.

It is probably widely known that wealthy families spend substantially more money on clothing and on personal and medical care. The derivative effects of these expenditures are probably not so widely recognized. By way of a particular example, it is known that self-acceptance is a high positive function of social acceptance. It is also known that social ratings of personal attractiveness are a high positive function of social position. This difference in social, hence self, rating with respect to attractiveness is rather definitely and substantially a derivative effect of the differential expenditures with respect to clothing, medical care, and personal care.

The greatest difference, either absolute or proportionate, in expenditures by poor and wealthy families occurs in the area of education. This difference undoubtedly has the effect of maintaining class lines at the extremes of the income continuum, since education is probably the primary avenue of class maintenance for the upper social classes and of upward mobility for the lower and middle classes in the United States.

Social Class and Personal Relations

183 From material given in Part 1, Unit 2, of this book, one can infer that self-approval is a positive function of social approval, and social approval is quite definitely a ________ ________ of social class.

positive function

184 In one study (Edmonds, 1955) a group of students from relatively lower-class families reported "feelings of inferiority" much more frequently than students from relatively higher-class families. Does this fact support the hypothesis? ________.

Yes

185 One would also expect that exaggeration of one's "good qualities" by oneself as well as by others would vary ________ with social class.

directly

186 Conversely, social and self-abasement would probably vary ________ with social class.

inversely (negatively)

187 It has been shown that the higher a person's social standing in a group, the ________ his performance is overrated by himself and by others (Harvey, 1953; Sherif, 1956).

more

188 Do these data indirectly support the general hypothesis that social and self-aggrandizement are direct functions of social class, whereas social and self-abasement are inverse functions of social class? ________.

Yes

In a study of nursery school children from one school, where the parents were largely professional, and from another school where the parents were largely workers, ratings were obtained relative to spontaneity of speech and drawing, persistence, cooperativeness, "poise," self-care, and play initiative (Gesell and Lord, 1927). All except self-care were more highly developed in the children with professional parents.

189 These data tend to confirm the hypothesis that the chances of developing a "socially useful" personality in American society varies ________ with social class.

directly

190 From the information we already possess, it seems probable that a person's chances of being "friendless" would be a ________ ________ of his social standing.

negative (inverse) function

191 In a study of people in Cambridge, Massachusetts, 30 percent of the unskilled workers, 13 percent of skilled, small business, and white-collar workers, and 10 percent of professionals and "top" business and government officials reported that they had no "close friends" (Kahl, 1953). It is obvious that the frequency of reporting no close friends correlates inversely with ________ ________.

social class

It has been rather firmly established that: (1) self-ratings are a high positive function of the imagined ratings of others, (2) imagined ratings by others are a high positive function of the real ratings by others, and (3) the real ratings of others are a high positive function of a person's status in a group or community. Therefore, on logical grounds one can infer that self-esteem is a high positive function of social class. The inference has been directly confirmed by at least one study.

Class and Caste Differences

Up to this point we have virtually ignored the differences resulting from differential caste membership entailed by the social statuses of Negro and white in the United States.

inferiority

192 The reader will, perhaps, recall that both "class" and "caste" refer to "differences of social superiority or ________ assigned to persons by members of a human community."

caste

193 A class stratification of a human population differs from a caste stratification in that a person can rise or fall from the position ascribed to him at birth in a class system, whereas a person's social position is unchangeable from that ascribed to him at birth in a genuine ________ system.

social class

194 Differences *within* the Negro or white communities constitute ________ ________ differences.

caste

195 Differences *between* Negroes and whites at least approach a pure ________ form of stratification in some parts of the Deep South.

castes

196 Figure 6 is the reported social class distribution of Negro and white ________ of a town of about five thousand in southeast Georgia.

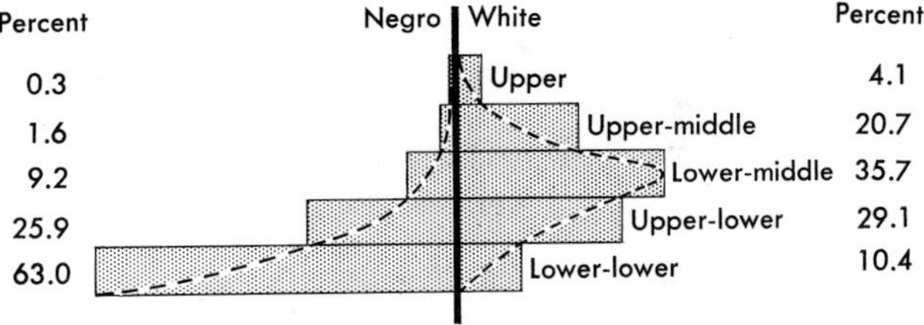

Figure 6. Social stratification of a small Deep South city. SOURCE: Mozell C. Hill and Bevode C. McCall, "Social Stratification in 'Georgia Town,'" *American Sociological Review,* 15:721–730, December, 1950. Used by permission.

more

197 It is apparent that Negroes, as compared with whites, were much ________ heavily concentrated in the lower strata of their own caste.

nine
four

198 Approximately ________ out of ten Negroes were lower class, whereas less than ________ out of ten whites were lower class.

twenty-five
two

199 Approximately ______ out of every hundred white people were in the two highest classes, whereas only ______ out of every hundred Negroes were in comparable class positions within their own caste.

Negro

200 In Mississippi, the average family income for white families was three times the average for ______ families in 1962 (CBS Reports, Sept. 25, 1962).

same

201 In 1959 the median family income for whites in the United States was $4,569, whereas the median family income for Negroes was $2,652 (Horton and Leslie, 1960). Although differences between whites and Negroes are less for the nation than for Deep South communities, such differences are still very marked and in the ______ direction.

lower-class

202 Assuming that the sources and functions of social class differences are very similar in both Negro and white communities, it is apparent that white and Negro differences would parallel middle-class and ______-______ differences.

lower-class

203 Speaking in terms of consequences, white communities are to Negro communities as middle-class communities are to ______-______ communities.

Baptist

204 From knowledge presented in this book, you could predict that very few Negro Protestants would be members of the Congregational Church, whereas many would be members of the ______ Church.

higher / higher
higher
more / fewer

205 You can, further, predict that Negroes, as compared with whites, have ______ psychoses rates, ______ general mortality rates, ______ infant mortality rates, ______ broken families, and ______ friends.

more

206 Likewise, you can predict that Negroes, as compared with whites, will be ______ conservative in every basic way except in their attitudes toward domestic welfare programs.[17]

[17] All the preceding "predictions," except the one predicting fewer friends, have been confirmed by many studies. The prediction concerning fewer friends is probably true, but the author does not know of any direct confirmation of it.

environmental

207 Since white-Negro differences so closely parallel middle-class–lower-class differences, it is probable that differences of behavior between Negroes and whites are largely, if not completely, due to ______ factors rather than to hereditary factors.

Stratification in the United States assumes a castelike hue with respect to the social standing of Negroes and whites in many areas of the United States. Something approaching a pure caste form of stratification occurs in the more isolated and rural areas of the Deep South.

Whites differ from Negroes in precisely the same ways that the higher classes within each race differ from the lower classes. Although this is an important bit of information in its own right, it is of further significance in indicating that the differences between whites and Negroes are due to the same environmental phenomena that make for class differences within each race.

SUMMARY

Stratification of religious bodies in America occurs between and within Protestant denominations and within the Catholic and Jewish denominations. When the major churches are arranged in order of decreasing aggregate prestige of their members, a consistent picture emerges of Congregational, Episcopalian, Jewish, Presbyterian, Methodist, Lutheran, Catholic, and Baptist. Folk knowledge of these prestige orders for denominational memberships is distorted certainly by ingroup aggrandizement and probably by prestige-selective attendance within the denominations.

Although there are many divergences from the central tendencies and evidence is not entirely consistent, the preponderance of evidence nonetheless indicates that religious behavior varies markedly with social class. Indifference combined with observance of religious rites of passage and religious holidays is more concentrated in the American upper class. Taking religion seriously seems to be typical for the American middle class, especially the lower-middle class. The American lower class seems to be polarized into hostile and zealous camps with respect to institutionalized religion, with the upper-lower class containing more of the zealots and the lower-lower class containing more of the antagonists.

There is apparently a widespread belief that the working classes are much more liberal than the middle and upper classes. It is perhaps easy to get this impression since government action aimed at helping the poor and generally underprivileged in this country is very probably the most widely discussed and debated dimension of political and economic liberalism. Here the working classes are the champions of liberalism that they are made out to be by the intellectuals, who are even still more liberal. This, however, is the only known area in which the working classes are more liberal than the middle and upper classes. When it comes to foreign aid, participation in international programs, civil liberties, equal rights for minorities, and religious ideology, the middle and upper classes are definitely more liberal than the lower class.

Available evidence suggests that psychoses occur with decreasing frequency as social class increases. Alternative hypotheses for explaining the high inverse correlations that have been obtained, namely, the differential treatment, horizontal drift, downward drift, and upward drift hypotheses, are disconfirmed by much relevant data.

Relationships between social class and neuroses are not so clear. Although positive relationships between social class and treated neuroses occur, treated neuroses rates may well reflect little more than ability to pay for the treatment, sensitivity to psychological sources of mental and physical difficulties, and attitude toward psychotherapy. In view of the low magnitude of the obtained relationship and what is known about the correlation between social class and chances of neurotics receiving psychotherapy, a negative correlation hypothesis is quite tenable though still unverified. Whatever may be true with respect to neuroses, as such, there is some direct evidence, and much indirect evidence, that happiness is a direct function of social class.

Physical illness parallels mental illness with respect to social class. Mortality rates at all ages, but especially during infancy, vary inversely with social class. The same is true for the frequency and severity of virtually all types of illnesses that have been studied. At the same time, the frequency of medical treatment is a high positive function of social class. The healthier that people, as class groups, are, the more likely they are to receive medical attention and treatment. This relationship apparently is contrary to the common belief that the poor and the rich receive much more medical attention and treatment than the middle-income groups. The rich do get more, but the poor get a lot less.

The impact of social class upon dating is apparently quite different for boys and girls. The relationship between social class and dating frequency is probably high and positive for boys but perhaps essentially curvilinear for girls. Adolescents have a strong tendency to date within their class, but when dating occurs outside an adolescent's class, the boy is far more likely to be in a higher social class than the girl. There is considerable evidence that, as the class difference with respect to the partners in a date increases, bargaining and exploitation, especially exploitation, also increase.

Marriage patterns closely resemble dating patterns. Marriages are essentially endogamous with respect to class, but when marriage outside one's class occurs, the husband is far more likely than the wife to have married "down." In a sense wives are indirectly purchased by their husbands in the United States.

The way people spend their money is highly correlated with how much they make. The absolute amount spent on the "necessities" of life has a very high positive correlation with family income. The proportion of total income spent on these "necessities" is a high inverse function of family income. Contrary to common belief, the poor do not spend disproportionate amounts of their income on automobiles or alcohol. Rather, the reverse is true, i.e., the wealthy not only spend much more on these items, but spend a greater proportion of their total income on them. Poor people apparently spend less money, both absolutely and proportionately, on education than on anything else. This has the effect of keeping them poor from one generation to the next.

Those who are admired and respected by others have a strong tendency to respect and admire themselves. Practically every kind of positively evaluated trait in our culture has been shown to correlate highly and positively with social class. These correlations are all the higher when they deal with personal traits as assessed by associates. Distorted assessments occur with considerable magnitude and frequency. When they occur they are in the approved direction for high-status persons and in the disapproved direction for low-status persons. Self-evaluations follow, and are very consistent with, social evaluations.

There are a vast number of other important functions of social class. Some of the most significant functions have been presented either because they are highly correlated or because they are unrecognized or distorted in traditional American social myths.

Social class differences in the United States parallel

racial differences, with most whites possessing the characteristics of the higher classes and most Negroes possessing the characteristics of the lower classes. If one assumes that social class differences are essentially due to environmental differences, then this social class-racial parallel suggests that racial differences are due to environmental differences.

SELF–REVIEW QUIZ

1 According to data presented, which rank order of denominations most correctly defines the aggregate prestige of their members? (Top ranking given first)

a. Lutheran, Episcopalian, Jewish, Methodist, Catholic
b. Methodist, Catholic, Episcopalian, Jewish, Lutheran
c. Jewish, Catholic, Lutheran, Methodist, Episcopalian
d. Episcopalian, Jewish, Methodist, Lutheran, Catholic

2–6 Match the following:

2. Upper class
3. Upper-middle class
4. Lower-middle class
5. Upper-lower class
6. Lower-lower class

a. Takes religion most seriously
b. Spends the least on education
c. Indifference combined with observance of religious rites and holidays
d. Most likely to belong to the "country club set"
e. Poor but respectable

7 Of the psychoses correlated with income and prestige, ________ (*a*, *b*, c, or *d*) is the only one which did not show strong inverse relationships.

a. schizophrenia, all types
b. manic-depressive psychoses
c. alcoholic psychoses
d. senile psychoses

8 Data from several studies (confirm/disconfirm) the idea that "poor people are the happiest people."

9 In the study of Elmtown, adolescents tended to date within their social class, but when a boy dated out of his class, it was likely to be with a girl of ________ status. When a girl dated out of her class, it was likely to be with a boy of ________ status.

10 Which is false?

a. Class differences in ratings of "good looks" are related to sums spent on personal care and clothing.

b. Tobacco expenditures are proportionately the same for both wealthy and poor families.

c. The poor spend proportionately more on alcohol than the wealthy.

d. The greatest proportional difference in spending between poor and wealthy is for education.

11 Exaggeration of one's "good qualities" by oneself varies (directly/inversely) with social class; self-abasement tends to vary ________ with social class.

12 Differences *between* Negroes and whites often approach a form of (caste/class) stratification in the Deep South; differences *within* the white community constitute ________ stratification.

13 It seems to be true that United States Negroes tend to be (more/less) conservative than whites in all ways studied except in their attitudes toward domestic welfare programs.

14 Available data suggest that, in the United States:

a. Social class differences parallel racial differences.

b. Racial differences are due to inherited qualities.

c. Most Negroes possess characteristics of the white middle class.

d. Social class differences do not parallel racial differences.

REFERENCES

Amidon, Beulah: *Who Can Afford Ill Health,* Public Affairs Pamphlet no. 27, Public Affairs Committee, Inc., Washington, D.C., 1944.

Berkowitz, Leonard: *Aggression: A Social Psychological Analysis,* McGraw-Hill Book Company, New York, 1962.

Bogue, D. J.: *The Population of the United States,* The Free Press of Glencoe, New York, 1959.

Bossard, J. H. S., and E. S. Boll: *Ritual in Family Living,* University of Pennsylvania Press, Philadelphia, 1950.

Campbell, Angus, et al.: *The American Voter,* John Wiley & Sons, Inc., New York, 1960.

Caplow, T. C., and R. J. McGee: *The Academic Marketplace,* Basic Books, Inc., Publishers, New York, 1958.

Centers, Richard: "Marital Selection and Occupational Strata," *American Journal of Sociology,* 54:530–535, 1949.

Centers, Richard: *The Psychology of the Social Classes,* Princeton University Press, Princeton, N.J., 1949.

Clark, R. E.: "Psychoses, Income, and Occupational Prestige," *American Journal of Sociology,* 14:433–440, 1949.

Conference on Economic Progress, *Poverty and Deprivation in the United States,* Washington, D.C., April, 1962.

Connelly, G. M., and H. H. Field: "The Non-voter: Who He Is, What He Thinks," *Public Opinion Quarterly,* 8:178, 1944.

Davis, Allison, B. B. Gardner, and M. P. Gardner: *Deep South,* The University of Chicago Press, Chicago, 1941.

Dollard, John: *Caste and Class*

in Southern Town, Doubleday & Company, Inc., Garden City, N.Y., 1957.

Dollard, John, et al.: *Frustration and Aggression,* Yale University Press, New Haven, Conn., 1939.

Edmonds, V. H.: "Value Empathy, Group Status, and Adjustment," unpublished master's thesis, Purdue University, Lafayette, Ind., 1955.

Farris, R. E. L., and H. W. Dunham: *Mental Disorders in Urban Areas,* The University of Chicago Press, Chicago, 1939.

Federal Security Agency, *Public Health Reports,* Washington, D.C., March, 1949.

Gesell, Arnold, and E. E. Lord: "Psychological Comparison of Nursery School Children from Homes of Low and High Economic Status," *Journal of Genetic Psychology,* 34:339–356, 1927.

Glock, C. Y., and Rodney Stark: "Is There an American Protestantism?" *Trans-Action,* 3: 8–13, 48–49, 1965.

Harvey, O. J.: "An Experimental Approach to the Study of Status Relations in Informal Groups," *American Sociological Review,* 18:357–367, 1953.

Henry, A. F., and J. F. Short, Jr.: *Suicide and Homicide,* The Free Press of Glencoe, New York, 1954.

Hill, M. C., and B. C. McCall: "Social Stratification in 'Georgia Town,' " *American Sociological Review,* 15:721–730, 1950.

Hollingshead, A. B.: *Elmtown's Youth,* John Wiley & Sons, Inc., New York, 1949.

Hollingshead, A. B.: "Class Differences in Family Stability," *Annals of the American Academy of Political and Social Science,* 272:39–46, 1950.

Hollingshead, A. B., and F. C. Redlich: *Social Class and Mental Illness,* John Wiley & Sons, Inc., New York, 1958.

Horton, P. B., and G. R. Leslie: *The Sociology of Social Problems,* 2d ed., Appleton-Century-Crofts, Inc., New York, 1960.

Jones, A. W.: *Life, Liberty and Property,* J. B. Lippincott Company, Philadelphia, 1941.

Kahl, J. A.: *The American Class Structure,* Holt, Rinehart and Winston, Inc., New York, 1953.

Lazerwitz, Bernard: "Some Factors Associated with Variations in Church Attendance," *Social Forces,* 39:301–309, May, 1961.

Lenski, Gerhard: *The Religious Factor,* Doubleday & Company, Inc., Garden City, N.Y., 1961.

Mayer, A. J., and Philip Hauser: "Class Differentials in Expectation of Life at Birth," in Richard Bendix and S. M. Lipset, *Class, Status and Power,* The Free Press of Glencoe, New York, 1953.

Mayer, A. J., and T. F. Hoult: "Social Stratification and Combat Survival," *Social Forces,* 34:155–159, 1955.

Miller, D. R., and G. E. Swanson: *Inner Conflict and Defense,* Holt, Rinehart and Winston, Inc., New York, 1960.

Meyers, J. K., and B. H. Roberts: *Family and Class Dynamics in Mental Illness,* John Wiley & Sons, Inc., New York, 1959.

Odoroff, M. E., and L. M. Abbe: "Patterns of Hospital Prepayment Coverage in the United States, 1956," *Public Health Reports,* 74:573–580, 1959.

Ogburn, W. F., and M. F. Nimkoff, *Sociology,* 3d ed., Houghton Mifflin Company, Boston, 1958.

Pope, Liston: "Religion and the Class Structure," *Annals of the American Academy of Political and Social Science,* 256:84–91, March, 1948.

Putney, Snell, and Russell Middleton: "Dimensions and Correlates of Religious Ideologies," *Social Forces*, 39:285–290, 1961.

Sherif, Muzafer: "Experiments in Group Conflict," *Scientific American*, 195:54–58, 1956.

Vernon, G. M.: "Religious Groups and Social Class: Some Inconsistencies," *Papers of the Michigan Academy of Sciences, Arts, and Letters*, 45:295–301, 1960.

Warner, W. L., et al.: *Democracy in Jonesville*, Harper & Row, Publishers, Incorporated, New York, 1949.

Woolston, Howard: "Religious Consistency," *American Sociological Review*, 2:380–388, 1937.

human learning and social control

human learning processes

VERNON H. EDMONDS

1 In this unit emphasis is placed upon those types of behavior that are more or less distinctively human. It is rather obvious that the life of people differs in many fundamental ways from the life of lower animals. Whether the differences, insofar as they are based upon learning, are due to fundamentally the same processes or to radically different processes is not obvious. The final answer is yet to be established. The procedure here is merely to catalog some of the basic differences and try to get some understanding of how they are acquired.

You will note that references are occasionally made to the Appendix, which deals with learning processes common to human and subhuman species. While the main emphasis here is on human learning behavior, the Appendix contains background information on learning processes which is necessary for a clear understanding of this unit.

The differences between man and lower animals may be matters of degree (quantitative differences) or matters of kind (qualitative differences). Neither type of difference is inherently more important than the other. Some degree differences, for example, the conceptual level of functioning, appear to have as much significance as some differences of kind, for example, the ability to create symbolic environments.

One can manipulate the number of qualitatively distinct human behaviors included in a list of such differences by manipulating levels of abstraction in one's classifying scheme. The higher the level of abstraction used the fewer distinctively human behaviors one can include in the list. The level of abstraction used in any classifying scheme is arbitrary; consequently, the number of distinctively human behaviors appearing in any list is arbitrary. It is not arbitrary, however, once a behavior class is clearly defined, to *inquire into its distinctiveness. Consequently, no attempt is made to enumerate qualitative differences. Rather, the procedure followed in this unit is to (1) carefully define a certain class of behavior, (2) inquire into its qualitative or quantitative distinctiveness, and (3) inquire into the processes through which the class of behavior is acquired by human subjects. In operations 2 and 3, one is forced to skim the surface of what is known, and what is known leaves much to be desired.*

Invention of and Response to Symbolic Environments

1 Some symbols are designative in the sense that they refer to some object or event. Which of the following symbols are designative?

a. Lyndon B. Johnson
b. people
c. subhuman animals
d. go

a, b, and *c*

2 Some symbols direct one to do something. Which of the following are *directive* symbols?

a. "Come."
b. "Close the door."
c. "The world is round."
d. A green light at an intersection.

designative

3 The third set of words in the preceding frame is made up of a series of ________ symbols.

4 Symbols may be *expressive* in the sense that they indicate some condition of the person emitting them. For example, emission of the word, "ouch," usually indicates the experience (condition) of pain on the part of the emitter. Which of the following symbols are expressive?

a. good
b. bad
c. round
d. reprehensible

a, b, and *d*

designative

5 Option c in the preceding frame is a ________ symbol.

refers

6 A designative symbol logically ________ to some object or event.

do

7 A directive symbol is one that makes another (feel/do/understand) something.

condition (state)

8 An expressive symbol indicates the subjective ______ of the person emitting the symbol.

directive

9 One can teach a dog to go, come, or heel. These are ______ symbols.

signs

10 Many subhuman species make noises and movements that indicate the presence of some internal condition. Such noises and movements are expressive ______. (See Appendix.)

symbols

11 Such noises and movements are, however, unlearned. They are natural signs of internal conditions, but they are not invented, arbitrary signs, i.e., ______, of these conditions.

designative

12 The type of symbol usage that is distinctively human is illustrated by a curved arrow on a road sign which, of course, indicates a right or left curve in the road ahead. This is a ______ type of symbol.

designative

13 When one person says, "The world is round," and another understands the expression, we have an example of an articulated series of ______ symbols.

designative symbol

14 The most distinctive type of symbol usage in man is ______ ______ usage.

symbolic environments

15 When one's effective environment largely consists of symbols one can sensibly speak of ______ ______.

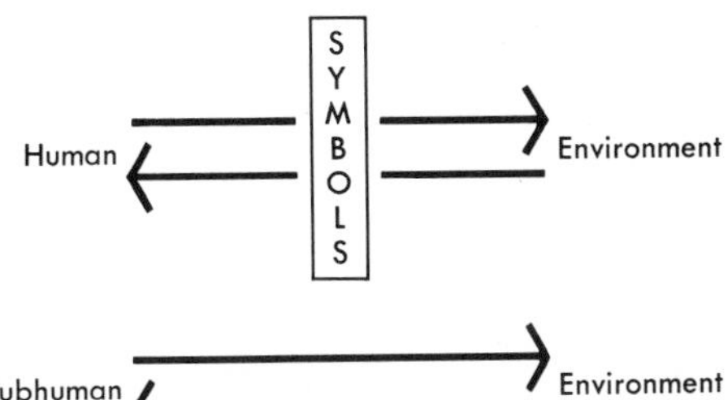

Figure 7. Human and subhuman environments.

symbolic

16 The symbolic environment is extremely important for the understanding of human behavior. Figure 7 indicates that a substantial degree of the human modification of the environment is by ______ means.

person (human)

17 Conversely, a substantial amount of environmental influence upon a ________ is either symbolic in itself or through symbolic events.

symbols

18 Subhuman animals, on the other hand, interact much more directly with their environment, and in their natural habitat rarely, if ever, invent or respond to ________.

environment

19 When a person says, "Bring me a glass of water," and the person addressed brings a glass of water, the first person's ________ has been modified by symbolic means.

symbolic environment

20 In one of the *Ways of Mankind*[1] recordings, a Kwakiutl Indian is depicted engaging in a ritual that will "appease the Salmon Spirit." The Salmon Spirit is not present in the sensory environment but definitely is a part of the Indian's ________ ________.

Salmon Spirit

21 Some years back many national magazines carried photographs of large groups of Texans praying for rain. In this case the Texans are asking their god to send them rain. God for these Texans is symbolically equivalent to the ________ ________ for the Indian.

white

22 It is estimated that from 25,000 to 200,000 Negroes "cross over" each year in the United States (Drake and Cayton, 1945). Crossing-over involves shifting one's public identifications from Negro to ________.

married

23 Assuming that marriage rates of these crossovers are similar to the marriage rates of Negroes generally and whites generally, one can conclude that approximately 90 percent of them will get ________.

white

24 Assuming that interracial marriage rates of these crossovers are similar to those of whites in general one can conclude that virtually all of them will marry people identified as ________.

few

25 Assuming that less than 1 percent of those who identify themselves as white marry persons whom they identify as Negroes, it is reasonably safe to conclude that very ________ of the persons who marry the crossovers would marry them if they knew of their crossing-over.

[1] Series of recordings by Walter Goldschmidt.

symbolic

26 The annual loss of Negroes from the Negro community via crossing-over dramatically illustrates that the same person is reacted to very differently for no other reason than the ______ usage of "Negro" in one case and "white" in the other.

symbolic environment

27 Consider those who would reject a prospective mate after being informed that the prospective mate is a cross-over. Such rejection would very probably be due solely to a change in the rejecter's ______ ______.

environment

28 The essential point with respect to the reactions people make to those who cross over is that the symbolic ______ makes all the difference.

designative

29 Man does, of course, invent and understand road signs and similar symbols. He, likewise, reads and understands books dealing with sociology, psychology, astronomy, etc. In short, much of man's symbolic environment consists of the use and understanding of ______ symbols.

increase

30 It is an open question whether the human use of symbols increases or decreases human contact with reality. There can be no doubt, however, that symbols greatly (decrease/increase) the chances of either type of development occurring.

For an amusing treatment of symbolic environments *see Box 1.*

Box 1. The Symbolic Environment of the Football Stadium

In the following passage Mr. Thomas H. Ferril, editor of *The Rocky Mountain Herald,* has depicted a football game as a Freudian anthropologist might depict it were he not too close to the system to analytically describe the symbols of football. The accuracy of the hypotheses are, of course, not vouched for.

Obviously, football is a syndrome of religious rites symbolizing the struggle to preserve the egg of life through the rigors of impending winter. The rites begin at the autumn equinox and culminate on the first day of the New Year with great festivals identified with bowls of plenty; the festivals are associated with flowers such as roses, fruits such as oranges, farm crops such as cotton, and even sun-worship and appeasement of great reptiles such as alligators.

In these rites the egg of life is symbolized by what is called "the oval," an inflated bladder covered with hog skin. The con-

vention of "the oval" is repeated in the architectural oval-shaped design of the vast outdoor churches in which the services are held every sabbath in every town and city, also every Sunday in the greater centers of population where an advanced priesthood performs. These enormous roofless churches dominate every college campus; no other edifice compares in size with them, and they bear witness to the high spiritual development of the culture that produced them.

Literally millions of worshipers attend the sabbath services in these enormous open-air churches. Subconsciously, these hordes of worshipers are seeking an outlet from sex-frustration in anticipation of violent masochism and sadism about to be enacted by a highly trained priesthood of young men. Football obviously arises out of the Oedipus complex. Love of mother dominates the entire ritual. The churches, without exception, are dedicated to Alma Mater, Dear Mother. (Notre Dame and football are synonymous.)

The rites are performed on a rectangular area of green grass oriented to the four directions. The grass, symbolizing summer, is striped with ominous white lines representing the knifing snows of winter. The white stripes are repeated in the ceremonial costumes of the four whistling monitors who control the services through a time period divided into four quarters, symbolizing the four seasons.

The ceremony begins with colorful processions of musicians and semi-nude virgins who move in and out of ritualized patterns. This excites the thousands of worshipers to rise from their seats, shout frenzied poetry in unison and chant ecstatic anthems through which runs the Oedipus theme of willingness to die for love of Mother.

The actual rites, performed by 22 young priests of perfect physique, might appear to the uninitiated as a chaotic conflict concerned only with hurting the oval by kicking it, then endeavoring to rescue and protect the egg.

However, the procedure is highly stylized. On each side there are eleven young men wearing colorful and protective costumes. The group in so-called "possession" of the oval first arrange themselves in an egg-shaped "huddle," as it is called, for a moment of prayerful meditation and whispering of secret numbers to each other.

Then they rearrange themselves with relation to the position of the egg. In a typical "formation" there are seven priests "on the line," seven being a mystical number associated not, as Jung purists might contend, with the "seven last words" but actually, with sublimation of the "seven deadly sins" into "the seven cardinal principles of education."

The central priest crouches over the egg, protecting it with his hands while over his back quarters hovers the "quarterback." The transposition of "back quarters" to "quarterback" is easily explained by the Adler school. To the layman the curious posture assumed by the "quarter-back," as he hovers over the central priest, immediately suggests the Cretan origins of Mycenaean animal art, but this popular view is untenable. Actually, of course, the "quarter-back" symbolizes the libido, combining two instincts, namely (a) Eros, which strives for even closer union and (b) the instinct for destruction of anything which lies in the path of Eros. Moreover, the "pleasure-pain" excitement of the hysterical worshipers focuses entirely on the actions of the libido-quarter-back. Behind him are three priests representing the male triad.

At a given signal, the egg is passed by sleight-of-hand to one of the members of the triad who endeavors to move it by bodily force across the white lines of winter. This procedure, up and down the enclosure, continues through the four quarters of the ritual.

At the end of the second quarter, implying the summer solstice, the processions of musicians and semi-nude virgins are resumed. After forming themselves into pictograms, representing alphabetical and animal fetishes, the virgins perform a most curious rite requiring far more dexterity than the earlier phallic Maypole rituals from which it seems to be derived. Each of the virgins carries a wand of shining metal which she spins on her fingertips, tosses playfully into the air and with which she interweaves her body in most intricate gyrations.

The virgins perform another important function throughout the entire service. This concerns the mystical rite of "conversion" following success of one of the young priests in carrying the oval across the last white line of winter. As the moment of "conversion" approaches, the virgins kneel at the edge of the grass, bury their faces in the earth, then raise their arms to heaven in supplication, praying that "the uprights will be split." "Conversion" is indeed a dedicated ceremony.

SOURCE: T. H. Ferril, *The Rocky Mountain Herald*, 97:52, Dec. 28, 1957. Used by permission.

Symbolic Learning

first

31 (See Box 1, Appendix.) In the Cook and Harris (1937) experiment a green light becomes a symbol of electric shock after a series of pairings in which the green light occurs ________ in the sequence. Some symbol learning is in keeping with the contiguity hypothesis.

symbol (arbitrary sign)

32 A child often learns that the word "bad" is a _______ of punishment. The learning process can be hypothetically diagramed as follows:

S ⟶ S ⟶ R
"bad" punishment pain & anxiety
S ⟶ R
"bad" anxiety

symbol

33 In the Harlow study (see Figure 16, Appendix) the color of the board is a _______ indicating whether the food is under the odd-shaped or odd-colored structure. This indicates that certain meanings of symbols are acquired in keeping with the effect hypothesis.

think

34 In studying the symbolic behavior of monkeys, one observes only what the monkey does and not what he "thinks." If, however, one is willing to assume that some of the monkeys eventually learn to consciously anticipate that food is under the odd-shaped structure when the board is of one color, and under the odd-colored structure when the board is of another color, then some of the monkeys have learned to _______ in a certain way.

contiguity

35 Consider the contiguity-learning hypothesis (see Appendix for a discussion of this theory of learning.) If cognitive anticipations are learned by the monkeys, then it is quite possible that they would have learned them with or without getting the food, provided they were permitted to frequently observe that when the board is one color the food is under the odd-shaped structure and that when another color the food is under the odd-colored structure. If so, then one could make a case for _______-type learning of the "meaning" of the different colored boards.[2]

sign (symbol)

36 A child early in life learns one meaning of the word "No" through trial and error. In this type of early learning, "No" becomes a customary _______ of punishment.

[2] One group of theorists, the best known of whom is E. C. Tolman (*Purposive Behavior in Animals and Men*, Appleton-Century-Crofts, Inc., New York, 1932), maintains that cognitive expectations are the things learned in effect-type learning and that the rewards and punishments affect performance but not the process of learning as such. There is no attempt to settle the issue here except to suggest that where cognitive expectations are acquired, rewards and punishments are irrelevant in the sense that one can learn to expect painful as well as pleasant events.

effect

37 Learning to stop doing something when a parent says "No" is, in its purely motor aspects, subsumable under ________-type learning.

contiguity

38 Sooner or later, cognitive expectations are learned, and these, perhaps, are learned in keeping with the ________ hypothesis.

Insight Learning

In the study by Cook and Harris (1937), some subjects were told that electric shock would follow presentation of a green light.[3] *The psychogalvanic response occurred in the absence of any exposure to green-light–shock sequences. Thus, subjects learned to react with anxiety to the green light in the absence of either neutral-stimulus–adequate-stimulus sequences or any kind of trial and error.*

insight

39 Unquestionably, we have an illustration of ________ learning, however contingent it might be upon a background of simple contiguity or effect learning.

shock

40 In this case the green light is a symbol of ________.

adequate

41 Note, also, the usual way a person learns the meaning of a word, such as "socialization." He usually reads a statement like, "Socialization refers to the process in which a person learns to conform to the norms of his group or community." One can, of course, think of socialization as a neutral stimulus and the process in which a person learns to conform to the norms of his group or community as a kind of complex ________ stimulus.

neutral

42 If, however, learning the meaning of socialization were purely and simply a contiguity-type process, analogous to the salivation learning of Pavlov's dogs, the ________ stimulus would have to occur first in the sequence.

is not

43 But, in this case, the order of occurrence of the defining term and the term to be defined makes little or no difference. Thus, learning the conceptual meaning of terms (is/is not) a pure and simple case of contiguity learning.

[3] See Box 1, Appendix.

The Conceptual Level of Functioning

44 A concept is defined as an awareness of something that is not present in the sensory environment. A commonly used word that usually means the same thing as concept is:

- *a.* action
- *b.* feeling (emotion)
- c. idea
- *d.* sensation

c (idea)

45 Concepts may be either abstract or concrete. A concept is abstract if it entails awareness of the common property of a number of things which in their totality are different. Which of the following words refer to abstract concepts?

- *a.* horse
- *b.* President Smith
- c. tree
- *d.* learning

a, c, and *d*

46 A concrete or specific concept entails awareness of some specific thing. Which of the following words refer to concrete concepts?

- *a.* The White House
- *b.* totalitarian government
- c. perception
- *d.* Yellowstone National Park

a and *d*

When one is aware of the common property or properties of a number of different objects or events one has an abstract concept. When one is aware of some particular object or event one has a concrete or specific concept.

47 Whether the concept is specific or abstract, the thing that one is aware of is not a part of the ________ ________ at the time the awareness occurs.

sensory environment

48 A person who is aware of the White House by virtue of looking at it would not be said to have a ________ of the White House.

concept

49 On the other hand, if the same person, while on a Florida vacation, was thinking of the appearance of the White House when he last saw it, he would be said to have a ________ of the White House.

concept

sensory

50 One never, strictly speaking, sees his idea of a horse, a girl, a book, etc. He sees some particular horse, some particular girl, some particular book, etc. Abstract properties per se are never a part of one's ________ environment.

Box 2. Significance of Conceptual Level of Functioning

Sherif and Sherif (*An Outline of Social Psychology*, rev. ed., Harper & Row, Publishers, Incorporated, New York, 1956, pp. 8–10) in commenting on the significance of man's conceptual level of functioning say:

The significance of this typical mode of human functioning is grasped more easily if its uniqueness in the animal kingdom is considered. Many of us have grown up interested in animals and pets. We have seen them do things which seemed remarkably like things human beings do. But in scientific study of human experience and behavior we must heed one of the lessons from the comparative study of various species: The comparative capacities of various species cannot be understood if we look only at their similarities and skip over the enormous differences between them. . . . The behavior of subhuman organisms may be suggestive for certain lines of investigating human experience and behavior. But in studying the interaction and social life of humans, the easy pleasure of simple comparison and analogy between human behavior and the behavior of pet dogs, laboratory rats, or chimpanzees has to be foregone. . . . The fact that man's typical level of functioning is conceptual means that seeing the world, feeling, discriminating, wanting and desiring attain properties not found in subhuman animals.

humans (persons, people, etc.)

51 It has been suggested earlier that some of the genuinely insightful solutions to problems by some chimpanzees involved an *imaginary* solution to the problems prior to actual mechanical solutions. If this is true, then the conceptual level of functioning is not limited to ________.

Hebb and Thompson (1954) describe the behavior of some chimpanzees at the Yerkes Laboratories that should leave little doubt on this issue. Some chimpanzees upon seeing a visitor being escorted through the colony will slip over to a water fountain, tank up, move quietly over to the side of the cage where visitors frequently pass, sit quietly with a mouthful of water until the visitor is within range, and then douse him with a pint or so of water.

prior

52 Such actions can hardly be accounted for without postulating that the sequence of acts is planned ______ to actual occurrence.

thinking

53 It is also apparent that such chimpanzees have the ability to act one way while they are ______ about acting in another way.

chimpanzees

54 Pfeiffer (1963) reports that chimpanzees in their natural habitat make simple tools, sticks of a standard length, and store them in a certain place. This indicates that ______ are capable of at least rudimentary thought processes.

thought (conceptual)

55 He also reports having observed a number of male chimpanzees, awaiting their turn to have sexual intercourse with a receptive female. This also indicates some kind of ______ processes occurring in these chimpanzees.

human

56 Other observations could be reported; however, these will suffice to show that the conceptual level of functioning is not a qualitatively distinct ______ trait.

conceptual

57 Of course, people would not be functioning on a very high level if they could only squirt water on people, store simple tools, and line up for sexual intercourse. Such things may be highly valued by some people, but they do not entail a high level of abstract ______ functioning.

Our next task is to achieve some understanding of how concepts are learned. It is plausible that the experimental studies of concept formation parallel the learning of concepts in everyday life. In a study carried out by Kenneth Smoke (1932) subjects were asked to select which card of a pair was a "zum." Smoke had decided in advance that a zum would be a red line trisected by two red lines. Each presentation of card pairs included a "zum" and another geometric design that violated one of the requirements of "zumness." When a subject could go through sixteen pairs without error it was assumed that he had learned what a "zum" was. After the subject selected a card he was told whether it was right or wrong.

is not

58 In one experiment twenty-three out of fifty-nine subjects who had learned the meaning of the word by Smoke's standard could not accurately define it. It is apparent that behavioral attainment (is/is not) contingent upon verbal attainment.

verbal attainment

59 On the other hand, once a subject correctly verbalized the concept the error rate immediately dropped to zero and remained there. Behavioral attainment invariably follows ________ ________.

verbal attainment

60 Which of these two types of attainment would be the better indicator of insight? ________ ________.

insightful

61 Since verbal attainment was common in Smoke's study we may conclude that ________ learning of concepts was also common.

Many of Smoke's subjects were observed to reason out loud or to report upon questioning that they covertly reasoned in a manner that we would normally think of as somewhat scientific. For example, they would say, "If a zum is a red line divided into three parts, then this card will be the zum." Upon being informed that it was or wasn't they would proceed on the same hypothesis or discard it for another.

hypothesis

62 Smoke called this "________ testing" and concluded that it was a basic procedure for learning concepts.

trial

63 As we have noted, a good many subjects mastered the concept in the operational sense of making sixteen correct choices without forming a correct hypothesis. Their reduction of error rates was comparatively slow and gradual. This type of concept learning most closely resembles the noninsightful, ________-and-error learning of subhuman animals.

Smoke has indicated three ways in which people learn concepts: trial and error, hypothesis testing, and insight, or sudden recognition of the meaning. Of course, one may maintain that all three processes are really the same thing in disguise, but as we have previously noted such a position is hardly tenable (See Appendix, pp. 444–461.)

contiguity

64 Hull (1920), using similar procedures, formulated his "principle of dissociation" to explain the learning of concepts. He put it this way, "What is associated now with one thing and now with another tends to become dissociated from either, and to grow into an object of abstract contemplation." This sounds more like a special form of the ______ hypothesis.[4]

contiguity

65 It is apparent that much concept learning does not involve a temporarily contiguous sequence in which a meaningless symbol (the term to be defined) is followed by a meaningful set of symbols or events (the defining term). Hence the ______ hypothesis is hardly an adequate explanation of all concept learning.

effect

66 Furthermore, the learning of concepts is often instantaneous, involving little or no previous trial and error. Concept learning can hardly be thought of as a process exclusively subsumable under the ______ hypothesis.

That neither effect nor contiguity principles are adequate explanations of concept learning is confirmed by the fact that there are large species differences in concept attainment. Even the existence of conceptual behavior in animals below the higher apes in the evolutionary scale is questionable. Furthermore, some studies in concept formation exclude the possibility of learning through trial and error or through contiguity of external stimuli (Hanfmann and Kasanin, 1937; Bruner, Goodnow, and Austin, 1956).

concept

67 Contiguity and effect processes, therefore, can hardly explain all ______ formation.

Box 3. Concept Formation

After reviewing many studies of concept formation, Bruner, Goodnow, and Austin (*A Study of Thinking*, Science Editions, New York, 1956, p. 79) say:

[4] It is recognized that Hull, being convinced at the time that all learning of all species was in keeping with the "law of effect," would not have accepted such an explanation. Later (1952) he expressed doubt that any principle of animal learning was adequate for explaining human thought processes.

Organisms do group the objects and events of their world into pragmatically useful concepts and they do so with regard to reality constraints. Psychology has been celebrating the role of "emotional factors" and "unconscious drives" in behavior for so long now that man's capacity for rational coping with his world has come to seem like some residual capacity that shows its head only when the irrational lets up. To account for the exquisite forms of problem-solving that we see in everyday life and may see in our laboratories any time we choose to give our subjects something more challenging than key-pressing to perform, highly simplified theories of learning have been invoked. One learns concepts by the association of external stimuli with internal mediating stimuli either by some simple law of frequency or contiguity or by a rather circular and over-begged law of effect. If we have at times portrayed conceptual behavior as perhaps overly logical, we will perhaps be excused on the ground that one excess often breeds its opposite. Man is not a logic machine, but he is certainly capable of making decisions and gathering information in a manner that reflects better on his learning capacity than we have been as yet ready to grant.

68 Although most, if not all, studies of concept formation involve the study of abstract concept formation, there seems no good reason to suppose that specific ________ ________ is any different, except where abstract intelligence is an important determinant of how quickly, or whether, the concept can be learned.

concept formation

The Use and Understanding of Propositional Language

69 Language is defined in the Appendix as the articulation of symbols (arbitrary signs) in such a way as to form words and ________.

sentences

70 Observe, for example, the following list of words: prevent, precursor, preliterate, preclude, prelude. In each of these words the ________ "pre" is articulated with other symbols to form words with different meanings in each case.

symbol

71 Observe, for example, the following sentences: "Social classes do not exist in any society which has no division of labor. Division of labor is the cause of social classes."[5]

[5] No one is being quoted. This is simply an illustration of how symbols are articulated to form sentences. The truth of these positions is, likewise, of no importance at this point.

sentence

Two terms, "social classes" and "division of labor," are articulated with other terms in each sentence in such a way that different meanings are conveyed by each ________.

propositional language

72 Propositional language is frequently referred to as "true language." True language is a synonym for ________ ________.

directive language

73 It is necessary, at this point, to make a distinction between propositional language, directive language, and expressive language. "Close the door" is an example of ________ ________.

expressive

74 "Ouch," "oh," and "wonderful" are examples of ________ language.

propositional language

75 "The world is round" is an example of ________ ________.

expressive

76 Expressive language, by definition, is produced by some condition of the emitter but does not combine designative subject and predicate terms in a conceptually meaningful manner. "Strawberry ice cream is good" is an example of ________ language.

symbol

77 The subject term "strawberry ice cream" logically refers to a general thing. "Strawberry ice cream" is, thus, a designative ________.

designative

78 On the other hand, the predicate term "good" does not refer to a general or specific thing. "Good" is not a ________ symbol.

predicate

79 This verbal expression is said to be an example of expressive language because (*a*) the predicate term "good" indicates some condition, probably pleasure, of the emitter, and (*b*) the nondesignative property of the predicate term makes it impossible for both subject and ________ terms to be combined in a conceptually meaningful way.

do not

80 Moral and aesthetic terms, since they only express some condition of the person using them, (do/do not) have designative properties.

refer

81 Hence, "Adultery is wrong," is an example of expressive language because the predicate term "wrong" does not *logically* ________ to some general or particular thing.

condition (state, feeling, etc.)

82 The word "wrong," like moral terms generally, indicates some ________, probably aversion, of the emitter, but it makes no logical reference to some object or event.

language

83 If either the subject or predicate term is devoid of designative meaning, the sentence as a whole is not in the category of propositional ________.

directive

84 When one says, "Hand me the keys," he is using ________ language.

do not

85 It is directive because (*a*) one person is trying to get another to act in a certain way, and (*b*) no statement, as such, is made. Directive expressions (do/do not) have the property of being true or false.

true / false

86 Expressive sentences, as well as directive sentences, do not have the property of being ________ or ________.

a and *d*

87 Which of the following verbal emissions are examples of propositional language?

a. The world is round.
b. Come in.
c. That's great.
d. The price of butter is higher than the price of margarine.

b and c

88 Which of the following verbal emissions are examples of expressive language?

a. Delinquency is common among children from problem homes.
b. Liberalism is an odious thing.
c. Adultery is unforgivable.
d. Alcoholism is more frequent in the lower class than in the middle class.

a and c

89 Which of the following verbal emissions are examples of directive language?

a. Please come in.
b. He came in the back door.
c. Leave the keys in the mailbox.
d. It is a simple matter of right and wrong.

directive

90 A chimpanzee trying to pull an object which is too heavy for it will frequently solicit help from other chimpanzees by doing such things as placing another chimp's hand on the rope, simulating pulling movements, etc. (Hebb and Thompson, 1954). It is apparent that such solicitations are functionally equivalent to the ________ language of people.

expressive

91 A cat can express its displeasure by meowing. It can express its pleasure by purring. In short, it can express some condition of itself and by doing so engage in something that is roughly equivalent to _______ language in people.

meowing

92 If the cat could talk it might say that stepping on a cat's tail is immoral. But in saying this it would undoubtedly be saying no more than it has by _______.

directive

93 One can, of course, teach a dog to come, go, sit, etc. A dog can learn to respond to _______ language.

propositional language

94 Not even the brightest chimp, however, could ever understand the expression, "The world is round." In other words, even the most capable of subhuman species cannot understand _______ _______.

No[6]

95 See the Appendix (p. 472) for a discussion of Blueboy, the Missouri parakeet that could recite the first two stanzas of "Mary had a little lamb" (Mowrer, 1960). Is Blueboy using and understanding propositional language? _______.

man

96 Man and some species of birds can express propositional language, but only _______ can understand it.

directive

97 One can teach a dog to retrieve a stick by saying, "Go get it." This, of course, is an example of _______ language.

environment

98 But what is more important, the "understood" subject of the sentence, "you," and the predicate, "it," are present in the sensory _______.

sensory environment

99 If one could tell a dog that his ancestors were all very intelligent and get the dog to understand it, then the dog would be responding to subject and predicate term referents that would not be—indeed, could not be—a part of the _______ _______.

understand

100 Learning propositional language involves both learning to use it and learning to _______ it.

[6] He is using it, but he does not understand it. If the reader is sufficiently naïve to ask, "How do you know he doesn't understand it?" let him simply ask Blueboy or any other parakeet such questions as "Who owned the lamb?" "What color was it?" and then wait for a relevant answer, which, one should note, is well within the vocabulary range of the bird.

understanding / propositional

101 There is probably no other class of behavior that is so distinctively human as the ______ of ______ language.

use

102 It is plausible that much early learning with respect to the ______ of words is the same for both children and the talking birds (see Appendix, p. 473).

pleasant

103 If so, then the beginnings of propositional language usage is a three-phase process. In the first phase, certain words are frequently heard in a ______ context.

reward

104 In the second phase, the child repeats words that are pleasant to hear because of the previous word-reward associations. The word sounds during this phase have their own built-in ______.

rewards
punishments

105 In the third phase, pronunciation and frequency of word usage are controlled by the frequency of ______ and ______ following the child's verbal emissions.

subject / predicate

106 Learning to understand propositional language is largely learning to understand the conceptual references of the subject term, the predicate term, and the (verbal) connective of the ______ and ______ terms.

world

107 How, for example, does one learn to understand the meaning of the statement "The world is round." One probably has to learn the meaning of the predicate term "round" before he can learn the meaning of the subject term ______.

dissociated

108 If a child learns the meaning of round in much the same way that experimental subjects learn the meaning of zum (see frame 63), then round is associated now with one object and now with another until it becomes ______ from either.

hypothesis

109 It is probable, however, that learning the concept of round involves considerable ______ testing and insight.

symbolic

110 Since the world, as such, cannot be observed, a child has to learn the meaning of "the world" through the use of some ______ procedures.

symbolic

111 He looks at globes and drawings and listens to verbal descriptions of the world. He apparently must learn the meaning of the word "world" through more or less insightful association of the word with ______ descriptions of it.

belongs to the class of

112 "Is" is a very abstract symbol meaning "belongs to the class of." To say that the world is round is to say that the world +++++ round objects.

same

113 The learning of the reference of "is" presumably comes about in much the ______ way that one learns the meaning of round.

contiguity

114 Mowrer (1960) tries to explain learning to understand propositional language by using the statement: "Tom is a thief." His point is that "Tom" becomes a partial substitute for the word "thief." Mowrer, thus, adopts a ______ explanation of this type of learning.

insightful

115 Somehow a child learns the conceptual and designative references of the words "world," "is," and "round." The learning of these conceptual references is almost certainly one of contiguity association, hypothesis testing, and more or less ______ reasoning.

explanation

116 Somehow he learns to put these concepts together in a logically meaningful way. To say that the process of logical integration of concepts involves logical intelligence is undoubtedly true, but such a statement is no genuine ______ of the process.

contiguity

117 In any case, the principles of effect and ______ can hardly constitute complete explanations of the process.

The Significance of the Conceptual-Linguistic Level of Functioning

Most of the phenomena enumerated here as functions of the conceptual-linguistic level of functioning are typically listed as the functions of "language" (Lindesmith and Strauss, 1956; Sherif and Sherif, 1956). Some go so far as to maintain that language determines the conceptual behavior of all people all the time (Whorf, 1940).

concepts

118 There can be no question that the child described in Box 4 is clearly aware of objects and events that are not present in her sensory environment. In other words, there can be no question that she has ______.

conceptual

119 Since she had been carefully tested to determine whether she could use or understand language, it is quite certain that the ______ level of functioning is not contingent upon the use or understanding of language.

Box 4. Conceptual Behavior without Language

McGinnis (*Aphasic Children*, Alexander Graham Bell Association for the Deaf, 1963, p. xiii) describes the conceptual behavior of an eight-year-old child who could neither speak nor understand language:*

That she had concepts was evident by the drawings she made of events in which she had participated and of the probable situations that led up to such events. In one instance, a teacher was absent. Assuming that the teacher was sick, the child drew a series of pictures. In the first picture she drew the teacher walking in the rain without an umbrella. The second picture showed the teacher in bed. A doctor was taking her pulse. In the third picture the mother was standing near the bed holding an umbrella and a pair of rubbers. The fourth picture depicted the mother spanking the patient.

* This condition, known as receptive and expressive aphasia, is caused by structural abnormalities, usually due to destruction of neural tissue, in the "speech area" of the brain.

thinking (understanding, conceptualizing, etc.)

120 Remember that Blueboy, the Missouri parakeet, could emit propositional language. It is apparent to anyone who listens closely to some sermons and convocation speeches that people are often in the same boat as the parakeet, i.e., they speak without ______.

think

121 Just as one can speak without thinking, one can ______ without speaking.

language

122 Many other illustrations of the behavior of aphasic children could be given that parallel that of this eight-year-old girl. They show beyond any reasonable doubt that conceptual behavior is not contingent upon either the use or the understanding of ______.

No[7]

123 A very common position is that thought, i.e., conceptual behavior, necessitates the manipulation of symbols. Does the behavior of the aphasic girl support this hypothesis? ______.

[7] From the information we possess, the girl might think without manipulating symbols, or she might have to manipulate symbols in some covert sense in order to think. Her case is irrelevant to this hypothesis.

124 The behavior of the aphasic girl, however, definitely disconfirms the hypothesis that conceptual processes are contingent upon either the use or the understanding of propositional ________.

language

125 The reader will recall that chimpanzees have been observed to do such things as making and storing tools, lining up for sexual intercourse, and tanking up on water, holding it in their mouths for several minutes, and then dousing visitors with it. All these behaviors indicate that chimpanzees are capable of operating on the ________ level.

conceptual

126 Chimpanzees neither use nor understand language. Conceptual behavior is not contingent upon either the use or the understanding of ________.[8]

language

127 Thus, thought can apparently occur without the use or understanding of symbols, broadly speaking, or of ________, narrowly speaking (cf., especially, Werner and Kaplan, 1963).

language

128 Nonetheless, language greatly facilitates thought and especially the communication of ________.

thoughts (concepts, ideas)

129 The following discussion will consist of those things which necessitate the ________ level of functioning, but not, in some cases, the linguistic level of functioning.

conceptual

130 The reason for speaking of conceptual-linguistic functions rather than conceptual functions is that the use and understanding of ________ language greatly increase the magnitude of these functions, and in some cases appear to be necessary for their existence.

propositional

131 We have emphasized that chimpanzees can plan a sequence of actions based upon the anticipation of some future event that takes place in a matter of:

a. minutes
b. hours
c. days
d. weeks

a

[8] There is no reason to suppose that chimpanzees are manipulating symbols when they are obviously thinking. At least, any such assumption is extremely gratuitous.

132 A student upon entering college is usually assuming that a college degree will bring certain rewards that are ________ away in time.

years

133 A man who takes out retirement insurance is usually basing his action upon an event that is typically decades away. It is obvious that man's actions, compared with those of the chimpanzee, are much less limited to fairly immediate ________ events.

future

134 Chimpanzees will regularly return to a certain box that they have seen food placed in, after being removed from the room that contains several boxes, provided that they are not removed for a period exceeding approximately five minutes (Yerkes, 1943). From this, it would seem that a chimpanzee's retention of an image of the box containing food is limited to a span of about ________ ________.

five minutes

135 Many old people, on the other hand, recall and react to things that happened in early childhood. This involves retention of experiences that extend ________ into the past.

years (decades)

136 Images of the past and future extend backward and forward only a little for chimpanzees but very much in the case of ________.

man (people, etc.)

137 Probably one basic reason that man's effective environment is so temporally extended over that of chimpanzees is that man possesses ________ language, whereas chimpanzees do not.

propositional

Furthermore, man's life is full of reactions to events that antedate his birth but are conveyed to him through the medium of propositional language. Although it rarely happens, these events could be communicated to people who haven't experienced them via nonlinguistic symbols, as, for example, in the picture stories of the aphasic girl (Box 4) or in the picture stories of the ancient Egyptians. Historical influences cannot occur in the absence of the use and understanding of designative symbols. Man is the only animal that uses and understands designative symbols. Man, therefore, is the only animal that is subject to historical influences.

Conceptual Codification

common

138 Let us now consider the process that we shall call "coding" or "categorization." Coding or categorization is said to occur when a person responds to the (common/unique) property (or properties) of a number of different objects or events.

common

139 There comes a time in the life of a child when he notices that Rover, Shep, Sport, and Tigue have something in ________.

coding (categorizing)

140 When he notices that Rover, Shep, Sport, and Tigue have certain things in common he is said to be ________ this part of his environment.

common

141 The word "dog" will be attached to these specific objects either before or after the child achieves some understanding of what they have in common. From this point he will, sooner or later, perceive that dogs, cats, and squirrels have certain things in ________.

more

142 They all have fur, teeth, four legs, give birth to and suckle their young, etc. His coding of his environment is now on a (more/less) abstract level than previously.

less

143 He may, once he learns the concept of dog, go in the other direction. He may learn that there are shepherds, bulldogs, cocker spaniels, etc. His coding of his environment is now on a (more/less) abstract level than when he was coding all of them as dogs. The coding process is diagramed below:

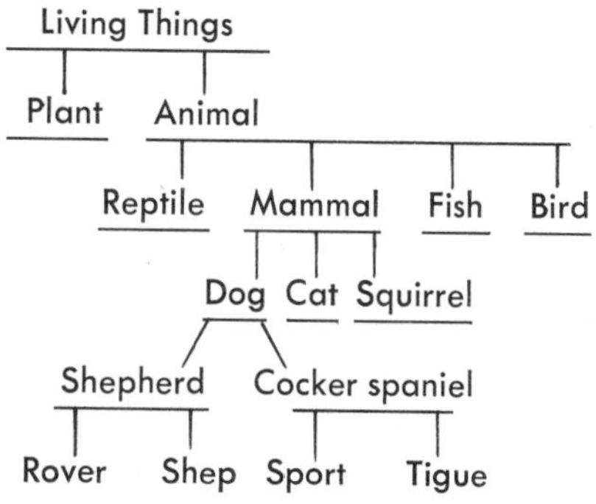

abstract

144 As one conceptually moves from Sport to living things the coding process becomes increasingly ________.

decreasingly (less)

145 As one conceptually moves from mammal to shepherd the coding process becomes ________ abstract.

coding

146 We have previously noted the phenomenon of crossing-over. It was stressed that probably most people who marry the crossovers are categorizing, i.e., ________ the crossovers as "white."

symbolic codification of their environment

147 The significant thing about this phenomenon is that such people are primarily reacting to their (real sensory environment/symbolic codification of their environment).

the symbolic code imposed upon the berries

148 Hallowell (1951) reports that the Northern Ojibwa classify (code) a variety of berries with different appearances as "snake berries." None of them is poisonous, but they are all avoided like poison. The Ojibwa are obviously responding to (physical aspects of the berries/the symbolic code imposed upon the berries).

reaction (response)

149 The physical and sensory properties of the snake berries do not determine the Ojibwa's ________ to them.

concepts elicited by the verbal stimuli

150 In Razran's study transfer of acquired responses to synonyms was greater than to homophones (see Appendix, Box 1). This indicates that subjects had typically learned to respond to the (concepts elicited by the verbal stimuli/physical properties of the verbal stimuli).

physically different

151 Once the physical environment gets coded in a certain way these coding processes "cut across" specific objects and events that are ________, and hence objectively, ________.

coded

152 It is probably correct to say that man typically responds to a symbolically ________ environment rather than to the sensory environment as such.

create (produce)

153 The lower animals, since they are incapable of genuine conceptual behavior, may learn to react to a perceptually coded environment. One could, for example, teach a white rat to avoid black rats, but it would be virtually impossible to teach him to avoid white rats with black rat ancestry. It could only be done by providing some sensory sign for such rats. The rat would never ________ such a sign on his own.

Self-concepts

A major function of the conceptual-linguistic level of functioning is the emergence of self-concepts and self-feelings.

images and feelings one has about oneself

154 The images and feelings one has about oneself are frequently referred to as "ego attitudes." Ego attitudes refer to +++++.

conceptual

155 In order to possess a more or less coherent self-image which includes judgments concerning one's intelligence, physical attractiveness, likableness, etc., one must operate on the ______ level, for these things are not a part of one's sensory environment.

c (think)[9]

156 In a word, one must be able to:

a. hear
b. see
c. think
d. smell

language

157 One can have a self-concept without the use or understanding of ______; however, the possession of a genuine propositional language would undoubtedly greatly facilitate the emergence of any person's self-concept.

Near the turn of the century C. H. Cooley (Human Nature and the Social Order, *Charles Scribner's Sons, New York, 1902, p. 184) coined a phrase "the looking-glass self" which, in his judgment, explained why people have certain self-attitudes. He said:*

As we see . . . our face, figure, and dress in the glass, and are interested in them because they are ours, and pleased or otherwise with them according as they do or do not answer to what we should like them to be; so in imagination we perceive in another's mind some thought of our appearance, manners, aims, deeds, character, friends, and so on, and are variously affected by it. A self idea of this sort seems to have three principal elements: the imagination of our appearance to the other person; the imagination of his judgment of that appear-

[9] A self-image could occur in the absence of any one of the others.

ance; and some sort of self-feeling, such as pride or mortification.

nonphysical (sensory)

158 Perhaps all analogies are to some extent misleading. One cannot see one's intelligence in a looking glass, but it is quite certain that people are always imagining how others appraise them in this respect. This analogy is a little misleading in that it does not convey the imagination of others' appraisal of the ______ aspects of oneself.

others

159 As a hypothesis it means that one's self-attitudes are determined by the attitudes ______ are imagined to have toward oneself.

Miyamoto and Dornbusch (1956) had subjects rate themselves on a five-point scale with respect to their intelligence, self-confidence, physical attractiveness, and likableness. The subjects also predicted how specific others would rate them on these traits and how others in general would rate them.

very intelligent

160 All four ratings were positively correlated. A person who, for example, rated himself as very intelligent usually thought that other specific people and people in general would rate him as ______ ______.

very intelligent

161 In such cases the specific others, who the subject thought would rate him as very intelligent, usually did rate him as ______ ______.

confirms

162 The correlation, however, between subject's self-ratings and the ratings *ascribed* to others was considerably higher than the correlation between subject's self-ratings and the *actual* ratings of the subjects by others. This particular result ______ Cooley's (1902) hypothesis concerning the source of self-attitudes.

ascribed (attributed, imputed, etc.)

163 To repeat, one's self-concept is more determined by the judgments of the self that are ______ to others than by their actual judgments.

subhuman

164 A major, if not the major, goal in life is the preservation and enhancement of one's self-esteem—a problem which ______ species do not have (Krech, Crutchfield, and Ballachey, 1963; Sherif and Sherif, 1956).

Imaginary Environments

an imaginary[10]

165 Another major function of the conceptual-linguistic level of functioning is suggested by the Kwakiutl Indians appeasing the Salmon Spirit and by the Texans praying for rain. In both cases the responses are made to (a real/ an imaginary) environment.

propositional language

166 Does the possession of propositional language lead one toward or away from reality? It is an open question, but the bizarre and fantastic world many people live in could not exist, even in imagination, if it were not for their use and understanding of _______ _______.

Box 5. The Imaginary Environment of a "Patriot"

There has been a substantial growth of far right-wing organizations in recent years. All these organizations apparently share the belief of imminent Communist take-over. Some of these organizations are quasi-military in character in that they emphasize the use of armed "patriots" as part of a necessary countermeasure to the imminent Communist conquest of the "free world." A portion of a letter written to a college student by a "lieutenant" in a patriotic "army" in St. Petersburg, Florida, is duplicated below. It clearly illustrates the point that man's ability to use and understand propositional language makes imaginary environments possible.

We are BROTHERS-IN-ARMS with the U.S. RANGERS, THE CALIFORNIA RANGERS, THE MINUTE MEN, THE TEXAS RANGERS, THE GREEN MOUNTAIN BOYS in New England, and many other smaller localized organizations all of which comprise a vast NATIONAL CHRISTIAN ARMY of over 10,000,000 PATRIOTIC MEN who are ready to defend this Nation against the RED HORDES that will soon attack the United States.
Each man needs the following basic equipment for GUERRILLA WARFARE OPERATIONS.

1. *Any Standard Rifle of at least .30 Cal.*
2. *One Good Quality Hunting Knife, 6" blade.*
3. *At least 1000 rounds of Ammunition.*
4. *Regulation Canteen-holder–webbed belt.*

[10] One may, of course, argue that the Salmon Spirit does exist and will be appeased and that God does exist and will send the Texans some rain. The point, in any case, is that there is no empirical evidence either of the existence of the spirits or of their presumed reactions to appeasing gestures.

5. *Any suitable type Back Pack on which can be mounted— A good quality sleeping bag—A good quality 2-man tent.*
6. *Three pair of camouflage fatigues of heavy duck cloth.*
7. *At least one pair of insulated paratroop type boots.*
8. *Seven day supply of concentrated food packs.*
9. *At least 500 water purification tablets.*
10. *Snake bite–and first aid kit.*
11. *One mosquito bar.*
12. *One camouflaged waterproof poncho.*

This is a basic equipment list that will allow you to operate as an effective Guerrilla Unit.

We shall fight from the fields, from the PLAINS, from the SWAMPS, and from the MOUNTAINS; and although OVERWHELMINGLY outnumbered in men and equipment we shall still be VICTORIOUS for we have ALMIGHTY GOD on our side and at the PRECISE MOMENT his Heavenly Armies will intervene and give us the VICTORY through the TRIUMPHANT RETURN OF HIS BLESSED SON.

Let us remember the words of our late Christian President who was ASSASSINATED by the ANTI-CHRIST JEW-COMMUNISTS, "I am a Berliner," and in the spirit of these brave people let us prepare to defend our CHRISTIAN HERITAGE for ALMIGHTY GOD, for CHRIST, and the NATION.

Specialized Cooperation

Another major function of the conceptual-linguistic level of functioning is the existence of purposive, specialized cooperation. Anyone familiar with the workings of ant colonies knows that ants specialize in their work. Some ants tend certain crops, others take care of the ant larvae, others fight off enemies, others do little more than breed, etc.

167 The behavior of such ants represents a highly ________ form of cooperation.

specialized

168 The behavior of a given ant type is, however, invariant within the species and occurs in its full-blown form in the absence of any experience with such behavior. This indicates that the specialized cooperation of ants is unlearned and, consequently, is not a purposive form of ________.

cooperation

169 Ants, in this respect, are not different from other "social" insects. While their cooperation is frequently highly specialized, it is by no means ________.

purposive

If chimpanzees engage in purposive, specialized, cooperative behavior, then such behavior cannot be contingent upon the use and understanding of language. Since chimpanzees, as intelligent as they are, can apparently learn only nonspecialized cooperation, and that only with considerable difficulty, it would seem that purposive, specialized, cooperation is unlikely to occur in the absence of the use and understanding of propositional language (true language). (Crawford, 1937; Kohler, 1925.)

Shortening of the Learning Process

Another major function of language is a very marked reduction or elimination of the drawn-out and continuous learning processes of acquisition and extinction.

neutral

170 In classical conditioning experiments a neutral stimulus is presented shortly before an adequate stimulus, and sooner or later the initially _______ stimulus becomes a partial substitute for the adequate stimulus.

never

171 The acquisition of the response to the initially neutral stimulus very rarely occurs after one sequential pairing of the stimuli and _______ occurs prior to one sequential pairing of the stimuli.

Cook and Harris (1937) instructed human subjects that a green light would be followed by electric shock. The galvanic skin reflex, an indicator of anxiety, occurred with full frequency and magnitude upon the first presentation of the green light and in the absence of electric shock.

propositional language

172 This indicates that the understanding of _______ _______ makes possible the acquisition of a conditioned response in the total absence of neutral-stimulus–adequate-stimulus occurrences.

not related

173 Further presentations of the green-light–shock sequence did not substantially increase either the probability or magnitude of the anxiety response. Thus the strength and frequency of the learned response were _______ to the number of sequential presentations of neutral-stimulus–adequate-stimulus sequences.

extinction

174 After the acquisition of the galvanic response to a green light some subjects were told that from that point on, the green light would not be followed by electric shock. The extinction of the galvanic skin reflex to the green light was extremely rapid for these subjects. Both acquisition and _______ of responses appear to be immensely truncated, when subjects capable of understanding propositional language are informed of the consequences.

different

175 One might tell a rat, a parrot, or even a chimpanzee the same thing, but we do not even have to conduct an experiment to know that the results would be very _______.

propositional language

176 Presumably the time required for acquisition of a response in effect-type learning could be greatly shortened and trial and error probably eliminated by simply informing a person capable of understanding _______ _______ that a given action would be followed by a given reward.

tenable

177 Many everyday observations indicate this, and the Cook and Harris study makes it eminently (tenable/untenable).

eliminate

178 In short, the use and understanding of a propositional language drastically shorten or even _______ the continuous processes of contiguity- and effect-type learning.

From these studies and reflections it should be clear that the use and understanding of a propositional language are matters of considerable significance in that they greatly facilitate, and now and then make possible, these forms of behavior which are distinctively human.

SUMMARY

In this unit emphasis has been placed upon those things which differentiate the human from subhuman animals. Pursuant to this objective considerable emphasis has been given to (1) the invention of and response to symbolic environments, (2) the conceptual level of functioning, and (3) the use and understanding of propositional language.

Although animals communicate via systems of natural signs that are occasionally fairly complex, they never utilize a system of arbitrary signs. Although they can learn to respond to symbols under human tutelage, they never invent symbols. Furthermore, even when animals are taught to respond to symbols their responses are in terms of feeling and action and rarely, if ever, in terms of thought.

There would seem to be little question that many of the reactions people learn to make to symbols are learned in keeping with the liberal interpretation of the contiguity hypothesis. This is, perhaps, especially true with respect to emotional and visceral reactions to symbols. There is, likewise, little question that much language usage is in keeping with the effect hypothesis in that people generally write and say those things which have been most frequently rewarded. But it is equally apparent that such simple hypotheses cannot at this time account for much symbol learning, particularly where the symbols are designative and combined to form propositions.

There can be no question that chimpanzees and people who are unable to use or understand language are capable of the conceptual level of functioning. The conceptual behavior of subhuman animals is, of course, very limited when compared with that of people with normal intelligence and probably limited to rather concrete forms of imagination. If subprimate animals are capable of operating on the conceptual level, the concepts are very rudimentary and are of little significance for understanding their individual or collective actions.

Although concrete concepts may frequently occur in the absence of things being associated with symbols, it seems that abstract concepts are typically, if not always, learned by a symbol becoming associated with the common property, or properties, of things that are, in their totality, each different from the other. Hull's (1920) principle of dissociation accurately describes the process; however, the precise learning dynamics are open to some question. Concept learning in human adults is accompanied by blind trial and error, rational hypothesis testing, and flashes of insight. Reward and punishment are probably not significant independent variables. Contiguity of symbol and thing symbolized is certainly involved, especially in the early learning of concepts in children. In any case, contiguity and effect hypotheses are inadequate explanations because sudden loss of errors, reverse order concept learning, and learning concepts that preclude trial-and-error acquisition are common phenomena in adult human concept learning.

Language, broadly speaking, is either expressive, directive, or propositional. It is with respect to the use and understanding of propositional language that man is most clearly and categorically differentiated from the lower animals. Some birds can be taught to express propositional language, but it is patently obvious that they do not have the slightest understanding of it. Other animals do not possess language as the term is used here. They do, however, possess approximate functional equivalents of expressive and directive language in their systems of natural signs.

The way a human learns to use propositional language, as distinguished from learning to understand propositional language, may in its early stages be similar to the way in which a talking bird learns to use language. If so, there is basically a three-phase process. In the first phase, children hear words repeatedly in a pleasant context. In the second phase, they form and repeat words because they sound pleasant to them. In the third phase, they alter the frequency and pronunciation of words because of their pleasant or unpleasant consequences. Of course this theory accounts for neither the infinite variations in the use of language that occur in normal adults nor the understanding of propositional language.

The understanding of propositional language is still largely unexplored territory. It seems unlikely that the "laws" pertaining to the simpler processes of animal learning will ever be equal to the task of explaining the process. With the present level of knowledge of both the laws and the process, the conclusion is much more definite—much more intelligent and more rational processes are involved than can be plausibly interpreted as the complex expressions of these simple laws.

There is a very widespread tendency to attribute the distinctive aspects of human life to the possession of language. A more careful study, however, reveals that most of these things can occur in the absence of language. It would be more accurate to attribute most of the distinctive aspects of human life to a comparatively high level of conceptual functioning, though some cannot occur in the absence of designative symbols. Nonetheless, propositional language greatly facilitates the emergence and growth of such distinctive aspects of human life, and the designative symbols that make some of them possible are almost always linguistic symbols. It is for these reasons that some distinctively human phenomena have been attributed to the conceptual-linguistic level of functioning. Among the more important human phenomena that are based upon the conceptual-linguistic level of functioning are: (1) responding to distant future contingencies, (2) responding to distant past contingencies, especially things that antedate the life of the individual, (3) self-concepts and feelings, (4) imaginary environments, (5) purposive, specialized cooperation, (6) the reduction or elimination of the normally continuous processes in contiguity-type learning, (7) the reduction or elimination of the normally continuous processes in effect-type learning, and (8) responding to an environment that is not only largely symbolic but also highly coded, or categorized.

SELF–REVIEW QUIZ

Select the one best answer for each question.

1 The most distinctive type of symbol that is used and understood by man is the
- *a.* designative symbol
- *b.* expressive symbol
- c. directive symbol
- *d.* moral symbol

2 Which of the following symbol sequences are presented in an order of increasing levels of abstraction?
- *a.* canary—bird—animal—organism
- *b.* canary—animal—organism—bird
- c. understand language of any form
- *d.* cat—mammal—organism—carnivore

3 Only man can learn to:
- *a.* express propositional language
- *b.* use language
- c. understand language of any form
- *d.* understand propositional language

4 A self-concept cannot exist in the absence of:
- *a.* language
- *b.* conceptual processes
- c. propositional language
- *d.* symbolic communication

5 The case of the aphasic girl who demonstrated human level conceptual processes through her drawings shows that:
- *a.* the conceptual level of functioning is not contingent upon the use or understanding of language
- *b.* conceptual processes are contingent upon the ability to use and understand designative symbols
- c. thought precedes symbolization
- *d.* thought and symbolization are reciprocally related in that neither occurs in the absence of the other

6 If the differences between human and subhuman behavior are always only a matter of degree, then the cheapest and simplest way to understand human behavior is to study the behavior of:
- *a.* amoebas

b. pigeons
c. rats
d. people

7 Which of the following is known to occur on the subhuman level?
a. conceptual behavior (thinking)
b. purposive specialized cooperation
c. self-attitudes
d. understanding propositional language

8 The phenomenon of crossing-over cogently illustrates the significance of:
a. ego attitudes
b. insightful learning
c. symbolic environment
d. coded environments
ANSWER: *a* and *b*; *b* and *c*; *c* and *d*; or *b* and *c*.

9 For a sentence to be included in the category of propositional language:
a. The subject term must consist of designative symbols.
b. The predicate term must consist of designative symbols.
c. Both subject and predicate terms must consist of designative symbols.
d. Both subject and predicate terms must consist of arbitrary (customary) signs.

10 The principle of dissociation accurately describes the early phases of:
a. emotional learning
b. concept learning
c. verbal learning
d. dissociation of personality traits

11 Even the brightest chimpanzee cannot learn to respond in a way very similar to that of a normal human adult to a verbalization like:
a. Get me a glass of water.
b. Close the door.
c. You have sinned deeply.
d. Protestants are more upwardly mobile than Catholics.

12 The human use and understanding of designative symbols greatly:
a. expands one's contact with reality
b. reduces one's contact with reality
c. does both of these things—neither effect being obviously dominant over the other
d. does both of these things—expanded contact with reality being clearly the dominant effect

13 The conceptual-linguistic level of functioning is a precondition of:

a. responding to things that are far removed from the "here and now"

b. self-attitudes

c. responses made to purely imaginary things

d. purposive, specialized cooperation

ANSWER: *a, c,* and *d; a, b, c,* and *d; a* and *c;* or *b, c,* and *d.*

REFERENCES

Bruner, J. S., J. J. Goodnow, and G. A. Austin: *A Study of Thinking,* Science Editions, New York, 1956.

Chamj, B. E.: "Paranoid Patriotism: The Radical Right and the South," *Atlantic,* 210:91–97, November, 1962.

Cook, S. W., and R. E. Harris: "The Verbal Conditioning of the Galvanic Skin Reflex," *Journal of Experimental Psychology,* 21:202–210, 1937.

Cooley, C. H.: *Human Nature and the Social Order,* Charles Scribner's Sons, New York, 1902.

Crawford, M. P.: "The Cooperative Solving of Problems by Young Chimpanzees," *Comparative Psychological Monographs,* 14:1–88, 1937.

Drake, S. C., and H. R. Cayton: *Black Metropolis,* Harcourt, Brace & World, Inc., New York, 1945.

Hallowell, A. I.: "Cultural Factors in the Structuralization of Perception," in J. H. Rorer and M. Sherif (eds.), *Social Psychology at the Crossroads,* Harper & Row, Publishers, Incorporated, New York, 1951.

Hanfmann, Eugenia, and Jacob Kasanin: "A Method for the Study of Concept Formation," *Journal of Psychology,* 3–4: 521–540, 1937.

Harlow, H. F.: "Love in Infant Monkeys," *Scientific American,* 192:68–74, May, 1955.

Harlow, H. F., and M. K. Harlow: "Learning to Think," *Scientific American,* 181:36–39, August, 1949.

Hayes, Catherine: *The Ape in Our House,* Harper & Row, Publishers, Incorporated, New York, 1951.

Hebb, D. O., and W. R. Thompson: "The Social Significance of Animal Studies," in Gardner Lindzey (ed.), *Handbook of Social Psychology: Theory and Method,* Addison-Wesley Publishing Co., Cambridge, Mass., 1954.

Hull, C. L.: "Quantitative Aspects of the Evolution of Concepts: An Experimental Study," *Psychological Monographs,* 28:1–85, 1920.

Hull, C. L.: *A Behavior System,* Yale University Press, New Haven, Conn., 1952.

Hunt, E. B.: *Concept Learning: An Information Processing Problem,* John Wiley & Sons, Inc., New York, 1962.

Kohler, Wolfgang: *The Mentality of Apes,* Harcourt, Brace & World, Inc., New York, 1925.

Krech, David, R. S. Crutchfield, and E. L. Ballachey: *Individual in Society,* McGraw-Hill Book Company, New York, 1962.

Lindesmith, A. R., and A. L. Strauss: *Social Psychology,* rev. ed., Dryden Press, New York, 1956.

McGinnis, M. A.: *Aphasic Children,* Alexander Graham Bell Association for the Deaf, 1963.

Miyamoto, S. F., and S. M. Dornbusch:" "A Test of the Interactionist Hypothesis of Self Conception," *American Journal of Sociology,* 61:399–403, 1956.

Mowrer, O. H.: *Learning Theory and the Symbolic Processes,* John Wiley & Sons, Inc., New York, 1960.

Pfeiffer, J. E.: "Human Tension: The Case of the Amiable Chimps and the Nervous Baboons," *Harpers,* 227:55–60, July, 1963.

Razran, G.: "Stimulus Generalization of Conditioned Responses," *Psychological Bulletin,* 46:337–365, 1949.

Sherif, Muzafer, and C. W. Sherif: *An Outline of Social Psychology,* rev. ed., Harper & Row, Publishers, Incorporated, New York, 1956.

Smoke, K. L.: "An Objective Study of Concept Formation," *Psychological Monographs,* 42:1–85, 1932.

Tolman, E. C.: *Purposive Behavior in Animals and Men,* Appleton-Century-Crofts, Inc., New York, 1932.

Werner, Heinz, and Bernard Kaplin: *Symbol Formation: An Organismic-developmental Approach to Language and the Expression of Thought,* John Wiley & Sons, Inc., New York, 1963.

Whorf, B. L.: "Science and Linguistics," *Technology Review,* 44:229–231, 247–248, 1940.

Yerkes, R. M.: *Chimpanzees,* Yale University Press, New Haven, Conn., 1943.

social control

VERNON H. EDMONDS

This unit involves a study in some depth of those processes and characteristics which increase compliance and conformity to some group, community, or societal norm. One basic source of compliance and conformity is the early learning of the infant and child. When this learning results in greater compliance to specified norms, "socialization" is said to have occurred. This general area is not dealt with in any considerable depth here, partly because it is dealt with elsewhere in this volume and partly because anything approaching an adequate treatment would make the unit longer than desired. Another general area of control, or at least of attempted control, is the whole governmental apparatus of attempted law enforcement. This area, too, is dealt with in a cursory fashion, partly because it is quite familiar to the student and partly because it is apparently not nearly so significant in determining compliance and conformity as the personal and group characteristics that are so much a part of everyone's existence. It is thus the personal and social forces operating at the moment of compliance that are extensively examined in this unit.

Basic Concepts

1 "Social control" is defined in the *Dictionary of Sociology* as "the sum total of the processes whereby society, or any subgroup within society, secures conformity to expectation on the part of its constituent units, individuals or groups" (Fairchild, 1944). Thus, any process which brings about an increase in compliance with the expectations of any given human group is, by definition, an instance of ________ ________.

social control

2 "Conformity" is a basic term in the above definition. Going along with the group is a common everyday definition of ______.

conformity

3 Given that behavior X is expected by the members of a human group, any member of the group would be said to be conforming who engages in ______ ______.

behavior X

4 One trouble with this definition of social control and conformity is that the word "expectation" is ambiguous. One man can expect another to behave in a given way either in the sense of *anticipating* that he will behave in that way or in the sense of *wanting* him to behave in that way. "Expectation," thus, means that certain behavior is either ______ or ______ of certain persons in certain situations.

anticipated / wanted (desired)

5 The "desired" reference of "expectation" will be used in this unit. Hence "social control" will be used to refer to all social behaviors and products of social behaviors that increase compliance with some commonly ______ behavior.

desired

6 The controlling agents are the ______ members of particular human groups and not society as such.

individual

7 Although one often hears that society expects, demands, or controls certain behavior, it is more appropriate to say that the individual members of the human groups are the real agents of social ______.

control

8 Of course, agents of social control are not always members of the social group to which a given controlled person belongs. Policemen, for example, often control people without, strictly speaking, being members of the ______ ______ that include these people.

social (human) groups

9 In either case, the controlling agents are individuals and not ______ per se.

society

10 After all, only ______ can engage in persuasion and the manipulation of incentives that constitute ______ ______.

individuals (people)
social
control

11 Societal control does, in a sense, exist. For example, in the United States there is a Federal law against kidnapping. Should a person kidnap someone, the Federal government is empowered to investigate, prosecute, and sentence. It should be noted, though, that the control agents are still ______ who are, presumably, carrying out the desires of most of the people of the United States.

individuals (persons)

conformity (compliance)

12 Societal control can thus exist either in the sense of the members of most groups effectively securing conformity with the same values or in the sense of special controlling agents more or less effectively bringing about some measure of ________ to prevailing social values.

society

13 In either case, individuals, but not ________ as such, are the controlling agents.

14 "Group" and "social group" are terms which have been used elsewhere in this book. They refer to "two or more people who engage in some form of interaction over a considerable period of time." Which of the following categories are social groups?

a. a neighborhood gang
b. a family
c. spectators at a football game
d. the teachers and secretaries of a small department at a college or university

a, *b*, and *d*

15 A distinction is made between social control and attempted social control. In order for any behavior to qualify as social control it must be effective. If a mother spanks her child for eating from the dog's bowl and the child continues to eat from the dog's bowl with undiminished frequency, then clearly there is no ________ ________ in this case.

social control

16 This is, on the other hand, clearly a case of ________ ________ ________.

attempted social control

17 Some years back a number of people asked President Eisenhower to exhort people to drive carefully over the Christmas holiday. He did. The number of people killed and injured substantially exceeded those killed the year before and the year after when the President did not exhort drivers to drive safely. It would appear that exhortation, so commonly relied upon, was not a ________ ________ in this case.

social control

Capital punishment is relied upon by many people in the United States and elsewhere as a means of preventing certain crimes. In the United States capital punishment is virtually limited to the crime of homicide. When one compares adjacent states, one of which has capital punishment and the other does not, homicide rates for the states with capital punishment are slightly higher than for the states without it (Sutherland & Cressey, 1955).

is not

18 One can amass much more evidence to support the same conclusion, but from this evidence alone it would seem that capital punishment as currently utilized in the United States (is/is not) a genuine means of social control.

social control

19 Just as there are many things that are supposed to be social controls but aren't, there are also many things that are not commonly thought of as means of social control that are. There is ample evidence that a fallacious argument made difficult by confusing statements will be much more readily accepted than if it were clearly stated. Thus, befuddlement is an effective means of social persuasion, and social persuasion is a particular type of ________ ________.

effective

20 For any behavior to be logically included in the category of social control it needs to be an ________ means of bringing about conformity with prevalent desires of a human group or larger collectivity.

works (is effective)

21 Consequently, even though a practice, such as capital punishment, be commonly recognized and intended as a means of social control it cannot logically be included in the category unless it ________.

Types of Social Control

One can, of course, analyze social control on many levels of abstraction and in terms of many defining characteristics. For purposes of communication and fruitful inquiry it is probably necessary to distinguish between two very general types of social control.

incentives (rewards and punishments)

22 One way to control others is to provide or promise rewards or punishments for some specified action. "Incentive manipulation" is, perhaps, the most useful label for this type of control. A mother who promises her child that she will take him to a movie on Saturday if he comes straight home from school each day during the week is attempting to control her child by manipulating ________.

social control

23 Another way to control others is to convince them that (*a*) a certain belief is true or false, or that (*b*) a certain way of reasoning is valid or invalid. "Persuasion" is probably the most useful label for this type of ________ ________.

persuasion

24 If one argues for the Supreme Court ruling that congressional districts within a state shall contain populations that are as nearly equal as it is possible to make them, by saying that only in this way can the representatives of a minority be prevented from having effective veto power over all legislation, one is attempting to control by use of ________.

b, *c*, and *d*

25 Which of the following are incentive methods of social control?

a. The editors of *Common Sense: Leader in the Nation's Fight against Communism* argue that fluoridation of the public water supply is part of a vast Communist conspiracy.

b. A professor chastises a student who is unprepared for class.

c. A husband chastises his wife for seeming to be too friendly with another man.

d. A judge gives a man a suspended sentence for reckless driving and then tells the man to drive carefully in the future.

a, *b*, and c

26 Which of the following involve persuasive methods of social control?

a. The graduate students in psychology at X University are all behaviorists. It is noted that, whatever their position upon entering X University, students are behaviorists by the time they graduate. The students, of course, are encouraged to "think for themselves."

b. A husband tells his wife that, although harsh and frequent punishment can produce a "good" child, the hostility and anxiety such treatment generates is too much of a price to pay for a "good" child.

c. When fluoridation is submitted to a referendum the proponents argue that it is a safe and effective means of preventing dental caries.

d. A student caught cheating on an examination is expelled from college.

27 It is clear from the preceding illustrations that persuasion very often consists of convincing others that a certain course of action will result either in nothing but rewards or a predominance of rewards over punishments. Conversely, if a certain form of behavior is disapproved of by any potential controllers they often try, if they utilize persuasion, to convince others that such behavior will be followed by either punishment or a predominance of _______ _______ _______.

punishment over reward

28 This type of persuasion is not clearly separable from _______ _______.

incentive manipulation

29 There is, however, some utility in maintaining the distinction. We shall, therefore, use the term "incentive manipulation" to refer to a means of control in which _______ and _______ are either meted out after some behavior has occurred or are promised as future payoffs for a given form of behavior.

rewards / punishments

30 All social influences that make a person maintain or change a previous position with respect to issues of truth or validity constitute social _______.

persuasion

31 In other words, social _______ consists of convincing a person, or persons, that a certain position is either sound or unsound.

persuasion

32 Although rewards are usually meted out by a person's friends and acquaintances, they are occasionally provided by agencies of the state. For example, medals of various kinds are given to military personnel in the United States and to both military and civilian personnel in the U.S.S.R. Legal rewards are, however, extremely (frequent/infrequent) as compared with nonlegal rewards.

infrequent

33 Rewards can be further analyzed as verbal, gestural, monetary, or physical. Classify each of the rewards listed below as one or more of these four types.

a. A little boy wipes his feet before entering his house. His mother says, "Good boy." _______.

verbal

b. A college student decides to dress in accordance with the campus fashion and he finds that the coeds now respond with friendly smiles when he speaks to them. _______.

gestural

c. The smiles elicited from an infant are found to be directly related to the amount of caressing the infant receives. _______.

physical for the infant; gestural for the adult

d. A professor at X University engages in scholarly research; as a result, his annual salary is increased significantly. _______.

monetary

yet to be performed

34 Verbal rewards, of course, may consist of either approval for acts already performed or promises for acts +++++.

legal

35 Punishments, unlike rewards, are frequently ________ in the sense that they are meted out by some functionary of the state.

legal

36 Agents of the state mete out ________ punishments by fines, imprisonment, physical punishment, or death.

frequent

37 Still the nonlegal punishments meted out by one's acquaintances, particularly one's friends, are far more ________ and are probably much more significant sources of social control.

38 The nonlegal punishments typically resorted to consist of verbal censures or threats, gestures of disapproval, monetary deprivations, physical punishments, ostracism, and banishment. Classify each of the following illustrations as falling logically into one of these six types.

gesture of disapproval

a. A new teacher in a high school in a small community wanted to buy an expensive sports car. When he applied for a loan from the local bank, the banker frowned and stared at him solemnly. ________.

ostracism

b. In an Old Order Amish community a person who has violated one of the mores is placed under a "ban" in which no one, not ever members of his family, will speak to him. ________.

verbal threat

c. A child is told that if he does not mow the lawn he will not receive money to attend a motion picture. ________.

banishment

d. A man who breaks the incest taboo in primitive society X is told that he must leave and never return. ________.

persuasion

39 The methods in which attitudes are changed typically consist of education, propaganda, and therapy. These are all forms of ________.

education

40 In one of these methods one gives the most complete and accurate information he is capable of giving. You will recognize this as the definition of ________.

propaganda

41 In another, the method consists of employing any kind of appeal, accurate or inaccurate, complete or incomplete, emotional or cognitive, that will bring about the desired change. This is typically called ________.

therapy

42 The other procedure consists of attempting to make some basic change in personality. This method is frequently employed in mental hospitals. It is ________ as we are using the term here.

education / propaganda

43 It is probably apparent that when one observes particular cases of social persuasion it is frequently difficult to distinguish between ________ and ________.

social control

44 So far we have discussed the typical devices used when one or more persons want to make one or more other persons comply with their wishes. There are a number of variables which affect compliance, but they are commonly neither conceived of nor deliberately used. These are the latent factors in ________ ________. They will be stressed in the next section.

Social Persuasion

Social control is dealt with at some length, though somewhat indirectly, in the units on human learning in this book. The choice must be made at this point between a rather superficial but inclusive treatment of social control or a rather intensive treatment of some aspect of social control. The latter alternative has been chosen. From this point on we shall be reviewing and interpreting experimental studies in persuasion. There is, perhaps, no particular advantage in emphasizing this aspect of social control except that the experimental studies in persuasion have been carried out with much greater scientific rigor than other types of studies in social control. The greater scientific rigor, in turn, has two advantages: (1) the reader can justifiably have more confidence in the truth of the conclusions derived from the studies, and (2) the material provides the reader with an excellent opportunity to increase his competence with respect to one of the most basic operations of science—the interpretation of factual information.

part

45 "Factor," as the term is used here, refers to "a part of the cause of any given event." The cause of an event would determine the event's occurrence and all of the variation that occurs as a part of the event's existence. A factor is only a ________ of the cause of an event.

factors

46 The type of event we are dealing with here is compliance. We shall, therefore, be studying the sources, i.e., the ________, of compliance.

47 In the following pages frequent use will be made of the terms, "positive factor" and "negative factor." A factor, as the term is used here, refers to a part of the cause of an event. A factor, then, occurs (after/before) the event in question.

before

48 If an increase in the factor is followed by an increase in the event being affected by it, the factor is said to be positive. Increased food consumption is followed by increased weight. In this example food consumption is a ________ ________ of weight.

positive factor

49 A factor is said to be negative when an increase in the factor is followed by a decrease in the event being affected by it. As the speed at which a given car is driven increases, the number of miles traveled per gallon of gasoline decreases. In this example speed is a ________ factor of the miles traveled per gallon of gasoline.

negative

50 The only difference between a positive factor and a negative factor is that as a positive factor increases, the event which it is affecting also increases, whereas as a negative factor increases, the event which it is affecting ________.

decreases

51 A negative factor (is/is not) as scientifically significant as a positive factor.

is

52 To say that we are studying the positive and negative sources of compliance is to say that we are studying the positive and negative ________ of compliance.

factors

53 Compliance, by definition, refers to "a process in which one or more persons change their behavior so as to bring it closer to, or in complete agreement with, the behavior that is ________ by one or more other persons."

desired

54 Once behavior is in line with specified individual or group desires, such behavior is then called "conformity." Thus conformity is the more or less stable outcome of ________.

compliance

55 In this section we are more concerned with the factors determining whether a person adopts a new position than with the factors which prevent his departing from a position once assumed. We are primarily concerned with ________ in this section.

compliance

One thing may produce some confusion. Most of the studies that are summarized here consist of experiments in which members of a rigged majority express, or the experimental subjects are led to think they express, a position on some issue. If an experimental subject goes along with this position he is said to be complying with the group. Such usage does not precisely fit our definition of compliance because the desires of the majority are absent, unknown, or artificial. Since, however, the experimental subjects do not know that the majority is rigged, i.e., told what to say in advance, they probably assume, if they assume anything, that the majority would like them (the experimental subjects) to agree with them (the majority). In any case, going along with, or agreeing with, the majority will be used as the operational definition of compliance.

pressure

56 We have specified that compliance involves a change. In the studies that are summarized, this change will be indicated either by (*a*) the performance of a comparable group of experimental subjects who are not under group pressure, or by (*b*) information pertaining to the experimental subject's own position prior to being exposed to group ______.

confederates

57 For the sake of convenience, and in keeping with common usage, the persons who are instructed, without the knowledge of the experimental subjects, to express specified positions when the occasion arises will be referred to as "confederates." ______ are usually hired to lie about something, but, in any case, they are instructed to express a given position whether they personally agree with it or not.

It will be useful to utilize two short terms for two generic types of experimental procedure. In one type of experiment, subjects are secreted in stalls or booths. They are asked to express their position on some issue. The experimenter informs them of the "positions of the others" participating in the experiment either by some electrical device or by handing them slips of paper. These positions taken by the others are really bogus positions made up by the experimenter. In this type of experiment the experimenter does not need any hired liars, or confederates, since he can lie for them.

In the other general type of experimental procedure, experimental subjects take a position around a table with a number of confederates. The experimental subjects do not, of course, know that the other subjects, usually constituting the great majority, are confederates. The experimenter usually asks for responses from most, if not all, of the confederates first. The confederates have been instructed to take a given position.

58 It should be noted that in the first type of experiment the behavior of the experimental subjects is anonymous in the sense that the other subjects do not usually know who specifically took a given position. In any case, they do not observe one another. This type of experiment shall be referred to as "type A." The "A" may be a useful memory crutch by indicating that the experimental subjects are in an anonymous situation in which their behavior is not ________ by other members of the group.

observed

59 In the second type of experiment, everyone is under observation. It is a personal face-to-face situation which (more/less) closely resembles the social pressures encountered in everyday life than does the type A situation.

more

60 This type of experiment, which entails personal face-to-face encounter, will be referred to as "type P." The "P" will, perhaps, serve as a reminder that the experimental subjects and confederates are under each others' scrutiny in a ________ face-to-face relationship.

personal

Issue Factors

In this section we shall study compliance insofar as it is affected by the difficulty level of a cognitive issue or by the amount of departure from a previously accepted norm that compliance with group expectations necessitates. We shall be particularly concerned with whether a group judgment can be so patently absurd that no well-educated and intelligent person will agree with the judgment when it is espoused by a majority of group members.

Difficulty of the Issue

61 The rigged or bogus majority usually takes an erroneous position. Sometimes the issue is a very simple and easy matter, and sometimes it is very complex and difficult. You can probably guess that difficulty would be a moderate to high (positive/negative) factor of compliance.

positive

difficulty

62 Asch (1952), using a type P procedure, asked subjects to state which line on a three-line card was equal to a line on another card. The confederates had been instructed to take an identical but erroneous position. By varying the discrepancy between the standard line and the line chosen as equal in length by the confederates, Asch provided an objective measure of the ______ of the problem.

positive

63 The results showed a high positive correlation between compliance and difficulty level. This experiment indicates that difficulty of the issue is a high ______ factor of compliance.

confirms

64 Coleman, Blake, and Morton (1958) using a type A procedure computed a correlation coefficient on difficulty of general information items and compliance. They obtained an r of $+.89$. This information (confirms/disconfirms) the hypothesis that difficulty of the issue is a high positive factor of compliance.[1]

difficult

65 One might conclude from the foregoing data that individuals comply with an erroneous group judgment only when the problem is too ______ for them to reach a reasonably definite conclusion.

easy (simple)

66 In one experiment (Asch, 1952) the standard line was 10 inches in length and the comparison lines were 3, 10, and 2 inches. When asked which comparison line was equal in length to the standard line, the confederates all said "line 1" (the 3-inch line). A substantial number of college students agreed with the confederates. Obviously, a problem can be extremely ______ and still a number of relatively intelligent and well-educated people will go along with an erroneous majority.

obvious (clear)

67 Asch deliberately tried to make the discrepancies between the line chosen by his confederates and the standard line so great that, presumably, no one would yield to the unanimous but wrong majority. He couldn't do this. Even when the discrepancy was as great as 7 inches a number of subjects would agree with the confederates. This experiment shows that some people will agree with an erroneous majority even when the error of the majority is extremely ______.

[1] See pp. 28–32 for information relating to the interpretation of correlation coefficients.

Box 1. The Bizarre World of the Conformer

In a study of compliance to "outlandish" group judgments concerning both information (I) and opinion (O) items, Read Tuddenham* has constructed a bizarre picture of the United States that a person would have who complied with the erroneous majority on all the items listed. A number of subjects, college students, did agree with the majority on all items.

According to the simulated judgments, the United States is something of a fairyland. For example, it is largely populated by old people, 60 to 70 percent being over 65 years of age (Item I–1). These oldsters must be almost all women, since male babies have a life expectancy of only 25 years (I–2). Though outlived by women, men tower over them in height, being 8 or 9 inches taller, on the average (I–4). The society is obviously preoccupied with eating, averaging six meals per day (I–5), this perhaps accounting for their agreement with the assertion, "I never seem to get hungry" (O–9). Americans waste little time on sleep, averaging only 4 to 5 hours a night (I–3), a pattern perhaps not unrelated to the statement that the average family includes five or six children (I–9). Nevertheless, there is no overpopulation problem, since the U.S.A. stretches 6,000 miles from San Franscisco to New York (I–6). Although the economy is booming with an average wage of $5.00 an hour (I–7), rather negative and dysphoric attitudes characterize the group, as expressed in their roundly rejecting the proposition, "Any man who is able and willing to work hard has a good chance of succeeding" (0–3), and in agreeing with such statements as, "Most people would be better off if they never went to school at all" (0–5), "There's no use doing things for people; they don't appreciate it" (0–6), and "I can not do anything well" (0–10). Such is the weird and wonderful picture of the world and of themselves, allegedly entertained by "the others in the group." The straight visual perception items are just as distorted.

* R. D. Tuddenham and P. D. Macbride, "The Yielding Experiment from the Subject's Point of View" *Journal of Personality*, 27:260, 1959.

Yes, of course.

68 Is it patently false that most people in the United States are over sixty-five years of age, that men are on the average 8 or 9 inches taller than women, that Americans average six meals a day? (See Box 1) ________.

No

69 A substantial number of college students complied with the majority on each of the items given in Box 1 and some college students complied with the majority on all of them. Does an issue have to be difficult for an individual to comply with an erroneous group judgment? ______.

comply (go along)

70 You will note from the last sentence in Box 1 that Tuddenham and Macbride (1959) exposed the subjects to erroneous visual perception judgments similar to those employed by Asch (1952). It would seem that a substantial number of college students, who are certainly above average in intelligence, education, and capacity for independent critical thought, will ______ with an absurd majority judgment.

Departure from Previous Norm

comply (conform)

71 Another factor that falls within the "nature of the issue" category involves the amount of departure from some previously accepted norm or practice. Jack and Schiffer (1948) present evidence which indicates that women in the United States will not follow the "dictates of fashion" with respect to hemlines when they get below 20 inches or above 30 inches from the ground. This leaves a variation of about 10 inches in which women will generally ______ with the dictates of fashion.

compliance

72 On the other hand, Kelley and Woodruff (1956) report that a bogus judgment of a reference group will have a "profound effect" upon a subject's judgment even when at marked variance with previously existing norms of that group. The evidence on the limits of compliance with a group judgment that increasingly departs from a previous norm is a bit sketchy. Nonetheless, a considerable amount of ______ with the deviant judgment can be expected.

By way of summary, it has been shown that the level of difficulty involved in making a cognitive judgment is a very high positive factor of compliance. Nonetheless, many persons of well above average intelligence and education will agree with an erroneous majority regardless of difficulty level. In fact, many will agree with group judgments that are as patently false as it is possible to make them. Departure from a previously accepted norm is probably a negative factor of compliance, but the evidence is sketchy with respect to this hypothesis.

Group Factors

In this section we shall be dealing with a hypothesis expressed by Becker (1932) as follows: "Whether arguments command assent or not depends less upon the logic that conveys them than upon the climate of opinion in which they are sustained." In doing so, we shall study the effects upon compliance of the following group characteristics: (1) level of consensus within the group, (2) desertion by a supporter, (3) number of people expressing a given judgment, (4) group cohesion, (5) prestige of potential influencers and attempts by group members to get subjects to agree with them, (6) amount of deviation of subjects' judgments from the modal group judgments, (7) presence or absence of an open expression of subjects' judgments prior to exposure to group pressure, (8) previous commitment, (9) subjects' status within the group, (10) diffusion of power within the group, (11) competition with other groups and competition within the group, (12) presence or absence of social ties outside the group, (13) whether subjects' judgments are anonymous or open to group observation, and (14) similarity of influence group to past groups in which subjects have been rewarded for compliance and punished for noncompliance.

Group Consensus

73 Edmonds (1964) using a type P procedure studied the effect of varying degrees of group consensus upon compliance. Group ________ refers to "the degree of agreement in a group."

consensus

In this study the subjects were graduate students and the task consisted of judging the validity of ten arguments similar to arguments encountered in everyday life. There were six confederates and one experimental subject in each group session.

74 In one experimental condition none of the experimental subjects was exposed to anyone else's judgment. The mean error for this group is indicated by the point directly above 0 on the horizontal axis in Figure 8. The mean error for this group was about ________.[2]

4.5

[2] Although exact figures are given as answers, the reader is not expected to be exactly right or to spend any additional time in trying to be.

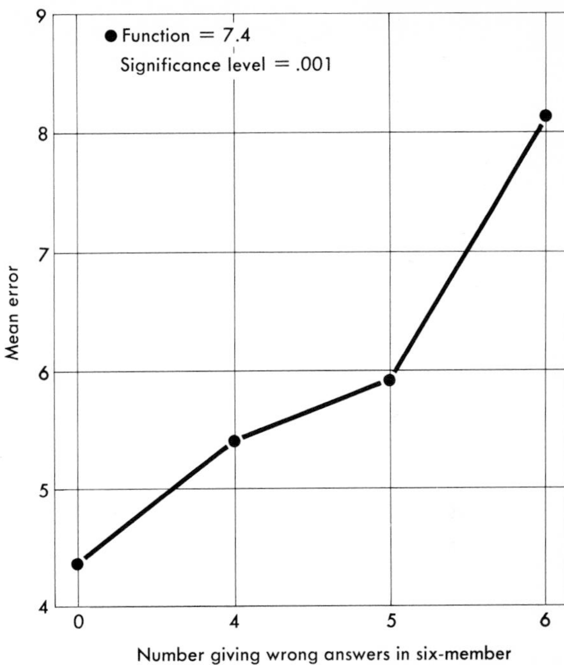

Figure 8. Mean errors for groups under different degrees of group consensus. SOURCE: V. H. Edmonds, "Logical Error as a Function of Group Consensus: An Experimental Study of the Effect of Erroneous Group Consensus upon Logical Judgments of Graduate Students," *Social Forces,* 43:35, 1964. Used by permission.

75 In one experimental group each experimental subject heard four out of six confederates give the wrong answer on each argument. The mean error for this group of experimental subjects is indicated by the point directly above 4 on the horizontal axis. The mean error for this group is
5.2 about ________.

76 In another experimental group each experimental subject heard five out of six confederates give the wrong answer on all ten arguments. The mean error for this group is indicated by the point directly above 5 on the
5.8 horizontal axis, and is about ________.

77 In another experimental group each experimental subject heard six out of six confederates give the wrong answer to all ten arguments. The mean error for this group
8.0 is about ________.

six

78 The degree of consensus is unanimous for the last group of experimental subjects because six out of _______ confederates gave the same answer on each of the ten arguments.

50

79 Median errors for the same four experimental conditions are 5, 5, 6, and 9 respectively. This means, for example, that the median error rate where two confederates were giving correct answers to each question was 5 out of 10, or _______ percent.

90

80 The median error rate where all of the six confederates gave wrong answers to all ten questions increased to 9 out of 10, or _______ percent.

positive factor

81 Under these experimental conditions consensus is demonstrated to be a high _______ _______ of compliance.

marked increase

82 Another way of saying the same thing is to say that as consensus within a group undergoes a marked increase, compliance subsequently undergoes a _______ _______.[3]

confirmation (support)

83 Becker (1932) once argued that "whether arguments command assent or not depends less upon the logic that conveys them than upon the climate of opinion in which they are sustained." Whether this hypothesis is, strictly speaking, verifiable, it is quite certain that Edmonds' (1964) study gives some _______ to it.

one

84 The largest break in this function relationship occurs between a consensus of unanimity[4] and unanimity minus _______.

less

85 Edmonds' (1964) study indicates that if even one person expresses a minority position there will be much _______ chance that others in the group will agree with the majority.

[3] Once upon a time one of the author's students, Harold Wickersham, had nothing better to do than derive a mathematical formula for this relationship, and came up with $P = KN^2 + C$ in which $P =$ probability of compliance, $K =$ a constant (in this case, .6), $N =$ number of people expressing a given judgment, and $C =$ a constant (in this case, 5.2). In other words, compliance varied directly as the square of the proportion of the group expressing a given judgment.

[4] Unanimity is defined in frame 78.

real

86 It is very difficult for people to express a minority position when no one is expressing a position the same as, or similar to, their own. It also seems to be true that perception of a high degree of consensus, even if inaccurate, prevents people from expressing their position (Cantril, 1958). The net effect would seem to be more apparent than ________ consensus.

self-fulfilling prophecies

87 A "self-fulfilling prophecy" is "a belief that creates conditions which make the belief true even though it was false at the beginning." Since believing that consensus is extremely high or unanimous on some things inhibits expression of disagreement, and since this inhibition further enhances the appearance of consensus, beliefs that a high degree of consensus exists are correctly labeled as ________-________ ________.

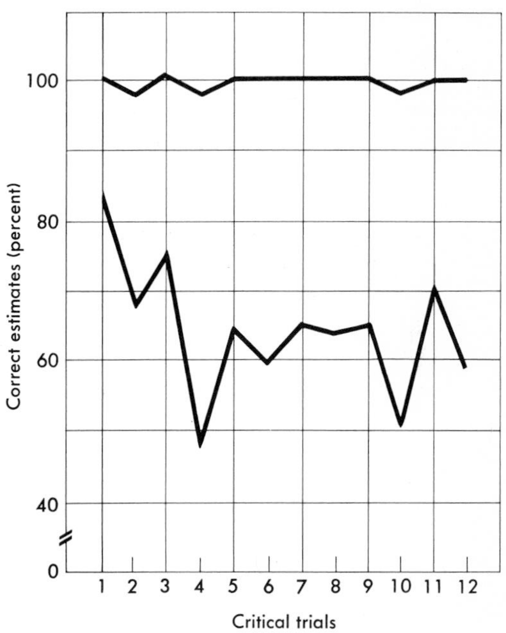

Figure 9. Error curve of 123 subjects, each of whom compared lines in the presence of six to eight opponents, is plotted in the bottom curve. The accuracy of judgments not under pressure is indicated in the top curve. SOURCE: S. E. Asch, "Opinions and Social Pressure," *Scientific American,* 193:35, November, 1955. Used by permission.

88 The effect of a unanimous but wrong majority of six to eight members upon the line-matching judgments of experimental subjects is depicted in Figure 9. Note that the average percentage of accuracy for those under no group pressure is about ________ percent.

99

89 When experimental subjects heard the confederates unanimously give the wrong answer on each of the twelve trials their average percentage of accurate judgments fell to about ________ percent.

65

90 It is apparent from the data contained in Figure 9 that the tasks are extremely (easy/difficult).

easy

91 There is no indication that anyone would have the slightest difficulty in selecting a line from three alternatives that is equal to the comparison line except for trials ________, ________, and ________.

2 / 4 / 10

92 Even on these trials there is apparently very little difficulty when the subjects are not exposed to the ________ judgments of others.

erroneous (false)

93 If one notices the proportion of correct estimates when the subjects are exposed to an erroneous and unanimous majority it is apparent that compliance is much greater on trials ________ and ________ than on any others.

4 / 10

94 We would have expected a comparable compliance-error score for trial ________, but for some reason this did not occur.

2

95 In general, though, it is apparent that ________ is a positive factor in determining the different degrees of compliance for the different trials.

difficulty

96 Different amounts of compliance for a situation in which everyone (in this case six to eight confederates) gives the wrong answer and a situation in which the experimental subject has a partner who doesn't always go along with the confederates are depicted in Figure 10. The presence of a supporter has a marked (positive/negative) effect upon compliance of the other experimental subject.

negative

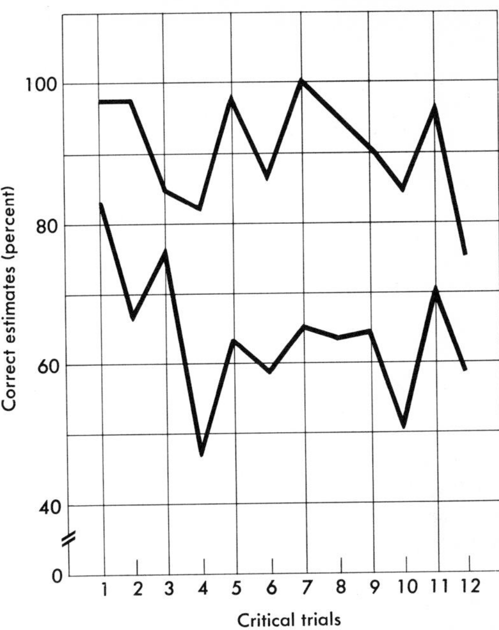

Figure 10. Two subjects supporting each other against a majority made fewer errors (top curve) than one subject did against a majority (bottom curve). SOURCE: S. E. Asch, "Opinions and Social Pressure," *Scientific American,* 193:35, November, 1955. Used by permission.

one

97 This datum confirms the hypothesis that a minority position can be substantially preserved if only ______ person will express that position.

confirms (supports, etc.)

98 Putney and Middleton (1961) have studied conformity with and rebellion against religious ideologies of parents. They find that compliance with the religious positions of the parents is at a maximum when religious positions are the same for both parents and for parents and the community. Here we have a real-life study which ______ the results of experimental studies dealing with the effect of consensus upon compliance.

positive

99 A rather large number of studies show consistently that consensus is a high ______ factor of compliance (see, e.g., Asch, 1952; Cantril, 1958; Edmonds, 1964; Putney and Middleton, 1961; Thorndike, 1938).

unanimity minus one

100 Two researchers (Asch, 1952; Edmonds, 1964) have shown that there is a precipitous break in this relationship between a condition of unanimity and ________ ________ ________ (see Figures 8 and 10).

Desertion by a Supporter

The subject loses a very substantial amount of his independence.

101 A factor that is closely related to consensus is desertion by a supporter. What happens when a partner deserts a subject by either leaving the scene or crossing over to the opposition? (See Figure 11.)

switching to the majority judgment

102 Which of the two types of desertion (switching to the majority judgment or leaving the group) has the greater effect? +++++.

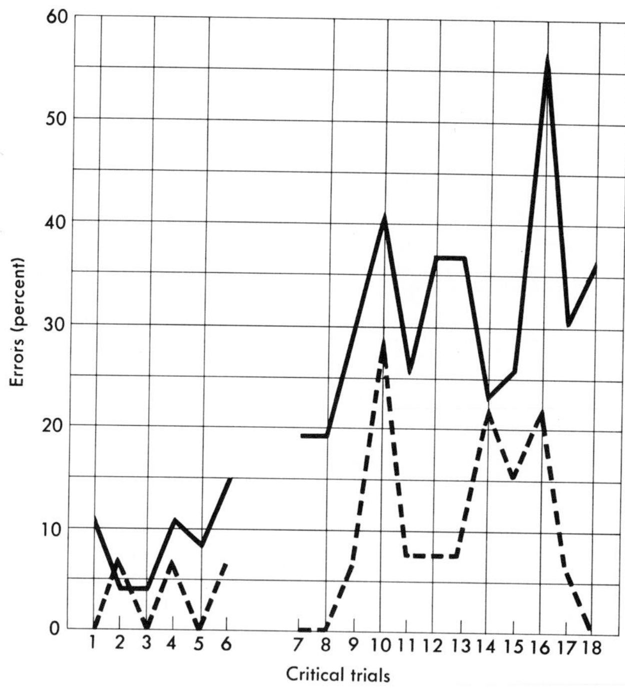

Figure 11. Partner left subject after six trials in a single experiment. Top curve shows the error of the subject when the partner "deserted" to the majority. Bottom curve shows error when partner merely left the room. SOURCE: S. E. Asch, "Opinions and Social Pressure," *Scientific American,* 193:35, November, 1955. Used by permission.

a single person initially agrees with him but later changes his position by deserting to the majority

103 Apparently a person's confidence in the accuracy of his judgments can be most effectively undermined by a situation in which +++++.

104 Harnack (1963), using a type P procedure, planted two confederates in each of his groups. One confederate took an extreme position on a "moral issue" at the beginning of the discussion period. The other one initially sided with the moral position of the subjects, usually numbering about six, but deserted to the extreme position of the other confederate during the last ten minutes of the discussion period. The moral judgments of the subjects shifted substantially toward the extreme position of the confederates in seventeen out of twenty groups. It would seem that the desertion of a partner to the opposition

minority

whether of a majority or a ________ substantially increases compliance with the position taken by the deserting partner.

desertion

105 It seems that in general a person's confidence in the soundness of his judgment is shaken by the ________ of a partner.

Group Size

106 Let us now consider the factor of group size. Assuming that we have instructed our faithful confederates to lie unanimously when we ask them for their judgment, will fifteen lying confederates produce greater compliance

Apparently not.

than five or six equally good liars? (See Figure 12.)

three

107 There is an extremely high positive correlation between the number of people expressing unanimous positions and compliance with that position up to a group size of ________.

seven

108 There are small increments in compliance with a unanimous majority up to an influence group size of ________.

three
seven

109 Compliance seems to approach a maximum with an influence group size of about ________ and reaches a maximum when the influence group size is about ________.

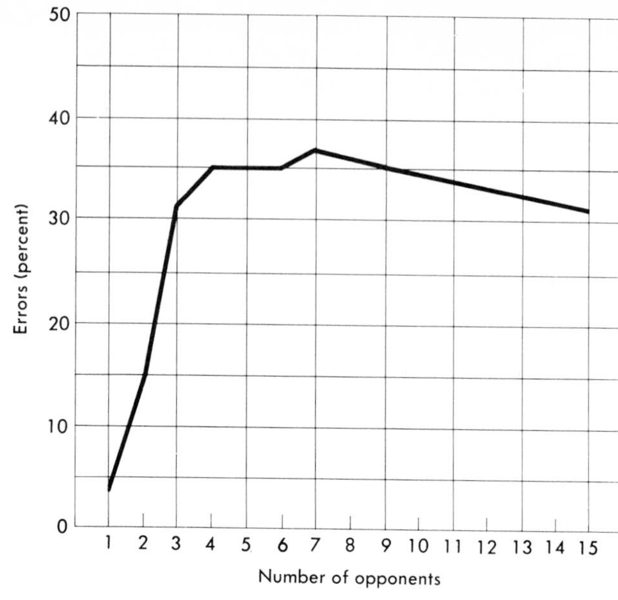

Figure 12. Size of majority which opposed them had an effect on the subjects. SOURCE: S. E. Asch, "Opinions and Social Pressure," *Scientific American,* 193:35, November, 1955. Used by permission.

(*a*) Compliance approaches a maximum with only three opponents.
(*b*) Compliance decreases slightly as the number of opponents increases beyond seven.

110 Although Asch's (1955) data confirm common beliefs about the direction of the correlation between the number of potential influencers expressing a unanimous position and the probability of complying with them, the results diverge from common beliefs in two surprising ways. What are they? (Take a *close* look at Figure 12.) (*a*) +++++. (*b*) +++++.

The data in Figure 12 seem to indicate that one person can exert little if any influence upon another. Common sense would tell us otherwise, at least for some subjects in some situations. Rosenbaum and Blake (1953) conducted an experiment in which the experimenter asked each of fifteen assembled people if they would participate in an experiment with him. In two of the experimental situations the first person asked was the experimenter's confederate. In one of these situations the confederate agreed and subsequently thirteen of the fifteen remaining also agreed to participate. In another experimental situation the confederate refused to participate, and in this group only four of the remaining fifteen subjects agreed to participate. With the confederate absent, eight out of fifteen persons agreed to participate in the experiment.

one

111 This experiment shows that ______ person, even though unknown to the others, can substantially influence their compliance with a request under certain circumstances.

positive factor

112 As a general conclusion, it seems reasonably certain that group size is a ______ ______ of compliance up to a size of three or four, and quite probably up to a size of six or seven where the majority is taking an erroneous position on some simple cognitive task.

Group Cohesion

113 A fourth factor of compliance is group cohesion. Group cohesion is usually measured by asking group members how much they like other members of the group, how much they would like to remain a member of the group, or how much they would like to engage in some activity with members of the group. There are other means of measurement, but it is apparent that "attraction to the group" is an approximate synonym for ______ ______.

group cohesion

114 A large number of studies have consistently shown group cohesion to be a high positive factor of compliance (see, e.g., Festinger, Schacter, and Bach, 1950; Seashore, 1954; Schacter, 1951; Schacter, Ellertson, McBride, and Gregory, 1951). It is rather certain that an increase in group cohesion will produce an ______ in compliance with group judgments.

increase

Festinger goes so far as to say that "covert changes in opinions and attitudes . . . can only be produced by a group by virtue of forces acting on the member to remain in the group." Both Asch (1952) and Edmonds (1964) interviewed subjects after they had been exposed to the experimental situations. Virtually all of Edmonds' compliant subjects and a very substantial proportion of Asch's said they were personally convinced of the accuracy of their judgments.

disconfirmed

115 Since there was no way for these subjects to remain in the group, and since there was no indication that they had the slightest desire to do so, Festinger's hypothesis that cohesion is a necessary condition of compliance is ______ by Asch's and Edmonds' studies.

false (in error)

116 Furthermore, there are many studies showing marked compliance of experimental subjects with the positions of others where the "definition of the situation" implies that the experimental subjects are unlikely to ever participate as a group with the others again. It appears quite certain that Festinger's hypothesis is ______.

Prestige of Influencers

A procedure for assessing group influence consists of placing subjects in a dark room that has a small fixed light, and under various conditions, asking them to estimate how much the light moves. Actually the light doesn't move at all, but it appears to, and is hence a sensitive means of measuring group influences upon judgment and perception (Sherif, 1937).

positive factor

117 In one of these studies (Sherif, 1937) experimental subjects were much more likely to agree with persons having high prestige than with those having low prestige. Prestige of influence persons appears to be a high ______ ______ of compliance.

prestige

118 There are a large number of studies that confirm this relationship between prestige of influence persons and compliance of influencees in that they consistently show a striking positive effect of prestige upon various kinds of individual judgments (Anon., 1957; Festinger et al., 1952; Moore, 1921; Sherif, 1937; Thorndike, 1935; Zaleznik, Christensen, and Roethlisberger, 1958). There would seem to be little question that ______ of potential influencers is a high positive factor of compliance with positions taken by the potential influencers.

Deviation from Group Mode

increasing

119 A sixth factor consists of one's deviation from the modal judgment of the group. We would expect that as a person's position becomes increasingly different from that held by most of the group there would be an ______ probability that the person would change his position in the direction of that held by the group.

In one study, some subjects were given the answers of others in the group which indicated that their judgments were very similar to those held by most of the group. Only 4 percent of these subjects changed their judgments. Other experimental subjects were given the answers of other subjects in the group which indicated that their judgments were very different from those held by most of the group. Under these conditions, 23 percent of these subjects changed their positions. This was a typical type A procedure. The majority judgments in both cases were bogus judgments supplied by the experimenter (Festinger et al., 1952).

confirms

120 The experiment described above _______ the hypothesis that deviation from the group mode is a positive factor of compliance. Other studies give further confirmation (Festinger, 1954; Hochbaum, 1954).

Group Pressure

increases

121 A seventh group factor consists of attempts to make the noncompliant subject "see his error," and agree with the majority. It will not be surprising to find that as the frequency of these attempts increases, the probability of a subject complying with the group _______ (Festinger, 1954; Festinger and Thibaut, 1951).

mode

122 A word of caution. It seems that these studies which involved different degrees of group pressure were always complicated by another known independent variable, namely, deviation from the group mode. It is possible, but perhaps rather unlikely, that the effect ascribed to influence attempts is really deviation from the group _______.

deviation

123 At least part of the effect attributed to influence attempts is probably due to _______ from the modal position of the group.

Previous Commitment

negative

124 Openness of prior expression, unlike the other group factors listed here, is a _______, rather than a positive, factor of compliance (Festinger, 1950; Sherif & Sherif, 1956).

less

125 This means that a person who has openly stated his position to a group prior to hearing their judgments is ______ likely to change his position in the direction of the majority than one who has not openly expressed his position.

confirmation (support)

126 This hypothesis is given some ______ by the fact that oral discussions of problems in which experimental subjects voice their opinions before hearing opinions from a number of confederates result in much less compliance than when communications are anonymous (Festinger, 1950).

b and *d*

127 This resistance to change after taking a stand is thought to be a product of "ego involvement" (Sherif and Sherif, 1956). Which of the following reactions would probably be aspects of "ego involvement" in this type of situation?

a. wanting to show off one's brilliance
b. being ashamed to "admit" that one was in error
c. a compulsive refusal to change
d. feeling ashamed that one is easily won over by the "crowd," that one can't "think for oneself"

Status in the Group

more

128 A ninth group factor is the potential influencee's status in a group or community. Hollander (1958) has hypothesized that "idiosyncrasy credit" is a positive function of a person's status. Some illustrations, such as the wining and wenching behavior of the English aristocracy in the seventeenth and eighteenth centuries, are given in support of it. The hypothesis means that as status, or prestige, in a group or community increases (more/fewer) departures from the group or community norms are tolerated.

noncompliance

129 We are, of course, studying compliance, and tolerance of ______ is not the same thing.

negatively

130 Still it is highly plausible to assume that tolerance of noncompliance and compliance are rather highly and ______ correlated.

confirmation

131 Bartos (1958), using a type P procedure and an "independence of judgment" questionnaire, reported that presidents of YMCA clubs were much more independent on both criteria than were "lieutenants" and the rank and file members. These data give some _______ to the hypothesis that status is a negative factor of compliance.

more

132 Sherif and Sherif (1953) report that as athletic competition between groups of boys increased, the lower-status members became much more vociferous in their expression of hostility toward members of the groups that were in competition with them than did the boys with higher statuses in the groups. Since "healthy, competitive games" always produce more or less intense amounts of hostility and aggression toward competing groups it would seem that the boys who are low on the totem pole are "showing their colors," i.e., complying with the group expectations _______ than the higher-status boys.

consistent

133 Sherif and Sherif thought the lower-status boys were trying to increase their standing in the group by providing a truculent display of one of the most prized group virtues. Although this information does not directly confirm the idiosyncrasy credit hypothesis, it is, nonetheless, (consistent/inconsistent) with it.

conformity

134 On the other hand, there is a considerable body of data indicating that the lower-middle class in America contains by far the largest proportion of rigid conformers (cf. Unit 3). The Warner school of social stratification has coined the term, "lower-middle-class morality" to refer to extreme forms of social _______ to the mores, especially those mores relating to religion, sex, and drinking.[5]

curving-line

135 The authors of *The Authoritarian Personality* (Adorno et al., 1950) believe that conformity is especially characteristic of the middle classes in Western societies. If this conclusion is correct then the relationship between social status and conformity in the society is a (curving-line/straight-line) function.

less

136 To say that the relationship between a person's social standing in a group and probability of compliance with group judgments is curvilinear is to say, in this context, that those near the top and the bottom of the group prestige structure are generally _______ compliant with group judgments than those near the middle.

[5] This type of morality is lampooned in G. B. Shaw's *Pygmalion*. The Broadway musical version of the play is entitled *My Fair Lady*. It is significant that this ascetic type of morality is referred to throughout the play as "middle-class morality."

middle

137 Two experiments (Dittes and Kelley, 1956; Harvey and Consalvi, 1960) studying small groups report that the highest level of compliance with group norms occurred among those who were well above average status in the groups but were still not at the top. These studies further confirm the hypothesis that compliance is highest somewhere in the ______ of the group status continuum.

lower

138 But from all stratification data we possess, the upper-middle class generally is much less conforming than the most conspicuously "respectable" class, the ______-middle class.[6]

verified (confirmed, etc.)

139 Berkowitz and Macaulay (1961) have come up with a theory that may be accurate. In any case, the theory is not definitely disconfirmed by the available data. They hypothesize that compliant and conforming behavior is a direct function of closeness to a status goal and the imagined chance of success in reaching it. Until we know more about the status goals of the individuals in groups and about people in the class positions in society, this aspect of the theory cannot be ______ by data dealing with differential conformity in the different classes.

more (higher, etc.)

140 The theory clearly implies that a society or group in which prestige positions exhibit high mobility, or change, would be characterized by ______ compliance and conformity than societies in which status positions are comparatively fixed.[7]

middle

141 Whatever the outcome of future research there are enough data to indicate that those somewhere in the ______ of a status hierarchy are probably the most conforming.

lower-middle

142 In small personal groups the most conforming segment may be an upper-middle position, but in the United States society at large there is little question that compliance with the mores is concentrated in the ______-______ class.

Concentration of Power

negative factor

143 Ross (1958) reports a low to moderate negative correlation between concentrations of power in some women's groups and the effectiveness of persuading women members to solicit money for philanthropic activities. Concentration of power was a ______ ______ of compliance in this case.

[6] See Box 1, p. 47 for a clarification of social class terms.
[7] This implication has not been verified to the author's knowledge.

parallels

144 Bovard (1951) reports more compliance with group expectations in "group-centered" groups than in "leader-centered" groups. Bovard's study (parallels/contrasts with) that of Ross.

Competition

positive

145 An eleventh group factor is competition *between* groups in which those making the right answer get some reward. Crutchfield (Krech, Crutchfield, and Ballachey, 1962) promised subjects that $50 would be given to the group that gave the correct answers to a number of factual and logical questions. Under this condition, subjects were somewhat more compliant to the bogus judgments attributed to the "others" than under a condition of no competition with other groups. The tentative conclusion indicated by this study is that competition between groups exerts a (positive/negative) influence upon compliance within a given group.

negative

146 The data on the relationship to competition *within* the group and compliance, as far as experimental research is concerned, are limited. However, there is some indication that as competition within a group increases, compliance with the group's positions decreases (Kelly and Shapiro, 1954). Competition within a group seems to be a ________ factor of compliance.

Social Ties Outside the Group

reduces (decreases, etc.)

147 Festinger, Schacter, and Bach (1950) studied conformity to certain norms of married students in a housing project at MIT. They found, among other things, that students who did not conform had much more "social life" with people outside the housing project. Whatever the particular explanation may be, and there can be several, it seems that having social ties outside a given group or neighborhood substantially ________ the probability of conforming to the norms of such a group or neighborhood.

greater (more)

148 Since the time sequence of these variables is unknown, and since there is no information that some other relevant independent variables were reasonably constant, the number of logical causal conclusions one can draw are ________ in number than is usually the case in the small-group experiments where both of these drawbacks are more or less eliminated, or at least substantially reduced.

less

149 It seems probable, however, that having more social ties outside an influence group would make a person ________ susceptible to the group's influence.

Observability

less

150 For some time we have been discussing type A and type P experimental procedures (see frames 58–60). When other things are held constant you can probably guess that substantially ________ compliance occurs in a type A procedure than in a type P procedure (Deutsch and Gerard, 1955; Levy, 1960).

observation (surveillance, etc.)

151 The main difference between type A and type P procedures is that in type A the experimental subjects are not under ________ of the rest of the group.

compliant (in conformity with)

152 Behavior that is actually observed is more likely to be ________ with group judgments than behavior that is not observed.

positive

153 Consequently, it is highly probable that potential observability of behavior is a ________ factor of compliance (Coser, 1961).

Similarity to Previous Socializing Groups

compliance / noncompliance

154 A fourteenth factor must be stated as a hypothesis with little or no direct verification but a vast amount of indirect verification. The variable alluded to is the similarity between the group situation and previous situations in which subjects have been rewarded or punished for compliance or noncompliance. Generally, of course, all but a few subjects would have been primarily rewarded for ________ and punished for ________.

positive

155 Hence, in general, similarity of the group to previous socializing groups would be a ________ factor in compliance.

P

156 It may be that many, possibly all, of these group situation factors are due, in part, to their similarity to past situations in which the subjects have been rewarded or punished for compliance. For example, anyone soon learns that one is much less likely to be punished for noncompliance when his behavior cannot be observed. Hence the difference in part between experimental procedures type A and type P may be due to the greater similarity of type ________ procedure to previous situations involving more punishment for noncompliance.

By way of summary, there is conclusive evidence that compliance with a group judgment is a positive function of (1) consensus within the group, (2) size of influence group, up to about a half-dozen persons, (3) group cohesion, (4) prestige of potential influencers, (5) attempts to get subject to agree with the group, (6) observability of the subject's response of agreement or disagreement with the group, and (7) similarity of groups and group situations to past groups and group situations in which the subject has been rewarded for compliance and punished for noncompliance. There is some evidence that deviation from the modal judgment of the group, diffusion of power within the group, and competition with other groups are also positive factors of compliance.

Compliance with a group judgment is rather definitely lowered by an open commitment to a position contrary to the group judgment prior to being exposed to the group judgment. Social ties outside a group also decrease compliance with the judgments and values of the group. Finally, there is some limited evidence that competition within the group is a negative factor of compliance with group judgments.

Personal Factors

In this section we shall study the effect upon compliance of the following personal factors: (1) self-confidence, (2) confidence in the accuracy of the judgments of potential influencers, (3) authoritarianism, (4) conservatism, (5) sex, (6) education, (7) intelligence, (8) prior frequency of reward for compliance and punishment for noncompliance, and (9) desire to express a correct judgment. This list does not exhaust the list of personal-biographical factors that have been studied in relation to compliance. They are discussed here because they appear to be relatively more significant and because evidence concerning their effects upon compliance is relatively substantial.

157 A good deal of variation of compliance is evident in all the studies where the issues and the group characteristics are constant. In such cases neither ________ nor ________ characteristics can be responsible for the differences of compliance.

issues
group

158 In these cases the sources of differential compliance have to be ________ factors. That is, they have to be due to individual differences.

individual (personal)

constant

159 The general premise upon which this deduction is made is: a variation can not be produced by a (constant/variable).

could not

160 In many of the experiments, issue and group situation factors have been constant. Therefore, they (could/could not) have produced the individual variations with respect to the amount of compliance.

Self-confidence

negative

161 Confidence in the accuracy of one's judgments would on commonsense grounds seem to be a high ______ factor of compliance.

negative

162 A glance at Table 12 will show that a rather high ______ correlation exists between initial level of certainty and subsequent compliance with an erroneous majority.

Table 12. Compliance as a Function of Initial Level of Certainty

Initial level of certainty of individual judgment on item	*Percent of subjects who yield to group pressure on item*
High (scale values 4, 5)	15
Medium (scale values 2, 3)	24
Low (scale values 0, 1)	36

SOURCE: D. Krech, R. S. Crutchfield, and E. L. Ballachey, *Individual in Society,* McGraw-Hill Book Company, New York, 1962, p. 510. Used by permission.

certainty (confidence)

163 Since the objective issues and group situation variables are held constant, it is highly probable that initial level of ______ is the cause, or at least a major part of the cause, of the variation in the amount of compliance.

compliance

164 Edmonds' subjects were asked to indicate how certain they were about the accuracy of their judgments on a five-point scale after the experimental exposure to varying degrees of erroneous group consensus (Edmonds, 1964). Virtually all of them checked the point on the scale that corresponded to a verbal description of "moderately certain." This was true even of the many subjects who went along with the erroneous majority ten times out of ten. Furthermore, it bore no relationship to their compliance-error score. Thus, in this study confidence was no indicator of either accuracy of judgment or ______.

negative

165 Although there are other studies (Boomer, 1955; Hochbaum, 1954; Johnson, 1940; Mausner, 1954) confirming Crutchfield's finding that confidence in the accuracy of one's judgment is a ______ factor of compliance, there is one study (Edmonds, 1964) that is not entirely consistent with it.

before (prior to)

166 Perhaps if Edmonds, like Crutchfield, had obtained a measure of confidence in the accuracy of subjects' judgments ______ exposure to the experimental conditions he would have gotten similar results.[8]

certainty (confidence)

167 The subjects who do not change their position in the direction of the majority undergo a marked reduction in level of certainty, even on very easy items (Krech, Crutchfield, and Ballachey, 1962). One "price" of not yielding is apparently a loss of ______ in the accuracy of one's position.

anxiety

168 Bogdonoff et al. (1961) correlated decrease in fatty acid levels in the blood with degrees of compliance with an erroneous majority and obtained an r of $-.63$. Assuming that fatty acid level is a good indicator of anxiety, another price of noncompliance is continuation of ______.

decrease (reduction, etc.)

169 In other words, persons who comply with the judgments of a group undergo a ______ in anxiety.

confirmation (support)

170 What happens to the level of confidence people have in the accuracy of their judgments after they change their position and agree with the erroneous, and bogus, "majority"? They are equally confident of their new judgments! Crutchfield states that this finding gives some ______ to the hypothesis that the "new believer" is especially likely to be the "true believer."[9]

very confident

171 In any case, a very confident person who is persuaded that his position is in error is also ______ ______ of the new position he is persuaded to accept.

[8] I am still puzzled by the fact that virtually all subjects, about half of whom were Ph.D. candidates, were so certain of the accuracy of their judgments even when they gave the wrong answer to every question.

[9] See Eric Hoffer, *The True Believer*, Harper & Row, Publishers, Incorporated, New York, 1951, for many real-life illustrations of this phenomenon.

Yes[10]

172 "Where mass movements are in violent competition with each other, there are not infrequent instances of converts—even the most zealous—shifting their allegiance from one to the other" (Hoffer, 1951). Do Crutchfield's small-group data parallel the phenomenon referred to by Hoffer? ________.

Confidence in Influencers

positive factor

173 Just as confidence in the accuracy of one's judgments is a negative factor of compliance, we would expect confidence in the accuracy of the others' judgments to be a ________ ________ of compliance. That such is the case can hardly be doubted either on the basis of commonsense observations or the basis of experimental data (Deutsch and Gerard, 1955; Mausner, 1954; Rosenberg, 1963).

not a necessary condition (not a precondition, etc.)

174 Deutsch and Gerard (1955) advance the hypothesis that one must have more confidence in the accuracy of others' judgments than in one's own to go along with the judgments of others. Rosenberg (1963) found that a number of subjects complied with the majority on items for which they indicated that they were more confident of the accuracy of their own judgments than of the judgments of the majority. Having more confidence in others' judgments than in one's own is apparently +++++ of complying with the judgments of others.

Desire to Be Right

less

175 Most of the experiments discussed have not provided a high degree of incentive to be right, or correct, in one's judgments. It would seem that under this condition the more capable subjects would be ________ likely to agree with an erroneous majority.

more

176 In one study (Festinger, 1954), subjects were told that an expense-paid trip to England might be given to the person in the group who gave right answers to the questions. Under this condition subjects were more compliant than under standard conditions. It seems that the desire to be right makes one ________, rather than less, compliant.

[10] There is at least a partial parallel. Crutchfield's data indicate that people who are certain about a given position become equally certain, once converted, about a position that is logically contradictory.

more

177 The reader will probably recall that Crutchfield's subjects were ________ compliant when they were told that a prize of $50 would be distributed equally to the members of the group making the largest number of correct responses.

No, because the reward in the latter case was to be given on an individual, rather than a group, basis.

178 Crutchfield thought the greater compliance under this competition with other groups might be due to a person feeling that, even though he disagreed with the others, he shouldn't spoil their chance of winning the prize. Can this explanation account for the results just mentioned in which subjects were more compliant when individuals were offered a free trip to England if they were correct in their judgments? Why? +++++.

compliant (conforming)

179 Crutchfield performed another experiment to eliminate this possible source of compliance. In this study, individuals were told that they were to be given $10 if their judgments were more accurate than any of the other individuals occupying the same booth in eleven other studies. In this case the students were no less compliant than when they were given no financial incentive to be right, but neither were they any more compliant. It seems that motivating a person to be right is not a very important factor where ________ behavior is concerned.

Age and Education

negatively (inversely)

180 A number of studies have correlated age with compliance. Berenda (1950), duplicating one of Asch's studies, obtained considerably more compliance with subjects seven to ten years old than Asch had obtained with his "adult" college students. Thus age was ________ correlated with compliance.

education

181 Marple (1933) had obtained similar results in a modified type A procedure. One cannot, of course, infer that age, per se, is the independent variable in the results of these studies. Among other things, the correlation between age and compliance is obviously contaminated by the variable of ________. (Note the obvious other difference that might, at least in part, account for the difference in compliance of Asch's and Berenda's subjects described in the preceding frame.)

is not

182 Edmonds (1964) correlated age and compliance-error scores for the graduate students in his sample and obtained an *r* of +.15. It is apparent that for Edmonds' graduate students age (is/is not) an important source of compliance.

cannot

183 If time, as such, cannot determine anything, then age, as such, ________.

prior to

184 Age could, of course, be a good indicator of certain other changes, such as level of general information, level of critical thinking, etc. Apparently this is the case for the years (prior to/after) about twenty years of age.

equal

185 In Table 13, groups IV and V are those experimental groups in which each experimental subject heard either four or five out of six confederates give wrong answers to questions concerning the validity of ten arguments. The mean number of errors under these low-pressure situations is about ________ for students who are candidates for both master's and doctor's degrees.

Table 13. Mean Errors of Candidates for Master's and Doctor's Degrees under Different Levels of Group Consensus*

Candidacy	*Groups IV & V*	*Group VI*	*Difference*
Master's	5.54	8.38	3.04
Doctor's	5.21	6.00	.79

* Difference in change = 2.95; $t = 2.14$; Sig. level = 0.025.

SOURCE: V. H. Edmonds, "Logical Error as a Function of Group Consensus: An Experimental Study of the Effect of Erroneous Group Consensus upon Logical Judgments of Graduate Students," *Social Forces,* 43:33–38, 1964. Used by permission.

60 (6 out of 10)

186 In group VI each experimental subject heard six out of six confederates give wrong answers on all ten logical arguments used in the computation. Under this high-pressure condition the compliance-error rate for candidates for the master's degree is about 84 percent (8.4 out of 10), whereas the compliance-error rate for students for the doctoral degree is only ________ percent.

more

187 There is little question that doctoral students are somewhat ________ independent than master's students under the conditions of unanimous consensus with items of this level of difficulty.

Yes, they made approximately the same mean errors under the comparatively low consensus conditions.

188 Is there any evidence that the difference in compliance with the erroneous majority in the group VI situation is not due to differences in reasoning ability of master's and doctor's candidates? (See Table 13.) +++++.

group pressure (group consensus)

189 The difference, thus, probably reflects a genuine difference in resistance to ________ ________ rather than any difference in reasoning ability.

190 Which of the following hypotheses, concerning the causal relationship between these variables of educational level and compliance, are tenable?

a. The experiences doctoral students are exposed to make them more independent.

b. Some common factor, or set of factors, such as, perhaps, social class, makes it more likely that certain students will be both comparatively independent and enrolled as doctoral candidates.

c. Doctoral candidates have more will power.

d. The association is almost certainly pure coincidence.

a and *b*. *c* is meaningless, and *d* runs counter to the evidence of this and other studies.

Previous Rewards for Compliance

occupations

191 Table 14 gives compliance-error scores for graduate students whose fathers were in different ________.

Table 14. Mean Logical Errors of Subjects Whose Fathers Are in Different Occupational Classes under Different Degrees of Group Consensus

Father's occupational class	*Groups IV & V*	*Group VI*	*Difference*
Professional	5.9	7.8	1.9
White collar	5.2	8.8	3.6
Labor	6.4	7.9	1.5
Farm	6.0	6.5	.5

SOURCE: V. H. Edmonds, "Logical Error as a Function of Group Consensus: An Experimental Study of the Effect of Erroneous Group Consensus upon Logical Judgments of Graduate Students," *Social Forces*, 43:33–38, October, 1964, p. 36. Used by permission.

erroneous (wrong, etc.)

192 The reader will probably recall that in groups IV and V each experimental subject heard either four, as in group IV, or five, as in group V, out of a total of six confederates give ________ responses to the experimenter's questions.

unanimous (complete)

193 In group VI the erroneous confederate consensus was ________ since six out of six gave wrong answers on each argument.

highest (largest, etc.)

194 Students whose fathers were white-collar employees made the ________ number of errors in the relatively high-pressure group VI situation where confederate consensus was unanimous.

smallest (least, etc.)

195 The same class of subjects made the ________ number of errors in the relatively low pressure group IV and group V situations.

No

196 Did students from any other occupational background change this much? ________.

No[11]

197 Is the greater compliance of students from white-collar backgrounds in the unanimous group situation due to less reasoning ability? (See Table 13 and frame 195.) ________.

white-collar

198 The conclusion should be very tentative, but it would seem that students from ________-________ backgrounds are more compliant when confronted with a unanimous but erroneous position than students from any other major occupational background included in these results.

punished

199 A tentative hypothesis advanced to explain these data is that students from white-collar backgrounds have been more frequently rewarded for compliant behavior and more frequently ________ for noncompliant behavior in their previous group associations.

confirmation

200 In 1940 Davis and Havighurst (1946) made a study of child-rearing practices in Chicago. They reported that, in general, middle-class mothers were much less permissive than lower-class mothers. If one assumes that Edmonds' white-collar students were from predominantly middle-class homes and that students from labor backgrounds were predominantly from lower-class homes, the Davis and Havighurst data give some ________ to this differential punishment hypothesis concerning the relatively high compliance of subjects from white-collar backgrounds as compared with those from labor backgrounds.

[11] At least this is most unlikely because they made the lowest number of errors in the comparatively low-consensus groups.

more

201 There is considerable evidence that the differential emphasis placed upon rearing "good," i.e., conforming, children switched directions for middle-class and lower-class mothers in the late forties or early fifties (Bronfenbrenner, 1958). Edmonds' subjects, however, were being socialized in the thirties and early forties when, apparently, the middle-class or white-collar mothers were still ______ likely to punish their children for nonconforming behavior.

c. *a is* a pseudo explanation. *b* is most unlikely in view of research reported on in the previous pages. *d* is simply absurd in that it implies either that the differences are not caused or that they can be constants.

202 Milgram (1961), using a wide variety of issues, found Norwegian students in Norway much more compliant than French students exposed to the same procedures in France. The most probable explanation for this is:

a. The French students are more able to think for themselves.
b. The French students are more concerned with being right than being liked.
c. The Norwegian students have been more frequently rewarded for compliant behavior and punished for noncompliant behavior than the French students.
d. The difference doesn't mean anything.

b. Such evidence as exists refutes *a.* Logical problems were not involved in most of these studies. If *d* is true it is probably a product of the process referred to in *b.*

203 Several studies (Applezweig and Moeller, 1958; Asch, 1956; Beloff, 1958; Tuddenham, 1958) disclose that females in the United States are substantially more compliant than males. The most probable explanation of this fact is:

a. Females are not as intelligent as males.
b. Females have been more frequently rewarded for compliant behavior and punished for noncompliant behavior than have males.
c. Females are generally dim-witted when it comes to problems of logic.
d. Females are generally more eager to please.

correlate

204 Personality psychologists have started studying personality correlates of compliance, and, as is usually the case when this happens in any area, the literature is literally swamped with a vast number of personality "traits" that have been found to ______ in some major or minor (usually minor) fashion with the thing under study.[12]

[12] The author readily admits that this morass of complicated confusion is largely inherent in the very complex nature of personality in a large multigroup society such as ours.

Authoritarianism

positive

205 Any attempt at a complete presentation of this research would be infinitely confusing since the personality traits listed are so numerous and their measurements so varied. One cluster of personality characteristics is, however, particularly worth stressing because it ties in with many other known aspects of compliant behavior. "Authoritarianism," as measured by the F scale,[13] correlated about +.50 (+.48 to be exact) with Nadler's measures of compliance in type P situations (Nadler, 1959). The correlation between authoritarianism and compliance is moderate and ________.

Box 2. The Authoritarian Personality

After the rise and successful grabbing of power by authoritarian fascist groups and organizations during the 1930s a number of scientists came to the tentative conclusion that there was a cluster of personality traits common to the supporters and leaders of these movements. Adorno and associates using a large number of complex procedures developed a portrait of "the authoritarian personality." The measurement of this cluster of traits is known to correlate positively with compliance with erroneous majority judgments. The trait cluster is listed and defined below.

The Authoritarian Personality

1. *Conventionalism: Rigid adherence to conventional, middle-class values.*
2. *Authoritarian Submission: Submissive, uncritical attitude toward idealized moral authorities of the ingroup.*
3. *Authoritarian Aggression: Tendency to be on the lookout for, and to condemn, reject, and punish people who violate conventional values.*
4. *Anti-intraception: Opposition to the subjective, the imaginative, the tender-minded.*
5. *Superstition and Stereotypy: The belief in mystical determinants of the individual's fate; the disposition to think in rigid categories.*
6. *Power and "Toughness": Preoccupation with the dominance-submission, strong-weak, leader-follower dimension; identification with power figures; overemphasis upon the conven-*

[13] The F scale was designed to measure "fascism" (hence the F) or "authoritarianism." The traits that constitute the authoritarian syndrome are listed and defined in Box 2.

tionalized attributes of the ego; exaggerated assertion of strength and toughness.

7. *Destructiveness and Cynicism: Generalized hostility, vilification of the human.*
8. *Projectivity: The disposition to believe that wild and dangerous things go on in the world; the projection outward of unconscious emotional impulses.*
9. *Sex: Exaggerated concern with sexual "goings-on."*

SOURCE: T. W. Adorno et al., *The Authoritarian Personality,* Harper & Row, Publishers, Incorporated, New York, 1950, pp. 248–250. Used by permission.

intelligence

206 Since authoritarianism, as measured by the F scale, correlated about −.50 (−.48 to be exact) with intelligence, as measured by the Stanford-Binet test (Adorno et al., 1950), it is conceivable that ______ might account for some of the correlation between authoritarianism and compliance.

increases

207 Whatever the particular explanation may be, we can tell from this correlation coefficient that as authoritarianism increases compliance ______.

Conservatism

positive

208 It is interesting to note that authoritarianism, as measured by the F scale, correlates about +.50 with certain measures of "politico-economic" conservatism (Adorno et al., 1950). From these data one can tentatively conclude that there is a ______ correlation between political and economic conservatism and compliance with an erroneous group consensus.

tentative

209 There is much information confirming this tentative conclusion, so that it really no longer needs to be ______ (Howells, 1930; Krech, Crutchfield, and Ballachey, 1962; Shuttleworth, 1927–1928; Sinclair, 1930).

Confidence in the soundness of one's judgments and confidence in the soundness of group judgments are rather definitely negative and positive factors, respectively, of compliance. It seems also that people will agree with group judgments even when the group judgments are rather obviously in error and even when they express more confidence in their own judgments than they express in the judgments of the group.

While there are, apparently, no experiments directly confirming the hypothesis that compliance with group judgments is a function of previous rewards for compliance and punishment for noncompliance, there is a large body of indirect evidence indicating that such is the case. It seems probable that the sexual, occupational, and national differences discussed here reflect aggregate background differences with respect to differential rewards and punishments for compliance. The same explanation is at least eminently plausible with respect to the fact that persons with conservative and authoritarian orientations are especially likely to comply with group judgments.

Finally, attempts to motivate subjects to express independent and correct judgments when confronted with the erroneous judgments of groups have not been successful. This tentatively disconfirms the hypothesis that subjects have generally agreed with erroneous group judgments because they had no good reason to do otherwise.

SUMMARY

Compliance with group, community, or societal values is the product of either incentive manipulation or persuasion. Although the logical distinction between these two general sources of social control is clear there are many specific cases of social control that are not clearly classifiable as one or the other. The incentive factors of reward and punishment may be either legal or nonlegal; however, in most societies they are almost always of the nonlegal type. The major types of nonlegal rewards consist of verbal approval, verbal promise, gestures of approval, monetary increments, or physical expressions of affection or approval.

Unlike rewards, punishments are frequently of the legal type in the sense that they are meted out by functionaries of governments. In this case they typically consist of fines, imprisonment, and, occasionally, physical punishment or death. Even so, the nonlegal punishments are much more important sources of social control. They typically consist of verbal censures, verbal threats, gestures of disapproval, physical punishment, ostracism, banishment and, occasionally, death.

Attitudes and beliefs are changed by many more things than those which are consciously and deliberately utilized. When certain things are deliberately utilized they typically consist of education, propaganda, or therapy.

The factors of social persuasion have been analyzed into issue factors, group factors, and personal factors. The central issue factor determining compliance with group judgment is rather definitely the difficulty of the issue. Although people may use their sensory experience and such logical reasoning as they possess on comparatively simple issues, they largely turn to group judgments as the issues become more complex and difficult. Social, rather than rational-factual, validation becomes the rule as issues become more complex and difficult. It is nonetheless true that the judgments of most people are greatly influenced by the "climate of opinion" regardless of level of difficulty. This is particularly true when the climate of opinion is unanimous. Furthermore, there are issues, such as those of ethics and aesthetics, that do not have the property of being accurate or inaccurate. Although precise comparative data are lacking, it seems that the judgments of individuals in these areas of opinion are even more susceptible to the climate of opinion than they are with respect to extremely difficult issues of truth or logical validity.

Group consensus, size of group, group cohesion, group pressure, prestige of influence members, deviation of influencee from the modal position of the group, observability of influencee's behavior, previous rewards for compliance, and previous punishments for noncompliance are all rather definite and important positive factors of compliance. Competition between groups and diffusion of power within groups seem to be positive factors of compliance. Status of influencees within a group, at this time, has not been shown to be either a positive or a negative factor of compliance; however, there is considerable evidence that those who are somewhere in the middle are most susceptible to group pressures toward compliance. In society at large it is the lower-middle class that is most conforming to the conventional mores, especially those pertaining to religion, sex, and drinking. Competition within the group seems to be a negative factor of compliance, but the evidence on this point is very limited.

Among the personal factors of compliance, confidence in the accuracy of one's own judgment is a definite high negative factor. However, we have the somewhat strange but interesting phenomenon wherein converts to the group's position take on the same level of certainty in the accuracy of their judgments that they had on the same issues before they were converted. It is also quite apparent that, aside from the more or less severe punishments usually meted out by groups to noncomplying members, those who fail to comply pay the price of loss of confidence and persistent anxiety.

Level of education is also a high negative correlate of

compliance, but the exact causal factor is uncertain. It is not solely a matter of ability. At the higher age levels, such as those characteristic of graduate students, it is not a function of age or anything highly correlated with age.

Females are more compliant than males, and subjects from white-collar backgrounds are apparently more compliant than subjects from professional, laboring, and farm backgrounds. Whether reward for compliance and punishment for noncompliance are the independent variables explaining these occupational differences is a bit difficult to say, but there is much indirect evidence indicating that such is the case.

Providing incentives for making correct judgments on cognitive issues seems to make little difference in the probability of compliance with an erroneous majority. If it does have any effect it seems to be positive rather than negative.

Finally, authoritarianism and conservatism correlate positively with compliance. Although part of this correlation may be due to variations in intelligence there is some evidence that most of it is due to previous learning experiences, especially those involving rewards for compliant behavior and punishments for noncompliant behavior.

SELF–REVIEW QUIZ

1 Two major sources of social control are ________ ________ and ________.

2 Rewards and punishments may be legal or nonlegal. Most types of such incentives are ________.

3 Typical legal punishments are ________, ________, and ________.

4–6 Match the studies with the type of persuasion involved:

4. Personal factor
5. Issue factor
6. Group factor

a. The Coleman, Blake, and Morton study of compliance and difficulty on general information items
b. Edmonds' study of the effects of group consensus on compliance
c. Bogdonoff's study of decrease in fatty acid levels in the blood with degrees of compliance with

an erroneous majority

a. "Volunteering" for a United Fund drive team when the boss suggests you would be "a good man" to do this.
b. Adults dancing the "frug" only when they chaperone a social dance.
c. Attempts to make a noncompliant person "see his error" and comply with the majority.
d. Getting the group to agree with you by getting the first person you ask to do so.
e. Presidents of clubs are more independent in judgments about club activities than are subordinate officers.

7–11 Match the factors related to consensus with the examples:

7. Group cohesion
8. Group pressure
9. Concentration of power
10. Observability
11. Status in the group

12 Generally speaking, there is a (positive/negative) correlation between education and compliance with suggestion.

13 Students from a [select one] (professional/white-collar/labor/farm) socioeconomic background are more likely to be compliant when faced with a unanimous but erroneous judgment.

14 Which of the following is *not* characteristic of "the authoritarian personality"?

a. anti-intraception
b. power and "toughness"
c. projectivity
d. little concern about sexual "goings-on"
e. cynicism and destructiveness

15 The soundness of one's judgment and confidence in group judgments are, respectively, negative and positive factors of ________.

REFERENCES

Adorno, T. W., et al.: *The Authoritarian Personality,* Harper & Row, Publishers, Incorporated, New York, 1950.

Anonymous: "Why White Collar Workers Can't Be Organized, *Harpers,* 215:44–50, 1957.

Applezweig, M. H., and G. Moeller: "Conforming Behavior and Personality Variables," Technological Reports no. 8, Contract NONR 996 (02), Connecticut College, New London, Conn., 1958.

Asch, S. E.: "Opinions and Social Pressure," *Scientific American,* 193:31–35, 1955.

Asch, S. E.: *Social Psychology,* Prentice-Hall, Inc., Englewood Cliffs, N.J., 1952.

Asch, S. E.: "Studies of Independence and Conformity: A Minority of One against a Unanimous Majority," *Psychological Monographs,* 70: 416, 1956.

Bartos, O. J.: "Leadership, Conformity, and Originality," unpublished paper presented at 1958 meeting of the American Sociological Society.

Becker, C. L.: *The Heavenly City of the Eighteenth Century Philisophers,* Yale University Press, New Haven, Conn., 1932.

Beloff, H.: "Two Forms of Social Conformity: Acquiescence and Conventionality," *Journal of Abnormal and Social Psychology,* 56:99–104, 1958.

Berenda, R. H.: *The Influence of the Group on the Judgments of Children,* Kings Crown Press, New York, 1950.

Berkowitz, Leonard, and J. Macaulay: "Some Effects of Differences in Status Level and Status Stability," *Human Relations,* 14:135–148, 1961.

Bogdonoff, M. D., et al.: "The Modifying Effect of Conforming Behavior upon Lipid Responses Accompanying CNS Arousal," *Clinical Research,* 9:135, 1961.

Boomer, D. S.: "Subjective Certainty and Resistance to Change," *Journal of Abnormal and Social Psychology,* 51:629–636, 1955.

Bovard, E. W., Jr.: "Group Structures and Perception," *Journal of Abnormal and Social Psychology,* 46:398–400, 1951.

Bronfenbrenner, U.: "Socialization and Social Class in Time and Space," in E. E. MacCoby, T. M. Newcomb, and E. L. Hartley (eds.), *Readings in Social Psychology,* Holt, Rinehart and Winston, Inc., New York, 1958.

Cantril, H.: *The Politics of Despair,* Basic Books, Inc., Publishers, New York, 1958.

Coleman, J. F., R. R. Blake, and J. S. Morton: "Task Difficulty and Conformity Pressures," *Journal of Abnormal and Social Psychology,* 57:120–122, 1958.

Coser, R. L.: "Insulation from Observability and Types of Social Conformity," *American Sociological Review,* 26: 28–29, 1961.

Crutchfield, R. S.: "Conformity and Character." *The American Psychologist,* 10:191–198, 1955.

Davis, A., and R. J. Havighurst: "Social Class and Colour Differences in Childrearing," *American Sociological Review,* 2:698–710, 1946.

Deutsch, M., and H. B. Gerard: "A Study of Normative and Informative Social Influences upon Individual Judgment," *Journal of Abnormal and Social Psychology,* 51:629–636, 1955.

Dittes, J. E., and H. H. Kelley: "Effects of Different Conditions of Acceptance upon Conformity to Group Norms," *Journal of Abnormal and So-*

cial Psychology, 53:100–107, 1956.

Edmonds, V. H.: "Logical Error as a Function of Group Consensus: An Experimental Study of the Effect of Erroneous Group Consensus upon Logical Judgments of Graduate Students," *Social Forces,* 43:33–38, 1964.

Fairchild, H. P. (ed.): *Dictionary of Sociology,* Philosophical Library, Inc., New York, 1944.

Festinger, L.: "A Theory of Social Comparison Processes," *Human Relations,* 7:117–140, 1954.

Festinger, L., et al.: "The Influence Process in the Presence of Extreme Deviates," *Human Relations,* 5:327–346, 1952.

Festinger, L., S. Schacter, and K. W. Bach: *Social Pressure in Informal Groups,* Harper & Row, Publishers, Incorporated, New York, 1950.

Festinger, L., and J. Thibaut: "Interpersonal Communication in Small Groups," *Journal of Abnormal and Social Psychology,* 46:92–99, 1951.

Harnack, R. R.: "A Study of the Effect of an Organized Minority upon a Discussion Group, *Journal of Communication,* 3:12–42, 1963.

Harvey, O. J., and C. Consalvi: "Status and Conformity to Pressures in Informal Groups," *Journal of Abnormal and Social Psychology,* 60:182–187, 1960.

Hochbaum, G. M.: "Relation between Group Members' Self Confidence and Their Reactions to Group Pressures to Uniformity," *American Sociological Review,* 19:678–687, 1954.

Hoffer, Eric: *The True Believer,* Harper & Row, Publishers, Incorporated, New York, 1951.

Hollander, E. P.: "Conformity, Status, and Idiosyncrasy Credit," *Psychological Review,* 65:117–127, 1958.

Howells, T.: "A Comparative Study of Those Who Accept as against Those Who Reject Religious Authority," *University of Iowa Studies in Character,* E. D. Starbuck (ed.), vol. 7, no. 2, 1958.

Jack, R., and Betty Schiffer: "The Limits of Fashion Control," *American Sociological Review,* 13:730–738, 1948.

Johnson, D. M.: "Confidence and the Expression of Opinion," *Journal of Social Psychology,* 12:213–220, 1940.

Kahl, Joseph A.: *The American Class Structure,* Holt, Rinehart and Winston, Inc., New York, 1961.

Kelley, H. H., and M. M. Shapiro: "An Experiment on Conformity to Group Norms Where Conformity Is Detrimental to Group Achievement," *American Sociological Review,* 19:667–677, 1954.

Kelley, H. H., and C. L. Woodruff: "Members' Reactions to Apparent Group Approval of a Counter Norm Communication," *Journal of Abnormal and Social Psychology,* 52: 27–74, 1956.

Kennedy, John F.: *Profiles in Courage,* Harper & Row, Publishers, Incorporated, New York, 1955.

Krech, David, R. S. Crutchfield, and E. L. Ballachey: *Individual in Society,* McGraw-Hill Book Company, New York, 1962.

Levy, L.: "Studies in Conformity Behavior: A Methodological Note," *Journal of Psychology,* 50:39–41, 1960.

Malinowski, B.: *The Father in Primitive Psychology,* W. W. Norton & Company, Inc., New York, 1927.

Marple, C. H.: "Comparative Susceptibility of Three Age Levels to the Suggestion of Group versus Expert Opinion," *Journal of Social Psychology,* 4:176–186, 1933.

Mausner, B.: "The Effect of Prior Reinforcement on the Interaction of Observed Pairs," *Journal of Applied Psychology,* 37:391–393, 1954.

McClelland, D. C., et al.: *The Achievement Motive,* Appleton-Century-Crofts, Inc., New York, 1953.

Milgram, S.: "Nationality and Conformity," *Scientific American,* 205:45–51, 1961.

Miller, D. R., and G. E. Swanson: *The Changing American Parent,* John Wiley & Sons, Inc., New York, 1958.

Moore, H. T.: "The Comparative Influence of Majority and Expert Opinion," *American Journal of Psychology,* 32: 16–20, 1921.

Nadler, E. B.: "Yielding Authoritarianism and Authoritarian Ideology Regarding Groups," *Journal of Abnormal and Social Psychology,* 58:408–410, 1959.

Putney, Snell, and Russell Middleton: "Rebellion, Conformity and Parental Religious Ideologies," *Sociometry,* 24: 125–134, 1961.

Rosenbaum, M., and R. R. Blake: "Volunteering as a Function of Field Structure," *Journal of Abnormal and Social Psychology,* 50:193–196, 1953.

Rosenberg, L. A.: "Conformity as a Function of Confidence in Self and Confidence in Partner," *Human Relations,* 16:131–9, 1963.

Ross, Aileen D.: "Control and Leadership in Women's Groups: Analysis of Philanthropic Money Raising Activity," *Social Forces,* 37: 124–131, 1958.

Schacter, S.: "Deviation, Rejection and Communication," *Journal of Abnormal and Social Psychology,* 46:190–208, April, 1951.

Schacter, S., N. Ellertson, D. McBride, and D. Gregory: "An Experimental Study of Cohesiveness and Productivity," *Human Relations,* 4: 229–238, 1951.

Seashore, S. E.: *Group Cohesiveness in the Industrial Work Group,* University of Michigan Press, Ann Arbor, Mich., 1954.

Sherif, M.: "An Experimental Approach to the Study of Attitudes," *Sociometry,* 1:90–98, 1937.

Sherif, M.: "Experiments in Group Conflict," *Scientific American,* 5:54–58, 1956.

Sherif, M., and C. W. Sherif: *Groups in Harmony and Tension,* Harper & Row, Publishers, Incorporated, New York, 1953.

Sherif, M., and C. W. Sherif: *An Outline of Social Psychology,* rev. ed., Harper & Row, Publishers, Incorporated, New York, 1956.

Shuttleworth, F. K.: "Measurement of Character and Environmental Factors Involved in Scholastic Success," *University of Iowa Studies in Character,* W. E. Starbuck (ed.), vol. 6, 1927–1928.

Sinclair, R. D.: "A Comparative Study of Those Who Report the Experience of a Divine Presence and Those Who Do Not," *University of Iowa Studies in Character,* E. D. Starbuck (ed.), vol. 7, no. 3, 1930.

Sutherland, E. H., and D. R. Cressey: *Principles of Criminology,* 5th ed., J. B. Lippincott Company, Philadelphia, 1955.

Thorndike, E. L.: *The Psychology of Wants, Interests and Attitudes,* Appleton-Century-Crofts, Inc., New York, 1935.

Thorndike, R. L.: "The Effect of Discussion upon the Correctness of Group Decisions, When the Factor of Majority Influence Is Allowed For," *Journal of Social Psychology,* 9:343–362, 1938.

Tuddenham, R. D.: "Some Correlates of Yielding to a Distorted Group Norm," Technological Report no. 8, Contract NR, 170–179, University of California, Berkeley, Calif., 1958.

Tuddenham, R. D., and R. D. Macbride: "The Yielding Experiment from the Subjects' Point of View," *Journal of Personality,* 27:259–271, 1959.

Verplanck, W. S.: "The Control of the Content of Conversation: Reinforcements of Statements of Opinion," *Journal of Abnormal and Social Psychology,* 51:668–676, 1955.

Zaleznik, A., C. R. Christensen, and F. J. Roethlisberger: *The Motivation, Productivity, and Satisfaction of Workers,* Harvard Business School, Cambridge, Mass., 1958.

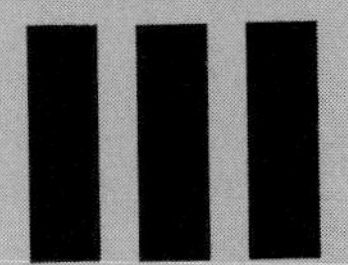

social institutions

An institution can be defined variously as an established custom or practice, as a recognized disposition or arrangement of things and/or people, or as a formal or informal organization of functions within a given structure. It is in the latter sense that we refer to social institutions. There is a variety of social institutions which shapes and controls human behavior. Some of them have already been referred to in previous chapters, but in a general or peripheral manner. It is reasonable to approach the socialization process from the viewpoint of specific, organized, social influences, such as the family and the school.

The family is the universal social institution by which man learns to be like, and to live with, other men. Marriage institutes the functions of the family but these functions vary from society to society. Particular emphasis is given in Part 3 to American family patterns and functions, but the reader will be able to contrast these with the patterns and functions of the family in other culture groups. Some of the dynamics underlying family separation and fractionation are presented with the hope that they will be personally, as well as intellectually, useful.

Next to the family, the school is probably the most influential institution in our society. The school promotes more than knowledge and skill in curriculum subjects. It also must deal with emotional, social, vocational, and ethical behavior. As you will see, Unit 3 of Part 3 discusses the school's attempts to incorporate learning for these competencies in the general educational program.

The teacher, who must serve as a surrogate parent as well as a fount of wisdom (particularly at the elementary school level), is of unique importance in the socialization process. Consequently, the role of the teacher, as representative of the school, is discussed in some detail. Of par-

ticular interest are the studies cited about teacher behavior. They lend some empirical credence to commonsense observations about effective teaching characteristics and may be compared with studies reviewed about parent behavior and child behavior in Human Behavior *(Malpass, 1965).*

The family and the school are presented as representative social institutions to demonstrate principles involved in behavior change associated with exposure to contact with institutions. The church and the job are other social institutions which bear consideration for similar reasons. To some extent, functions of these institutions will be included in succeeding units.

family structure

DONALD E. ALLEN

1

The family is the basic institution of all societies and represents the logical foundation for all cultural development. Although the family varies in form from one society to another, every society maintains some constant typical family system. The family form peculiar to a given society is usually regarded, either explicitly or implicitly, as a primary value within the society. If a society deprecates family values or manifests indifference to them, the anthropologist or sociologist looks for other signs of incipient breakdown and decay in the society as a whole. The vitality of the society as a whole is closely related to the vitality of the family as an institution on which society is founded.

The present unit will survey the principles and forms of family organization. The survey will demonstrate first that family organization offers a considerable array of workable alternatives. Second, it will demonstrate that development, alteration, or improvement of the technology of a society tends to produce related modifications of family organization. The relativity of family organization to both cultural variation and social change will be presented.

Concepts of the Family

1 The term "structure" refers to the static interrelations among groups of objects which constitute an organized unit. If we define the family by the relationship of its separate objects we are defining it by its ________.

structure

2 The overall structure or pattern of organization of a family may also be referred to as its form, and denotes the formal character of the family. A definition which specifies the form of the family is a ________ definition.

formal

3 The formal or structural definition, though it specifies the appearance and makeup of the family, tells us little about the functional aspects of the family. The function of a family indicates what it does, how it operates, and what it achieves. A more adequate definition should specify both the ________ and the ________ of the family.

structure / function

4 The U.S. Bureau of the Census (1959) defines the family as a group of two or more persons related by blood, marriage, or adoption, residing together in the same household. This is primarily a (structural/functional) definition.

structural

5 Families are conventionally expected to include parents and children. The family, however, as defined by the Census Bureau (must/need not) include children.

need not

6 By the Census definition, two brothers living together as a household would constitute a ________.

family

7 By the Census definition two brothers rooming together at a college dormitory would not constitute a family because they do not reside in a separate ________.

household

8 Robert MacIver (1937, p. 196) defines the family as the conjugal union of a man and a woman sufficiently precise and enduring to result in the bearing and upbringing of children. This is a ________ rather than a structural definition.

functional

9 To say that a man and a woman are joined in a conjugal union is to say that they are ________.

married

10 MacIver's definition stresses that the family must provide for the ________ and ________ of children.

bearing / upbringing

11 MacIver's definition does not account for all the forms of the family, since it is possible to have a family-type group which does not include ________.

children

12 MacIver's definition stresses a basic function of the family, but it is inadequate to deal with variations in the ________ of the family.

structure

13 Queen (1961, p. 11) states that in the sociological sense we think of the family "as an intimate group of persons mostly . . . related by . . . blood . . . who are regarded . . . as a distinctive social unit." This is also a ________ definition.

structural

14 The individual is incorporated into society in the first instance as a member of a ________ which is the basic organized social group in all ________.

family
societies

15 George Murdock (1949, p. 1) defines the family as a group of "adults of both sexes, at least two of whom maintain a socially approved sexual relationship, and children, own or adopted, of the sexually cohabiting adults." This definition requires that the sexual relationship be ________ ________.

socially approved

16 Of course, the accepted method of gaining social approval for sexual cohabitation and the bearing of children in our society is the ________ ceremony.

marriage

17 Some form of marriage ceremony is employed in virtually all societies to establish recognition of the new ________ relationship between adults.

family

18 The anthropologist, Malinowski (1930, p. 140), notes that marriage is not primarily to legitimize sexual cohabitation between men and women, but rather to legitimize the bearing of ________.

children

19 Since society in all cases regulates and controls the establishment of families, it may be inferred that the family is an important basic element in ________.

society

20 Typically the individual attains his position in society by virtue of having been born into an acknowledged ________ in that society.

family

21 Since the individual receives his original orientation in society by having been a child in his own family, we may indicate the family from which he comes as his family of ________.

orientation

22 Bearing children constitutes the process of procreation. Therefore, the new family which one establishes when one marries may be termed the family of ________.

procreation

23 Although the family may be variously constituted, it depends originally on a stable and socially responsible relationship between parents and ________.

children

24 Since the family occurs always in a larger society, and is recognized and controlled by society, it is clearly a ________ institution.

social

procreation

25 The family which a man establishes with his wife is called a family of ________.

In summary, a satisfactory definition of the family should include both structural and functional elements. From the several definitions cited, we may conclude that the family is a socially approved group of sexually cohabiting adults who accept responsibility for rearing the children they produce. The family originates in a dependency relationship between parents and their minor children. It functions during the period required for the full socialization of the children. The family is an integral part of the larger society on which it depends. It must therefore adapt its members to the cultural milieu, the social norms, and the institutional mechanics of the larger society.

The Sexual Nexus of the Family

bisexual

26 Man shares the biological characteristics of bisexual reproduction with other mammals. That there are two sexes is implied by the term ________.

sex drive

27 Among the quadruped mammals, such as cattle, horses, and dogs, a mating or sex drive may be coupled with a maternal drive. However, the female manifests a much more passive interest in sexual union than the male, and a much more active interest in caring for her young. Thus, the maternal drive is stronger than the ________ ________ in the female quadruped.

reproduction

28 The female quadruped will accept the male in sexual union only during the few days following ovulation, when she is said to be "in oestrum" and can be impregnated. At all other times she will repel any suggestion of male interest. This suggests that copulation among female quadrupeds has the exclusive function of ________.

passive

29 During the few seconds that copulation occurs, the female quadruped manifests no excitement or physical reaction. The female animal has no such function as the sexual climax. While the behavior of the male during mating is very active, terminating in the sexual climax, that of the female is relatively ________.

young

30 Although the female is unresponsive during copulation with the male, she shows marked interest in her young and becomes excited if the young are threatened or if she is separated from them. The female's excitability and responsiveness in reproduction centers not on sexual union with the male but on protecting her ________.

oestrum (heat)

31 The male quadruped typically shows little interest in the young and seeks contact with the female only when her scent or behavior indicates that she is in ________.

copulate

32 Some males, such as wolves and lions and many species of birds, stay with the female to assist in caring for the young. The male's concern in such cases cannot be ascribed to sexual attraction to the female, since the female will not allow the male to ________ during this period.

female

33 It would appear that sexual excitement in the male is not triggered spontaneously by internal physiological processes, but rather by evidence that the ________ is in oestrum.

continuous

34 Human beings have a reproductive system similar to that of other mammals, but the adult human being maintains a relatively continuous capacity for sexual behavior. For this reason, the female constitutes a continuing attraction to the male, which forms a basis for a ________ relation between the sexes.

women

35 Men are inclined to place greater emphasis on sexual gratification than are ________.

men

36 Women are inclined to place greater emphasis on their children than are ________.

woman

37 If a man has a greater need for sexual gratification, and a woman is the source of such gratification, then the person in the stronger position to reward and to control the behavior of the other is the ________.

control

38 Since a man's behavior is often controlled by the woman's behavior, we may apply the definition of Thibaut and Kelley (1959, p. 103) stating that the woman often exercises behavior ________ over the man.

vary

39 This power of behavior control operates when the woman, by varying her behavior, can make it desirable for the man to ________ his behavior, too.

wife (woman)

40 The long-term values of children, home, and family are likely to be of greater concern to the ________.

control

41 A wife may give limited rewards to her husband with a loving smile or a pleasant remark. Her ability to dispense a wide variety of rewards to her husband gives her some degree of ________ over his behavior.

control

42 Since the wife usually has a less compelling interest in immediate sexual gratification than her husband, she may be in a position to exercise behavior ________ over him.

threatened (endangered, etc.)

43 Maternal concern for the child is manifested by the mother's anxiety when the child's welfare is ________.

affection

44 In another way, the mother's concern for the child is also usually shown by her many affectional gestures toward the child. In time, most children begin to respond with similar gestures of ________.

children

45 The husband, if not prevented by other cultural values, can share closely in his wife's affection if he adopts an affectionate nurturant attitude toward their ________.

The process of the human child's reaching physical and social maturity is termed the "maturation" process. In primitive families this process requires about fifteen years; in industrial societies, it usually requires eighteen to twenty years.

In the modern family, the last child usually is born by the mother's twenty-seventh year; the last child typically completes maturation before the mother has completed menopause.

maturation

46 Basically, it is the slow ________ of children which requires the long continuation of the nurturant family.

maturation

47 The object of the family with regard to children is to bring each child through the ________ process.

Thus, we see that the male mammal is attracted to the

female through his interest in sexual gratification. Among men this attraction operates continuously rather than seasonally and provides a motivational basis for continuous association in marriage. The wife, because she is the source of sexual gratification, is in a position to influence her husband's behavior. She is also the source of affectional gratification to her children. The wife therefore constitutes the central and controlling figure with regard to social and expressive relationships within the family. Owing to the slow maturation of the children, it is necessary for her to maintain this position for about three decades.

Family Structure and Societal Factors: Incest, Exogamy, and Endogamy

48 Man universally manifests a social inclination and prefers to live and work with others in a relatively standardized, ordered social system. To say that man normally lives in organized social groups is another way of saying that man is ________.

social

49 The family is a subsystem of society. Therefore, the family must be integrated with ________.

society

50 A shared language, a shared system of values, and shared techniques of production, education, and protection constitute some of the support which the family derives from ________.

society

51 If the family as a subsystem and society as a system are formed from constituent elements structured from a common set of fixed relations, we may infer that both the ________ and the ________ are structurally interdependent.

family / society

52 The basic role positions of male and female parents and male and female offspring are constituent ________ of the family structure.

elements

53 Society is organized from families and other groups of persons ordered into institutional structures, including religious, educational, economic, recreational, and military organizations. Such organized groups are ________ ________ of a society.

constituent elements

54 Order and integration in a society require that the various classes of constituent elements be structured according to some basic and generally required pattern. Rules are required to maintain such ________.

patterns (structures)

55 Unrelated societies may apply widely differing patterns and systems of ordering relationships within themselves, since there are usually a number of alternative means for achieving the essential goals of any ________ organization.

social

56 The family is the primary structural unit in ________.

society

57 The groups composing any one society must be able to interact, exchange members, and work toward common ________.

goals

58 If the individual families of each class in society must be able to cooperate and exchange members with other families, the patterning of the different ________ must be relatively uniform.

families

59 One of the most fruitful examples of cooperation among the families of a society is the exchange of mature daughters or sons to establish new ________.

families

60 All societies require the constituent families to exchange mature sons and daughters with other families in establishing marital unions. Young adults must thus ________ outside their immediate families.

marry

61 The out-marrying requirement is indicated from the Greek roots ex meaning "out," and *gamos* meaning "mate." Thus, the term "exogamy" means ________-________.

out-marriage

62 If a mature male and female of the same immediate family were to mate or marry, they would violate the principle of ________ and would break the taboo of incest.

exogamy

63 A taboo is a stern prohibition of an act or condition. ________ is strictly tabooed in all societies, primitive and modern.

Incest

64 A prohibition enforced by extremely heavy penalties which are strongly supported by public opinion is called a ________.

taboo

65 A few societies of the past required that their royal families remain "pure" by marrying only within the immediate family. Thus, for the ancient Egyptians, the Incas, and the Hawaiians, brother and sister married and occupied the throne jointly. These royal marriages were ________ (Chinoy, 1961, p. 116).

incestuous

66 Within these royal families, the incestuous marriage served to isolate the royal family from the rest of society. If incestuous marriage were generally applied, families of the society would be ________ from each other.

isolated

67 In bisexual reproduction, offspring share the genetic material of their parents. If the two parents are unrelated, the offspring represent a new pooling of genes. The children of the same parents, however, share a common ________ pool.

gene

68 If brother and sister formed an incestuous union, their offspring would share the same gene pool from both parents. The offspring would lose the benefits of diverse gene pools, which is the primary advantage of ________ ________.

bisexual reproduction

69 The social resources of two families are recombined and may provide for improvements from complementary resources, such as power, property, influence, skill, or prestige in cross-family or ________ marriage.

exogamous

70 An expanded society provides a wide variety of potential mates for each nubile individual. The ________ individual is one ready for marriage. A wide selectivity of potential mates provides a better chance to match desired social or biological characteristics.

nubile

71 Siblings are defined as two or more children born of the same parents and hence related to each other as ________ or ________.

brother / sister

72 An incestuous principle of mate selection would be impractical because of the extremely limited ________ and because of a frequent disbalance of the two sexes, among the ________ of each individual family.

selectivity

siblings

73 In virtually all societies, the structure of families is maintained by rather rigidly confining the approved sexual relations for mature adults within the ________-________ relationship.

husband-wife

74 The restrictive rules of family organization serve to provide a permanent and socially operable relationship between the parents and their ________, who are the primary structural elements in families.

children

household

75 Incest taboos prohibit mating or marriage between members of the same family. Since the family conventionally makes up a household, we may generalize that incest taboos apply to members of the same ________.

primary relatives

76 Incest taboos apply universally to primary relatives. One's father, mother, brother, sister, daughter, and son are ________ ________.

secondary relatives

77 Secondary relatives are those who are primary relatives to one's primary relatives. Therefore, the father, mother, brother, or sister of one's own father or mother are ________ ________.

taboo

78 Although societies vary, secondary relatives, such as uncles, aunts, nieces, nephews, grandparents, and grandchildren, are usually included under the incest ________.

affinal

79 Affinal relatives are the primary relatives of one's spouse. In general, incest taboos may also apply to ________ relatives, who are related by marriage.

exogamy

80 The term "endogamy" refers to the process of selecting a marriage partner *within* the limits of a specified group, which is generally regarded as similar in social status. The opposite, requiring marriage outside a defined group of kindred, is ________.

exogamous

81 Since sons and daughters are required to marry outside their own family, the family can be called an ________ social unit.

endogamous

82 One of the tests of social equality is that of the permissibility of marriage between two groups. Two such groups make up a larger ________ whole.

endogamy

83 Some religious groups require their members to marry only within the group. Some states permit marriages only between members of the same race. In India, caste and subcaste members must marry within their caste or subcaste. These are applications of the principle of ________.

social classes

84 Members of a social class observe the principle of endogamy when they insist that their children marry in the same social class. Marriages across class lines tend to obscure the distinctions between two ________ ________.

exogamy

85 The principles of exogamy and endogamy relate to isolation of social groups. Maintaining ______ ensures that the individual family will not become socially and biologically isolated from other families.

isolation

86 A caste, religious sect, or ethnic group also may seek to preserve its ______ from other groups by maintaining a rule of endogamy.

socialized

87 In all societies, children must be ______ so that they can be exchanged as members between social units.

endogamy

88 The principle of ______ applies to the marriage of two persons regarded as members of basically equal social classes.

family

89 The typical basic unit for economic production and consumption in most societies is the ______.

structure

90 From the foregoing, it may be hypothesized that changes in the structure of the system of production may bring about changes in the ______ of the family.

fixed

91 An agrarian economy with fixed holdings of land for each family will tend to produce a ______ pattern of lineal descendants to own and control the property.

father

92 The lineage or line of descent in the fixed agrarian economy may be paternal or maternal. If power and control are transmitted through a paternal lineage, it is necessary to know certainly who one's ______ is.

monandrous

93 Reckoning descent on the paternal lineage normally imposes a strict requirement of monandry (having only one husband) on each mother. In order that her children can be ascribed to one specific father, the mother is restricted to a ______ marriage.

generation

94 In the fixed agrarian pattern the younger generations remain dependent upon, and under the control of, the older ______.

independent

95 Under the factory system of production, as soon as a son has a regular job at cash wages, he becomes largely ______ of his father.

independent

96 Under the factory system, with a variety of jobs and cash wages, each new generation tends to detach itself from the older generation and to establish an ______ family.

nuclear

97 A family consisting of a man, his wife, and their minor children is a nuclear family. Since it is unencumbered with other relatives, the ______ family is relatively mobile.

nuclear family

98 The modern nuclear family is usually interested in augmenting both its income and its standard of living. Since it is mobile, versatile, and committed to the idea of progress, the ______ ______ is efficient for an industrial society.

production

99 Family structure and functioning is strongly influenced by the prevailing patterns of economic ______ in a society.

In summary, then, families exist only in societies and in conjunction with other families. A social order provides a system of rules regulating the relations of individuals within families and between families. The taboo of incest prohibits marital or sexual unions within families and forces maturing young people to find mates outside their immediate families. The rule of endogamy places outer limits on the field of eligible mates and requires the young to marry within a socially defined stratum. The individuals born into a social order must be socialized to uniform patterns of behavior and expectations, so that they can enter other families and other social units and interact with other individuals effectively.

Principles of Family Organization

generations

100 A family is an institution for generating new social beings and consists of a long-continued relationship between parental and filial ______.

The family arises from the generative union of male and female and from the long-enduring relationship of these parents with their new offspring. Since one's lineage can be reckoned on either paternal (father) or maternal (mother) lineage, the resultant patterns of organization are called patrilineal or matrilineal.

patrilineal
matrilineal

101 The Hebrews of Biblical times reckoned descent through a line of fathers. The Hopi Indians of the Southwestern United States reckon lineage through a line of mothers. The Hebrews are ______, while the Hopi are ______.

lineage (family)

102 In the matrilineal or patrilineal system, if the descendant can recall four direct-line progenitors, he can keep track of his ______ for four generations.

bilateral

103 Some societies reckon bilateral lineage, recognizing both male and female progenitors. In four generations, a descendant has two parents, four grandparents, eight great grandparents, and sixteen great great grandparents, totaling thirty names. Obviously, it is far more difficult to distinguish ______ lineage.

thirty

104 Each person's bilateral lineage doubles with each generation, exceeding 1,000 lineal ancestors in ten generations, 1 million in twenty generations, and 1 billion in thirty generations, a period of six to seven hundred years. However, one's direct paternal lineage would include only thirty forefathers in ______ generations.

consanguine

105 Those having the same ancestors have a common biological heritage or a congenital relationship by virtue of their birth. The conventional term for this relation is based on the notion of inherited "blood" (Latin *sanguis*), or consanguine relation. "Blood relatives" are ______ relatives.

congenetic

106 Biological science shows that the gene patterns in cell nuclei are centrally significant to our genetic pattern of inheritance. Although characteristics of blood are inherited, they are of little significance to the total genetic pattern. Therefore, it would be more appropriate to speak of ______ relatives.

congenetic
spouses

107 The congenetic family is described by Linton (1936, p. 139) as a "nucleus of blood relatives surrounded by a fringe of spouses." The ______ relationship is primary, and the ______ occupy a secondary rank.

The Protogenerational Family

108 *Proto* is a Greek prefix used to indicate "first" or "preceding." If we combine this prefix with "generational," we describe a family system which stresses preceding and elder generations, as ________.

protogenerational

109 Families organized primarily on the protogenerational basis stress kinship relations or having common ________.

ancestors

110 The protogenerational family consists of three or more generations of congenetic relatives and their spouses. Primary recognition goes to the oldest living progenitor. The family is extended and tends to incorporate collateral lines deriving from the offspring of the same sex as the oldest living ________.

progenitor

111 In protogenerational families, the congenetic relationship is stronger than are the conjugal relationships by which the spouses are attached. Therefore, the security and attachment of the children lies through their congenetic relationship to the oldest ________.

progenitor

112 The protogenerational family maintains a lifelong interdependency among congenetic relatives. Maximizing numerical size and temporal duration results in an extended ________.

family

113 The basic tie in protogenerational families is the ________ relation.

congenetic

114 The oldest progenitor of the extended family usually retains control of the family's power and physical resources. Younger members find themselves more or less completely under his ________.

control (authority)

115 Since the values and traditions of the oldest progenitor are carefully conserved in the protogenerational family, this family system tends to be highly ________.

conservative (traditional)

116 All societies experience some pressure for change, but the highly traditional protogenerational family is a stabilizing factor in the larger society because it tends to resist innovation or social ________.

change

The Neogenerational Family

neogenerational

117 Neo is a Greek prefix meaning "new" or "recent." If the family organization primarily stresses the new generation, we may term such an organizational type as ________.

children

118 By definition, the neogenerational family is oriented not to precedent, but to present and new generations. It is centered on the conjugal relationship of a parental pair and their ________.

neogenerational

119 The family which centers its interests on the needs of the children can be called a ________ family.

neogenerational

120 In contrast to the large extended protogenerational family, the ________ family includes only a father, a mother, and their minor children.

minority

121 The neogenerational family maintains its primary function of rearing children only until the children have passed through their ________ period.

secondary

122 The neogenerational family tends to be child-centered and child-oriented. The interests of the children are primary and the interests of the parents tend to become ________.

future

123 The neogenerational family orients to the present, is less influenced by traditional values, and looks forward to achievements in the ________.

parents

124 The neogenerational family tends to be socially and emotionally disjoined from the grandparental generation. The children, on reaching maturity, likewise tend to disjoin from their ________.

children / parents

125 The parents of the neogenerational family have typically severed close relations with their own parents. As their children mature and enter the period of dissociation, there is a period of readjustment which may be difficult for both the ________ and the ________.

dissociation

126 The modern neogenerational family is oriented against tradition and against the preceding generations. It creates a distinct requirement for ________ and independence for its maturing children.

matrilineal

127 The lineages of protogenerational families in their most extended duration were patrilineal or ______. By contrast, the neogenerational family pays little heed to grandparents and may well be described as alineal (without lineage).

alineal

128 A society which ignores both paternal and maternal lineage has an ______ family system.

Protogenerational and Neogenerational Families Compared

accumulate

129 The protogenerational family accumulates members both through the addition of generations and through the retention of collateral lines. Paralleling its accumulation of persons, it tends to ______ lands, animals, natural resources, money, or other forms of economic wealth.

expand (extend)

130 Thus, we can say that the general trend of the protogenerational family, regarding size, is to ______.

economic

131 The head of the protogenerational family retains position and power in the family by virtue of the control he retains over the ______ resources of the family. Such a family tends to be stable in terms of the fixation of its resources.

economic power

132 The protogenerational family relies on an accumulation of economic resources. The economic power of the matriarch or patriarch is great because he controls these resources. By contrast, the young adult has very little ______ ______.

consumption

133 The neogenerational family retains a minimum of members and a minimum of economic resources. Production of income is intended for relatively immediate ______.

restrict (control)

134 The main trend in the neogenerational and nuclear family is to ______ its size.

marriage / childbirth

135 The protogenerational family tends to find satisfaction in increase of membership and in increase of resources. It rejoices in marriage and childbirth. Typically, it encourages early ______ and uncontrolled ______.

protogenerational (extended)

136 A fixed agrarian system of landholding is best suited to the ______ family type.

children

137 In the agrarian situation, the protogenerational family found children an economic asset. In some societies, as in the Russian *mir* system, allocation of land was based on the number of mouths to be fed. Such a family could profit from having many ______.

two

138 The neogenerational family manifests a tendency toward diminution. Its minimum size is ______ persons.

five

139 Typically in the United States, the average wife produces fewer than three children (Vital Statistics of the United States, 1962). Most of these neogenerational families will not exceed ______ members while all minor children are still at home.

decrease

140 Since the modern neogenerational family depends on a relatively fixed current income, the per capita consumption of members in the family will ______ rapidly as the number of children increases.

$2,000

$1,000

141 If three people live on a $6,000 income, the per capita income, or income per person, is ______. If there are six persons, the amount available for each person is ______.

doubling

142 A neogenerational family can easily cut its standard of living in half by ______ the size of the family.

original (minimal)

143 After the children complete their socialization and find employment, the neogenerational family tends to revert to its ______ size.

neogenerational (nuclear)

144 In an industrial society, considerable advantages in mobility and flexibility may be claimed for the ______ family.

The two alternatives for family orientation are the protogenerational family and the neogenerational family. With the protogenerational family type, authority, influence, values, and identity remain with the preceding or elder generation. Children, lands, and goods remain under the control of the surviving progenitor. The family maximizes in size, reveres tradition, and stresses its hereditary identity. It is relatively inflexible and immobile, and thus provides long-term stability.

The neogenerational family places emphasis on the new generation and withholds recognition and authority from the older generation. The grandparental generation retains little if any power or control over the adult children or the grandchildren. The neogenerational family separates itself physically from the grandparental domicile, in a new and independent household. It tends to a minimal size, restricts the number of children, and is highly mobile. The neogenerational family is less stable, but is more adaptable to new opportunities and to the changing demands of a complex industrial society.

Patterns of Marriage

The premarital period provides for some process of selection and adjustment to the prospective husband and wife to match male with female in an enduring marital union. Premarital relations between sexes are virtually uncontrolled in some preliterate societies and rigidly controlled in others.

145 Whatever their attitudes and practices regarding premarital relations, all societies are relatively strict in their control of ________ relations.

marital

146 The people of the Trobriand Islands place no restrictions on sex relations among children and adolescents prior to marriage, though they forbid as "indecent" any manifestation of affection in public. They strictly enforce incest taboos and rigidly prohibit adultery after ________.

marriage

147 The Hopi Indian girl receives all-night visits from a number of suitors. When she becomes pregnant, she selects her favorite suitor as a ________.

husband

148 The monogamous union is relatively stable thereafter, though the Hopi husband lives as a guest in the house of his wife's mother. From this it is apparent that the Hopi are ________.

matrilineal

149 Many societies place great value on the chastity of women and the virginity of brides. In patrilineal agrarian societies one's social status, economic status, and family identity derive from an assured paternity by the legitimate husband of one's ________.

mother

150 Chaperonage may be used to safeguard the chastity of virgins. In Latin countries of South America, when a suitor calls on an upper-class girl, an elderly female relative remains in the room as a ________.

chaperone

virgin
chaste

151 The patrilineal Veddah of Ceylon, the Semang people of the Malay Peninsula, and the Buganda of East Africa insist that brides be ______ and that wives be ______.

marriage

152 Another technique employed to safeguard women's chastity until marriage was the precontract, as used by the Hindus. Girls were contracted in ______ as infants, and even before birth.

contract

153 Having contracted a daughter to a specific marriage, the parental family maintained the ______ by assuring the chastity of the girl.

husband / wife

154 In the United States, both the religiocultural traditions and the laws of the several states rigidly assert a doctrine of suppression of sexual behavior except between ______ and ______.

marry

155 In our agrarian past, a young man called on a young lady only with "honorable" intentions. If he called more than once, his behavior was termed courtship, and was taken as an earnest of his serious intent to ______ the girl if her father would consent.

premarital

156 However, even in colonial times, there were serious violations of moral standards. At the Puritan Church of Groton from 1761 to 1775, of 200 persons confessing at baptism, 66 confessed the sin of fornication (Calhoun, 1944, p. 133). Fornication defines ______ sex relations.

sex

157 In the United States today the average boy and girl start having intermittent dates at about age fourteen and marry at age twenty for girls and age twenty-three for boys (Kephart, 1961). Throughout this long period of dating, they have ample opportunity to improve their adjustment to individuals of the other ______.

marry

158 Dating of young people is aimed at having a good time and getting to know each other. It has no implication of intent to ______.

only (solely, exclusively)

159 Going steady is a preemptive form of dating which incorporates a mutual agreement to date ______ with the other person, and to be available when either desires to date.

engagement

160 The third and final period before marriage includes an explicit declaration of intent to marry, freely entered upon by both parties. This is the ______ period.

control

161 A long premarital dating pattern gives the girl the possibility of learning to generate and control the boy's responses. She may also learn to generate her own "echo responses" without herself losing ________.

74

162 In the free, voluntary self-selective dating pattern, 92 percent of the women marry and about 80 percent of these marriages are permanent (Kephart, 1961). Thus, for (92 percent × 80 percent) of women, or ________ percent, the dating pattern leads to a permanent marriage.

child

163 One of the purposes of marriage is to ensure that a specific man is identified as the father of each ________. This is known as the legitimacy principle.

legitimacy

164 The child is assured of an accepted place in the society through the ________ principle, which specifies his father officially.

legitimacy principle

165 The child is afforded an identity, a name, and a recognized status through the ________ ________.

social

166 The socially recognized father is usually the biological father, but for social status, the ________ relationship is more important than the actual biological relationship.

elder brother

167 The ancient Hebrews, according to the Levirate ("law of Levi"), required that a younger brother marry the widow of his elder brother and rear any children he had by her as the heirs of his ________ ________, and not as his own children.

children

168 Some societies accept pregnancy as a precondition of marriage. The Hopi Indians and the Andaman Islanders do not consider a marriage complete until a child is born. In all societies, the expectation of and provision for ________ is an integral part of marriage.

identity (recognition)

169 In all societies marriage provides a basis of social ________ for the child.

father

170 Among the matrilineal Nayar of India the husband stays with the bride only three days, and then leaves her permanently. She accepts various lovers, but her husband is the acknowledged ________ of her children, and her brothers fulfill the fatherly duties for her sons.

Monogamy and Polygamy

171 Two Greek prefixes *mono* for "one" and *poly* for "many" are combined with three Greek suffixes *gamos* for "mate," *andros* for "husband," and *gyne* (pronounced guy-nay) for "wife" to form the descriptive terms for the various forms of _______.

marriage

172 Monogamy is defined as the marriage relation in which each spouse has only _______ mate.

one

173 Polygamy is defined as a marriage relation in which one spouse has _______ mates.

many

174 Polyandry specifies a marriage relation in which one wife has many _______.

husbands

175 Polygyny indicates a marriage relation in which one _______ has many _______.

husband / wives

176 Monogamy is the most universal pattern of marriage and is accepted in many societies which give preference to other forms of marriage. Monogamy means single _______. It is the most practicable marriage form in societies where the sexes are about equal in number.

mate

177 Monogamy is the preferred form of marriage where there is relative equality of right and status. Where there are gross inequalities, such as slavery, or where there is a gross difference between the status of men and women, some form of _______ is likely.

polygamy

178 In group marriage, two or more men are married to two or more women. We can combine the terms "polygyny" and "polyandry" to indicate a _______ marriage.

polygynandrous

179 Wives are often an economic asset, as among the Baganda of Africa. The Baganda wives labor in gardens and increase the husband's wealth. The Baganda combine labor and productivity with a _______ marriage system.

polygynous

180 Among the Todas of southern India, a woman is married to a group of brothers, and becomes the wife of any younger brother as he matures enough to be a husband. When a woman has several husbands, this form of marriage is called _______.

polyandry

181 The traditional practice of female infanticide among the Toda made polyandry necessary, owing to the resulting shortage of adult _______.

females

polygynous

182 Some societies have several forms of marriage simultaneously. Most Arabs are monogamous, but the wealthy have up to four wives and thus are ______. The Tibetan nobility are polygynous, while the peasants are polyandrous.

polygynandrous

183 The Kaingang Indians of Brazil allow a surprising variety of marriage patterns. Of their people, 60 percent are monogamously married; 18 percent are polygynous; 14 percent are polyandrous; and 8 percent are involved in group or ______ marriage.

polygyny
polyandry

184 Polygamous forms of marriage include both ______ and ______.

extended

185 The monogamous marriage occurs in both patrilineal and matrilineal families, and assumes three forms. The largest of these is the extended family, another is the stem family, and the last is the nuclear family. Of these, the largest in size is the ______ family.

generation

186 The extended family involves more than two generations, the eldest usually being the grandparental ______. The extended family often includes a number of married sons and daughters and their children.

extended

187 The polygynous marriage system, being made up of the patriarch, his wives, his sons and their wives, and his grandchildren, such as that of the ancient Hebrews, permits the ______ family.

extended

stem

188 The stem family is a reduction of the ______ family, and is made up of a father and mother, one of their sons and his wife, and their grandchildren. In rural Ireland, only one son usually can remain at home without splitting the small landholding. Other sons and daughters of the ______ family must migrate.

two

189 The stem family is not much larger than the nuclear family, having only ______ more persons than the nuclear family which it includes.

extended

190 The stem family is a restricted form of the ______ family.

nuclear

191 A family consisting solely of a man, his wife, and their minor children is a ______ family.

maturity

192 The nuclear family is the smallest in size and is held to its minimum size in the United States through birth control and through the separation of children when they reach social ______.

The most universal marriage relationship is that of monogamy, which in the great majority of cases consists of a lifelong marital relation between each marital pair. In societies where there is a marked unbalance in the numbers of the two sexes, some form of polygamy may be expected. Extensive female infanticide may produce a drastic shortage of females and result in a polyandrous marriage pattern, in which each wife has several husbands. Male infanticide, military and religious service, and poverty may create a reduced proportion of available husbands and result in a system of polygyny.

Any of the patterns of marriage may be associated with a nuclear family system, an extended family system, or a stem family system. The nuclear family maintains minimal size, and consists only of a husband, a wife, and their minor children. The nuclear family reduces to a two-person unit when the last child reaches maturity and establishes a detached family of his own. The extended family preserves the close family relationship of three or more generations, including collateral lines, and maximizes its size. The stem family is a reduced version of the extended family which maintains the close family relationship between the grandparents and only one of their children and his spouse.

The Fractional Family

blood / marriage / adoption

193 The U.S. Bureau of the Census (1959) defines the fractional family as a group of two or more persons, related by ______, ______, or ______, residing in the same household, which lacks either the father, the mother, or minor children of the nuclear family.

fractional

194 About 10 percent of all married women are unable to bear children, owing to the infertility of either the husband or the wife, or the couple's unwillingness to have children. Such married couples would constitute a ______ family.

195 In recent years in the United States, the average wife marries at age twenty, bears her first child at twenty-one, her last child by age twenty-seven, and the last child leaves home at age twenty (Duvall, 1962, pp. 14–19). The total period of minority children at home in this "average" family totals ______ years.

twenty-six

196 The average husband marries at age twenty-three and dies at age sixty-nine. His total span of married life, if he is among the 80 percent that does not divorce, will be ______ years.

forty-six

197 Therefore, the average husband and wife live together after their minor children have matured and left home for approximately ______ years.

twenty

198 Minor children are sometimes cared for by maternal or paternal grandparents, thus constituting an alternate-generation family. In this case the ______ generation has been removed.

parental

199 A family arising from the continued association or reassociation of adults living together in the same household and related through an earlier nuclear family would also constitute a ______ family.

fractional

200 Elderly parents, often in an impecunious condition or having modest pensions, live in a subordinate position in the home of one of their children. They invert the old relationship of seniority and control and accept ______ by their child.

control

Divorce and Separation

201 Divorce may be defined as a socially recognized and permanent ______ of a marriage.

end (dissolution, etc.)

202 Separation may be defined as the absence of either spouse from the common domicile, with no presumption of ______.

reunion

203 In 1957 there were about 25 divorces for each 100 marriages. Of the 25 divorces, 5 were among persons previously divorced. But most divorced persons remarry. Therefore, the proportion of divorces represents in part persons in a transitional state between ______ (Kephart, 1961).

marriages

Table 14. Years' Mean Duration of Marriage

No. of marriages for:				
Husband	*Wife*			
	1	*2*	*3*	*4*
1	6.3	3.9	3.0	2.1
2	4.6	3.2	2.4	2.2
3	3.7	2.8	1.8	1.6
4		2.5	2.1	1.2

SOURCE: F. P. Monohan, "The Duration of Marriage to Divorce," *Journal of Marriage and Family Living,* 21:137, 1959. Used by permission.

falls

204 Monohan's data in Table 14 show that duration of marriage steadily (rises/falls) with successive marriages.

women / men

205 It is also clear that the duration of marriage declines faster for ______ than it does for ______ in successive marriages.

206 If you doubt this, compare any column (varying man's marriage) with the same numbered row (varying woman's marriage). The figures going down the column are consistently ______ than the figures going across the row.

greater

207 From this generalization we would predict that the average marital union of a man in his fourth marriage with a woman in her third marriage will continue for ______ months longer than that of a man in his third marriage to a woman in her fourth marriage.

five

Table 15. Marital Status for Age 14 and Over

	Men	*Women*
Single	25%	19%
Spouse present	66	62
Spouse absent	4	4
Widowed	3	12
Divorced	2	3
	100%	100%

SOURCE: U.S. Bureau of the Census, *Census of Population: 1960.* PC. (2) 4B, 1964, p. 7.

widowed

208 The greatest difference between men and women is in the ______ category (see Table 15).

women

209 The proportion of ever-married population separated from the spouse for all causes, including death, is higher among ______.

3

210 Although there are about twenty-five divorces for each hundred marriages, only about ______ percent of all people are divorced at any one time. It is apparent that most divorced persons do not stay divorced.

9

211 Of the men who have married, the proportion separated from their spouses through divorce, death, desertion, or other causes is about ______ percent.

19

212 Of the total female population, the proportion separated by divorce, death or desertion, or other causes is about ______ percent.

Table 16. Selected Age Categories of Women Who Will Marry or Remarry

	Divorced	*Widowed*	*Single*
Age 20	93%		89%
Age 30	94	60%	48
Age 45	50	18	9

SOURCE: Arnold W. Green, *Sociology,* 4th ed., McGraw-Hill Book Company, New York, 1964, p. 436. Used by permission.

poorer

213 From Table 16 it is clear that a single girl has a (better/poorer) chance to marry than a divorcee the same age has to remarry.

twice as good

214 The thirty-year-old divorcee has about (twice as good/the same/half as good) a chance to remarry as a thirty-year-old single girl.

less likely

215 The thirty-year-old widow is (more likely/as likely/less likely) to remarry than the thirty-year-old divorcee.

divorces

216 Of eighteen states reporting in 1960, 40 percent of all divorces involved no children (see Table 17). The remaining 60 percent of the ______ involved an average of two children each (Statistical Abstract of the United States: 1964, Table 77, p. 67).

Table 17. Divorces and Annulments by Number of Children

Number of children	*Percent of divorces and annulments*
0	39.8
1	23.3
2	18.9
3	10.2
4	4.5
5+	3.3

SOURCE: Vital Statistics of the United States, Washington, D.C., 1962, vol. III, table 2–7.

divorce / annulment

217 As the number of children increases, the probability of ________ and ________ decreases.

no

218 The greatest probability of divorce exists for couples that have ________ children.

four-child

219 The magnitude of the effect of children appears in dividing, say, the 5 percent divorce ratio for four-child couples into the 40 percent ratio for childless couples. Divorce is eight times more prevalent among childless couples than among ________ couples.

Table 18. Divorces and Annulments by Duration of Marriage

Years' duration of marriage		*Percentage distribution* 1953	1962
<1		6.8	5.1
1		10.0	8.6
2		9.7	8.3
3		8.0	7.6
4		7.1	6.6
5		6.9	7.0
6		6.6	5.1
7		6.0	4.9
8		3.9	4.4
9		3.0	3.9
10–19	Annual average =	2.0	2.5
20–39	Annual average =	.5	.6

SOURCE: Vital Statistics of the United States, Washington, D.C., 1962, vol. III, table 2–5.

less

220 Table 18 suggests that the longer the marriage endures, the (more/less) chance of divorce.

first

221 Apparently, the ________ year is the most critical for marriage.

reduction (decrease)

222 Comparing the 1953 and 1962 percentages of divorces through the first three years shows that there was a ________ in the proportion of divorces in 1962.

increase

223 Comparing the percentage distribution of divorces for the eighth through the thirty-ninth years of marriage shows that there was a consistent ________ in the proportion of divorces in 1962.

later

224 These figures indicate that divorcing couples tended to terminate their marriage somewhat ________ in 1962.

SUMMARY

Although the family varies in the details of its organization, it is based on a relatively permanent relationship between a cohabiting pair of mature adults and their minor children. If the ties of power, authority, locus, and dependency are maintained after the children mature and marry, we have a protogenerational family which tends to expand in numbers and to revere tradition. If the parental ties are broken more or less abruptly and completely when the children mature and marry, we have a neogenerational pattern of family organization which closely limits the period of intimate contact to the minority of the child. This period terminates when the child completes his training for adult participation in the society. The protogenerational family tends to be stable, rigid, traditional, and authoritarian. In contrast, the modern neogenerational family is more unstable and manifests highly discrete stages of child rearing and postchild companionship. The neogenerational family tends to be flexible, child-centered, and democratic. The highly mobile neogenerational family is better adapted to a rapidly developing industrial society. The protogenerational family is better adapted to a fixed agrarian pattern of society.

In a biological sense, most families center primarily on the female. It is the female's cycle of ovulation, gestation, and lactation which triggers the succession of events in reproduction. Man has converted the mating and child-rearing functions into the permanent social institution of marriage but here, too, the female has a natural advan-

tage because partial or full sexual gratification is more rewarding to the male than to the female (Kinsey et al., 1948, 1953). If the female can maintain a monopoly over her mate's sexual behavior, she can maximize her influence over him. Women thus attain maximum power and influence over males in a system of completely monogamous marriage, under conditions of high sexual morality.

The family structure must be integrated socially and biologically into the larger society. The relationship between the family and the society is regulated by an elaborate set of rules. These rules define functions and obligations for the basic family positions and for the relation of members of families to other institutions which make up the organizational pattern of the society. The incest rule requires that maturing children must mate with those emerging from other families than their own and that the reproduction function be confined exclusively to husband and wife. The complementary rule of endogamy, ensuring that the maturing young person must marry within his recognized society, is of declining importance in the modern era, owing to the universalization of industrial society. Modern society no longer opposes international marriages, say, of a Frenchman to an Italian, and religious groups are only moderately successful at maintaining endogamy among their membership.

The universal and predominating pattern of mating in human societies is monogamous marriage. The alternative form, polygamy, is found occasionally among primitive societies and among nomadic and agrarian societies. Here it tends to be confined to the wealthier and more powerful members. Nearly all cases involve one relatively powerful husband with a plurality of wives. Only three societies manifest polyandry, where one female is the wife of a plurality of husbands. In fraternal polyandry, the husbands are a group of brothers. In primitive societies polygamy is often associated with infanticide of females in the case of polyandry, and infanticide of males in the case of polygyny.

Fractional families result when some portion of the nuclear family pattern is not present, or is substituted, owing to death, divorce, or separation of parents, or to the absence of children because of the sterility of parents or the death or maturation of children. Fractional families are smaller, more limited in function, and typically somewhat impaired in social status vis-à-vis conventional families. Since the children of broken families tend to remain with the mother, an aunt, or a grandmother, women predominate among adult heads of fractional families. It is evident that the structure of the family varies considerably among societies. The basis of family organization may be altered to conform to permanent disbalance between the sexes, to disbalance in wealth and authority, and to the influence of religious, economic, and political factors.

Finally, the typical nuclear family alters its structure as it passes through the reproductive, nurturant, and post-child phases of the family cycle. This succession of structural phases in the family cycle has implications for housing, health, education, welfare, income, patterns of consumption, religion, and recreation. At the same time, members of families have the problem of altering their behavior, life patterns, and systems of resource allocation to conform to changing requirements of the family cycle.

SELF-REVIEW QUIZ

1 The pattern of organization of a family indicates its basic ________.

2 Family structure begins with the presumably permanent ________ ________ of a man and a woman, for bearing and rearing children.

3 The individual typically becomes a member of society in the first instance by becoming a structural part of the ________ into which he is born.

4 The family into which an individual is born is his family of ________.

5 The family which an individual generates as a parent is his family of ________.

6 The family brings the child to adulthood through a ________ process.

7 The modern family maintains its basic structure as a child-rearing unit for about ________ years.

8 The wife, as a source of affectional gratification for husband and children, constitutes the ________ figure with regard to social and expressive relationships within the family.

9 The family is a basic ________ within the larger social system.

10 Since families must be able to exchange members with other families in establishing new conjugal units, family ________ must be relatively uniform within endogamous strata of the society.

11 All societies in modern times apply ________ ________ in forbidding marriage or sex relations between congenetic relatives in the nuclear family.

12 Affinal relatives are primary relatives to one's ________.

13 Extreme stability, traditionalism, and a retention of power and authority in the oldest progenitor mark the ________ type of family.

14 The family type best adapted to periods of rapid social change is the ________ family.

15 The most universal pattern of marriage relation is ________.

16 The stem family is a modification of the ________ family.

17 Fractional families are generally defined as those which have lost some element of the ________ family.

REFERENCES

Bogue, Donald: *Population of the United States,* The Free Press of Glencoe, New York, 1959.

Calhoun, A. W.: *Social History of the American Family,* Barnes & Noble, Inc., New York, 1944.

Chinoy, Ely: *Society,* Random House, Inc., New York, 1961.

Christiansen, Harold T.: "Studies in Child Spacing: I. Premarital Pregnancy as Measured by the Spacing of the First Birth from Marriage," *American Sociological Review* 18: 55, 1953.

Duvall, Evelyn M.: *Family Development,* J. B. Lippincott Company, Philadelphia, 1962.

Ehrmann, Winston: *Premarital Dating Behavior,* Holt, Rinehart and Winston, Inc., New York, 1959.

Green, Arnold W.: *Sociology,* 4th ed., McGraw-Hill Book Company, 1964.

Kephart, William C.: *Family, Society and the Individual,* Houghton Mifflin Company, Boston, 1961.

Kinsey, A. C., et al.: *Sexual Behavior in the American Male,* W. B. Saunders Company, Philadelphia, 1948.

Kinsey, A. C., et al.: *Sexual Behavior of the American Female,* W. B. Saunders Company, Philadelphia, 1953.

Landis, Paul H.: "Sequential Marriage," *Journal of Home Economics,* 42:625–628, 1950.

Linton, Ralph: *The Study of Man,* Appleton-Century-Crofts, Inc., New York, 1936.

MacIver, Robert: *Society: A Textbook of Sociology,* Holt, Rinehart and Winston, Inc., New York, 1937.

Malinowski, Bronislaw: "Parenthood: The Basis of Social Structure," in Calverton and Schmalhausen (eds.), *The New Generation,* Macauley Company, New York, 1930.

Malpass, Leslie F. (ed.): *Human Behavior,* McGraw-Hill Book Company, New York, 1965.

Monohan, Francis P.: "The Duration of Marriage to Divorce," *Journal of Marriage and Family Living,* 21:137, 1959.

Murdock, George P.: *Social Structure,* The Macmillan Company, New York, 1949.

Queen, S. A., Habenstein, R. W., and Adams, John B.: *The Family in Various Cultures,* J. B. Lippincott Company, Philadelphia, 1961.

Thibaut, J. W., and Kelley, H. H.: *The Social Psychology of Groups,* John Wiley & Sons, Inc., New York, 1959.

U.S. Bureau of the Census, *Current Population Reports,* ser. P–20, no. 81, March, 1958, table 1.

U.S. Bureau of the Census, *Current Population Reports,* ser. 20, no. 96, March, 1959.

U.S. Bureau of the Census, *Census of Population: 1960, United States Summary.*

U.S. Bureau of the Census, *Cen-*

sus of Population: 1960, PC (2) 4B, *Persons by Family Characteristics,* 1964.

U.S. Bureau of the Census, *Statistical Abstract of the United States,* 1964.

Vital Statistics of the United States, 1953, vol. 1, and 1962, vol. III.

Westoff, C. F., et al.: "Fertility through Twenty Years of Marriage," *American Sociological Review,* 23:549–556, 1958.

family functions

DONALD E. ALLEN

2

A description of function requires a discussion of the family's primary operating goals and the main features of the mechanics for achieving these goals. The functional interpretation views the family as a dynamic enterprise and incorporates the notion of growth, change, and adaptation. It involves the changing relations among the structural elements within the family. Central to the concept of function is the idea that the family is a subsystem of the larger society and that the family operates through the instrumentality of a culture.

The objectives of the family cannot be viewed as relevant chiefly to the criteria of satisfaction or gratification of the individual member. Families sustained primarily by personal satisfaction are feeble in the extreme and tend to fail in their larger purpose with regard to the society which they help to constitute. They also tend to fall short of their supposed purpose of individual gratification, since the satisfaction of the individual is often transient and sometimes illusory.

That the family functions in part to integrate persons into the parent society helps to explain the limiting effects which society imposes on it. Quite apart from the personal satisfaction or desires of individuals, every culture incorporates various compulsory pressures on all members of the family to maintain a series of more or less onerous duties between spouses, parents and children, and kinsmen. Although most societies make provision for severing marital relations, the divorce process is almost universally viewed as dysfunctional to the society.

Finally, in its functioning the family provides both the short-term and the long-term inputs from the parent society. These two classes of exchange factors make up a reciprocal and mutually reinforcing pattern which serves to maintain and strengthen the whole social system. A description of the family as the elemental social unit will help to explain why the individual is constrained to accept a relatively rigid and relatively elaborate social discipline the better to meet his unique personal and private needs.

Elements of Family Function

1 In scientific usage, the term "function" indicates a relationship between two events. The analysis of function helps to define or to clarify a relationship. In mathematical usage, for example, if the term *X* varies in a consistent way regarding variation in *Y*, then *X* is a ________ of *Y*.

function

2 The mathematical use of function can be applied to the relationship between early marriage and the birthrate. If the birthrate is high in societies which encourage early marriage, then a high birthrate is a function of ________ ________.

early marriage

3 Function can be used in a less precise application. For example, we may demonstrate that more married couples indicate satisfaction with marriage where there is a good adjustment of the personalities of the two spouses. Personality adjustment appears to be a ________ of satisfaction in marriage.

function

4 The concept of function also applies to a means or method of operation between parts or elements in a larger organism or organization. If the wife conventionally prepares meals for other members of the family, we may generalize by saying that the wife usually has the ________ of cooking.

function

5 A function may also be viewed as relating an activity to a goal. One studies French 101 to ________ ________.

learn French (get an A? enter French 102?)

6 A goal is a condition which is to be achieved at some future time. If a family seeks to rear children to maturity, to bring them to a particular level of formal education, or to acquire ownership of a home by paying off a mortgage, these are future ________.

goals

7 A goal may also be in the process of being achieved, or it may refer to a desirable state or condition which is a normal function of the family. A goal of maintaining the health and providing food for a family applies not to some future state, but to a ________ condition.

present

8 A family is a group of related persons interacting with one another. To organize their behavior, different members play roles appropriate to their position in the ______.

family

9 Consequently, the basic behavioral pattern for performing the functions appropriate to a specific position in the family is called ______ behavior (hereafter, role).

role

10 Cottrell (1942) defines a role as an internally consistent series of conditioned responses by one member of a social situation representing a stimulus pattern for a consistent series of responses of the other. Cottrell's definition requires at least ______ persons for role play.

two

11 Sarbin (1954) says that a role is a pattern of learned actions performed in an interaction situation. He does not imply that the behavior in role play is confined to conditioned responses, but he does stress that the behavior has been ______.

learned

12 The term "function" provides a conceptual tool for describing what a family does, what it aims to achieve, and how it operates. The term "role" is similar, but identifies some region of behavior in a social context. "Role," like "function," is a ______ ______.

conceptual tool

13 Parsons (1951, p. 38) calls the role a sector of an actor's[1] system to meet expectations. It is based on a set of values and is played with the actor in a complementary role. Parsons emphasizes that any role an actor plays is only one role out of a number of ______ available to him.

roles

14 The different roles which an actor could play are called his repertoire. To interact with another actor, the actor must select a role from his ______.

repertoire

15 We have noted in the foregoing definitions that an actor can learn a pattern of behavior for various interaction situations and that he has a choice from a ______ of roles. These two facts imply that the persons in a family can ______ new roles and can adapt behavior to new situations.

repertoire

learn

[1] An actor is defined as a person performing a recognized role in a social situation.

16 This suggests that the family is an active dynamic group which can evolve new behavior patterns or new _______ over a period of time.

roles

17 Roles are patterned systems of behavior designed to meet various social situations. It would appear that if a person learned a variety of roles, he would be able to function in a variety of _______ _______.

social situations

18 Role playing occurs usually in interaction with another person who is also playing a role. If the first person changes his orientation or his role, this will probably produce a change in the _______ or role of the other person.

orientation

19 Playing many roles and shifting readily from one role to another require poise and flexibility. A person who needs to interact with only a few well-known friends and kinsmen would probably lack _______ in his role play.

flexibility

20 If one's life situation requires interaction with a great variety of people, one requires the _______ of a large role repertoire.

flexibility

21 Families function simultaneously in several time frames. For example, biological functions, such as eating meals and sleeping, occur in a diurnal or daily _______ _______.

time frame

22 Periodic religious activities, attendance at school, and most regular employment operate in a _______ time frame.

weekly (seven-day)

23 Family activities involved in birthdays, anniversaries, holidays, and seasonal activities operate in an _______ time frame.

annual (yearly)

24 Some time frames are indefinite, such as military service in wartime or the duration of a chronic illness in the family. Some fill a major part of a lifetime. Death of one spouse ends the _______ time frame and the twenty-first birthday ends the period of legal _______.

marriage
minority

25 Many interaction patterns of the family are rhythmic. The direction of action reverses between actors, as in conversation, in play, and in disciplinary relations. Thus, the parent's question is matched by the child's _______.

response (answer)

cycle

26 The basic patterns of action in the family are cyclic. Any action which goes through a series of steps and continues to revert to a starting point is essentially circular and may be termed a ________ of action.

dynamic

27 The time frames afford a scale to permit counting and coordinating interaction. Cycles relate to the dynamics of family growth and change. An appropriate daily diet leads to growth of the young. Annual cycles of schooling lead to graduation. Time frames provide a static notation system, but cycles constitute a ________ process in the family.

continuous
cumulative

28 Some cycles are related only to continuing functions which do not vary materially. Other cycles relate to cumulative functions which modify steadily until a distinctly new condition is attained. Sleep represents a ________ function; education represents a ________ function.

cumulative

29 Functions that lead to nodal points which signal some major change in family functioning are ________.

retirement

30 The nodal points become the focus of special planning; once they are reached, some reorganization of elements and/or routines is required. For example, a father's working career eventually ends in ________.

family

31 Functions always involve a conceptual orientation and refer to some broader framework, such as the family or society, or to historical perspective. The function of preparing meals, for example, refers most immediately to the ________.

society

32 The function of formal schooling for children is of concern to the family, but formal education is undertaken as a function of ________.

dysfunction

33 Merton (1957) defines "dysfunction" as observed consequences which lessen the adaptation of adjustment of a system. Anything which impedes, retards, or prevents some essential process, goal, or relationship in a family would be an example of a ________.

dysfunction

34 Marriage is usually essential to the security of the family. Continued conflict between husband and wife or the withholding of support or affection by either is a ________ of marriage.

dysfunctional (injurious)

35 A married woman who maintains extramarital sexual relations is violating her marriage contract and is breaking the law. Such behavior is ________ to the marital relationship.

manifest

36 Functions are normally concepts or understandings of the relations, operations, and goals of a system. They may be manifest or latent. Those which are normally known and agreed upon are manifest to everyone. Thus functions which contribute to the adjustment or adaptation of a system and are intended and recognized by participants of the system are ________ functions (Merton, 1957).

latent function

37 Functions may be latent; i.e., they may operate in the system, but be neither intended nor recognized. The manifest function of the automobile is to provide transportation, but it has also provided opportunities for romance. The automobile has had the ________ ________ of abetting romance (Merton, 1957).

society (family, species, etc.)

38 One of the basic manifest functions of the family is to produce children. This has the broader latent function of assuring survival of the ________.

dysfunctional

39 If the death rate is suddenly lowered without a lowering of the birthrate, the population suddenly expands and overpopulation and pauperdom may ensue. In such a case, retaining the earlier high birthrate becomes ________ (check response 35).

value orientation

40 The functions of the family are deeply influenced by the world view, philosophy, or, as the sociologist Talcott Parsons might say, the value orientations of the society. The primitive warrior society, such as that of the Plains Indians, stressed courage, bravery, daring, endurance of pain. The ________ ________ of this society centered on efficiency in warfare.

father

41 The ancient Romans believed that the father gave life to his children and, as their creator, should have supreme power over them. This belief led to the *pater potestas,* which is Latin for the power of the ________. The Roman father could order his children killed at birth, or at any time after, if he chose.

Several kinds of functions can be identified in family operations. One characteristic, such as personality adjust-

ment, may vary consistently with a second characteristic, such as satisfaction in marriage; the second characteristic may be a function of the first. A second use of the functional concept relates to a working part of the family which determines the operation of other parts. The chief income earner has the function of providing for the family's material needs. Third, the concept of function may relate to attaining some future goal. The school cycle has the function of educating the child for later social needs. The explicit goal is graduation.

Family operations are carried out through role play. Within the family, members learn and carry out a number of social roles which together constitute a role repertoire. Individuals who must work and interact in many and varied social settings must develop a suitable role repertoire and must be flexible in playing the appropriate roles, as the social situation may demand. Finally, failure to perform suitable roles may impair the operation of the family. Such failure would be dysfunctional to the family.

Regeneration, Providing Domicile, Socialization, and Social Integration

The family is a basic social unit which develops and maintains personalities in a cultural medium. Its functions include (1) regeneration, (2) providing domicile, (3) socialization, (4) control and boundary functions, and (5) social integration.

family
society

42 The basic social unit is the ________. Its main function is to relate individual personalities to ________.

regenerative

43 Altogether the regenerative cycle includes copulation, gestation, infancy, childhood, and adolescence. The family must make provisions for all five of these stages in the ________ cycle.

regeneration

44 The regenerative function embraces the replacement of adult members of the society. The procreation of infants is only a first step in the process of ________.

childhood

45 The second, third, and fourth steps for regenerating adult members of society are gestation and bringing the newborn through the period of infancy and ________.

adolescence

46 The fifth step in regeneration is to bring a child through his period of ________, which generally covers the period from puberty to maturity.

marry

47 The end of the regenerative cycle for the individual is marked by his readiness to ________ and become a parent.

maturity

48 The conventional length of the regenerative cycle varies with the amount of training required to reach ________ in a given society.

fourteen, give or take a year

49 For example, in primitive societies (and in some agrarian societies) maturity is considered complete soon after puberty, or by about age ________.

socialization

50 The family is the primary socializing agent. The process of acquiring the values, attitudes, language, and techniques and skills needed in playing social roles is termed ________.

socialization

51 The child must incorporate the culture as habits of speech and thought and action. We say that he must internalize the culture. This process of acquiring mastery of a basic culture is included in the process of ________.

parents

52 Children in a family develop mastery of the culture by internalizing the behavior, ideas, values, speech, and thought patterns they observe in their parents and others. Enculturation usually begins in early infancy and is initiated by the ________.

function

53 Adolescents acquire much of their knowledge and skill in the culture from sources outside the family, but they manifest their new talents in the family, where they are appreciated, critiqued, and/or modified. Socialization continues in part as a family ________ during adolescence.

socialization

54 It seems clear that members of the family participate in a continuing process of ________.

control

55 The family usually asserts continuing control over its members. In complex cultures, family obligations and controls are sustained by official agencies of the state. The marriage contract is established under state authority and is enforced by the state. It operates as a ________ over both parties to the marriage.

control
parents

56 Young children are typically under the ________ of the ________, although the parental control tends to decrease as the child gets older.

57 As the parental control over the adolescent declines, the adolescent assumes increasing responsibility for his own ________.

behavior

58 The adolescent is expected to be responsible, to exercise due care over the safety and welfare of others, and to plan for his own future status as an ________.

adult

59 The boundaries demarcating the family in Western societies are probably the most clearly drawn of any in modern culture. Only spouses, their children, and congenetic relatives resident in the home are accepted as members of the ________.

family

60 As children grow up and leave home, the family contracts until it has reverted to its original regenerative dyad, the pair of ________.

spouses (parents)

61 The family boundary is demarcated by several categories of behavior differentials. A consistent and demonstrable difference in behavior which an individual directs to different persons indicates a ________ ________.

behavior differential

62 Family relations are demarcated from nonfamily relations by the amount and kind of services which family members provide one another. When outsiders receive personal services within the family, the outsider is usually in the special status of ________.

guest

63 A pattern of mutual obligation binds family members and distinguishes them from nonmembers. The child acknowledges a complex of mandatory relationships to parents, siblings, and others living as members of the family. Outsiders are excluded from this system of ________.

obligations

64 Families provide ascribed status to their members. Statuses which the individual receives automatically with no effort on his part, such as sex, citizenship, and childhood, are examples of ________ ________.

ascribed status

65 The family provides the motivation and necessity for the husband and wife to perform occupational functions appropriate to their position in the ________.

society

66 Western society expects the father to be successful in his ________ for the sake of his family.

occupation (career)

67 Through the socialization process, the family integrates persons into society. The induction, commitment, and incorporation of persons into social units constitutes the process of social ________.

integration

68 Induction requires only that the person be introduced into a social ________ in some clearly defined status, such as student, member, or worker.

institution

69 A ceremony, set of symbols, or prescribed regimen may be used to help the inductee to acknowledge, understand, and internalize his new ________.

status

70 Commitment of the person is the most crucial of the three steps. It requires that the person himself accept his newly defined status as a member of an institution and that he be willing to control his behavior and strive to conform to the requirements of the ________.

institution

71 Incorporation of a person into an institutional group is a process which follows induction and which depends in part upon ________.

commitment

72 When the person has become capable of meeting normal requirements of membership, is regarded by himself and others as a regular member, and is depended upon to discharge social roles as a member, we may say that he is ________ into the institutional group.

integrated

In sum, the family serves the long-term function of regeneration, which is defined as the production and socialization of children to full adulthood. This stage has been reached when the young adults have demonstrated their readiness to enter marriage and resume the regenerative cycle with their children. The operation of the family requires the fulfillment of the domiciliary function, the full socialization of the children into a sufficient number of socially viable roles, and the maintenance of the boundaries which compartmentalize the family as a distinct functional unit in the larger society.

As a socializing agency, the family trains the child in the basic values, norms, techniques, and language systems of the culture. The socialization process also involves training the child to a satisfactory level of performance in suitable social roles. In maintaining its internal relationships, socialization functions, and boundaries, the family must assert control over its members. After sufficient socializa-

tion, the children internalize the values and norms of the society and can effectively control themselves.

Continuous Family Functions

73 There are three classes of intrafamily functions. These are (*a*) continuous functions, (*b*) cumulative functions, and (c) achievement functions. Those functions which operate daily within the family to maintain the minimum essentials of family living and to meet immediate needs we may call ______ ______.

continuous functions

74 Continuous intrafamily functions necessary for the daily life of the family include *domiciliary functions, interpersonal functions,* and *social functions.* The daily routine involved in maintaining the home or household are clearly ______ ______.

continuous functions

Domiciliary Functions

women

75 Home-keeping is traditionally the function of ______ in the family.

domiciliary

76 Children are often socialized into work roles when they contribute to ______ functions at home.

living

77 The modern home is a "machine for family living." It is constantly occupied and provides a storehouse for various necessities of daily life, such as clothes, linens, food, and tools. We might summarize these as ______ utensils.

consumption

78 The family is a consumption center in which goods are made available for actual use in living. Most modern families use a wide variety of goods and services. The final goal of most productive effort is ______ in the family.

consumer

79 The family is the primary consumer unit in all societies except in rare cases of communally organized societies. In other societies, nearly all the productive effort is to serve the ______ needs of the family.

family

80 Early human societies apparently provided only water, food, and simple utensils (tools), and these items were probably gathered or fashioned by the ______, as a cooperative unit.

father

81 In modern society the production of commodities has been specialized and moved outside the family as a producer unit. The primary responsibility of providing for commodity needs falls on the ________.

services

82 One of the most critical domiciliary functions of the household is that of managing and organizing the consumption of goods and services. The mother is the primary source of ________ in the family.

Interpersonal Functions

interpersonal functions

83 The family maintains various levels of interpersonal functions ranging from the most intimate, at the erotic level, through affectional, sympathetic, companionable, and general supportive relationships. Intimacy of association in ________ ________ is a basic aspect of family life.

small groups

84 The family has been likened to other small groups (Turner, 1958). It is a highly specialized form of small group with differentiated statuses and functions, and has much more intensive association between members than is found in other ________ ________.

love

85 Intrafamily association is sustained by continuing erotic relationships of warmth, affection, and mutual support. The most intensive of these relationships is expressed in physical manifestations of ________.

erotic

86 The erotic relationship (from the Greek word for love, *eros*) consists of physical contact on the skin and of pressure, patting, stroking, or rubbing some area of the skin. The entire skin surface is sensitive to ________ stimulation, and the mucous tissues of the body openings are highly sensitive to such stimulation.

mother

87 Companionship operates in a manner varying with the relation of the two family members involved. The need of small children for companionship is initially filled by the ________.

function

88 Daily life in the family offers opportunities for the individual to discover, exercise, and develop special talents and to explore interests. Reinforcement and support of a person's individual qualities is a continuing ________ of the family.

89 The family also has the function of recognizing and modifying individual qualities which might hinder adjustment in later life. Protuberant teeth can be straightened. A stammer can be treated clinically. These exemplify the idea that ________ may be improved.

adjustment

90 The mother receives support or pressures to fill her status as a mother when her children demand care, love, and other maternal functions. Being expected to fill these functions supports her in her maternal ________.

status

91 Expression of approval gives support to a family member who is filling a status position. Most people require the ________ of others.

approval

92 The family is the nucleus of social life, including living, maintenance, and gratifications for each individual family ________.

member

93 As a subsystem of the larger society, the family maintains a continuing exchange with the larger society. This continuing exchange constitutes the social ________ of the family.

function

94 The family provides not only a nuclear region where its members live, but also a focal area from which they emerge to effect linkage with some institutional element of the larger ________.

society

95 According to the mores (i.e., moral customs) of the community, the family has a ________ function to operate as a part of a community system.

continuous

In summary, continuing functions are repetitive and constant. They represent a major part of the family's daily activity in the home. The organization, planning, and fulfillment of the continuing functions rest primarily on the mother or homemaker. The homemaker imports consumer goods into the home and processes and distributes them in final form for consumption or use by individual members of the family. She also provides affective and expressive outputs to family members. The reciprocity of the other family members in demanding and responding to the maintenance and affective services of the mother supports the mother in her maternal status. Finally, the family has the continuing function of maintaining the nexus between individual family members and the larger society.

Cumulative Family Functions

96 Several family functions evolve and grow through a single long-term cycle in the family. The fact that they are ________ means that they operate continuously, but change by increments which are detectable only after a period of time.

cumulative

97 Cumulative functions in the family tend toward an end state which alters the basic position of those exercising the ________.

function

98 Cumulative functions are directed to their own completion and to transformation to some postfunctional ________ ________.

end state

99 Since the cumulative function of the family progresses through a cycle by imperceptible increments, those concerned can never ________ precisely where they stand on the cyclic continuum.

know

100 The child may know much more English than his parents suspect, or understand much less than they assume—or both. A dramatic event merely reveals that some stage has already been reached at some unknown time in the ________ or that it has not yet been reached.

past

101 Erotic behavior tends to dominate the preparental period. It provides much of the binding force for the regenerative dyad. (A married couple constitutes a ________.)

dyad

102 Near the beginning of the parental period, the marital relationship has two foundations. The original erotic-affective monopoly is broken, and the joint responsibility for the ________ brings a new phase.

child (children)

103 As infants arrive, the marital relation may be modified, interrupted, or distracted from its purely gratificatory ________-________ relationship.

erotic-affective

104 The interaction system between the marital pair usually reaches its broadest variety and maximum intensity during the parental period. All the complex manifestations of ________ involvement are incorporated.

family

105 Although the menopause does not affect the erotic capacity of the wife, it does mark the end of the woman's ________ period.

fertility (childbearing)

menopause

106 The marital union may regain something of its preparental intimacy after the ________.

grandparents

107 There may be parental echo functions with the grandchildren, but the involvement of ________ in family functions is usually peripheral.

socialization

108 Socialization is the process of training a person to participate in a social environment. It involves internalizing a symbol system, a set of values, a normative system, and a technology which are already shared in the wider cultural milieu. One of the primary functions of the family is the ________ of children.

setting

109 Socialization operates in a discontinuous series of social settings. Symbols are repeated and are joined with new symbols and with social and physical objects in the social ________ (Barker and Wright, 1954, pp. 45ff).

cumulative

110 The socialization process operates throughout childhood and the early adult years. Socialization is therefore a ________ function.

social

111 Each increment of the socialization process occurs in a specific social setting. Thus, the dining room where one learns how to share the eating behavior with the family exemplifies a ________ setting.

symbol

112 In the social setting there is applied a specific symbol set, a technology, a value set, and a system of norms. The terminology for tableware, prepared foods, etc., constitutes the ________ set in our example.

technology

113 The skills involved in manipulating food constitute a ________ of dining. (If you think there is no technology in eating, try eating fried rice with chopsticks.)

value set

114 (Reread frame 108.) For example, there are ratings of foods, cookery methods, and appurtenances related to dining. There are also prescribed combinations, quantities, and sequences of foods. All these together constitute a ________ ________ with regard to dining.

symbol set

115 As another aspect of socialization, the young child's language generally serves as a rough indicator of his maturity level. He continues to learn new symbol sets for broadening and more varied environmental situations. The child's facility for internalizing a new ________ ________ is in evidence throughout later life.

116 Family members, particularly the mother in our society, teach the normative system of the culture through language. Ways of thinking about time, space, personal relations, nature, tools, animals, and natural process are ________-bound.

culture

117 A child's idea of time may be quite different from his parents'. The mother tells the child, "Be home at three o'clock," having a definite time span in mind. A child who has just learned to read a clock may interpret this position of the clock hands as a chance event in the unanticipated ________.

future

118 He lives in the present, which includes time only in a vague, unconvincing way. Many American Indians and rural Mexicans have similar trouble with precise accounting for ________.

time

119 As the child becomes more familiar with the parent culture, he begins to parallel more closely the general system of ________.

values

120 He absorbs prevailing concepts of time, locus, and process. The effect is cumulative. The concepts tend to become more rigid than the associated language ________.

symbols

121 The behavior of his culture, once internalized, will be modified by the child only with difficulty and reluctance. Once he has accepted it, he has no adequate basis for abandoning it. The behavior seems natural and obvious, and he finds it impossible to understand or to tolerate contradictory ________.

behavior

122 The cumulative effect of rationalizing the norms of a culture is to manifest the culture as a member in good standing. The new member is no longer regarded as a novice, because he appears to behave like the other ________.

members

123 One test of fitness in the cultural rationale is that of conventionality. When one has learned to behave like everyone else in his group, he may be termed a ________ member.

conventional

124 Innovation violates secure conventional standards. We know where we are, and are secure in this. We do not know where innovation could lead us. Therefore, it is easy to reject ________.

innovation

behavior setting

125 After childhood, the development of a number of technologies for a variety of behavior settings is mandatory. Mastery of technology is marked by acknowledgment of full status in a ________ ________, as in a work place, a classroom, or a basketball court.

technologies

126 The top level of technology is reached by a few of the highly placed, and sets an ideal for others. At other levels, both children and adults master a large variety of ________ which are available thereafter.

community

127 If the family is effective in its broader functions of growth, training, control, and career, it gains status in the ________.

status

128 Any major change requires mobilization in the family. Shifting from one social stratum to another, the family may experience either a gain or a loss in socioeconomic ________.

mobile

129 Families are frequently required to mobilize their household effects to move to another area. In industrial societies families are relatively ________, moving on the average of once every five years.

home

130 In societies operating above the subsistence level, families acquire rights or property in a cumulative process. The Baganda boy (Africa) accumulates a bride price. The Kwakiutl Indian family (Canada) accumulates goods for potlatches or spending competitions. American families (United States) pay on a mortgage to acquire ownership of their ________.

education

131 The family supports the educational process for the young. The educational process accumulates stages of accomplishments pertinent to social and economic functions. A boy becomes qualified for a ceremony, for using weapons or tools, or for receiving a college ________.

education (courses)

132 In Western society, adult members of families are often maintained in educational and training processes. Professional men and business leaders often undertake advanced ________ to improve their professional skills.

authority (control)

133 The family tends to mirror the prevailing philosophy of government in its application of control and authority in the family. In the autocratically ruled state, the father's ________ may be punitive and tyrannical.

134 In a democratic state, the concept of equality of persons in the state apparently supports this same ideological concept of persons in the family. The authority of the parents is limited, and the ideal of democratic ________ is applied.

equality

135 Within the United States family, children tend to be given increasing degrees of autonomy until they have reached relatively full autonomy by the time of late ________.

adolescence

136 In all societies the family has some responsibility for inculcating attitudes toward religious, sacred, or supernatural functions. Older family members acquaint the young with ________ concepts.

religious (sacred, supernatural)

137 All societies with an integrated system of religious beliefs maintain some system for initiating their members into religious ________.

functions (ceremonies, etc.)

138 The family functions described in this section are concerned with incremental changes in family behavior eventuating in another stage of socialization. They are called ________ functions.

cumulative

Cumulative family functions, then, are fulfilled by imperceptible increments which slowly modify the capabilities of the individual family member and which depend on the support and assistance of other family members. After a period of such gradual modification, a nodal point is reached which comes to be identified as an end state and marks a new status level. Cumulative functions are carried out in a process of socialization, in which the individual gradually internalizes the symbols, value set, normative system, and technology incorporated in the function. Cumulative functions include, for example, developing proficiency in language, social relationships, and technological capacities. The individual gains further acceptance as an active member within the family and in the larger society as the cumulative functions are fulfilled. The end state becomes manifest when it is recognized that the developing individual can perform like other accepted members of the social group with regard to a specific function. When this point is reached, the individual is usually ready to undertake a further stage of adjustment in a sequential cumulative function. A series of cumulative functions are mastered within the family. When the developing child reaches maturity and emerges from the family as a young adult, he has learned how to undertake further cumulative functions required for his socialization into social units in the larger society.

Achievement Functions

family

139 Family "achievement functions" refer to goals which are essential to the formation and fulfillment of the ________.

change (alteration, etc.)

140 When an achievement function is completed, the family undergoes a major change in status, structure, and condition. This may require extensive ________ in routines, resource allocation, and intrafamily relations.

Establishing a Home

marriage

141 The major achievement which makes a family socially possible to begin with is ________.

marriage

142 Marriage typically marks the culmination of a sorting and matching process. As individuals mature physically, socially, and economically, they are ready for ________.

United States

143 Matching for marriage may be accomplished by parents, as in classical China; by purchase of a bride, as among the Baganda of Africa; or by the random-trial, free-enterprise dating system of the ________ ________.

home (domicile)

144 After marriage, the next major achievement is the establishment of a ________.

change

145 Most married couples desire and have children. Conception places the family on a new footing. A distinct ________ in family status occurs.

Role Differentiation

home / mother

146 The achievement function, on completion of a segment of the growth continuum, requires reorganization of routines and the imposition of new roles. The wife who has just delivered her first child must reorder the routine of her ________ and adopt the new role of ________.

The wedding establishes the new family. (*Wide World Photos*)

147 The adoption of new roles as a consequence of achieving a segment of a growth continuum also may necessitate the relinquishment or modification of old ________.

roles

148 Achievement functions may be referred to a conceptual scale of adequacy of achievement. It may be fulfilled or not. Thus the family may fail in its regenerative function by not having ________.

children

149 In most societies, marriage requires career viability of the male spouse. He is expected to support his wife and any children that she may bear. Therefore, marriage usually requires the qualification of the male for an ________.

occupation (career)

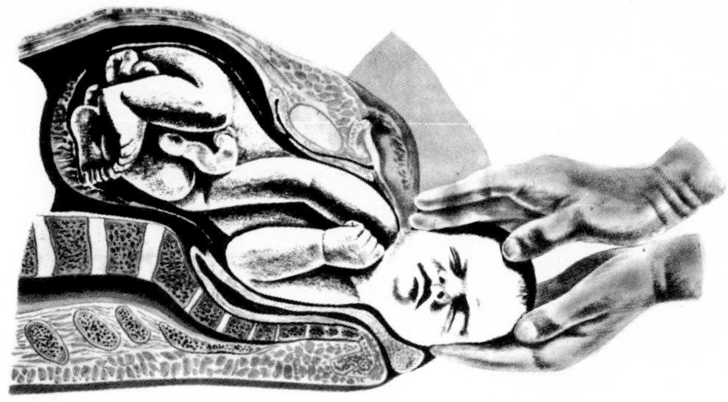

Delivery of a child means a major achievement in the family. *(McGraw-Hill Book Company. Used by permission.)*

150 Marriage ordinarily requires economic adequacy. The marital pair must have sufficient ________ resources to meet their needs as a family.

economic

151 (Refer to Figure 13 for information relative to the next sixteen frames.) The family seeks placement of its members in appropriate roles. Sons require roles for instrumental objectives. Masculine role sets incorporate skills in handling objects, machines, and persons for ________ goals.

instrumental

152 The family must achieve generalized expressive and instrumental roles which are integrated with those involved in sex identification. The boy elaborates his masculine identification with male ________ of performer, achiever, and responsible agent.

roles

153 The family also sustains a series of roles primarily concerned with expressive functions. The expressive behavior serves internal needs of its members and conveys orientations to social objects in the environment. Expressive gestures and communications generate interaction within the nuclear ________.

family

154 As shown in Figure 13, the father is the superior instrumental member of the nuclear family: he links the family to the external world. He provides goods, skills in handling instruments, and objective standards in ________ family affairs.

managing (handling)

155 The realist and the technician of the family is typically the ________.

See Figure 13.

Superior instrumental (father)		Superior expressive (mother)	
Universal	Particular	Universal	Particular
Technical expert	Executive (instrumental leader)	Expressive virtuoso, cultural expert	Charismatic leader (expressive leader)
Inferior instrumental (son)		**Inferior expressive (daughter)**	
Universal	Particular	Universal	Particular
Adequate technical performer	Cooperator	Willing, accommodating person	Loyal member

Figure 13. Eightfold differentiation of role types. SOURCE: Talcott Parsons and Robert Bales, *Family: Socialization and Interaction Process,* The Free Press of Glencoe, New York, 1955, p. 51. Used by permission.

See Figure 13.

156 The one who sets up objective criteria for skills and performance is typically the ________.

skills

157 The son is expected to emulate his father and to achieve adequate social and technical skills by objective criteria. The son also manifests particularistic ________ in cooperating in the performance of objective tasks.

man

158 He is expected to judge himself and others by non-personal objective standards. He must "stand on his own two feet," and seek to be adequate as a ________.

role model

159 The son needs a role model to guide him to full masculinity. He achieves a series of standings with the help and support of his family. The father typically serves as a ________ ________ for the developing masculinity of the son.

visible (available)

160 The son's task of developing suitable roles, using his father as role model, may be difficult if the father's role as worker and producer is not readily ________ to the son.

role

161 The son is also vulnerable to unforeseen changes in his father's primary masculine role as breadwinner. If unemployment or technological change interrupts or terminates the father's effectiveness, the son has to determine other ways to fill his ________.

Daughter applies affective skills. (*Wide World Photos*)

162 In America, the mother is usually the family manager. The mother sustains her daughter through a series of achievement levels in her role as expressive authority in the ________.

home

163 The daughter may practice as a mother, first, with inanimate models such as dolls and toy houses. Then she begins to apply her skills in the play group, with her agemates of the same sex as ________. Mother's clothes, shoes, and cosmetic arsenal come in for exercise at an amateur level at this stage.

models

164 After puberty, the daughter may begin to apply some of the mother's broader social and affective-erotic ________.

roles (skills)

parental

165 As the son and daughter go through the achievement stages, they gain autonomy. In the later stages of development they may assume a large portion of the ________ skills and orientations.

authority differential

166 The authority differential is nearly absolute for the infant, but as children become adults, they approximate more and more closely to the general power and maturity levels of their parents. The ________ ________ approaches zero as the child matures to full adulthood.

Status

family

167 The status-achievement level applicable for any individual regenerative dyad depends on the members' own conception of the status norm appropriate to their ________.

status achievement

168 Once this norm is agreed upon, the dyad ordinarily strives to maintain or to attain this norm of ________ ________.

control

169 Status retention requires that the primary members of the family remain employed. The family is, therefore, vulnerable to forces operating in the larger society and outside its own area of ________.

status norm

170 A family may be satisfied with a given status level because it has achieved the status norm which it conceives as appropriate. If the norm conceived appropriate is higher than the attained norm, as with the ambitious middle-class family, the family must strive to reach a level more proximate to its assumed ________ ________.

behavior

171 The family orients the child to its assumed status norm by explicit and implicit attitudes and by indoctrination. The child usually internalizes the parental status norm and orients his ________ to retain or to attain this level of status achievement.

acceptance (approval)

172 The American family seeks to place the child in a selected status or in a situation which will give him access to it. The working-class family typically takes pride in this status. The family orients the child to ________ of the workman's way of life.

achievement

173 The foregoing illustrate the concept that the family provides ________ functions for its members.

The first day at school. (*Wide World Photos*)

174 The family operates as a subsystem of society. Therefore, the functions of the family may also be defined from the more generalized viewpoint of the larger ________.

society

175 The family is the original unit for the orientation and control of persons. The family is the primary unit with facilities and resources for providing the extensive personal contact which children need to develop into socialized adults. The prime function of the family is to ________ people.

socialize

176 The family has an equally important function of "sexualizing" its members, so that they may later participate in a normal ________ function of the family.

regenerative (sexual)

The college graduation achievement. (*Wide World Photos*)

functions

177 The etiology of normal sexual maturation is not known, but it is evident that the family is intimately connected with the development of sexualization. This probably occurs in most families through the affective-erotic ________ of the mother.

functions

178 The family provides members to participate in society. These people are trained, socialized, and sexualized. They thus attain a concatenation of features which enable them to fill an extensive set of needed and highly specialized ________ in society.

A specialized function for a mature man. (*Wide World Photos*)

179 The family operationalizes, generates, and regenerates culture. It therefore preserves the characteristics of a culture as it ________ culture to the children.

transmits

180 In the process the family contributes minor additions to the overall culture and contributes to the evolution of ________.

culture

181 By virtue of its ability to transmit cultural elements, the family is highly flexible and can adapt to far-reaching environmental and technological and social changes. The fact that the family is a highly flexible and highly mobile growth unit makes it ________ in the face of changing requirements. This is one of the most basic functions of the family.

adaptable (flexible)

SUMMARY

The family functions simultaneously in three temporal dimensions. The first of these is the ongoing present, in which the continuous functions take place as a primary objective. Interest centers in performing a job, eating a meal, or putting things away. These functions are carried out for and within the family, and are basically under the mother's direction, although they involve behaviors originating with the mother and radiating to all members of the family. Echo behaviors, or reactions to the behaviors of the mother as the directing agent, provide the response step which repeats until a specific function is carried to completion.

In carrying out the continuous functions, the mother performs a remarkable variety of duties in which she incorporates manual labor on the semiskilled level, planning, resource allocation, the direction of social, play, work, and maintenance activities, and the direct emotional and physical stimulation of the members of the family. The husband may share in many of these functions, or he may remain relatively aloof to them. In either case, the responsibility for carrying out these duties falls on the mother in most families.

Although continuous functions are most obvious and require the bulk of the family's resources, they are a vital part of the family's operation. Cumulative functions are fulfilled in a process of incremental development associ-

ated with biological maturation and social adjustment. Cumulative functions can be fulfilled only if the social environment provides inputs to those who are developing. Thus, the infant slowly acquires the ability to respond to and with verbal symbols. Similarly, the child learns to interact with other children and to initiate, direct, and evaluate group behavior. But he can do this only if he has opportunity to maintain such associations. Finally, there is no fixed time when a cumulative function is completed.

Achievement functions mark nodal points in the family's development. Unlike the cumulative functions, achievement functions are highly definitive and are marked by status change. Many achievement functions are ritually marked by a ceremony to establish the new status, such as a marriage, the birth of a child, or the conferral of membership in a recognized social or professional group. Achievement functions require planning and effort. Usually there is some uncertainty as to whether the achievement functions will be completed. In some cases they require the consent or assistance of other parties. In other cases an element of chance may contribute to completion of the function or may forestall its accomplishment. Examples are sterility, mental retardation, and malformation.

Finally, the family is geared into the larger society of which it is the smallest and the most basic constituent element. Except in times of revolution or disaster, there is a complex mutual interdependence between the family and the society which demands a system of standardized expectations regarding both intra- and extrafamily behavior. These fixed relationships, established by custom and usually sanctioned by law, enable the family to undertake long-term obligations with reasonable assurance that the society in general, and the particular individuals concerned, will continue to support them.

The society is involved in all the family functions. It provides a framework, a system of organized production and use of resources, and a reservoir of other families which make the maturational process meaningful. The society also maintains a reservoir of culture, including a history, a system of values, a technology, and some understanding of desirable and acceptable goals for the future. Therefore, the family functions of personal maintenance have their reflection in the larger society which has a function in making available the raw materials for living. Cumulative functions of the family confer skills on individuals which enable them to fulfill role expectations both *within a family of procreation and in the larger society. The achievement functions likewise are recognized by the society in much the same terms as they are recognized by the family. In fact, we might say that the formal interpersonal and interinstitutional relations are an extension of relations which had their genesis in the family.*

SELF-REVIEW QUIZZ

1 The things the family does, the way it operates, and the goals which it strives to achieve are the ________ of the family.

2 Individual members of the family assist the functioning of the family by performing their various ________.

3 Each actor in the family group learns to perform a number of specific roles which together make up his ________.

4 The basic functions of the family include provision for (*a*) ________, (*b*) ________, (*c*) ________, (*d*) ________, and (e) ________ ________.

5 The regenerative function is completed by bringing ________ to ________.

6 The end of the regenerative cycle is indicated by the readiness of the grown son or daughter to marry and become a ________.

7 The boundaries of the family are usually demarcated by the ________ in which the family lives.

8 The various services which must be repeated daily with little change over time are denoted as ________ ________.

9 Continuous functions are primarily managed and maintained by the ________ of the family.

10 Cumulative functions involve small incremental changes which in time evolve to a recognized ________ ________.

11 The acquisition of skill in the use of the native language exemplifies an ________ ________.

12 The achievement functions are most clearly represented in modern society by the successive levels of ________ the child is expected to master.

13 From the viewpoint of the family the final achievement function for a daughter is to get her successfully, satisfactorily, and legitimately ________.

14 The modern family must learn to adapt its socialization processes to the needs of the larger ________ in which it functions.

REFERENCES

Barker, R. G., and H. F. Wright: *Midwest and Its Children,* Harper & Row, Publishers, Incorporated, New York, 1954.

Broom, L., and P. Selznick: *Sociology,* 2d ed., Harper & Row, Publishers, Incorporated, New York, 1958.

Burgess, E. W., Locke, H. J., and Thomas, M. M.: *The Family: From Institution to Companionship,* 3d ed., American Book Company, New York, 1963.

Cottrell, L. S., Jr.: "The Adjustment of the Individual to his Age and Sex Roles." *American Sociological Review, 7,* 618-625, 1942.

Lindzey, Gardner: *Handbook of Social Psychology,* Addison-Wesley Publishing Company, Inc., Reading, Mass., 1954.

Lundberg, G. A., Schrag, C. L., and Larsen, O. N.: *Sociology,* Harper & Row, Publishers, Incorporated, New York, 1958.

Merton, R. K.: *Social Theory and Social Structure,* The Free Press of Glencoe, New York, 1957.

Parsons, Talcott: *The Social System,* The Free Press of Glencoe, New York, 1951.

——— and R. F. Bales: *Family, Socialization and Interaction Process,* The Free Press of Glencoe, New York, 1955.

Sarbin, R. T.: "Role and Theory," in G. Lindzey (ed.), *Handbook of Social Psychology,* Addison-Wesley Publishing Company, Inc., Reading, Mass., 1954, vol. I, chap. 6.

Simmel, Georg: *Soziologie,* Duncker & Humblot, Berlin, 1958.

Turner, R.: "The Family," in L. Broom and P. Selznick, *Sociology,* 2d ed., Harper & Row, Publishers, Incorporated, New York, 1958.

Winch, Robert F.: *The Modern Family,* rev. ed., Holt, Rinehart and Winston, Inc., 1963.

the school as a social institution

DONALD L. LANTZ

As a social institution, the school is second only to the family in terms of amount of interpersonal contact involved and, in all probability, in its influence on individual behavior. Education is a full-time occupation or a time-consuming avocation for about one-third of the population of the United States. In 1965 there were almost 47 million elementary and secondary pupils, and about 5 million full-time or part-time college students in our country. Over 2 million teachers, professors, and administrators served the students in 137,000 schools and colleges. Practically all elementary and secondary school pupils spend as many of their waking hours in direct contact with their teachers and their classmates as with their families. Many children spend more time with their teachers than with their mothers. Few Americans have not been significantly influenced and affected by their experiences in school.

The school exerts a variety of influences on child behavior. Not only does it provide curricular information of the usual type, but modern schools also have accepted as necessary the responsibility of helping children learn other kinds of behavior—social competence, vocational training, driver education, dramatics, individual and group sports, journalism, and other extracurricular activities. All these learning activities contribute to the socialization process.

For the majority of children, the teacher is the most important source of social stimuli. For that reason, the interaction between teacher and student deserves considerable attention. Other motivating influences, such as achievement criteria and the peer group, are also extremely important in the socialization process to which the school, as a social institution, contributes.

Educational Functions of the School

To many people the function of the school is to facilitate the process of learning to read, write, and work arithmetic, to understand history, and so forth. Many people, on the other hand, prefer a broader function for the school that includes teaching ethical behaviors, values, aesthetic development, and understanding of social relationships. Differences of opinion exist about what ought to be the specific function of the school at all levels. Two broadly differing viewpoints of the function of the school will be discussed in the following section.

1 Education has been defined as the "progressive or desirable changes in a person as a result of teaching and study" (English and English, 1958). The process of helping people develop intellectual ability, social competence, and optimum individual potential can be called the ________ process.

educational

2 Every society prepares its members for a role in that society through a system of providing reinforcement and punishment. This process of preparing individuals for a role in a society is known as ________ or socialization.

education

3 A school is an "organized group of pupils pursuing defined studies and receiving instructions from one or more teachers" (English and English, 1958). The organized agency of society that provides the environment for the experiences necessary for the education of individuals is the ________.

school

4 The environment of the ________ provides an organized sequence of experiences for students which are designed to promote behavioral changes consistent with expected behavior in a ________.

school

society

5 The school is responsible for providing efficiently the educational experiences necessary to bring about desirable behavior changes in individuals. It is a special environment which provides an organized ________ of educational experiences that will facilitate learning.

sequence

6 The development of education in most societies has been evolutionary. When *informal* education alone failed to prepare people for society, schools ________ to provide the basis for ________ education.

evolved (emerged, etc.)

formal

7 In its broadest sense, education includes all those influences of society which help determine human behavior. It includes learning situations found not only in the school, but also in out-of-_______ learning situations.

school

8 For example, in some communities in America, Negro youth learn to "know their place." This type of learning is not the result of formal instruction, but rather of _______ learning.

informal

9 The home and peer groups provide informal education, while the school provides _______ education.

formal

10 The formal educational experiences provided by the school obviously are not confined to classroom or book learning. Extracurricular activities provided by the school may be considered _______ education when these activities are also designed to provide an educational experience.

formal

11 A school dance is a situation provided by the school environment in which students can have fun. It may also facilitate learning social competence. This situation provides for _______ learning much as a biology class provides for "academic" learning.

social

The discussion of school in this chapter is concerned primarily with public schools. A public school is usually defined as a school with (1) elementary or secondary grades, (2) organized under a school district of the individual state, (3) supported by tax revenues, (4) administered by public officials, and (5) open to all.

12 Public schools are supported by _______ _______ and are organized under a _______ _______.

tax revenues
school district

13 Public schools are administered by _______ _______ and are open to _______.

public officials
all (everyone)

14 Schools perform two basic functions for society which seem to be paradoxical at first glance. They (*a*) preserve society, yet (*b*) they effect changes in _______ (Havighurst and Neugarten, 1962).

society

15 Some people believe the school's primary function is to preserve the culture of our past. Such people would not design school curricula for living in a contemporary culture, but for a culture of the _______.

past

Schools play a basic role in preparing children for society.

to preserve society
to effect changes in society

16 Society has commissioned schools with two major functions. They are _______ _______ _______ and +++++.

changes

17 The school functions not only to mirror society and perpetuate the *status quo* but also to effect _______ leading toward a more ideal society.

preparing people to live in contemporary society

18 Of the two basic functions of education, the one that predominates is that of preserving the contemporary society. Even in nonliterate societies, the role of education is predominantly that of preparing individuals for contemporary life. The dominant function of education is +++++.

preservation

19 The school transmits the culture of society by reflecting the dominant mores and values of society. This function is related to the _______ of society.

Yes

20 During periods of rapid social change or unrest, education seems to effect more changes in society than during periods of tranquility. Would you have expected this function (effecting changes in society) to be prevalent during the Great Depression? _______.

to effect changes leading toward a more ideal society

21 A social studies lesson was designed to teach pupils that all citizens should have equal rights at the voting polls. Which function of education does this illustrate? +++++.

22 A history lesson was designed to show students where we have erred from the mark of ideal democracy and how we might make a better approximation of the ideal. Which function of education would this demonstrate? +++++.

to effect changes in society

REVIEW: *The two basic functions of the school are to preserve society and to effect changes in society. These sometimes interact to create conflicts in education.*

23 School integration problems illustrate how the interaction of the two principal functions of schools can lead to the creation of difficulties. Thus, the basic functions of the school may ______ to create problems.

interact

24 Changes in educational needs are related to changes in society. Conversely, changes in society have instigated changes in education. As society has made technological advances, schools have reflected these ______ in society.

changes (advances)

25 Some educators advocate that schools should teach students how to use their leisure time. This in part reflects the changes that have occurred in society during the past fifty years regarding how much time is spent on the job. For example, millinery is not taught in home economics courses now, as it was fifty years ago, because society has ______.

changed

26 Like the family and the church, the school is one of society's institutions that helps to ______ the child.

socialize

27 The specific aspects of the socialization process for which the school is responsible have varied from time to time and from society to society. For example, driver education is one aspect of ______ that United States schools were not responsible for in 1930.

socialization

28 Correspondingly, schools in Brazil currently do not provide ______ ______ for their students.

driver education

29 Schools exist for the purpose of educating and socializing the child to function as a member of a particular ______.

society

Table 19. Percentage of Persons 25 Years Old and Over: Years of School Completed, by Color and Sex, 1962

Color, sex	Years of school completed			Median school years completed
	College (4 years)	*High school*	*Eighth grade*	
Total	9.0%	46.4%	80.6%	11.4
Male	11.4	45.0	79.1	11.1
Female	6.7	47.5	81.9	11.6
White	9.5	48.7	82.9	11.8
Male	12.2	47.4	81.8	11.6
Female	7.0	49.9	84.1	12.0
Nonwhite	4.0	24.8	58.6	8.6
Male	3.9	23.2	54.6	8.3
Female	4.0	26.2	62.2	8.9

SOURCE: U.S. Department of Commerce, *Statistical Abstract of the United States,* 1964, p. 113.

30 Table 19 presents the percentage of individuals twenty-five years of age and over in the United States who have completed college, high school, and eighth grade.
80 Approximately ______ percent of the adult population has completed the eighth grade.

31 Now study the table in terms of race as it relates to completion of the eighth grade. The percentage of white
higher adults who completed eighth grade is (higher/lower) than the percentage of nonwhite adults.

32 In 1962, approximately 40 percent of the males and 43 percent of the females in the United States who were at least twenty-five years old had completed at least four
one-half (50 percent) years of high school. Less than ______-______ of the adult United States population has graduated from high school.

33 Table 19 indicates that the percentage of white adults who completed high school is higher than the per-
75 centage of nonwhite adults. Approximately ______ percent of nonwhite adult population had not completed high school when the table was compiled.

34 In 1962, approximately 10 percent of the males and 6 percent of the females at least twenty-five years of age had completed at least four years of college. Less than one-tenth of the adult population in the United States had earned a ________ degree.

college

REVIEW: *Since virtually all children in our society attend either public or private schools, it seems safe to assume that only the family, as a social institution, has more potential influence on child behavior than the school.*

The School as a Subculture

Differences in school subcultures are not always obvious to the outside observer, but there are marked variations from one community to another with regard to promotion, grading, grouping, and the amount of departmentalization. School culture is also affected by the attitudes and values of students.

35 Schools transmit the culture of society and facilitate an improved culture by teaching the dominant knowledge, skills, values, and mores of ________.

society

36 The present school system is one of the cultural products of the society it serves and must be regarded as part of the total ________.

culture

37 The school is not an isolated institution of society but is part of the total cultural framework contributing to the ________ of the child.

socialization

38 School subculture may vary considerably within a community in such a way that the opportunities to learn are restricted for some groups and expanded for other groups. Conant's *Slums and Suburbs* (1961) indicates the great contrast between nonwhite slum schools and schools in the ________.

suburbs

39 The difference in suburban school culture and slum school culture is partly due to the fact that schools reflect the culture of the area they serve. Would you expect the subculture of a school in the slums to provide its students the same kind of stimulation for achievement as the subculture of a school in the suburbs? ________.

No

subculture

40 Each school has its own complex set of values, replete with traditions and taboos, which differs slightly from that of other social institutions and from the dominant mode of American culture. In other words, every school has its own ________.

subculture

41 School subculture is in part determined by the interaction of several factors, namely, the peer culture, the values of educators, and the culture of the community. The resultant school ________ determines the kind of interpersonal relations that will occur at school and even, to some extent, how students will learn.

subculture

42 For example, in some schools children sit in fixed rows with little opportunity for interacting with fellow students; in other schools children are seated in different ways, depending on the activity, and are involved in group work frequently. These differences are the result of the particular school ________.

lower

43 In most school subcultures, particularly for lower- and middle-class children, there is some pressure exerted on students to master subject matter through competition with other students. The middle class tends to place a higher value on academic achievement than the ________ class.

middle

44 Learning competitiveness via academic achievement in school tends to be valued most by which social class? ________.

academic

45 The student peer society and community are frequently at variance with the school culture regarding achievement. For example, in many schools students place a higher value on extracurricular activities, such as athletics and social competence, than on ________ achievement.

extracurricular

46 One reason for this difference is that academic learning may not have as great prestige value as certain ________ activities.

achievement (success)

47 Some extracurricular activities have more prestige value than academic achievement because often more privileges and approval are given for success in extracurricular activities than for academic ________.

Very few. Honor assemblies are sometimes held.

48 The cheering crowd and the sports page publicity are forms of social rewards. What rewards are given for successful academic achievement? +++++.

set of values

49 The phrase "set of values" means a preference for a particular pattern of behavior based on an individual's or institution's concept of what is desirable. An individual's behavior is determined in part by this preference or ________ ________ ________.

set of values

50 Each social institution teaches a set of values derived from its particular subculture that may distinctly influence the behavior of the child. The set of values taught the child at home or church may or may not be the same ________ ________ ________ taught to the child at school.

grade level

51 One of the ways in which a child gains status is his identification with his grade level. Sometimes teachers also identify themselves in terms of the grade level they teach. Thus, a facet of school culture (for better or worse) is the ________ ________ orientation.

school

52 Grade levels, report cards, grouping, and routine time schedules are examples of elements of ________ culture.

school (teachers)

53 The set of values taught in the child's home may either reinforce or contradict those taught by the ________.

values

54 The set of values taught at home may not always be reinforced by the ________ taught in school.

social positions

55 People occupying several social positions have status relationships with one another within the school. Administrators, faculty and staff, and pupils represent different ________ ________ within the school.

pupils

56 Administrators, who work for a local board of education, typically occupy the top rung of social positions in the school. They exert a direct influence on teachers, who in turn exert a direct influence on ________.

middle of the roaders (conservative, etc.)

57 Pressures exerted on the school by the community ordinarily result in schools being somewhat conservative. Administrators usually select teachers who they feel will not "rock the boat." Most teachers in our public schools tend to be +++++.

faculty

58 Within the school there are also many formal and informal organizations which encourage different relationships among ________ and students.

formal

59 A group of friends would constitute an informal organization, while the dramatics club would constitute a ________ organization.

formal
informal

60 A class in English literature constitutes a ________ organization; a lunchroom clique represents an ________ organization.

REVIEW: *Different social positions and formal and informal organizations within the school indicate that the school can be considered a particular type of subculture.*

Interaction of the School and Other Social Institutions

The home, neighborhood, and church affect attitudes of students toward school and, in turn, toward learning in school. Some students come from homes that encourage hard work and appropriate behaviors in school. Some come from homes that do not have high expectations of the school and may actually encourage behaviors that reduce the efficiency of the school.

home (family) / school

61 The two major institutions that are responsible for the education and socialization of the child are the family and the school. This is a shared responsibility; hence, cooperation between ________ and ________ is needed.

education (socialization)

62 Historically, the early schools in our society were simply institutions that supplemented the educational function of the family by teaching the three R's. Society increasingly has asked the school to assume more responsibilities until now, all too often, the school must turn to the family and ask parents to assist in the ________ of the child.

values

63 A number of factors influence the interaction of values learned in school and values learned at home. Some of these are (*a*) ethnic origin, (*b*) religious background, (*c*) regional differences, and (*d*) social class. More than one factor may influence the ________ taught at home.

ethnic

64 Take ethnic origin as a case in point. Children from a Chinese-American home may develop values that vary somewhat from those of other ________ groups, including those of the dominant American group.

ethnic origin

65 Similarly, children from an immigrant European family will vary in behavior from native-born American school children because of differences in ________ ________.

different

66 Differences in religious background may cause variations from the dominant American culture among families. For example, children from Christian Science families may be expected to hold values related to health and medicine somewhat ________ from the dominant American attitude toward health.

religious

67 Some school children are excused from dancing in gym classes because of the ________ convictions they (or their parents) hold.

values

68 Regional differences account for some of the variations in the mainstream of American culture. Values learned by children raised in homes of the Deep South differ in some aspects from the ________ learned by children raised in New England.

regional

69 Differences in reaction to school integration typically are related to ________ considerations.

middle-class

70 Possibly the most important factor resulting in differences between value patterns in American culture is socioeconomic class. Children of lower-class homes most likely have a different pattern of values from children of ________-________ homes.

social class

71 As we have already seen, social class tends to differentiate school behavior of children. So far as school behavior is concerned, social caste[1] is not so important a determiner as ________ ________.

class

72 Negro children from middle-class homes have values more similar to those of white children from middle-class homes than to those of Negro children from lower-class homes (Davis and Havighurst, 1946). This emphasizes the importance of social ________.

caste

73 Social class has been more important than social ________ in influencing school behavior.

[1] As used here, social caste (color caste) implies social separatism based on skin color.

REVIEW: *The four factors that influence the interaction of values learned in the home and the school are ethnic origin, religious differences, regional differences, and social class.*

social class

74 Each social class has a culture of its own which is a variant of the dominant American culture. Members of each _______ _______ likewise have different attitudes toward education.

social class

75 The set of values taught the child by his family is in a large measure a function of the family's _______ _______.

In a previous unit, American society was stratified according to particular criteria. For convenience, we shall divide society into five major social classes, subdividing the lower and middle classes but not the upper class. Thus, we can refer to the lower-lower and upper-lower class, the lower-middle and upper-middle class, and the upper class. The criteria given in Part I, Unit 2 for identifying these social classes can be used for our purpose.

schools

76 The various social classes found in society can also be identified in the public _______.

upper
formal

77 The upper social class regards formal education as a matter of proper rearing. Formal education is important in the same way that learning the desirable social graces is important. If they are to be reared "properly," _______-class childen must receive a distinctive _______ education.

social

78 Education for upper-class children is almost synonymous with acquiring desirable _______ conduct.

They represent a small percentage in the total population and tend to be enrolled in private schools.

79 Children from upper-class families constitute a small minority in public schools. What factors do you think account for this fact? +++++.

upper-middle

80 Education is also extremely important to the upper-middle class. Parents from the _______-_______ class tend to manifest anxiety if their children do not receive high grades in school (Havighurst and Neugarten, 1962).

upper-middle

81 Older children in the upper-middle class learn that rewards for educational achievement may be delayed. A college education is usually considered a minimum preparation for entrance into ________-________-class adult status.

college

82 Most upper-middle-class parents feel that it is essential for their children to attend ________ in order to maintain their social class status.

lower-middle

83 People in the United States lower-middle class view a high school education as very important, and approximately one-third of the young people from the ________-________ class will attend college.

jobs (employment, positions)

84 Education is usually considered important, not so much for its own sake as for the fact that it is essential for good ________.

high school

85 Parents in the upper-lower class usually expect their children to go further in school than they did. Children whose parents attended but did not complete high school are expected to finish ________ ________.

value

86 Most upper-lower-class parents do not consider education especially important except for its immediate, practical results. Parents from this class tend to place a greater ________ on vocational-type curricula for their children than on the college preparatory curriculum (Havighurst and Neugarten, 1962).

lower-lower

87 People in the lower-lower class often view education with some skepticism, perhaps because they sense that it teaches values which contradict those they hold. Many values taught in ________-________-class homes do not tend to be reinforced by school personnel.

social class

88 Our society is becoming more homogeneous with respect to attitudes toward school, but differences can still be detected by which (typically) membership in a particular social class may be designated. Attitudes toward school are usually reflections of one's ________ ________.

middle-class

89 Teachers predominantly hold a middle-class set of values even though their origin is not always middle class. Accordingly, we might expect most teachers to represent ________-________ behavior.

discriminated

90 Some teachers display discriminatory attitudes toward lower-class children. This may be a result of teachers' rejecting their own social class origin and of their desire to identify with upper-middle-class pupils. Lower-class children frequently are ________ against because of teacher attitudes toward lower-class behavior.

value

91 Children establish value patterns from their relationships with their parents before they come to school. When children enter school, they may begin to identify with admired teachers. If they identify themselves with teachers, they tend to take on the teacher's ________ pattern.

middle

92 Approximately two-thirds of the public elementary school students come from lower-class homes (Davis, 1948). The majority of these students have not learned the ________-class values and behaviors which most teachers demonstrate.

conflicts

93 A child's first conflict over values may occur when the values he learns at home do not match those he learns in the lower elementary grades. Children from lower-class homes frequently tend to demonstrate ________ between values.

middle-class

94 Children from lower-class homes tend to be rejected both by some of their classmates and their teachers, who typically represent ________-________ values.

lower class

95 Children from the lower socioeconomic classes are more likely to hold antischool attitudes than those from the middle and upper classes. Many more students from the ________ ________ than from other classes drop out of school because of such attitudes.

lower-class

96 Since the majority of children in elementary classrooms come from lower-class homes, we would expect that most of these children have learned ________-________ values.

class

97 Lower-class children learn early that most rewards in school are given to middle-class children. This may be reflected in the inverse relationship between school dropouts and social ________.

dropout
rewards

98 The ________ rate is highest for lower-class children. It may well be the result of fewer ________ in school.

middle-class values
lower

99 In many areas served by schools, middle-class values are nonrepresentative. Yet many teachers may attempt to impose ________-________ ________ upon pupils who are predominantly from the ________ class.

educational aspirations

100 The educational aspirations of children and adolescents decrease from the upper classes to the lower classes. Children from the middle class tend to have higher ________ ________ than children from lower-class homes (Kahl, 1953).

REVIEW: *Children from lower-class homes tend to be rewarded less in school than children from middle-class homes. For example, high grades do not tend to have so high a reward value for lower-class children as for middle-class children (Raths and Abramson, 1951).*

The one-third of children that come from the lower-lower class slum population often find schools quite uncongenial. Many people believe that one of the most urgent tasks today in education is learning how to educate the culturally disadvantaged child. Several attempts have been made to stimulate more able students from culturally deprived homes. An example is the Higher Horizons Program in New York which was aimed at enriching the child culturally, supplying remedial services, and attempting to involve parents.

Higher Horizons
parents

101 The ________ ________ Program was designed to assist the culturally disadvantaged child. One of the features of the program was the involvement of ________.

teacher

102 The Higher Horizons Program resulted in some improvements in academic achievement, attendance rates, discipline problems, and teacher morale. This program apparently not only benefited the pupils but also improved ________ morale.

higher (better)

103 One study (in which the IQ of the subjects was controlled) showed that a disproportionately larger number of children from upper-middle-class homes receive ________ grades than children from lower-class homes (Havighurst, Bowman, Liddle, Matthews, and Pierce, 1962).

104 The verbal discipline customary in middle-class schools has a different effect on children from lower-class homes. These children are conditioned to harsher punishment, such as being beaten or sworn at. The reprimand, "Please be quiet," will ________ in meaning for children from lower-class and middle-class homes.

differ

105 Some behavior of children from lower-class homes (e.g., cursing) often appears to be immoral to teachers who hold middle-class values. Such behavior is not immoral to those who hold ________-class values.

lower

106 In school, pupils from lower-class homes receive more physical punishment than middle-class children and likewise receive less praise. Many times this differential proportion of punishment and praise is a function of the teacher's ________-________ value system (Hollingshead, 1949).

middle-class

107 There is a tendency for students from the upper-middle class to participate more frequently in extracurricular activities than students from ________-class groups.

lower

108 We might expect that the greater proportion of students participating in the senior play would be from ________-________-class homes.

upper-middle

109 The "hidden tuition" (costs for books, supplies, participation in extracurricular activities, etc.) prohibits many lower-class pupils from full participation in the total school program. The inability of pupils from the lower class to participate in extracurricular activities because of financial considerations often results in programs sponsored by the public schools essentially for pupils from middle classes because they can afford to pay the ________ ________ costs.

hidden tuition

110 Many extracurricular activities provide an environment in which students can learn desirable social behavior. The extent of participation in ________ activities varies widely among the social classes.

extracurricular

111 In the classic sociological study of Elmtown (Hollingshead, 1949) the proportions of students who participated in at least one of the twenty-three activities studied were 100, 75, 57, and 27 percent respectively, from the highest to the lowest status. Participation in extracurricular activity (decreases/increases) from the high- to the low-status groups.

decreases

extracurricular

112 Young people from lower-class homes do not tend to receive as much financial support from their parents to participate in ______ activities as young people from economically secure homes.

middle

113 Lower-class children must attend classes, but they often discover that extracurricular activities are designed for ______-class pupils.

REVIEW: *Current educational practices eliminate from school a disproportionately large number of children from lower-class homes. These children are referred to as drop-outs.*

total amount of schooling, drop-outs, participation in extracurricular activities, etc.

114 Social class position can be used for prediction of achievement in schools. Name some other behavior in school that can be predicted by social class. +++++.

individual

115 If you were to use social class to predict such behavior, it should be noted that you are predicting for differences in group averages only and not for individual students. Social class data (relative to the items above) are inadequate for predicting the success of any given ______.

REVIEW: *There are several important educational implications raised by a knowledge of social class differences. Values, aspirations, participation in extracurricular activities, and dropout behavior are all related to social class. The present educational system in the United States tends to give the middle-class child an advantage over the lower-class child.*

increases

116 Amount of formal education is positively correlated with social class (Hollingshead, 1949). As social class level increases, at least through the upper-middle class, the amount of formal education ______.

expected

117 The amount of education expected of children in different social classes has changed during the last forty years in the United States. In 1920, a high school education was expected of the middle class; in 1966 some college work is ordinarily ______ of the middle class.

college

118 In 1920, a college education was an avenue up the status ladder for an individual in the lower-middle class. In may be that, by 1970, a ________ education will be expected to maintain even the lower-middle-class status.

The amount of change in education from 1920 to 1960 among the middle class has not resulted in changes of class structure per se. More education has resulted in greater knowledge and skills; consequently, people have been more productive. This productivity has resulted in a higher standard of living for members of all classes.

standard of living

119 An individual's ________ ________ ________ may be raised as a result of education, while his social status may not be affected.

longer

high school

120 It would be expected that the children of high school graduates would remain in school ________ than the children of high school dropouts. It would also be expected that children of high school graduates might attain some post-________ ________ education.

The School and Social Mobility

intelligence / motivation

121 American schools serve as an upward escalator in terms of socioeconomic class for those who have the necessary intelligence and/or motivation. Many intelligent pupils from the lower class do not persist in school and fail to move up the escalator because they do not have the necessary ________ and/or ________.

Usually, if a person is to elevate his social class level, he must adopt a new way of life. Social mobility affects many factors about an individual, including his speech, manners, dress, and attitudes toward education. Many young people from the lower class, when faced with the necessity of remaining in school in order to increase social mobility, realize they may be isolating themselves from their families and old friends.

mobility
motivation

122 In such instances, social ________ is presumed to be an extremely strong ________.

123 Encouragement from an interested teacher is often the factor that enables an intelligent student, whose parents are disinterested in education, to persist in school. In this case the teacher provides the stimulation which enables the school to be a vehicle of ________ ________.

social mobility

124 Sometimes the discovery of a particular talent (e.g., athletic prowess or dramatic ability) encourages a student from a lower class to increase his ________ ________ level through continued educational effort.

social class

125 There is still another consideration related to social mobility and education. Technological advances decrease the number of unskilled jobs, but at the same time they increase the number of skilled jobs. This suggests that schools must prepare more students for ________ jobs than they have in the past.

technical (skilled)

126 The middle class is not meeting the demand for skilled jobs; thus, recruits must come from the lower class. Those who have the necessary intelligence and ________ are likely to be in the stream of upward mobility.

motivation

REVIEW: *Several factors just considered encourage lower-class children to remain in school. They are interested teachers, discovery of talent, and meeting the demand for skilled jobs.*

127 Schools tend to perpetuate social class differences in various ways. In addition to the differential reward system accorded middle- and lower-class children, different curricula (e.g., business, secretarial, shop, and college preparatory) contribute to perpetuation of social class differences. Most pupils who enter the college preparatory curriculum tend to be from the same ________ class.

social

128 Another way schools tend to perpetuate the *status quo* in social class is by use of grouping procedures. Homogeneous ________ generally tends to place students of the same social class in the same classroom. Social class behaviors thus tend to be reinforced and perpetuated.

grouping

129 Downward social class mobility is defined as not maintaining the educational status of one's parents. Children from middle-class homes who drop out of high school often demonstrate +++++ later in life.

downward social class mobility

REVIEW: *Educational achievement is an important vehicle for social mobility. Children who attain significantly higher school achievement than their parents have a better chance of upward mobility. Those who do not achieve the same level of education as their parents risk downward mobility.*

The Church and the School

During colonial times and the early years of our Republic the first compulsory public schools were clearly sectarian. The impetus for changing sectarianism in public schools was the changing social scene and Protestant groups who resented their children being taught specific Protestant creeds. Horace Mann, who marshaled support from the dissenting Protestants, was influential in bringing about the beginning of a secular public school system.

130 The initial breakdown of sectarian public schools came from dissenting ________ groups and the leadership of ________ ________.

Protestant
Horace Mann

131 The pressure from the various Protestant groups resulted in a Protestant school system in which the specific creeds were not taught, but children were indoctrinated in the common Protestant tenets. The first step in the secularization resulted in what might be called a ________ school system.

Protestant

132 The Protestant view remained dominant until tension was produced by increased Roman Catholic immigration during the middle of the nineteenth century. These new immigrants did not wish their children to be indoctrinated in Protestant teachings and quite naturally resisted such ________ teaching in the public school.

sectarian (Protestant)

133 Because of the resistance of the Catholics, many Roman Catholic children were poorly treated by public school officials. The schools gradually changed, becoming increasingly secular as a result of pressure from ________ ________.

Roman Catholics

134 The Roman Catholics did not want secular schools, but they preferred them to ________ schools.

Protestant

135 The Protestants did not want secular schools either but preferred them to providing tax support for Roman Catholic schools or permitting ________ ________ indoctrination in the schools.

Roman Catholic

secularization

136 In one sense schools in the United States became Christian in their orientation. This might be considered the result of the second step in the ______ of the schools.

By the time of the large Jewish immigration (latter part of the nineteenth century), the schools had become largely secular, and Jewish children did not suffer the humiliation that Catholic children received earlier. They were, however, subjected to a "Christian" view. It is quite possible that the pressure to conform is greatest when religious observances are broadly nonsectarian, such as observances at Christmas.

Christian

137 The tendency for Jewish children to be subjected to dogmatic indoctrination of any given creed was slight, but they were/are subjected to a ______ view. Generally speaking, however, the Jewish community is satisfied with the public school system.

litigation

138 The early secularization of the schools was the pragmatic accommodation to the competition between the creeds and was not guided by constitutional principles. Since World War II, however, the secularization of schools has been primarily through litigation (judicial process of the courts). ______ might be considered the third step in the secularization of the schools.

religious

constitutional

139 The initial step in the secularization of public schools came as a result of competition between ______ creeds. The basis for recent secularization of schools has been ______ principles.

no establishment / free exercise

140 Most of this litigation has centered around the First Amendment in our Bill of Rights: "Congress shall make no law respecting an establishment of religion, or prohibiting the free exercise thereof. . . ." This clause states two broad principles: ______ ______ of religion and the ______ ______ of religion.

secularization / First

141 The Supreme Court decision in the Schempp case (1963) is an example of recent litigation regarding ______ based on the limitations imposed by the ______ Amendment.

Bible

142 The Schempp case resulted in a decision outlawing public school prayer and devotional Bible reading. The Supreme Court considers devotional ______ reading unconstitutional.

prayer and Bible reading

143 The Schempp case is important both for what it forbids and for what it explicitly permits. The practices it forbids are devotional practices such as +++++.

devotional (religious)

144 It apparently does not forbid a religious census of pupils or baccalaureate services, as indicated by the Chamberlain case (1963) from Florida. The decision of the Supreme Court definitely prohibits ______ exercises in public schools.

(*a*) Yes
(*b*) No, providing there was no devotional exercise connected with it.

145 (*a*) Does the Supreme Court decision (Schempp case) apply to a practice of daily prayer by a teacher in a public school without direction from anyone in authority over her? ______. (*b*) Would a manger scene in a classroom at Christmas violate the Supreme Court decision? +++++.

The freedom to worship as one pleases is considered a basic freedom in American democracy. It is strongly believed by many that any sectarian teaching would be a denial of religious freedom. On the other hand, many parents are concerned with the lack of religious training in public schools.

sectarian (religious)

146 They are sending their children to parochial schools where they will get a ______ education as well as a secular education.

secular

147 Some churches in America view the public schools with skepticism and dissatisfaction. This has come about with schools professing secularism. Some churches view the public schools as "godless" and "antireligious" because the schools profess to be ______.

antireligious

148 The schools profess to be secular but not antireligious. The schools are concerned with teaching children and youth the moral and ethical principles common to the Judeo-Christian heritage. Secularism is not synonymous with the idea that public schools are ______.

health

149 The beliefs of several small religious groups occasionally create problems within the public schools. For example, one sect believes that health is a religious matter and is likely to object to ______ programs in the school.

150 Members of one religious group claim that it is immoral to salute the flag of the United States because it is a form of image worship. Since flag saluting is part of the opening exercises in most schools, we may occasionally expect a conflict to arise between school officials and members of this ________.

sect (religious group)

151 Those churches which accept a very literal interpretation of Genesis are likely to reject the teaching of the biological concept of ________.

evolution

152 Some churches (e.g., Roman Catholic, Lutheran) perceive religious training to be an integral part of the school curriculum. These churches sponsor their own parochial schools so that the school curriculum will include ________ training.

religious

153 Many churches are dissatisfied with public schools because, they say, there is no Christian emphasis. On the other hand, some Jewish communities are dissatisfied because they believe too much ________ emphasis is found in the public schools.

Christian

154 Certain Christian holidays observed by public schools may cause friction between the Christian and Jewish communities. Schools are likely to depart from their secular orientation when observing the Christian holidays of ________ and ________.

Christmas / Easter

155 Many nonreligious people, agnostics, and even members of some religious sects became disturbed with public schools for promoting religion. These people have sometimes sought court action to keep ________ out of the public schools.

religion

156 The parochial school is one approach to the solution of conflict between church and public school. In such schools religion is fused with the school ________.

program (curriculum)

157 Some religious groups use a program of released time for voluntary religious instruction. In such programs pupils are generally ________ from the public school one period a week to attend classes of religious education by a teacher provided by the church.

released

158 A program of religious instruction held during the school day but for which the church is responsible is termed ________ ________.

released time

may not

159 The Supreme Court has also made some decisions relative to released-time instruction. The McCollum case prohibits religious instruction conducted in public school buildings. The Zorach case, however, sustained a program of religious instruction in which students were released to attend classes in neighboring churches. Released-time religious instruction (may/may not) be held in public school buildings.

church / state

160 Other churches believe that with cooperation of the Sunday church school and the home they can provide children the necessary religious instruction. Such churches are usually careful not to infringe on the principle of separation of ________ and ________.

religious

161 Conflict between religious bodies can be divisive in American society. A function of the public schools is to teach religious tolerance so that differences in ________ views may exist and yet promote dignity for every human being.

tolerance

162 Religious ________ can do much to reduce conflict in public education.

REVIEW: *Secularism in public schools is the result of the principle of separation of church and state. That schools are secular does not mean that they are antireligious. The immigration of Catholic and Jewish people resulted in the public schools becoming less Protestant and more secular in nature. The extent of religious instruction in public schools has decreased since the early days of public education. The Supreme Court decision in the Schempp case declared prayer and devotional Bible reading in public schools unconstitutional.*

SUMMARY

The school is one of the three major social institutions that assist in socializing the child. The function of the school is to teach certain knowledge and skills that will not only preserve the society but also assist in effecting changes in society.

The success of the school in fulfilling its role in the socializing process is partially dependent on the relationship between the school and other social institutions. The relationship between the family and the school is close. One very significant variable related to whether or not a child will be receptive to the school is the level of social class of the family. The school teaches the value system of the middle class, which is alien to many children from lower-class homes.

The school functions in many ways to maintain the existing status quo of students, yet in many ways encourages an upward mobility of students. Placing students with similar backgrounds together in certain curricula (such as agriculture, business, technical) limits their contacts with pupils who have different backgrounds and thus tends to maintain their existing status. Similarly, the location of the school tends to maintain the status quo of students. Students tend to come from rather homogeneous neighborhoods. Upward mobility of students is often fostered by a close student-teacher relationship in which the teacher perhaps serves as a model for behavior for the student or encourages raising of the student's goals.

The public school was clearly sectarian in colonial times, but pressure from the churches themselves caused the schools to move to a nonsectarian point of view. Since World War II, the schools have become increasingly secular, owing to litigation based on the idea of separation of church and state. Even though the schools are basically secular, they are not antireligious.

SELF–REVIEW QUIZ

1 The educational function of the school is which of the following:

a. transmission of academic skills and culture of contemporary society

b. teaching pupils to do better the things they would do anyway

c. to effect changes leading to a more ideal society

d. both *a* and *b*

e. both *a* and c

2 Approximately ________ percent of all Americans over twenty-five years of age have completed a high school education.

a. 25

b. 50

c. 75

d. 85

3 Approximately ________ percent of all Americans over twenty-five years of age have completed four years of college.

a. 5

b. 10

c. 25
d. 45

4 The subculture of a school is determined in part by:
a. peer culture
b. values of educators
c. culture of the community
d. all of the above
e. *a* and *b*

5 As a social institution, the school is second only to the ________ in terms of its potential influence on individual behavior.
a. church
b. family
c. press
d. television
e. peer group

6 The middle-class home emphasizes the importance of education because:
a. It teaches democratic procedures.
b. It improves the mind.
c. It provides opportunity for achievement striving.
d. All of the above.
e. *b* and *c*.

7 Children from the ________ class are most receptive and responsive to the typical school curriculum.
a. lower-lower
b. middle
c. upper
d. upper-lower
e. none of the above

8 Adolescents from the lower class tend to:
a. drop out
b. persist
c. make better grades than average, if they stay
d. participate in many extracurricular activities

9 Children from the lower class comprise approximately what fraction of our elementary school pupils?
a. one-fifth
b. one-third
c. one-half
d. two-thirds

10 The Supreme Court decision in the Schempp case declared which of the following unconstitutional in the public schools?
a. prayer
b. course in comparative religion
c. secular festivities at Christmas
d. baccalaureate service

REFERENCES

Conant, J. B.: *Slums and Suburbs,* McGraw-Hill Book Company, New York, 1961.

Davis, A.: *Social Class Influences upon Learning,* Harvard University Press, Cambridge, Mass., 1948.

Davis, A., and R. J. Havighurst: "Social Class and Color Differences in Child Rearing," *American Sociological Review,* 11:689–710, 1946.

English, H. B., and Ava C. English: *Dictionary of Psychological and Psychoanalytical Terms,* Longmans, Green & Co., Inc., New York, 1958.

Havighurst, R. J., P. J. Bowman, G. P. Liddle, C. V. Matthews, and J. V. Pierce: *Growing Up in River City,* John Wiley & Sons, Inc., New York, 1962.

Havighurst, R. J., and Bernice L. Neugarten: *Society and Education,* Allyn and Bacon, Inc., Boston, 1962.

Hollingshead, A. B.: *Elmtown's Youth,* John Wiley & Sons, Inc., New York, 1949.

Kahl, J. A.: "Educational and Occupational Aspirations of 'Common Man'," *Harvard Educational Review,* 23:186–203, 1953.

Raths, L. E., and S. Abrahamson: *Student Status and Social Class,* Modern Education Service, Bronxville, N.Y., 1951.

U.S. Department of Commerce: *Statistical Abstract of the United States,* 85th ed., 1964.

the school and the socialization process

DONALD L. LANTZ

The potential behavior that students learn at school covers an exceedingly wide range. Besides teaching academic competency, one of the major purposes of schools is to help students learn behavior that is healthy and useful. The extent to which schools accomplish these purposes is dependent on the interaction and effects of certain variables. The teacher is responsible for creating situations in the classroom in which socialization occurs, but teacher behavior is only one of the variables that influence student learning. At least four classes of variables influence the quality of the socialization process in the schools. These variables are: (1) environment, (2) pupil, (3) teacher, and (4) the interaction of pupil and teacher behavior.

Much of the behavior that a student learns is contingent on environmental variables, such as school location (slums or suburbs), school organization (traditional or "activity" oriented), and community economic factors.

The variables associated with the learner—his attitudes, interests, and abilities—are crucial in their influence on what he will learn, how well he will learn it, and what changes will occur in his behavior.

Teachers' personalities and professional characteristics are two of the variables that influence the socialization process in the classroom. Many educators assume that certain personality traits of teachers, such as attitudes toward pupils, affect what pupils learn. The specific knowledge and skills that a teacher has acquired through professional training constitute a second component of teacher variables.

Classroom behavior variables include not only the behavior of the teacher and pupils but also the interaction of the two. The classroom provides a situation in which the teacher can translate her professional learning into actual behavior designed to effect changes in pupil behavior. However, teachers and pupils alike are influenced by environmental variables and by the way they perceive each other's behavior.

The Socialization Process

The child is socialized in part by a process of reinforcing some behavior and withholding reinforcement for other behavior. This is perhaps an oversimplified description of the process of socialization, but a tenable one. During the process of socialization, children learn certain patterns of behavior. The following are two examples:

1. *A student who continuously strives for high achievement in school exhibits a pattern of behavior that is sometimes labeled a "need to achieve."*
2. *A student who is constantly fighting or looking for fights with other children exhibits a pattern of behavior that is frequently labeled a "need for aggression."*

1 A student who continuously strives for high achievement in school is said to demonstrate a ________ ________ ________.

need to achieve

2 Since the process of socialization varies, different patterns of behavior may be acquired. Children who have been raised differently acquire different patterns of ________.

behavior

3 The process of socialization varies for children raised in different social classes. We would expect that children from different social classes would have ________ patterns of behavior. Sometimes these various patterns of behavior are labeled as various ________.

different

needs

4 If children from different classes have different patterns of behavior, the acquisition of the different patterns of behavior is induced in part by differences in the ________ process.

socialization

5 Children from different status groups seem to be motivated differently by incentives offered by the teacher. Differential student motivation to a given incentive is due in part to differences in the ________ of students.

needs

motivated

6 Incentives represent goals which serve to satisfy acquired needs. Let's say that a gold star on a paper represents teacher approval. A child who "needs" this type of approval presumably will be _______ to obtain a gold star on his paper.

goals/routes

needs

7 The teacher, to a large extent, controls both the need-satisfying goals that are available to students and the available routes to these goals. Teacher behavior usually determines both the _______ and the _______ to these goals in the classroom that will satisfy psychological _______ of students.

socialization

8 The child learns what behavior is desirable and what behavior is undesirable in school by the _______ process.

socializing

9 The teacher helps to perform the function of _______ the child.

behavior

10 A teacher helps to perform this function by organizing learning experiences which permit the learning of behavior desired by society. The process of socialization involves changes in _______.

teacher

11 As a socializing agent, the teacher communicates the expectations of society to students. Students are made aware of the behavior expected by society through the _______.

values (expectations)

12 The teacher may not be aware that he is communicating these expectations, but he has internalized these values and his behavior is influenced by them. During a spelling bee the teacher teaches not only spelling but also _______ of society.

values (expectations)

13 The way in which a teacher communicates the expectations of society may be illustrated by his behavior in giving a spelling test. He states the word that is to be spelled and then uses it in a sentence as follows: "Property—You must respect the property of others." The teacher is teaching not only spelling but also the respect of others' property, which is one of the many _______ of society.

communicate (teach)

14 Teachers who have internalized a middle-class value system unconsciously tend to _______ middle-class values to students.

encourage (reinforce)

15 A child learns that academic achievement is important because parents and teachers ________ behavior which represents this value.

reinforced
punished

16 An individual who has been exposed to vulgar language at home does not learn that this kind of verbal behavior is in poor taste unless he is exposed to situations in which such behavior is not ________ or in which he might be ________ for it.

teacher

17 As in the family, the child learns in school what adult standards are. He finds out what acceptable standards are by a system of rewards and punishments controlled by the ________.

As one phase of the socialization process, the school has assumed the responsibility of teaching patterns of behavior that presumably are consonant with democratic ideals. The school cannot assume that appropriate behavioral patterns will be learned simply by exposing students to facts. Schools in the United States are responsible for teaching not only academic fundamentals but also behavior patterns valued in a democracy.

The Identification Process

identification

18 In the identification process, an individual acquires without direct teaching the attitudes and values of another person or group. A student who accepts as his own the values of his favorite teacher may have learned them in part through the process of ________.

attitudes (values) /
behavior

19 As students identify with an individual or group, they tend to acquire not only the ________ but also the ________ of the group or individual, provided these are reinforced.

reinforced

20 Students will identify with teachers if the behavior and attitudes they identify with are ________.

relationship

21 Cogan (1956) found a significant positive relationship between (*a*) self-initiated and required work performed by students and (*b*) teacher behavior that students perceived as warm and friendly. This suggests that the identification process of student with teacher might contribute to the ________ that exists between perceived teacher behavior and amount of work done.

attitudes (values, etc.)

22 It is assumed in Cogan's study that, through the process of identification with the teacher, students acquired intellectual ________ and hence did more required and self-initiated work.

A study at Bennington College (Newcomb, 1958) investigated the attitudes of girls toward public affairs over a four-year period. The purpose of this study was to determine whether or not the college atmosphere had any effect on changing attitudes of the girls. This study was conducted during the Great Depression and the New Deal, i.e., the 1930s. Many of the girls had conservative social and political views, whereas the faculty generally supported a liberal point of view. It was found that the girls who most strongly identified with their parents were the girls whose attitudes changed least.

greatest

23 Girls who identified themselves with the college community changed their attitudes to the ________ extent.

identification

24 The Bennington study indicates that a college can influence student attitudes about public affairs, but the extent of the influence is partly dependent on the ________ of the students with the college community.

perception

25 The teaching-learning process is influenced by perceptions which the student and teacher have of each other. An important aspect of the teaching-learning process is students' ________ of teacher behavior.

parent

26 Children tend to perceive teachers, like parents, as authority figures. In the classroom the child is always in a role that is subordinate to the teacher. In the elementary grades, at least, the teacher becomes a ________ surrogate.

perception

27 In a sense, the teacher is a stimulus event which influences the student's behavior. A student's behavior is influenced by his ________ of the teacher's behavior.

teacher

28 Likewise, we can conclude that his own perception of students' behavior often influences the ________.

needs

29 A teacher's behavior may be modified by his inferring student needs from student behavior and attempting to help students satisfy these ________.

need

30 If a teacher's behavior is in part determined by his perception of the student's needs, then the teacher may present appropriate goals for the student that will be _______ satisfying.

REVIEW: *The interaction that takes place between the teacher and student is in part a function of the perceptions that the teacher and student have of each other. The purpose of the teacher in the interaction is to stimulate goal direction that will satisfy student needs and bring about desirable changes in student behavior. Students who identify with teachers and the school would be expected to exhibit high morale and fewer discipline problems than students who do not identify with teachers and the school program.*

Studies of Teacher Behavior

Considering the importance we assume classroom behavior to have, we know little about it and its effects on learning. Some important studies which assess the relationship of teacher behavior to pupil behavior are described in the following section.

Dominative and Integrative Behavior

One of the earliest significant studies concerned reliably observing and recording teacher and pupil behaviors. This study was conducted with elementary children by Anderson and his colleagues. Various behavior categories were determined which resulted in the description of two main types of teacher behavior, namely, dominative and integrative behaviors (Anderson et al., 1945, 1946a, 1946b).

dominative

31 Using physical restraint or punishment, applying verbal threat or ridicule, and demanding rigid conformity to rules were operational examples of _______ behavior in this study.

dominative

32 An elementary teacher who remarks, "Stop! Don't do it that way! I'll tell you how to do it, and if you can't do what you're supposed to do, you'll have to go out into the hall," illustrates _______ teacher behavior.

Teacher behavior often may be a more important factor in determining what a student learns in the classroom than the curriculum itself.

In the Anderson studies, dominative teacher behavior tended to restrict the child's activities and lead to distracted, aggressive, noncooperative conduct from the pupils. Integrative teacher behavior was defined as that which expanded the child's opportunities for self-direction and for cooperative behavior with the teacher and peers.

dominative

33 Behavior characterized by constant control in the form of commands and criticism was classified as ________ behavior.

integrative

34 Teacher behavior that permits a child to use and develop his own ideas was classified as ________ behavior.

integrative

35 Encouraging pupil participation, asking questions of pupils, and showing interest in pupils were operational examples of ________ behavior on the part of teachers.

Teacher behavior patterns in the classroom tend to filter down to the students.

dominative

36 Teachers use a variety of teaching techniques. Seldom does one find a teacher whose behavior in the classroom is either totally dominative or integrative. Many teachers, however, exhibit a higher proportion of ______ behavior than integrative behavior.

dominative

37 The behavioral pattern of teachers in the classroom tends to diffuse among the students in the classroom. Domination tends to spread throughout the classroom of a teacher whose behavior consists predominantly of ______ contact with students (Anderson et al., 1945, 1946a, 1946b).

Children in rooms with teachers rated as dominative were rated resistant to authority and nonconforming. These pupils whispered more, paid less attention to what the teacher was saying, and did not *persevere as much with their lessons in class.*

dominative
nonconforming

38 This suggests that ______ behavior on the part of teachers leads to more ______ behavior on the part of students.

frustration

39 Reactions to the dominative type of teacher suggest that the children were more frustrated and more hostile toward dominative behavior. Anderson indicates that these reactions are consistent with the ______-aggression hypothesis.

REVIEW: *Information derived from the above frames indicates that domination on the part of the teacher tends to elicit nonconforming and frustrated behaviors on the part of students.*

integrative

40 Children in rooms of teachers rated as demonstrating essentially integrative behavior were themselves also rated as showing more ______ behavior.

integrative behavior

41 A teacher whose behavior consists predominantly of integrative contact with students encourages further ______ ______ on the part of students.

42 Anderson's studies suggests that a teacher's behavior generalizes among pupils even when the teacher is no longer in the room. We would then expect a class which had a teacher rated high in dominative behavior to tend to behave in a ______ and ______ way when the teacher was absent from the room.

frustrated / nonconforming

In the Anderson studies, children who were studied in grade 2 were also studied in grade 3. Some children's behavior in grade 3 was different from that in the second grade, being more consonant with the behavior of the new teacher in grade 3.

43 Teachers tended to behave the same way (integratively or dominantly) year after year, but children's behavior tended to vary with the teacher they had. For example, most children were rated cooperative, spontaneous, and interested in their work under an ______ teacher.

integrative

44 When children were passed from an integrative teacher to a dominative teacher, they were then rated as more ______ in their behavior.

uncooperative (routinized, nonspontaneous and disinterested)

45 Perhaps one of the most important implications of these studies is that dominative teachers may get outward submission from pupils, but they do *not* tend to elicit cooperation and ______ in schoolwork.

spontaneity (interest)

46 The teacher more than any other individual sets the behavior pattern for the class. The main direction of behavior influence in these studies was from the ______ to the pupils.

teacher

REVIEW: *A high proportion of dominative teacher contacts results in pupils being more easily distracted from schoolwork and showing greater compliance to, as well as rejection of, the teacher domination. Other things being equal, pupils who find it difficult to work during a teacher's absence from the room are likely to have a teacher who tends to be dominative (Anderson, 1945, 1946a, 1946b). A high proportion of integrative teacher contact results in pupils showing more spontaneity, initiative, voluntary social contribution, and acts of problem solving. A classroom that shows a high proportion of self-initiated work is more likely to have a teacher whose behavior tendency is integrative (other things being equal).*

At this point, perhaps, it is significant to point out a study by Jersild (1954). A survey of students at all levels of primary and secondary school indicated that more negative than positive reactions toward school were given. Presumably, these student reactions are related to the ways in which teachers react to children. Jersild's and Anderson's studies with children of elementary school age clearly indicate that the type of leadership in the classroom is associated with changes in student behavior. Much more research needs to be conducted before we can make estimates of the effect of classroom leadership on the behaviors of high school and college students.

maladjusted

47 Snyder (1947) suggested that some evidence indicates that maladjustment in teachers is related to _______ behavior in pupils.

maladjustment

48 Snyder's view should be tempered with the realization that some kinds of teacher maladjustment are more likely to be related to pupil _______ than others.

teacher maladjustment

49 Some research studies lead us to assume that teacher maladjustment is not necessarily traumatic to children. Thompson (1952) has pointed out that problems of _______ _______ are partially mitigated "by the remarkable resiliency with which children respond to social pressure from all adults."

Autocratic, Democratic, and Laissez-faire Leadership

Lewin, Lippitt, and White (1939) studied the effects of controlled leadership behavior on eleven-year-old boys. This study used informal boys' play groups rather than formal school classes. The leadership techniques (autocratic, democratic, and laissez-faire) and the leaders were rotated for each of the play groups, and the technique was also rotated among the leaders. The technique of leadership used by the leaders was refined by extensive training to minimize differences among leaders.

In the authoritarian group, the activities of the group were determined by the leader. The outcomes indicated that the play groups under an authoritarian leadership technique spent a high percentage of their time on productive work (50 to 80 percent) when the leader was present, but exhibited many expressions of discontent and little interest in their work. In the laissez-faire group, the boys were free to do as they pleased. The play groups with laissez-faire leadership spent much of the time loafing, exhibited low morale, and produced few outcomes that were satisfying to the group or to individuals when the leader was present. In the democratic group, the leader acted as part of the group, and activities were the result of group decisions. The play groups under a democratic leadership technique spent approximately 50 percent of the time on intensive work, exhibited high morale, and showed high interest in the outcome of their projects.

training

50 The technique of leadership used by the leader was refined by ______ and was rotated among each of the play groups and among the leaders for purposes of controlling the experiment.

leadership

51 The ______ techniques were labeled "autocratic," "democratic," and "laissez-faire."

leadership

52 In the rotation of the leader and the technique of leadership, it was found that the ______ technique was highly related to the outcomes of the play groups, whereas the group leader as a person was not highly related to the outcomes of the group.

interest

53 Boys under authoritarian leaders spent a good deal of time at work on projects in the presence of the leader but demonstrated little ______ in the projects.

less (reduced)

54 When the authoritarian leader left the room, the percentage of time spent in work dropped considerably (dropping from 50 to 80 percent down to 17 to 30 percent). Under authoritarian leadership, the work involvement is considerably ______ when the leader is absent compared with when he is present.

present

55 When the laissez-faire leader left the boys, the percentage of time spent in work involvement increased. Boys under laissez-faire leadership spent a greater portion of time in work involvement when the leader was absent than when he was ______. A possible reason for increased productive activity when the leader was absent was that one of the boys assumed leadership.

laissez-faire

56 High morale was *not* characteristic of play groups under either authoritarian or ______ techniques of leadership.

democratic

57 Play groups that exhibited the highest morale were influenced by ______ leadership.

presence

58 Boys under democratic leadership spent approximately the same percentage of time on work whether or not the leader was present. The amount of time spent on work under democratic leadership was not dependent on the ______ of the leader.

democratic

59 Children who decorated their rooms with their projects most likely made their projects under ______ leadership. (Remember that in the Anderson studies children who were in classrooms of an integrative teacher showed more interest in schoolwork than children under a dominative teacher.)

autocratic

60 Children who threw their projects away after they made them most likely made their projects under ______ leadership.

REVIEW: *It is not likely that one would find classroom teachers whose leadership behavior is consistently autocratic or laissez-faire, as in the Lewin, Lippitt, and White study, but the importance of this study lies in the suggestion that the leadership role of an adult is a strong determinant of child behavior.*

Direct and Indirect Influence

Flanders (1963, 1965) studied the influence of teacher verbal behavior on students' freedom of action, attitudes, and achievement. Teachers control students' freedom to respond by both direct and indirect influence. Student behaviors indicating autonomy of decision were designated as freedom of action.

It was found that teachers who used a high proportion of indirect influence but were flexible in the type of influence used to control students' freedom increased both student participation in the classroom and independence of the teacher. Generally speaking, teachers who exhibited a high proportion of indirect influence to direct influence also were flexible in the pattern of teacher influence. Flanders also reported that scores on an inventory developed for measurement of classroom attitudes and achievement were positively related to scores for indirect influence and flexibility of the teacher.

freedom

61 Student behaviors indicating choice of action were designated as ________ of action.

indirect

62 Teachers control students' freedom to respond by direct influence as well as by ________ influence.

direct

63 A teacher who gives facts, opinions, directions, or commands to which a student is expected to reply would be classified as a ________ influence.

indirect

64 Teachers who accept student feelings and ideas, who praise and encourage them, and who ask questions of students were classified as demonstrating ________ influence.

teacher

65 It was found that teachers who tended to be inflexible and who used predominantly direct influence in the classroom increased student dependence on the ________.

Flanders reported a decrease.

66 Would you expect a (decrease/increase) in voluntary student participation and a restriction of learning activities when teachers control student behavior by direct influence?

indirect influence

67 Above-average scores on an inventory of classroom attitudes were associated with above-average scores for ________ ________ of the teacher.

positively

68 Teachers who had above-average scores for indirect influence were perceived by students as above average in "fairness" in the classroom. Students' perceptions of teachers' fairness with rewards and punishments were (positively/negatively) related to above-average scores of indirect influence.

positively

69 Students in classrooms (social studies and mathematics) in which the teacher had a flexible pattern of influence and a high ratio of indirect influence achieved more than students in classrooms in which direct influence predominated. Student achievement was (positively/negatively) related to above-average scores of indirect influence.

REVIEW: *Flanders' studies point out that the kind of teacher influence used in the classroom is related to students' classroom attitudes, dependency on the teacher, freedom of action, and, finally, academic achievement.*

Some years ago, Jersild (1940) reported a study of children's preferences in teacher behavior. American school children rated the following teacher characteristics:

Physical appearance—attractiveness in dress and person

Disciplinary qualities—fairness, impartiality, consistency in administering punishment

Teaching qualities—presenting material in interesting, enthusiastic, democratic way

"Human" qualities—kind versus "mean"; even-tempered versus "hot-tempered"; cheerful versus "grouchy"; etc.

Jersild:
1. "human"
2. discipline
3. physical appearance
4. teaching

70 Try to guess the order in which American school children rated the teacher characteristics. Rank them 1, 2, 3, and 4, and then compare your rankings with those actually given by the children. Remember, you are concerned with what children *like* about teachers.

human / disciplinary

71 Leeds and Cook (1947) reported the same ranking for children in upper elementary grades as Jersild did for children in lower grades. If "human" and "disciplinary" qualities are important reinforcers for student behavior, it seems evident that a teacher should demonstrate these ________ and ________ qualities as part of her repertoire of general characteristics.

No

72 Does the above study indicate that teachers should behave as students desire them to? ________.

Teacher Values

It is assumed by some (e.g., Warner, 1953) that the pattern of teacher behavior in the classroom stems from the teacher's own personal standard. On the basis of this assumption, we would expect the internalized values of a teacher to be positively associated with his pattern of behavior in the classroom.

middle class

73 Warner (1953) estimated that 94 percent of American teachers were from the middle class. That is, the overwhelming proportion of teachers in public schools are members of the ________ ________.

punishments

74 The middle-class value orientation taught in the public schools is usually not part of the formal curriculum but rather is taught informally through a system of rewards and ________ administered by the teacher.

middle-class

75 On the basis of the assumption in the information above, we would expect most teachers to reinforce student behavior that is oriented toward ________-________ values.

rewards

76 Davis and Dollard (1940) reported that teachers distribute rewards and punishments initially on the basis of social class status and not on students' classroom performance. Lower-class children tend to receive a preponderance of punishment while middle-class children have a monopoly on social ________.

punishment

77 The middle-class child learns to discriminate what behavior will be reinforced. The lower-class child, on the other hand, learns to avoid ________.

distribution

78 The middle-class set of values of the teacher is a major determinant in the distribution of social rewards (privileges and approval) and punishment in the classroom. This orientation of values in part determines the ________ of social rewards and punishment and likewise determines the kind of pupil behavior that reinforces the teacher (Miller and Dollard, 1941).

reinforce

79 A teacher who socially reinforces a middle-class child may enable that child to maintain good grades and citizenship. The student's good grades and citizenship in turn ________ the teacher's behavior.

middle-class
lower-class

80 This interaction between child and teacher creates a phenomenon of circular reinforcement which results in the teacher's giving preferential treatment to ________-________ children and discriminating against ________-________ children.

teacher

81 Not all educators share the assumption that social class values are manifested in teacher behavior (Dahlke, 1958). It is possible that the frame of reference for classroom behavior is not the internalized values of the ________ but those stemming from his professional training.

REVIEW: *Assuming that most teachers are members of the middle class and that teacher behavior in the classroom is derived from middle-class values, the difference in school experience that we would predict for middle- and lower-class children is middle class—success in school and lower class—failure and frustration.*

Socialization and School Achievement

Teachers use an ordinary system of rewards—grades, promotion, compliments, honors, and leadership positions —according to some judgment of student performance. Many times there are grade expectations for achievement, and the child is judged by how he measures up to these expectations.

The following section discusses a few studies concerning the relationship between teacher behavior and students' perception of teachers, and the achievement of students.

Student Attitudes

82 Teachers are obviously important sources of information as well as means by which students learn to gauge adult reactions and behavior. In other words, teachers are responsible for a student's ______ level as well as for his social conditioning.

achievement

83 Much speculation and relatively little research has been presented about the relationships between children's perceptions of school and their ______ in school.

achievement

84 One study has indicated that there are positive relationships between students' ______ of school and their achievement (Malpass, 1953).

perceptions

85 Relationships were found between students' reactions to school and the grades they received, but not between their perceptions of school and scores on standardized ______ tests.

achievement

Schools assist students to acquire attitudes associated with responsible citizenship.

subjective

86 In other words, students' subjective reports about school were related to ______ reports about students from teachers.

achievement

87 However, subjective reactions about school were *not* related to objective ratings of school ______, i.e., standardized test scores.

Box 1. School Achievement and Pupil Behavior

A major study relating school achievement to pupil reactions was proposed by Sears (1940). She devised a reliable method for designating students' level of aspiration about school achievement. The subjects for this study were students from the fourth, fifth, and sixth grades; they were selected on the basis of their history of success or failure in reading and/or arithmetic. Another criterion for selection of subjects was their serious concern about the quality of their performance on the experimental task. The experimental task for the students was to estimate the time it would take them to complete a task in the area of reading and/or arithmetic. The first part of the study consisted of asking the children to estimate their performance (level of aspiration) in reading and arithmetic under neutral conditions. It was presumed that their successes or failures in school would affect their level of aspiration. The children who had a history of failure were more variable in estimating their expected performance than the children who had a history of success. Also the discrepancy between the level of aspiration and the actual performance tended to be larger with children who had experienced failure than with those who had experienced success.

The second part of the study consisted of experimentally inducing success and failure. Half of each group were told that they did very well on the task, and the other half of each group were told that they had done very poorly. Being told how they had performed was presumed to affect level aspiration on succeeding achievement tests. When asked about their expectations on subsequent tests, the praised group showed an expectation of improvement and actually did perform better. The group that were told they had done poorly tended to show unrealistic levels of aspiration. These pupils either tended to set their goals too high or were too low in their score expectancy.

The effects of immediate success and failure as induced in this experiment are similar to the effects of long-term success and failure.

aspiration

88 In the Sears (1940) study, the pupils' achievement level was related to expectation. The study strongly suggests that level of _______ influences school performance.

level of aspiration

89 Students who had a history of success in school tended to be realistic in setting their _______ _______ _______.

unrealistic

90 Students who had experienced considerable failure tended to be _______ in setting their level of aspiration.

performance

91 Under experimentally induced success conditions, the students' level of aspiration tended to correspond realistically to their _______.

level of aspiration / performance

92 Under experimentally induced failure conditions, there were large differences between students' _______ _______ _______ and their _______.

raise

lower

93 Students who experienced success tended to _______ their level of aspiration on the next task while students who experienced failure tended to _______ their level of aspiration.

expectation

94 A special reward may be attractive to a child, but because of his past experience of working for such a reward, he has little hope of attaining it. The child's past experience and his concept of his ability to achieve the reward influence his _______ of achievement (Worell, 1956).

expectation

95 As an example, a student may place a high value on a high honor point ratio but have little _______ of attaining it because of his past experience.

Motivating Factors in Achievement

Thompson and Hunnicutt (1944) investigated the effect of praise and blame on the work achievement of introvert and extrovert fifth-grade children. Praise consisted of a G (meaning "Good"), and blame consisted of a P (meaning "Poor") placed on pupils' papers.

introvert

96 Figure 14 shows that the extrovert-blamed group made the largest achievement gains, and the _______-blamed group made the least achievement gains.

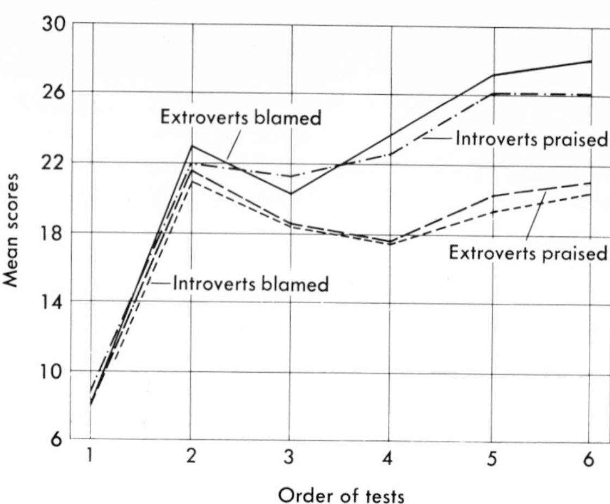

Figure 14. Effects of praise and blame on "introverts" and "extroverts." SOURCE: Adapted from G. G. Thompson and C. W. Hunnicutt, "The Effects of Repeated Praise or Blame on the Work Achievements of Introverts or Extroverts," *Journal of Educational Psychology*, 38: 264, 1944. Used by permission.

extroverts

97 The study also showed that praise increased the work output of introverts until it was higher than that of introverts who were blamed or ________ who were praised.

personality (behavior)

98 This study does not suggest recipes for applying praise or blame in the classroom. It does demonstrate that praise and blame have different effects on children with different ________ traits.

teacher

99 The chain of interaction between teacher and pupil is arbitrarily considered to start with behavior of the ________, which may be thought of as a source of stimuli for pupils.

the behaviors of teachers and pupils

100 (Refer to diagram, page 309.) The central concern of Cogan's study is the relationship between +++++.

perceptions

101 This study reported that pupils' perceptions of teacher behavior tended to keep the pupils and social interaction central to the objective of teaching and that pupils' ________ were positively related to the amount of required and self-initiated work done by them.

Cogan (1958) studied the relationship of students' perceptions of teacher behavior and the amount of required and self-initiated schoolwork performed by students in response to teacher stimuli. This study assumed that teacher behavior as perceived by students influenced the nature and extent of schoolwork done by students.

Chain of Teacher-Pupil Interaction

The behaviors of teachers as perceived by pupils	influence the nature and extent of	1. The motivation of the pupils 2. communications with pupils 3. the classroom experiences	which may instigate

pupil behaviors 1. required schoolwork 2. self-initiated schoolwork	which may result in	pupil behavior change

perceptions
self-initiated

102 Pupils' _______ of teacher behavior that indicated teachers were interested in pupils were associated with the amount of required and _______-_______ work performed by pupils.

This study also showed that teacher behavior which gives pupils a position on the periphery of objectives shows an inverse relationship (though not statistically conclusive) to required and self-initiated work scores of pupils.

self-initiated

103 Students who perceived teachers as *not* interested in students tended to accomplish a lesser amount of required and _______-_______ work.

work

104 This study illustrates that certain teacher behaviors (as perceived by students) are significantly related to the amount of required and self-initiated _______ done by students.

105 Low achievers tend to receive more teacher contact than high achievers, but high achievers receive a higher quality of contact than _______ achievers (Hoehn, 1954).

low

106 Both the quantity and quality of contact a child receives from a teacher is partially dependent on his level of _______.

achievement

107 A caution should be introduced at this point. Are social class and achievement highly correlated? _______.

Yes

108 If teachers do in fact discriminate against lower-class children, would you expect this to lead to differential achievement? _______. Would differential achievement tend to reinforce teacher discrimination? +++++.

Yes
Yes, assuming Davis and Dollard's studies are valid

Most teachers encounter cheating in classroom examinations. It is possible that cheating occurs because a greater emphasis has been placed on winning (competitiveness for grades) than on learning.

109 An unwarranted emphasis on marks and grading may result in more _______ than would occur if emphasis were placed on learning.

cheating

REVIEW: *The studies presented in this section used different labels for teacher behavior. The important outcome derived from the studies is that teacher behavior is related to student behavior. The Anderson studies indicate that the direction of behavioral influence in the classroom is from the teacher to the student. Cogan's study demonstrated the importance of students' perceptions of teacher behavior. Students' perceptions of teacher behavior were related to the amount of required and self-initiated schoolwork performed by students. Flanders' study indicates that teachers may increase or decrease the dependency of students on teachers by controlling students' freedom to respond. The Lewin, Lippitt, and White study suggests that differences in leadership (teaching) technique are related to differences in child behavior. Leadership technique differences were more important than differences among leaders themselves.*

Peer Relationships in School

The influence of social relationships in school increases throughout the school years. The social relationships established at school by adolescents are much more influential than those established at school by younger children. The peer group is important in teaching the adolescent social skills, attitudes, and ways of adult living. The peer group also provides many identificands which are important in the socializing process. The peer group constitutes the group with whom an individual associates. Usually, the various members are approximately equal in status.

peer	***110*** The group of individuals with whom a child associates is typically designated as a ______ group.
socialization	***111*** Much of the child's experience at school involves social contacts with other pupils. These contacts influence the process of ______.
peers	***112*** A large portion of the child's school experience constitutes contact with his peers under the supervision of parent surrogates. A large amount and a wide variety of social learning will result from the child's contact with his ______.
peer	***113*** In the peer group, a child has approximately equal status with other members of the group. High school students and junior high school students do not typically belong to the same ______ group.
A "drugstore clique," members of a school athletic team, etc.	***114*** Peer groups are of many different kinds, ranging from informal play groups to highly organized clubs. Can you think of some examples? +++++.
more	***115*** The peer group in school becomes more important as a socializing agent as the child grows older. A student in high school is ______ likely to be influenced by his peer group than is a student in elementary school.
peers	***116*** As children grow older, they feel less bound to conform to adult patterns. Thus, the peer group creates its own standards of conduct. High school students are more concerned about how their ______ dress than the way adults dress.

117 A reference group is one in which an individual accepts as his own the standards of behavioral attitudes of the group. The peer group is the ________ group for students' learning appropriate sex roles and other behavior.

reference

118 The influence of intimate peers is greater during adolescence than at any other time, particularly as it relates to moral values (Peck and Havighurst, 1960). The development of a standard of moral behavior for an adolescent is influenced not only by his family but also by his ________ ________.

intimate peers

119 Conflict occasionally occurs between school officials and students concerning standards of dress and grooming. The wearing of shorts to class is one example of such ________. Perhaps you can think of others.

conflict

REVIEW: *The peer group helps determine what goals and knowledge are important to the individual. If the peer group believes that information about countries behind the iron curtain is important, a social studies unit on the iron curtain will provide goals that are need satisfying because they are related to peer approval.*

120 If a boy receives more reinforcement from being accepted by his peers than from receiving good grades, we may expect his behavior in the future to be less ________ oriented.

academically

121 Good grades and academic achievement have relatively low status for many peer groups. This situation exists because these goals are not so ________ as other activities in school.

reinforcing

122 The peer group influences the attitudes of its members because of pressures to conform set up by the ________ ________.

peer group

123 The pressure to ________ to attitudes in a peer group comes in the form of rejection of deviant members.

conform

124 Occasionally a role is learned that is not appropriate for the peer group. For example, a girl who had previously been an A student in arithmetic began making C's. When she was questioned about her change in performance, she replied, "Girls are not supposed to be good in arithmetic." This illustrates a conflict of values between the classroom and the ________ ________.

peer group

peer

125 Many students who are honest in other situations cheat on examinations. A possible reason for their cheating and not feeling dishonest is that the ________ group approves of cheating and the simple rationalization that "everyone cheats—it's a game."

norm (reference)

126 Occasionally, an individual may be a member of a group but not look to the group for a pattern of behavior. In this case, the individual is simply a member and does not use the group as a ________ for his behavior.

middle-class

127 The peer group usually reinforces the set of values of any given social status. A peer group composed of students from middle-class homes most likely reinforces ________-________ values.

did not

128 "The peer group appears to be less an organization than a reinforcer of moral values and behavior patterns . . ." (Peck and Havighurst, 1960, p. 182). The moral values reinforced within a peer group probably (did/did not) originate within the group itself.

middle-class

129 The peer group may become a means by which a lower-class boy learns the social mores of the middle class and thereby aspires to raise himself to ________-________ status.

sociometric

130 Sociometric tests are used to estimate the social interaction in a group. The extent of student interrelationships could be studied by a ________ test.

rejection

131 A typical question asked on sociometric tests is, "Whom would you like to work with on a project?" The intent of this question is to measure the extent of acceptance or ________ of individuals to the interaction of a group.

interaction

132 The extent of acceptance or rejection indicates the interaction of the group. There are many different kinds of questions that could be used in measuring the social ________ of a group.

sociogram

133 The data collected from a sociometric test can be plotted on paper as a diagram of the social interaction. The plotted information is then known as a ________.

sociometric

134 Some children seem always to be left out of activities by their peers. These children receive few choices by their peers on a ________ test.

135 Children who receive few, if any, choices from their peers for social interaction are frequently called neglectees and isolates (Gronlund, 1959). Children who are either overlooked or perceived as having an unpleasant appearance, being socially ineffective, or being socially aggressive are called ______ and ______.

neglectees / isolates

136 Children classified as neglectees on a sociometric test receive relatively few choices from their peers. Children classified as isolates receive no choices from their ______.

peers

137 Children who tend to be rated high in social and athletic skill are often designated as ______.

stars

138 A major characteristic of dropouts from school is their inability to find belongingness in a group. We might expect a greater number of ______ and ______ to drop out of school than stars.

neglectees / isolates

REVIEW: *Sociometric tests help us identify three classes of students based on the number of times they are chosen by their peers. These classes are stars, neglectees, and isolates.*

139 The sociogram indicates only the interrelationship of children. A sociogram indicates which children are popular but does not tell us ______ they are popular.

why

140 After the interrelationship of students has been determined, teachers are interested in finding the causes of social maladjustments and then in designing a program to promote ______ maturity and greater acceptability.

social

REVIEW: *A graphic representation of the association of children (such as mutual pairs, cliques, or isolates) is called a sociogram.*

SUMMARY

The school not only teaches certain basic knowledge and skills but also provides many opportunities for social interaction. Thus, a child learns the ways of society through social relationships at school. The teacher, by virtue of her position, frequently becomes a "significant other" to stu-

dents. Thus, teachers become models for students' attitudes and behaviors. It is important to remember, however, that teachers do not become models for all students.

Because students spend a great deal of time in classrooms, teachers are potentially important agents in the process of socialization. Teacher behavior is assumed to be probably the most important ingredient in education. Although they use different terminology, the independent studies of teacher behavior by Anderson, by Lewin, Lippitt, and White, by Cogan, and by Flanders support one another concerning the effects of teacher behavior on student behavior. A major finding of the Anderson studies was that teachers who behave in a particular way evoke similar behavior from students. The Lewin, Lippitt, and White study indicated that the particular type of leadership used in boys' clubs had an effect on the type of behavior exhibited by the boys and on their orientation to their tasks. Flanders' study points out that teacher flexibility and the kind of influence used are related to student attitudes and achievement. Cogan's study indicated that students' perceptions of teacher behavior were related to the amount of required and self-initiated schoolwork of students. A note of caution must be exercised here. Although a number of studies relating teacher behavior and student behavior and learning show signs of promise, we do not have conclusive and definite answers to questions of teacher behavior and its effect on students.

The peer groups with whom students interact at school also have a large effect on student behavior. As students progress through school, there is a succession of peer groups to which they belong; each group has its own norms and values which it transmits to the child. Some of the peer values may reinforce those which the school teaches, and others may encourage the child to reject certain values which the school teaches.

SELF–REVIEW QUIZ

1 In the Bennington College study, the girls who changed their attitudes least while at Bennington were those who:

a. were most influenced by their immediate friends
b. were most strongly identified with their parents
c. were identified with the college community
d. were in strong conflict with their families

2 Because of the value system that most teachers hold, they are most likely to have conflicts with children from the:

a. lower class
b. middle class

c. upper class
d. both *b* and c
e. both *a* and *b*

3 Children having a dominative teacher are likely:
a. to develop a respect for people in authority
b. to develop a high interest in the task
c. to develop behavior patterns similar to those of the teacher
d. to depend on their own ingenuity
e. none of these

4 The Lewin, Lippitt, and White study indicated that:
a. The laissez-faire group stopped work in the leader's absence.
b. The authoritarian group work involvement was highest when the leader was absent.
c. High morale was characteristic of the laissez-faire group.
d. Activities in the democratic group were determined entirely by the boys.

5 Teachers who use a preponderance of direct influence and who are also inflexible tend to:
a. increase students' freedom to respond
b. increase students' achievement level
c. enable students to set realistic goals
d. increase students' dependency
e. increase students' work output

6 In Cogan's study, students' perceptions of teacher behavior were related to:
a. amount of self-initiated schoolwork
b. amount of required schoolwork
c. both of the above
d. neither *a* nor *b*

7 The Sears study compared pupils with histories of failure in reading and arithmetic with those having histories of success. It was found that the successful students were more inclined to:
a. set their level of aspiration realistically
b. set their level of aspiration unrealistically high
c. set their level of aspiration unrealistically low
d. be extremely variable in goal-setting behavior

8 Students' level of aspiration ordinarily:
a. increases following failure
b. decreases following success
c. both of the above
d. neither *a* nor *b*

9 Children who are likely to drop out of school frequently receive scores on a sociometric test that are labeled:
a. neglectees and isolates

b. stars
c. passive
d. loners
e. cliquish

REFERENCES

Anderson, H. H., and Helen M. Brewer: "Studies of Teachers' Classroom Personalities: I. Dominatively and Socially Integrative Behavior of Kindergarten Teachers," *Applied Psychology Monograph,* no. 6, 1945.

Anderson, H. H., and Helen M. Brewer: "Studies of Teachers' Classroom Personalities: II. Effects of Teachers' Dominative and Integrative Contacts on Children's Behavior," *Applied Psychology Monograph,* no. 8, 1946. (a)

Anderson, H. H., J. E. Brewer, and Mary F. Reed: "Studies of Teachers' Classroom Personalities: III. Follow-up Studies of the Effects of Dominative and Integrative Contacts on Children's Behavior," *Applied Psychology Monograph,* no. 11, 1946. (b)

Cogan, M. L.: "Theory and Design of a Study of Teacher-Pupil Interaction," *Harvard Educational Review,* 26:315–342, 1956.

Cogan, M. L.: "The Behavior of Teachers and the Productive Behavior of Their Pupils," *Journal of Experimental Education,* 27:89–124, 1958.

Dahlke, H. O.: *Values in Culture and Classroom,* Harper & Row, Publishers, Incorporated, New York, 1958.

Davis, A., and J. Dollard: *Children of Bondage,* American Council on Education, Washington, D.C., 1940.

Flanders, N. A.: *Helping Teachers Change Their Behavior,* School of Education, University of Michigan, Ann Arbor, Mich., 1963. (Multilith.)

Flanders, N. A.: "Teacher Influence, Pupil Attitudes, and Achievement," *Cooperative Research Monograph,* no. 12 (OE–25040) U.S. Department of Health, Education, and Welfare, 1965.

Gronlund, N. E.: *Sociometry in the Classroom,* Harper & Row, Publishers, Incorporated, New York, 1959.

Hoehn, A. J.: "A Study of Social Status Differentiation in the Classroom Behavior of Nineteen Third Grade Teachers," *Journal of Social Psychology,* 39:269–292, 1954.

Jersild, A. T.: "Characteristics of Teachers Who Are Liked Best and Disliked Most," *Journal of Experimental Education,* 9:139–151, 1940.

Jersild, A. T.: *Child Psychology,* Prentice-Hall, Inc., Englewood Cliffs, N.J., 1954.

Leeds, C. P., and W. W. Cook: "The Construction and Differential Value of a Scale for Determining Pupil-Teacher Attitudes," *Journal of Experimental Education,* 16:149–159, 1947.

Lewin, K., R. Lippitt, and R. K. White: "Patterns of Aggressive Behavior in Experimentally Created Social Climates," *Journal of Social Psychology,* 10:271–299, 1939.

Malpass, L.: "Some Relationships of Students' Perception of School and Their Achievement," *Journal of Educational Psychology,* 44:475–482,1953.

Miller, N. E., and J. C. Dollard: *Social Learning and Imitation,* Yale University Press, New Haven, Conn., 1941.

Newcomb, T. M.: "Attitude Development as a Function of Reference Groups: The Bennington Study," in E. E. Maccoby, T. M. Newcomb, and E. L. Hartley (eds.), *Readings in Social Psychology,* Holt, Rinehart and Winston, Inc., New York, 1958, pp. 265–275.

Peck, R. F., and R. J. Havighurst: *The Psychology of Character Development,* John Wiley & Sons, Inc., New York, 1960.

Sears, Pauline: "Levels of Aspiration in Academically Successful and Unsuccessful Children," *Journal of Abnormal and Social Psychology,* 35: 498–536, 1940.

Snyder, W. U.: "Do Teachers Cause Maladjustment?" *Journal of Exceptional Children,* 14:40–56, 1947.

Thompson, G. G., and C. W. Hunnicutt: "The Effect of Repeated Praise or Blame on the Work Achievement of Introverts and Extroverts," *Journal of Educational Psychology,* 38:257–266, 1944.

Warner, W. L.: *American Life: Dream and Reality,* The University of Chicago Press, Chicago, 1953.

Worell, L.: "The Effect of Goal Value on Expectancy," *Journal of Abnormal and Social Psychology,* 53:48–53, 1956.

the church as a social institution

HERSCHEL E. ASELTINE

The behavioral scientist is concerned with understanding, explaining, and, hopefully, predicting human behavior. At physiological levels, where deprivation, pain, or pleasure are directly related to behavior, even a nonscientist can perceive how food deprivation will result in food seeking, electric shock will lead to withdrawal, and so on for both human and subhuman species. There is another type of behavior, however, which is of a different order. It is not observed among rats or pigeons, sheep or goats, mice or monkeys. On the other hand, it can be observed among men of all races and cultural backgrounds. Its manifestations include sitting or kneeling quietly, often with bowed heads or folded hands; it may be fervent and dynamic, catching up a whole group of people in various ceremonies and rituals; it may be engaged in individually or in company of thousands of others. The perceptive person will recognize these forms as religious behavior.

Evidently the same set of conditions does not apply to both respondent and religious behaviors. Since the behavioral scientist is concerned with repeated patterns of behavior, he notes that many people engage in religious forms of behavior regularly with no observable stimulus to initiate it. Why do men pray? What other patterns of behavior belong to this same spectrum of human activity? What are some of the social conditions and consequences related to these behaviors? Why do people in our society join together in groups (usually, but not always, called churches) where they affirm various moral, ethical, and ideological beliefs and reinforce these with various ritualistic behaviors? In part, this unit will attempt to provide answers for these questions.

Criteria for Religious Behavior

Webster's dictionary gives the following among its definitions of religion: "a pursuit, an object of pursuit, a principle, or the like, arousing in one religious convictions and feelings such as great faith, devotion, or fervour, or followed with religious zeal, conscientiousness or fidelity."

behavior

1 In this definition of religion, the first-named characteristic is "pursuit." The primacy of this word indicates that, if a choice is to be made between belief or behavior as a criterion of religion, the emphasis is placed on ________.

feelings

2 Lundberg, Schrag, and Larsen (1963), speaking of examples of religious behavior, state: "They represent a complex of emotional feelings and attitudes on the part of their adherents toward the mysteries and perplexities of life." Both Webster and these authors agree on emotional ________ as a characteristic of all types of religious behavior.

problems

3 Yinger (1957) states: "Religion, then, can be defined as a system of beliefs and practices by means of which a group of people struggles with these ultimate problems of human life." Both Lundberg et al. and Yinger, in defining religion, agree that it involves the ultimate ________ of life.

problems

4 Allport (1950), a Harvard psychologist, regards religion metaphorically as a "crucible in which life's residual problems are resolved." Again, there is an emphasis on the importance of religion for dealing with ________.

spiritual beings

5 The term "religion" is often limited to "belief in spiritual beings" (Tylor, 1958). The above definitions indicate that from a scientific viewpoint religion is something more than belief in ________ ________.

religion

6 The central object of concern may vary widely, but where there is a set of beliefs, emotional attitudes involving some degree of commitment, and a set of typical behavior patterns or rituals common to members of a group, there is a form of ________.

religion

7 In their attempts to be strictly "scientific," many scientists have avoided religious phenomena. For example, Terman (1938) included only one religious factor in his marital-happiness study; other writers omit making any reference to ________ as a factor in family behavior.

8 Human behavior, however, is not adequately explained without taking into account both *beliefs* and *attitudes*, e.g., a high school graduate applies for admission to a university because:

a. He has an instinct or drive for learning.
b. He believes university training will aid him in reaching life's goals.

b

9 To the Hindu, the cow is sacred. Although he is practically starving, he will not kill and eat a cow because:

a. He believes he should not eat beef.
b. Man should not eat beef.

a

10 The influence of attitudes on behavior was tested by Levine and Murphy (1943). They found that subjects given material that was congenial to their prior views tended to learn more rapidly than did subjects exposed to material that was uncongenial. Since the two groups had shown equal learning ability on neutral material, the difference in learning can best be attributed to ________.

attitudes

11 On the basis of behavioral facts such as those cited above, the cliché, "It's what a man does that counts," does not adequately explain much of human behavior. One must also consider, "It's what a man ________ that counts."

believes

12 In addition to biological and social factors, then, an adequate explanation of human behavior must consider both ________ and ________.

beliefs / attitudes

REVIEW: *The three criteria which distinguish religious behavior are sets of beliefs, emotional attitudes, and ritual behavior.*

13 Magic is sometimes confused with religion—traditionally "belief in unseen powers" and "ritualistic behaviors" have been ascribed to both. Note, however, that a scientific definition of religion as used in this unit does not rest on beliefs in ________ ________.

unseen powers

14 Malinowski (1925) distinguishes between religion and magic on the basis of goal-directed behavior patterns. The religious response is one of human impotence; the object of faith may be petitioned but it cannot be manipulated to ensure the success of a particular ________.

goal

magic

15 Magic is an attempt to control unseen powers for specific ends. A shaman might recite an incantation over an effigy of an enemy, and then throw the effigy into the fire to destroy the enemy. His behavior, directed to a specific goal, is an example of ________.

No

16 Malinowski states that magic and science are akin in that both have definite aims intimately associated with human pursuits; both develop sets of special techniques; both are surrounded by strict conditions in the performance of their rites. Does this mean that magic and science are identical? ________.

No

17 Magic and religion both arise in situations of some emotional stress; both offer escapes from such situations; both are surrounded by various taboos. Do these similarities make magic and religion identical? ________.

magic

18 According to Malinowski, then, a practical art relating to unseen powers and consisting of acts which are only means to a definite end expected to follow later on is ________.

religion

19 A body of self-contained acts relating to the unseen, and being themselves the fulfillment of their purpose, are not of the order of magic but of ________.

Man lives in an empirical world where things can be observed, counted, and measured. He also lives in a mental and emotional world of nonempirical phenomena. The "things" in this world are not observable, yet they often represent the ultimate realities in human affairs. Whether things are empirically verifiable or not, man can refer and relate to them through symbols. A symbol, simply stated, is something which stands for or suggests something else —it is a visible sign of something invisible.

symbol

20 A flag is, essentially, a piece of cloth. The United States flag, however, stands for the nation. It is not merely a colorful piece of cloth; it is a ________ of the nation.

love

21 A diamond is merely a piece of carbon. However, mounted in a finger ring, it is a favorite gift for young men in love to give to their young ladies. The carbon is not the love, but it is a symbol of that invisible, precious, and brilliant feeling called ________.

One piece of cloth, the National Flag, symbolizes the attributes associated with the concept "nation."

22 Insofar as religion deals with nonempirical entities, i.e., beliefs, sentiments, attitudes, it must refer to its subject matter by means of ________.

symbols

23 At the most abstract levels, some ideas can be symbolized only by analogies. The poet wrote: "My love is like a red, red rose." Jesus said: "The kingdom of God is like a treasure hid in a field." Can either statement be empirically verified? ________.

No

24 Does this mean that there are no such concepts as "love" or "the kingdom of God"? ________.

No

25 Behavior which relates to attitudes, beliefs, sentiments, or ideologies finds expression in symbolic forms. This may be referred to as ________ behavior.

symbolic

26 A person engaged in shaking hands, in saluting the flag, or in praying is involved in ________ behavior.

symbolic

Animals can be trained to respond to symbols. If a dog were trained to salute the flag, this could not be called symbolic behavior. It does not seem likely that the dog would know that the flag symbolizes the nation.

27 Man uses symbols to refer to which of the following:
  a. visible things
  b. invisible things
  c. actions
  d. all the above
  e. *a* and c above

d

28 Man shares many types of behavior with the subhuman levels of life, but the greatest difference between them lies in man's mental life, which is the source of his ________ ________.

symbolic behavior

A sociological definition of religion, based on emotional and ritualistic behavior patterns, is much broader than a definition based on some particular belief. At the same time the point is stressed that beliefs, religious or otherwise, do significantly influence human behavior. Magic and religion, although alike in some respects, are distinguishable in terms of their functions, i.e., the ends toward which the behavior is directed. Finally, much of man's nonempirical world of thought and communication is made real by means of symbols, and a large part of his response to his life situation is in terms of symbolic behavior.

Forms of Religion

29 One of the most elementary forms of symbolic behavior occurs when an individual attributes special powers to some "lucky piece." This emotional attitude and its attendant beliefs has some of the characteristics of a ________.

religion

30 An object regarded as possessing some special power for its individual owner is called a fetish. An aborigine might find a peculiarly shaped object one day and then note that he had a run of exceptional good fortune after he had taken the object home. He might attribute his good fortune to some power in his object, and it would then be a ________.

fetish

31 Lundberg, Schrag, and Larsen (1963) report that some soldiers in the world wars carried special charms to ward off danger. This behavior illustrates a modern form of ________.

fetishism

The Seal of the University of South Florida uses the lamp of learning as a symbol of education.

32 Sometimes a clan or tribe regards a specific object or animal as having special powers and a supranatural relationship to the tribe. This object is known as a totem, and the form of religion associated with it is ________.

totemism

33 The modern practice of athletic teams having a mascot which symbolizes the team may be regarded as a mild form of ________.

totemism

34 When the unseen forces which seem to influence man's destiny are conceptualized as living beings, these are known as gods. In ancient Assyro-Babylonian mythology the origin of the world was attributed to the ________ Apsu and Tiamat.

gods

35 Theism (from the Greek word for God: *Theos*) is used to distinguish those religions based on beliefs in gods. These are called ________ religions.

theistic

36 According to the *World Almanac* (1964), three persons out of five of the world's population believe in gods of one type or another. According to this source, then, the majority of the world's population are ________.

theists

37 Monotheism and polytheism are different versions of theism. Judaism, Christianity, and Islam are based on a belief in one Supreme Being. This belief is known as

monotheism _______.

38 Greek mythology and Hinduism have many gods and

polytheistic are classified as _______ religions.

39 A number of modern nontheistic belief systems have arisen which put some secular entity at their center. These "isms," according to Lundberg, Shrag, and Larsen (1963), sometimes manifest the characteristics of religion and may

religions be regarded as secular _______.

40 Dedicated communists display behavior patterns

communism which suggest that their religion is _______.

41 The humanist is devoted to the goal of bettering man's lot in this world. Dedication to this ideology is known

humanism as _______.

42 A widespread emotional-ideological-ritualistic system found throughout the modern world stresses loyalty to nationalistic values and goals. In a sociological perspective, then, a current form of religion is to be found in

nationalism _______.

43 Lundberg, Schrag, and Larsen (1963) point out that some modern scientists reject traditional forms of religion, and then devote themselves to "the pursuit of knowledge," scientific rituals, and emotional behaviors in a way which

scientism makes them followers of _______.

REVIEW: *As a result of your study you can match the following forms of religion with their main ideological base.*

1. *Fetishism with an individual and his "lucky piece"*
2. *Totemism with a tribal sacred object*
3. *Nationalism with statism*
4. *Islam with monotheism*
5. *Hinduism with polytheism*

Practically any ideology can serve as the basis of some form of religion. Religious forms can arise out of emotionally charged situations and may involve either theistic or nontheistic belief systems. For the majority of people, however, the belief system does extend to a theistic dimension.

Functions of Religion

Where there is a wide range of religious manifestations, such as those listed above, the question arises, Are there some common elements or needs which are met in various ways by all religions? This is called the "functional analysis" approach and has been used by many anthropologists and sociologists (e.g., Durkheim, 1915; Malinowski, 1925; Yinger, 1957).

44 For the individual, questions arise demanding an explanation of the mysteries of life. These questions, moreover, demand answers which are both rationally and emotionally satisfying. Many people believe that religious answers are the most ________ and ________ satisfying in many cases.

rationally / emotionally

45 One of life's major perplexities which men have to face is death. Science cannot peer beyond the grave; philosophy cannot pierce the shades of doubt; but traditional religions affirm that life continues after ________.

death

46 A firm belief in immortality is a source of great comfort and strength when one is faced with bereavement and with the imminence of one's own ________.

death

47 Problems of suffering and of evil are almost universal. A religious belief in a future life, where righteous living will reap its due reward, is an aid to many people, both to accept the fact of death and to bear their ________ in this life.

sufferings

48 Evil, whether it be in the form of misfortune, injustice, or malicious design, is common to the experience of all men. Religion affirms, however, that ultimately good will triumph over ________.

evil

49 From infancy onward, man experiences continuing frustration. The normally adjusted person eventually works out a set of beliefs, attitudes, and responses to deal with his ________.

frustrations

50 A young child often reacts to frustration by breaking things or engaging in other forms of deviant behavior. A Muslim says: "It is the will of Allah," and thereby resolves his frustrations calmly within his ________ ________.

religious beliefs

purpose (meaning)

51 Religion also gives meaning and purpose to life. One prominent sociology text (Young and Mack, 1965) states that an essential element for a successful social system is a sense of ________.

sense of purpose

52 Many secularistic moderns refer to their work as a "rat race." St. Paul could say, "I press toward the mark of a high calling . . ." (Phil. 3:14). St. Paul, through his religious motivation, had a definite ________ ________ ________.

mental serenity

53 Mental serenity is generally adjudged to be a desirable state. Some modern psychiatrists have adopted W. H. Auden's phrase to describe this era as "an age of anxiety." At the same time the authors of several best sellers (e.g., Joshua Loth Liebman, Norman Vincent Peale) advocate religion as the road to ________ ________.

mental serenity

54 The prophet Isaiah wrote, "Thou wilt keep him in perfect peace whose mind is stayed on Thee." Isaiah lived in an age of wars, invasions, and the downfall of nations —politically, an age of anxiety. Religiously, however, he had achieved ________ ________.

mental serenity

55 The Muslim's fatalistic attitude not only serves to blunt the force of his frustrations but also to resolve his anxieties in favor of ________ ________.

mental serenity

56 Buddha taught that men are distressed and disappointed when they do not get what they desire in life. To avoid distress and disappointment, he advocated the cultivation of an attitude which would eliminate desire. "No desire, no distress" is another path which religion has provided to ________ ________.

anomie

57 Durkheim (1915) postulated that social disorganization results from "anomie," a state of normlessness resulting from a lack of authoritative standards for behavior. Juvenile delinquency reflects in part ________ in modern society.

anomie

58 Durkheim also regarded religion as a basic means of providing standards of behavior for members of a society. Where there is a unified religious system, as in medieval Europe, there is a minimal level of ________.

moral

59 Just as a society needs a set of norms for integration, so, too, individuals need a personal code around which they can integrate their moral behavior. Such a code, with its definitions of what is right and wrong, is known as a _______ code.

moral code

60 Allport (1950) sees religion as a major source for providing time-tested guides to conduct. In other words, religion provides its adherents with a _______ _______.

moral code

61 In reply to a question on premarital intercourse (Burgess and Wallin, 1953) the majority of respondents said, "I do not think it right." For these respondents, their behavior was governed by their _______ _______.

In this section some of the functions of religion, both for individuals and for whole societies, have been considered. For many persons religion provides rationally and emotionally satisfying answers to some of life's major questions relating to death, evil, suffering, and residual problems. It is also a source of inspiration in the search for meaning and purpose in life, for mental serenity, and for a moral code as a guide to conduct. For a society, religion can provide an integrating set of norms which will minimize anomie and provide approved standards of behavior which will meet with the widest expectations.

This is not to say that religion in the traditional sense is the only approach to these problems—nor that all nominally "religious" people are well adjusted. It does say that religion as generally understood can and does serve the functions enumerated.

The Church as a Social System

The preceding section presented the definition, the forms, and the functions of religion. Durkheim (1915) maintained that each form, in large measure, encompasses all the functions of religion for the adherents of that form. The most familiar form of institutional religion in America is commonly referred to as "the church." This does not mean any particular church; it is not concerned with particular beliefs; it is a generalized concept of the church as a social institution.

One of the simplest models for analyzing a social system is provided by Talcott Parsons, a prominent Harvard sociologist, who regards all significant behavior as value-oriented, i.e., goal-directed. Social behavior is varied, but seldom completely random; it becomes patterned into social systems and society is the major system.

Social systems develop around four basic "functional imperatives," i.e., the basic activities which are necessary for a system to continue. There must be some mode of adaptation to the environment (an economy), some means of regulating goal achievement (rules or government), some integrative set of common values and norms (both secular and religious values), and some structure for pattern maintenance (the family. Parsons uses the term "latency.") Each of these imperatives develops a social subsystem having the same imperatives, and each subsystem has boundary relationships with the other three subsystems.

To illustrate how this model can be used, adaptation (the economy—the means of getting a living) is achieved by the Eskimo through hunting and fishing, by the Chinese through rice growing, by Americans through the development of the industrial arts and money economy.

In the following analysis of the church, the Parsonian model will be used as a framework for discussing the church, both as a subsystem and in its relationships with the other subsystems in the society.

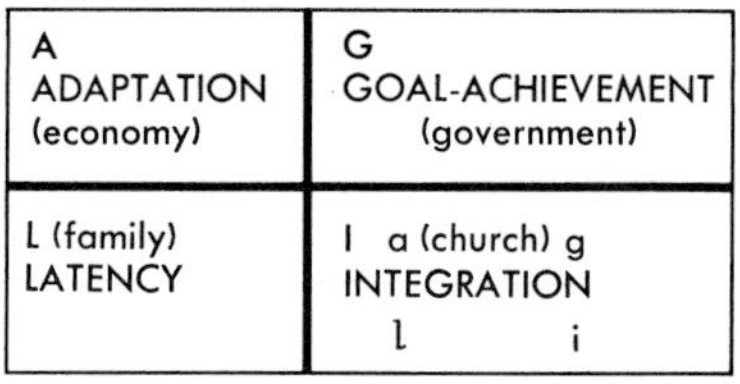

A ADAPTATION (economy)	G GOAL-ACHIEVEMENT (government)
L (family) LATENCY	I a (church) g INTEGRATION l i

Figure 15. Diagrammatic model of the Parsonian social system.

Adaptation: Adjustment of the Church to Its Environment

62 The Christian church developed out of Judaism. Paul began his missionary work in synagogues but the old religious leaders could not ________ to his new doctrines.

adapt

63 The early Christian church also challenged the established customs of the Roman Empire and met with severe opposition. In time, however, as the church gained acceptance, it began to ________ to the society.

adapt

64 The major social institution in the Roman Empire was the civil government with its hierarchy of officials from the Emperor down to the local level. As the Christian church[1] became institutionalized it adopted a similar form of organization with a ________ of officials.

hierarchy

65 The economy (tithes) of the church, like that of the government, rested on collections from the people. The government collected taxes; the church collected ________.

tithes

66 A tithe is a tenth part of one's annual produce or earnings. Many modern churches recommend that their members support the church by giving a ________.

tithe

67 In addition to tithes, churches have also depended on ownership of property for income. In the Middle Ages, a mutual service society based on large, landed estates prevailed. During this period, the church produced various monastic orders which obtained large landed ________. Many of these provided a continuing economic base for the church.

estates

68 In the United States church-owned property customarily has been tax-exempt. Some churches have tried to conduct profit-making enterprises for supplementing church income, but these properties have generally lost the privilege of tax ________.

exemption

69 In addition to tithes and landownership, churches have depended on voluntary contributions for their continuance. By its nature, then, the church, as a voluntary association, depends in part for its support on voluntary ________.

contributions

REVIEW: *In meeting the functional imperative* of adaptation, *over the centuries the church has been supported through tithes, landownership, and contributions.*

Goal Achievement: Church Polity; Forms of Organization

The goals of the church are primarily concerned with relationships of man with God and of man with man. The principles involved in these relationships are regarded by devoted church members as life's ultimate goals.

[1] For convenience, the word Christian will be omitted hereafter in referring to the Christian church. In the plural form, the term refers to separate denominations, usually Christian.

70 To achieve its goals, the church has developed several types of social organization (i.e., government or polity). In the first reported instance of collective action by the church (Acts I) the members *elected* Matthias to take the place of Judas. Such election by popular consent exemplifies ________ government.

democratic

71 From the Latin, *gregare,* "to assemble," and *com(n),* "together," a congregation is a group "assembled together" and acting jointly. Where members of churches act jointly, there is a ________ form of organization.

congregational

72 Among modern denominations, the members of the Baptist, Congregational, and Disciples Churches act jointly in church matters. These churches have a ________ form of polity.

congregational

73 In many societies the old men (Greek: *presbuteroi*) constitute a council to guide in social problems. An organization based on a council of elders or presbyters is called ________.

presbyterian

74 The Presbyterian Church is distinguished from others, not for its theological beliefs primarily, but for its ________ form of organization.

presbyterian

75 Among the early Christians, the apostles provided a leadership council for the group. Thus, some Christians maintain that the early church was ________.

presbyterian

76 One problem which arises in social organization is that new members often are not fully educated as to the bases and goals of the movement. A trained leader or "overseer" (Greek: *episcopos*) is then appointed to guide the group. In missionary churches Paul appointed such ________.

overseers

77 A natural extension of this form of organization is the appointment of bishops (Greek: *episcopos;* Latin: *biscopus*) to supervise a number of churches. Based on the Greek word, this form of church polity is known as the ________ organization.

episcopal

78 The Roman Catholic, the Episcopal, and the Methodist Churches are episcopal in their organization; they are governed by ________.

bishops

REVIEW: *Three major Protestant denominations which are named for their form of organization rather than for their particular doctrines are the Congregational, the Presbyterian, and the Episcopal.*

The imperative of goal achievement does not specify the goals to be achieved, but rather the forms and norms whereby the goals are to be achieved. The church as a social system does not operate by divine fiat but by the various forms of organization similar to those used by other social systems.

Integration: Consensus and Cohesiveness in the Church

Parsons (1951) maintains that every social system needs an integrating system of values held by the majority of members of the society. In general, each religious group subscribes to a particular set of beliefs and practices to maintain its integration.

79 In totemism, consensus with respect to the beliefs and attendant values symbolized by the totemic object serves to ______ the clan.

integrate

80 In the Christian church a set of theistic beliefs and values based on the life and teachings of Jesus provide the primary source of ______.

integration

81 The church is also a social institution in which sets of beliefs and values relating to the form of the organization (congregational, etc.) develop. Integration will depend, then, on consensus regarding both the theistic and the organizational sets of ______ and ______.

beliefs / values

82 In some cases a leader will arise who redefines or reinterprets the beliefs in a new and different way. As he gains followers the new group may separate from the older one, but both groups tend to maintain integration through their chosen sets of ______ and ______.

beliefs / values

83 Martin Luther "protested" against some of the beliefs and practices of the medieval church. His followers united on the basis of his doctrines, and a new type of church arose which is known as a ______ church.

Protestant

doctrines

84 Solidarity is threatened when new doctrines arise, either from within the system or from competing systems. Luther was a monk and priest within the church and the official leaders threatened to kill him in order to silence his variant ________.

isolation

85 Some groups attempt to maintain their solidarity by providing isolation from competing doctrines. Thus, the Mormons moved from Nauvoo, Illinois, to Salt Lake, Utah, to preserve their integration through ________.

isolation

86 Physical isolation becomes increasingly difficult to achieve in a complex society. Groups like the Amish and Missouri Synod Lutherans attempt to maintain their identity by practicing partial social ________.

cohesiveness

87 In addition to self-isolation, groups seek cohesiveness, or integration, by developing shared rituals and ceremonies. Durkheim (1915) regarded such congregational participation as very important in providing ________.

Integration in the church arises from consensus regarding particular sets of beliefs and values which relate to both the theistic and organizational aspects of the group. When solidarity of the group is threatened by new doctrines, the preservation of the old is attempted through both discipline and isolation. Ritualistic reaffirmations of the central doctrines reinforce the cohesiveness of the congregation.

Latency: Membership Maintenance in the Church

The "latency" *imperative involves the addition and replacement of members to keep a social system operating. In the larger social system the family is the major institution to provide for latency.*

latency

88 In medieval European society, people were born into membership in the family, the church, and the state. In that society, the family provided the ________ function for the church.

coercion

89 At times in the past new members have been added to both church and state through coercion. The modern church has no legal means for gaining new members through ________.

voluntary

90 A voluntary association by definition is an organization which a person joins of his own free will. The churches in America now are constituted of ________ membership of adults.

voluntary

91 Some churches baptize infants and count them as members, but the vows made at the time of baptism are expected to be "confirmed" by the child when he is old enough to understand what is involved. While the infancy rite is imposed from without, the confirmation represents a ________ assent to belonging to the church.

REVIEW: *In modern society the voluntary enlistment of new members in the church meets the functional imperative of latency.*

evangelistic

92 Evangelism is a term used to refer to the church's program for recruiting new members. When special services are held to attract new members these are called ________ services.

evangelist

93 Billy Graham is a world figure, noted for his work as an ________.

church

94 Evangelism is the chief means of reaching the unchurched, but the major source of new church members is the children of existing members. Religious education is the major technique used to gain these potential members for the ________.

education

95 Sunday schools, vacation Bible schools, and parochial (church) schools are some of the approaches to recruiting children through religious ________.

education

96 Some churches have special classes for adult instruction in the doctrines of the church. In these situations the evangelistic approach is supplemented through ________.

REVIEW: *The function of membership maintenance in the contemporary Christian church is carried on through evangelism and religious education.*

The church depends for its continued survival on voluntary enlistment of new members. The main techniques of persuasion are evangelism and religious education. Since 49 percent of the population were counted as church members in 1940 and the percentage had risen to 63.4 percent in 1962, it appears that the membership maintenance or latency function of the church is being served more or less successfully by its present programs.

Boundary Relationships of the Church and Other Social Systems

In the Parsonian model of the social system (see page 330), each subsystem has boundary relationships with the other three subsystems. This section will explore some of the relationships between the church and the economic order, the political order, and the family. In simple societies, the religious system is inseparable from the rest of the cultural ethos. In modern societies scholars have distinguished three main patterns or roles which various branches of the church have assumed in their relationships with the rest of society. These are the ecclesia, the sect, and the denomination.

97 The *ecclesia* type of church seeks to provide the integrating system of norms for the society as a whole. The medieval church in Europe is an example of the ________.

ecclesia

98 The ecclesia aligns itself with various power structures in society and supports the existing social, political, and economic orders. The official state churches of the Scandinavian countries are examples of the ________.

ecclesia

99 Sects arise when people feel that a state church tends to compromise with the corruption in the social order; also that it does not meet with personal religious needs of people. Consequently, some groups have withdrawn from state churches and have become ________.

sects

100 The denomination stands somewhere between the ecclesia and the sect. Both the social normative structure and personal religious needs are encompassed in the doctrines of the ________.

denomination

In the modern era a church may or may not assume the role of the integrator of society. There are three possible postures for an institution to take, and misunderstandings can and do arise as critics use an irrelevant criterion for assessing the relationships of the church and the social system. It also follows that where two or more belief systems exist in the same society and each one strives to be the one and only integrating system for the whole, then the result will be divisive rather than integrative for the larger system. Europe went through a period known as the Hundred Years' War in which Catholicism and Protestantism each tried to annihilate the other.

The Church and the Economic Order

Examples of boundary relationships between the church and the economic order are legion. They will be examined in both simple and complex societies, under both rural and urban or agrarian and capitalistic economies.

101 The Hopi Indians are an agricultural people in the arid Southwestern region of the United States. Feeling that they could not depend on nature to provide needed moisture for their growing crops, they developed the rain dance to implore their rain god to give the needed ________.

rain

102 The ancient Hebrews were a pastoral people. When they settled in Palestine and began farming, some noted that the native farmers and baal-worshippers had better crops. Many of the Hebrews then concluded that they should adopt baal-worship in order to grow good ________.

crops

103 In a study of a French-Canadian parish, H. W. Miner (1963) reported that the mass of St. Marc's day is followed by a special ritual. The priest blesses a large bowl full of assorted seeds. A man takes a handful of the blessed ________ home and these are the first to be planted.

seeds

104 Many rural Protestant churches in the United States remind their members of the divine element in crop growing on "Rural Life Sunday" in May. These ceremonies affirm the farmer's dependence for the life and growth of crops on ________ ________ beyond his technological controls.

divine elements

105 Ancient Israel, modern Canada, and the United States had and have religious ceremonies to celebrate the harvest. The national festival in the United States occurs in late November and is called ________.

Thanksgiving

REVIEW: *In rural societies ranging from simple tribesmen to modern scientific farming communities one can find evidences of the techniques of crop growing accompanied by various religious rituals.*

The relationships between the church and the modern economic order are less direct than in rural societies, but many customs can be traced to religious sources. A common example is the seven-day week, which stems from the Old Testament Commandment, "Remember the sabbath day to keep it holy. Six days shalt thou labor and do all thy work, but the sabbath is the Lord thy God's. In it thou shalt do no work" (Exodus 20:8–10). Property rights were established in ancient Israel by the Commandment, "Thou shalt not steal" (Exodus 20:15). American lawmakers, following these traditions have passed laws regarding both Sunday observance and stealing. Weber (1930) and Tawney (1948) trace the roots and rise of modern capitalism to religious forces in Protestantism—particularly the Calvinistic branches—as follows.

106 John Calvin, a famous Protestant reformer who lived between 1501 and 1564, claimed that Christ is King of this world and that, therefore, all of life is under divine jurisdiction. Every honorable vocation—farmer, businessman, or politician—is a divine calling for the individual in that ________.

vocation

107 Eternal salvation was the ultimate goal of Calvin, and the best assurances he could have of his salvation were various "signs of grace" showing that he had won God's favor. Prosperity and business success were regarded as due to divine favor and were, therefore, ________ ________ ________.

signs of grace

108 Profit in business was desired, not only for its economic value (many Calvinists lived very unostentatiously) but for its religious significance as a ________ ________ ________.

sign of grace

109 The economic system which uses capital goods to produce other goods for profit is known as capitalism. As the Calvinist sought to maximize his signs of grace (i.e., his profits), he became, in economic theory, a ________.

capitalist

110 To make big profits, the capitalist needs large sums of money, much of which he borrows and on which he makes payments of ________.

interest

interest

111 The medieval church, by forbidding usury, made it difficult for individuals to borrow large sums of money. Calvin, however, rationally interpreted a payment for the use of money as the same principle as the payment of rent for the use of land. Such a payment was not usury but ________.

capitalism

112 The primary goal of the Calvinist was eternal salvation, but his pursuit of economic success as a sign of grace led to the development of ________.

profit
interest

113 Calvinism, then, provided a religious sanction for two of the key elements in modern capitalism, viz.: a specific motivation for ________ making and legitimizing the payment of ________.

wealthy (rich)

114 Of course, moneymaking depends on resources and technology as well as on motivation. Calvinism is very strong in the Highlands of Scotland, but most of the people there are not ________.

resources

115 On the other hand, Weber points out that China has great resources and, until modern times, a more advanced technology than Europe. China has remained economically backward, however, evidently because of its backward-looking religious ethic rather than its lack of ________.

religious system

116 India, too, is a land of considerable resources and boasts an old civilization, but its dominant religious system has stressed mystical experiences rather than rational economic policies. It would seem, then, that India's economic plight may be related in part to its dominant ________ ________.

economic

117 In the twentieth century, Western world capitalism is not dependent on a traditional religious drive, but has developed a drive of its own. Men now engage in economic activity as an end in itself where the goal is ________ success.

religion

118 Lundberg, Schrag, and Larsen (1963) have pointed out that for some people capitalism is pursued with such emotional fervor, firm beliefs, and ritualistic behaviors that it is more than a vocation for them; it has become a ________.

119 Let's review some of the foregoing concepts in the next three frames. According to Weber, the modern economic system developed primarily out of which of the following:

a. man's scientific progress
b. America's rich natural resources
c. the ethic of Protestantism
d. modern economic theory

c

120 The economic system which uses capital goods to produce other goods for profit is ________.

capitalism

121 The dominant related belief systems underlying the modern economic order in the twentieth century are which combination of the following:

a. Calvinism
b. Catholicism
c. capitalism
d. communism

a and c

The preceding frames have suggested some striking relationships between the religious ethic of a society and its economic development. Reference has also been made to technology, and the question may be raised, What, if any, relationships are there between the rise of technology and religious belief systems? Since technology is commonly used as a synonym for "applied science," Merton's essay, "Puritanism, Pietism, and the Rise of Science," (1957) may provide some pertinent material in answer to this question.

122 The Puritans, an ascetic branch of English Protestantism, believed that the study of God's works in creation was a means of coming to know God better. The religious motivation toward study led many Puritans to become ________.

scientists

123 The Puritans were a minority group in seventeenth-century England, but 62 percent of the founding members of the Royal Society of Science were Puritans. This indicates a high relationship between the Puritan ethic and an interest in ________.

science

124 In Europe (1666–1883), excluding France, there were 107 million Catholics and 68 million Protestants, yet the Academy of Paris list of scientists named only 18 Catholics as compared with 80 Protestants. These data suggest that interest in science was more pronounced among the ________.

Protestants

scientists

125 Merton (1957, p. 575) states: ". . . Certain elements of the Protestant ethic had pervaded the realm of scientific endeavour and had left their indelible stamp upon the attitudes of ______ to their work."

God

126 Robert Boyle was writing religious essays by the time he was twenty-one. In his last will and testament he petitioned the Fellows of the Royal Society ". . . to discover the true Nature of the Works of ______."

Biblical

127 "The Bible, for Newton, was the true basis of his faith" (Sootin, 1955). This refers to an incident which took place at Cambridge when Newton was about thirty-three years old. Forty-nine years later, the biographer reports, ". . . He occupied himself with the study he loved best—______ research."

REVIEW: *The rise of science was, to a great extent, a result of certain elements of the Protestant (Puritan) ethic and its influence upon the attitudes of scientists to their work.*

Merton's conclusion to his essay is: ". . . Finally, the highly visible interaction of the institutions of science and religion—as in the so-called war between the two in the nineteenth century—may obscure the less visible, indirect and perhaps more significant relationship between the two" (1957, p. 606).

The Church and the State

The church and the state have come into being as major institutions to meet the functional imperatives of integration *and* goal achievement *(laws to regulate relationships) in the social system. According to Parsons (1956) the two are inevitably tied together through their boundary relationships. Evidence of these relationships is found in various official ties, in sharing similar attitudes and values, and where traditional religious forms are rejected, the setting up of new ideologies which are basically religious.*

church / state

128 Ancient history records indicate that the world's first empire, Sumer (ca. 4000 B.C.) was ruled by a priest-king. The office of priest-king demonstrates a unification of the two institutions, the ______ and the ______.

church / state

129 In England at the present time, 6,000 years after Sumer, the monarch, though not regarded as a priest, still is the official head of both the ______ and the ______.

divine right

130 The doctrine of "divine right" to rule was long used by monarchs in Western Europe as a justification for their autocratic rule. Under this claim, a subject who disagreed with the king was guilty of denying his ______ ______ to rule.

divine right

131 During the Middle Ages, the divine right claim was strengthened by the practice of rulers seeking the anointing of the Pope, head of the Church in Rome, to establish the validity of their ______ ______ to rule.

emperor

132 In another version of the inseparability of church and state, the ruler claimed to be divine, the actual god of his people. Roman Emperors claimed such a status and one of the serious problems of early Christians was the decree that all citizens must worship the ______.

worship

133 This version has persisted down to modern times. In Japan, the emperor was regarded as "the son of Heaven" by Shrine Shinto and, until Japan's defeat in 1945, the law of the land required emperor ______.

REVIEW: *The institutions of church and state have been joined in the person of their leader in various highly advanced societies over a period of 6,000 years. The main approaches to this unification have been through the priest-king, the divine right to rule, and the concept of the divine ruler.*

Societies which have unified the church and the state in the person of the ruler would appear to have been well integrated and relatively long lasting. After all, critics could be and were readily eliminated, since they were considered both heretics and traitors.

Continuities in Western Church-State Relationships since the Middle Ages

The rise of modern states in Western civilization shows close relationships between new religious and new political interpretations of the nature of things. There was rebellion against both of the old institutional forms of church and state. Three new alternatives developed: one which modified the old forms and retained the traditional norms, one which tended to continue with the old forms, and one which attempted to reject both forms and norms and develop new integrating systems.

134 The Protestant Reformation began about 1500 A.D. in an era when both kings and priests were absolutists. At first the protests arose against some of the teachings and practices of the ______.

priests (church)

135 Martin Luther taught two new principles: (*a*) justification by faith, and (*b*) the priesthood of all believers. This means that the individual is saved, not by the institution of the church but by his own ______, and that a person does not need an official priest to intercede for him but he himself serves as his own ______.

faith

priest

136 Luther's doctrines transfer the emphasis in religion from the rituals of the institution to the faith of the ______.

individual

137 The medieval church had two classes: the clergy and the laity. Luther's "priesthood of all believers" implies the equality of all men. This undercuts special claims to privilege by a priestly class and makes all believers ______.

equal

138 People still gathered for religious services but the rule of the priests had been rejected. A new form of rule by the people had to be developed by the congregation. This new type of autonomy arose in England (ca. 1600 A.D.) and is known as ______.

congregationalism

REVIEW: *The teachings of Luther and other Protestants produced three major innovations in the church as an institution. These were an emphasis on the individual, a recognition of the equality of men, and the development of rule by the people, i.e., congregationalism.*

139 The leaders of the Protestant Reformation did not reject much of the traditional content of religion as they knew it. Their concern was with its institutional expression. This is indicated by the term, the ______.

Reformation

140 Rulers in the Northern kingdoms of Europe were more receptive to Protestantism than those in the South. Scandinavian countries, Germany, and England established state churches which were ______.

Protestant

141 By the eighteenth century the principles of newfound religious freedom for the people began to be applied to the political order. Political philosophers in England could argue that the divine right to rule did not rest in a single person, the king, but in all the ________.

people

142 The American Revolution against the king of England was justified on the basis of sovereignty being a natural right of the ________.

people

143 The American revolutionaries restated the principle of equality in political terms. The Preamble to the Constitution states that "all men are created free and ________."

equal

144 The new form of government in the former Colonies followed the example of the congregational churches. In its application to government, the principle of rule by the people (Greek: *demos*, "people") became known as ________.

democracy

145 The Revolution in the eighteenth century, then, appears to be the second step in the Reformation begun in the sixteenth century. Both church and state in the old autocratic institutional forms were rejected. Both continued, however, in new, ________ institutional forms.

democratic

146 The Constitution of the new Republic stated that the state would not establish a formal state church or interfere with the free exercise of ________ by its citizens.

religion

147 Under this principle, American society in the past has operated on a democratic, religiously pluralistic basis in which each institution is largely independent of the other, but they support each other insofar as they share the same ________.

principles

REVIEW: *In the eighteenth century the American colonists extended the principles of the church Reformation to revolutionize the political system and church-state relationships: any divine right of government does not rest in the ruler but in the people; the Constitution states that "all men are created equal"; the form of government which is based on the rule of the people is democracy.*

Church and state were long united in the figure of the national leader. The Reformation, in a larger sense, demonstrated that they could be separated and yet maintain boundary relationships under the principles of individual-

ism, equality, and democracy. Another alternative developed in Southern Europe, however, in which the old forms tended to continue.

148 In Italy both church and state continued along the traditional autocratic lines, opposed to both reform and democracy. In government, this trend reached its zenith under Mussolini, who was noted for his ______ rule in the period preceding World War II.

autocratic

149 Spain continued to maintain its close ties with the Church of Rome and its monarchs maintained their autocratic rule into the 1930s. General Franco, the head of the Spanish government, was another example of an ______ ruler.

autocratic

150 South America was colonized by the Southern European powers and, again, the trend of government produced leaders such as Peron in Argentina and Batista in Cuba who were ______.

autocrats (dictators)

151 The third alternative developed in Western countries was a strong authoritarian type of church supported by and supporting an autocratic ruler. Revolutions there had to attack both church and state in their entirety. This was the case in France in 1789 and in ______ in 1917.

Russia

152 Revolutionaries, however, need an integrative institution to support their new social system. In France an attempt was made to substitute deism in a form dedicated to the goddess of reason and nature as a new form of ______.

religion

153 In the case of France it appears that the revolution never did become a full Reformation. The old authoritarian church became reestablished and the civil government depends for stability upon ______ leadership such as that provided by de Gaulle.

autocratic (authoritarian)

154 Russian revolutionaries, following Karl Marx, rejected orthodox religion along with czarism. Their new integrative system was based on a set of beliefs based on the doctrines of ______.

Marx

155 Russian communism now has its set of beliefs; a founder—Marx; a prophet—Lenin; a "sacred" tomb—Lenin's; its scriptures—e.g., the *Manifesto* and *Das Kapital;* its symbols—hammer and sickle; its rituals—e.g., May Day parades in Moscow. Under the criteria set forth in frames 1 to 12, these criteria are basic to ______.

religion

Nazism

156 Adolph Hitler, the leader of the Nazi party, came to power in Germany in 1933. Hitler is noted for his anti-Semitism but he was also anti-Christian and antiliberal. He rejected the traditional church and substituted his ideology of ______.

religion (church)

157 Like deism in France a century earlier, Nazism was able to integrate the society for a short period of national crisis, but when things returned to more normal levels the nation returned to its traditional ______.

integration

158 The next three frames review the major concepts in this section. The cases cited above support the hypothesis that societies develop some system of "religion" to integrate the society; also that practically any ideology will serve as a "religion" to provide ______.

"religious"

159 From the sociological point of view, complete separation of church and state is an unrealistic notion. The choice lies between competing forms of ______ systems.

deism
communism / Nazism

160 Examples of nontheistic ideologies elevated by political rulers to national religious status in the modern era have included: ______ in the eighteenth century in France; ______ in Russia, 1917; and ______ in Germany, 1933.

The church-state relationship is often blurred by ignorance of the basic issues involved. Religion is not "the Protestant religion," or "the Moslem religion," or any other specific "sacred" institution alone and in its entirety. Lundberg, Schrag, and Larsen (1963), Yinger (1957), and others have named capitalism, communism, nationalism, humanism, and even scientism as religions for *some people who demonstrate attitudes of emotional attachment to some particular beliefs along with a set of ritualistic behaviors to accompany the beliefs.*

In Western society, religion has found its dominant institutional expression in "the church." Whether people like it or not, society is inextricably bound up with the church in many ways. In Western countries that have rejected the church in its Christian form, i.e., institutionalized religion, alternative systems have arisen; within the Christian nations, various forms of Christian churches have arisen—just as various forms of government have flourished in different times and places. In most cases, however, the church and state have developed mutually compatible boundary relationships which have met the functional imperatives of integration and goal achievement for the particular social system.

The Church and the Family

The family is the oldest, most universal, and most basic of social institutions. Some behavioral scientists (e.g., Freudians) regard sex as the prime mover in human behavior and they see marriage and the family resulting from man's sex drive. Long before the rise of behavioral science, however, marriage and family relationships were matters of religious concern and remain so to the present.

161 Assyro-Babylonian mythology, in its *Epic of Creation* (Larousse, 1959), the oldest religious documentation, states that the gods, Apsu and Tiamat, gave birth to the world. This myth, then, regards marital relations as the origin of _______.

creation (the world)

162 The *Epic* also points out that: "Like men, the gods had wives and families." This indicates that marriage was not regarded as a matter of mere human sexual activity but was practiced by the _______ themselves.

gods

163 The origins of both marriage and religion were explained in Egyptian mythology as follows: The goddess Isis married the god Osiris and bore a son. Isis then instituted marriage among men and Osiris instituted _______.

religion

164 The Biblical account in Genesis states that God created both the world and man. He then saw man's need for companionship so He created woman, thereby instituting marriage and the _______.

family

165 In ancient Israel, family roles were regarded as divinely established; e.g., God spoke to Eve saying: ". . . Thy desire shall be to thy husband and he shall rule over thee" (Genesis 3:16). This gave the man the dominant _______ in the family.

role

166 The Commandment, "Honor thy father and thy mother (Exodus 20:12), states that parental _______ are superior in prestige and power to those of children.

roles

role

167 The father was not only the titular head of the family but also its high priest. In the Old Testament book of Job (1:5), we read: "He would rise early in the morning and offer burnt offerings for his family." This function of the father was a priestly ______.

God (divinity)

168 According to the Biblical view—a view still widely accepted by the church—marriage and marital roles do not arise from biological drives and tension release but are ordained by ______.

covenant

169 The newborn child is a source of major concern to members of Hebrew-Christian religions. The mark of the covenant, for the ancient Hebrews, was the rite of circumcision. Thus, Moses' wife circumcised her newborn son with a sharp stone so that he would be under the ______.

sin

170 The Roman Catholic Church teaches that children inherit Adam's original sin and that immediate baptism is necessary to wipe out that stain of ______ and bring the baby into the church.

church

171 Many Protestant churches practice infant baptism; others observe a ceremony of infant dedication. This is a commitment by the parents to train the child in the ways of their particular ______.

REVIEW: *According to the most ancient documents, religion provides answers to questions about marriage origins, family roles, and newborn rites.*

Granted that religious institutions have made it their business to be concerned with rites, roles, and rules pertaining to marriage and the family, the question arises, Is there any evidence that religious beliefs, attitudes, and doctrines are reflected in patterns of family behavior? Terman (1938), a noted psychologist, implies that emphasis on religion in family life may be very risky (". . . the ogre that threatens domestic happiness"). But Burgess and Wallin (1953), in their study of several hundred young married couples, reported positive relationships between religious factors and marital adjustment. Terman used only two items pertaining to religion in his survey. Burgess made provision for over one hundred responses in his questionnaires. On the basis of adequacy of information gathered about religion and family life, the Burgess survey would appear to be more reliable than Terman's. In the following discussion some positive correlations will be shown between religious factors and marital adjustment. Two points must be kept in mind, however: (1) correlation does not imply causation, and (2) religious differences can cause unhappiness—just as differences of opinion over money, in-laws, or other issues can.

Religion and Marital Adjustment

religious affiliation

172 Burgess (1953), in a study of 1,000 engaged couples, reported that couples with the same religious affiliation (Catholic, Jewish, Protestant) manifest the highest proportion of *unbroken* engagements (73.1 percent) as compared with those unions of mixed faiths (58.8 percent). Where both state no religious affiliation, there is a higher percentage of *broken* engagements (69 percent). These findings suggest that a good predictor of a successful engagement is same ________ ________.

ministers (priests)

173 In a continuing study of the same couples, Burgess reported high adjustment scores for those whose marriages were performed by clergymen, i.e., ________.

Table 20. Survival Rates per 1,000 Marriages, Various Combinations of Religious Affiliation, Iowa, 1953–55

Religious affiliation of husbands and wives	*Number of marriages*	*Survival rate*
Catholic-Catholic	5,598	974
Protestant denominational combinations	2,708	962
Protestant denomination same	19,924	911
Protestant*-Protestant*	2,363	589
Catholic-Protestant*	359	557

* Protestant here refers to such vague affiliation that no information on denomination was given.

SOURCE: Unpublished data from a study made by Lee Burchinal, University of Iowa, Iowa City, Iowa. Used by permission.

religious affiliations

174 The data in Table 20 show that the survival rate of marriages was less than 60 percent where there was little religious support, but it jumped to over 90 percent where there were similar and positive ________ ________.

divorce

175 Churches tend to stress the undesirability of divorce and Table 20 suggests that where church relatedness is weakest there is more likelihood of ________.

divorce

176 Mixed marriages (Catholic-Protestant) are often regarded as most likely to end in divorce due to different religious beliefs. Table 20 suggests that where there are very vague religious beliefs there is practically the same likelihood of the marriage ending in ______.

grievances

177 "Differing in religious beliefs" was included in Terman's list of "grievances" which would affect marital happiness. It ranked forty-seventh for husbands and forty-fourth for wives among the various ______. It would appear that similar religious affiliations can favorably affect the survival rate of marriages.

REVIEW: *According to the data of Burgess (1953) and Burchinal (Table 20) one of the most positive predictors in both engagement and marriage survival is same religious affiliation between partners.*

Presumably childbearing characteristics are randomly distributed over all the biologically mature women in a population. If there are consistent differences between different religious groups it seems logical that the religious beliefs may have some relationship to the differences in behavior. Studies by Blood and Wolfe (1960) provide some data on this point.

Table 21. Childbearing Preferences, Performances, and Expectations by Wife's Church Preference

	Church preference			
Children	*Catholic*	*Protestant*	*Jewish*	*Greek Orthodox*
Preferred number of children	3.63	3.18	3.15	3.31
Number born to date	2.17	2.01	1.65	1.44
Expected number	2.79	2.66	1.77	1.40

SOURCE: Robert O. Blood, Jr., and Donald M. Wolfe, *Husbands and Wives,* The Free Press of Glencoe, New York, 1960. Used by permission.

Protestants

178 The women in each of the categories (Table 21) prefer more than three children. The closest fit between "preferred" and "expected" numbers in any one category is to be found among ______.

Greek Orthodox

179 The greatest discrepancy between "preferred" and "expected" numbers is to be found among the ________ ________.

180 The greatest difference in number of children born to date is that between the

a. Catholic - Protestant
b. Protestant - Jewish
c. Jewish - Greek Orthodox
d. Greek Orthodox - Catholic

d

181 Assuming that Blood and Wolfe controlled for other pertinent factors in childbearing, the conclusion which can be drawn from the data in Table 21 is that both performance and expectations are modified by the wife's ________ preference.

church

Burgess devised a Marital Adjustment Scale with a possible range of 0 to 194 for an individual (0 to 388 for a couple), and calculated the score for each of his respondents. Using the Burgess data, Aseltine (1958) made a study of religious activity and marital adjustments by comparing the highest- and lowest-scoring couple with respect to their religious activity (as measured by church attendance) and a number of other variables.

Table 22. High and Low Scoring (Marital Adjustment Scores) Samples and "Common Interests"

	Number of respondents	
Type of interests	*High*	*Low*
Recreational (e.g., music, dancing, travel)	48	54
Social (e.g., friends, social activities, cards)	26	26
Religious (e.g., church, scouts, ideals)	16	3
Family (e.g., home, children, family activities)	37	22

SOURCE: Unpublished data from a study made by H. E. Aseltine, The University of Chicago Press, Chicago, 1958.

182 "Common interests" are often taken as a guide for predicting success in marriage. Table 22 indicates that there are very few differences between high- and low-scoring marriages in this sample as far as ________ and ________ interests are concerned.

recreational
social

religious / family

183 The common interests which are mentioned more often by the high scorers are ______ and ______.

dancing

184 Which of the following common interests is least likely to lead to a high marital adjustment score: dancing; participating in family activities; attending church? ______.

Not necessarily. Their religious interests are not common interests (see also Table 21).

185 John attends the Catholic Church regularly; Mary teaches Sunday school in the Baptist Mission. Would their religious activity indicate that they would make a happily married couple? +++++.

REVIEW: *The study of religious activity and marital adjustment suggests that the most significant common interest in the high-scoring sample is that of religious interests.*

Boundary relationships between the church and the family are evident in the oldest recorded documents. While strong religious differences can adversely affect marital happiness, the evidence provided by the research cited indicates that the church continues to contribute positively and significantly to engagement stability, marriage survival, and better marital adjustment.

The Church in Modern Society

Critics of the church and prophets of doom and gloom have long forecast the early demise of both the family and the church in America. Both of these social institutions have experienced cataclysmic changes in the past century; both have lost many of their former functions; both now seem to depend for their existence on nonrational, nonempirical, and nonutilitarian factors, such as affection, emotional attitudes, beliefs, and ritualistic behaviors often regarded by the critics as mere nonsense. In spite of the dire prophecies, however, empirical evidence indicates that both institutions are gaining rather than disappearing, both in absolute numbers and in proportions relative to the population as a whole. In the case of the family, in 1910, 54.2 percent of the male population of the United States was married; fifty years later the percentage had increased to 69.6 percent (Census, 1960). In the case of the church, in 1910, 43 percent of the population of the country was reported as church members; half a century later the reported percentage had risen to 63.4 percent (Landis, 1964).

The critic may be simply embarrassed by the evidence. It behooves the behavioral scientist, however, at least to explore objectively the more obvious facets of what is happening to the church in modern society and to offer some explanation as to why.

A modern suburban Protestant Church.

Table 23. Value of New Construction of Religious Buildings by Decade, 1930–1960

Year	*Value*
1930	$ 135,000,000
1940	59,000,000
1950	409,000,000
1960	1,016,000,000

SOURCE: Benson Y. Landis (ed.), *Yearbook of American Churches,* National Council of the Churches of Christ in the U.S.A., New York, 1964. Used by permission.

186 "Money talks" is a commonplace criterion in modern society. The data in Table 23 indicate that Americans place a money value on new religious buildings of approximately
1 billion ________ ________ dollars a year.

construction

187 Even taking inflation into account, the 1960 dollar was worth about half the value of the 1940 dollar. There was over a 200 percent increase in the money spent on ______ for new religious buildings in 1960.

church

188 When other expenses—maintenance of existing buildings, salaries, and operating expenses—are taken into account, it appears that large sums of money are being spent every year on the life and work of the ______.

voluntary

189 It may be noted, also, that church moneys are not collected by compulsion as are tax moneys. Rather, the church in America depends for its support on the ______ contributions of members.

Table 24. Population of the United States and Percentages Reported as Church Members, by Generations, 1850–1962

Date	*Population*	*Percent*
1850	23,191,876	16
1880	50,155,783	20
1910	91,972,266	43
1940	131,668,275	49
1962	185,822,000	63.4

SOURCE: Population: U.S. Bureau of the Census, *Statistical Abstract of the United States, 1964; Percentage:* Benson Y. Landis (ed.), *Yearbook of American Churches,* National Council of the Churches of Christ in the U.S.A., New York, 1964. Used by permission.

increased

190 Table 24 indicates that over the past century the percentage of church members in the United States population has (increased/decreased) by 300 percent.

voluntary

191 In medieval society the church could enforce compulsory membership so that church membership was universal. In modern America, however, church membership is not coerced. Like the monetary support, membership is ______.

monetary support
membership

192 The answer to the question of what is happening to the church in modern society may be confusing in some respects but one fact is clear: the institutional church, depending almost completely on voluntary response, has grown with respect to both ________ ________ and ________.

church

193 In some respects the church appears to be a declining phenomenon. In medieval society, the functions of education, welfare, and community recreation were carried on by the ________.

commercial

194 The recreational function once performed by religious holidays and festivals has now become commercialized and is performed for profit. Fairs, carnivals, sporting events, and other kinds of entertainment are now carried on by ________ operators.

church

195 A century ago American society was almost entirely dependent on church-established colleges and universities. Since that time state governments have poured millions of dollars into new campuses, but it was not until 1950 that enrollments in state institutions exceeded enrollments in private and ________-related institutions of higher learning.

state (public)

196 When comparing the present performance of the church and state in elementary education, we must keep in mind that the state compels every local taxpayer to support the public schools. Families sending their children to church schools have to pay fees to the parochial schools as well as taxes for the ________ schools which they are not using.

church

197 Welfare has been associated traditionally with religious institutions since ancient Sumer. Until the 1930s welfare in America depended to a great extent upon voluntary agencies and ________-related agencies.

state

198 Of the voluntary agencies, Bornet (1960) has stated that these were often sponsored by religious bodies, or laymen founded them and gave long hours in their service. At present the public welfare programs are so extended that writers often refer to the present era as the age of the welfare ________.

REVIEW: *Many of the service functions formerly provided chiefly by the church are now being preempted by the state and commercial interests. Examples of these functions are recreation, education, and welfare.*

The church is growing, but its service functions are declining. How is this paradox to be explained? It appears that the church pioneered, directly or indirectly, in providing society with various services which have now become functionally autonomous and have left the church. The continued growth of the church under these circumstances suggests that the role of the church is something more than that of a humanitarian agency; it deals with man's ultimate concerns, and these concerns may well be increasing in spite of advances in science and technology.

199 Man's basic emotional problems remain—the facts of death, of frustration, of suffering, and of evil. The growth of church membership suggests that for the majority of people satisfactory answers to these problems can still be found in the ________.

church

200 Man seems to need a sense of purpose, some measure of mental serenity, some code to guide his daily living. These are needs which are peripheral to science but central to ________.

religion

201 As was pointed out earlier, Durkheim (1915) concluded that both personal and social disorganization arise out of anomie, that is, a state of normlessness. In his view, religion, with its sets of beliefs, norms, and rituals, can and does counter the development of ________.

anomie

202 Burgess's marital-adjustment investigation shows positive correlations between religious activity and marital adjustment. This suggests that the religious ethic provides guides to conduct which enable men to live relatively better-________ and more satisfying lives.

adjusted

203 Herberg (1960) sees the growth of church membership related to the need of the individual for a sense of identity. Western mass culture, according to the popular diagnosis, produces alienation. The major religious groups (Protestant, Catholic, Jew) help to provide the individual with an ________.

identity

problems / norms
identity

204 Why is the church still around and still growing? Possibly because it still serves some of man's most basic needs; e.g., it provides: answers to basic emotional ________, a set of ________ to live by, and an individual ________.

The family appears particularly suitable as a foil and an analogy for evaluating the church or any other social institution. There are harsh, unloving, and bigoted parents and similarly harsh church leaders; there are homes which stand in the way of developing personalities and churches which have been backward in their social concern; there are children who flout the best efforts of their parents and there are church members who are poor examples of the standards expected of religious persons. In spite of these liabilities, however, the evidence suggests that both the church and the family as social institutions play major roles in modern society and will continue to do so.

SUMMARY

Religious behavior is universal. It is found in the lives of individuals, in various institutional forms, and in value-oriented boundary relationships with other institutions. Religious behavior appears in many guises; the devout churchman, the ardent patriot, the dedicated scientist, and the avowed atheist—all display behavior patterns which are by definition religious.

In America, the manifest form of institutionalized religion in the traditional sense is often referred to as "the church." It has all the characteristics of other social institutions, and its boundary relationships with the other major institutions are evident throughout the American way of life.

The church—like the family—has been divested of many of its service functions by the state and special agencies. Both institutions, however, show remarkable virility and ability to thrive on such intangibles as providing affection in the family and symbolic values in the church.

As a human institution the church is subject to all of mankind's genius for imperfection; as an integrative system its efficacy, adaptability, and universality merit serious consideration by the behavioral and social scientists. The material, substantive, and secular aspects of life are sometimes symbolized by the word "bread." The Founder of the Christian church stated the case for religion succinctly in the words, "Man shall not live by bread alone. . . ."

SELF-REVIEW QUIZZ

1 The chief criteria for identifying religious behavior are ________ ________ and ________ ________ ________.

2 Religion and magic share many features in common but can be distinguished on the basis of their functional ________.

3 Praying, reciting the pledge to the flag, or presenting a medal "for valor" are examples of ________ behavior.

4 Where some object is regarded as having some special power for and relationship to a tribe, and rituals are performed in connection with it, there is a form of religion known as ________.

5 A general characteristic which distinguishes Christianity, Islam, and Hinduism from more elementary forms of religion is the ________ belief system.

6 Among problems common to all men, and for which religion alone provides rational and emotionally satisfying answers, are ________, ________, and ________.

7 A code of right and wrong standards of behavior for the individual is provided by most religions. This is known as a ________ code.

8 Where a whole society follows the same behavioral codes, anomie is minimized and the society tends to be well ________.

9 With no legal means of enforcing membership, the church with over 100 million members is the nation's largest ________ organization.

10 The terms Congregational, Episcopal, and Presbyterian refer to differences in church ________.

11 The major techniques for gaining new church members are ________ and ________ ________.

12 In America, a church body of 1 million members, in which people find their religious needs met but are also urged to be good citizens and to support societal values, is commonly referred to as a ________.

13 Calvinism provided a rational and religious sanction for two of the key elements underlying modern capitalism. These were making of ________ and payments of ________.

14 Congregational forms of conducting church affairs developed into ________ forms of political government.

15 The Burgess and Burchinal marital studies indicate that one significant factor in making these lasting relationships is the same ________ affiliation.

16 The church in twentieth-century America has shown an increase from 43 percent to ________ percent.

17 The continued growth of the church in the twentieth century suggests that man has basic needs which are being served, for the majority of people, by ________ ________.

REFERENCES

Allport, Gordon W.: *The Individual and His Religion,* Macmillan Company, New York, 1950.

Aseltine, H. E.: "Religious Activity and Marital Adjustment," unpublished paper, The University of Chicago Press, Chicago, 1958.

Blood, Robert O., Jr., and Donald M. Wolfe: *Husbands and Wives,* The Free Press of Glencoe, New York, 1960.

Bornet, Vaughn: *Welfare in America,* University of Oklahoma Press, Norman, Okla., 1960.

Burchinal, Lee: "Religious Affiliation and Marriage Survival," unpublished paper, University of Iowa, Iowa City, Iowa, 1960.

Burgess, Ernest W., and Paul Wallin: *Engagement and Marriage,* J. B. Lippincott Company, Philadelphia, 1953.

Durkheim, Emile: *The Elementary Forms of the Religious Life,* trans. by Joseph Swain, George Allen & Unwin, Ltd., London, 1915.

Eighteenth Census of the United States: 1960, Vol. I, Part A, Population, U.S. Bureau of the Census, Washington, D.C.

Herberg, Will: *Protestant, Catholic, Jew,* Anchor Books, Doubleday & Company, Inc., Garden City, New York, 1960.

Landis, Benson Y. (ed.): *Yearbook of American Churches,* National Council of the Churches of Christ in the U.S.A., New York, 1964.

Larousse Encyclopedia of Mythology, Batchworth Press, Ltd., London, 1959.

Levine, J. M., and G. Murphy: "The Learning and Forgetting of Controversial Material," *Journal of Abnormal Social Psychology,* 381:507–517, 1943.

Lundberg, George A., Clarence C. Schrag, and Otto N. Larsen: *Sociology,* 3d ed., Harper & Row, Publishers, Incorporated, New York, 1963.

Malinowski, Bronislaw: *Argonauts of the Western Pacific,* Dutton & Co., Inc., New York, 1922.

Malinowski, Bronislaw: "Magic Science, and Religion," in Joseph Needham, *Science Religion, and Reality,* The Sheldon Press, London, 1925.

Merton, Robert K.: *Social Theory and Social Structure,* rev. ed., The Free Press of Glencoe, New York, 1957.

Miner, Horace: *St. Denis, A French Canadian Parish,* The University of Chicago Press, Chicago, 1963.

Needham, Joseph: *Science, Religion, and Reality,* The Sheldon Press, London, 1925.

Parsons, Talcott: *The Social System,* The Free Press of Glencoe, New York, 1951.

Parsons, Talcott, and Neil J. Smelser: *Economy and Society,* The Free Press of Glencoe, New York, 1956.

Sootin, Harry: *Isaac Newton,* Julian Messner, Inc., New York, 1955.

Statistical Abstract of the United States, U.S. Bureau of Census, Washington, D.C., 1964.

Tawney, Richard H.: *Religion and the Rise of Capitalism,* John Murray (Publishers), Ltd., London, 1948.

Terman, Lewis: *Psychological Factors in Marital Happiness,* McGraw-Hill Book Company, New York, 1938.

Tylor, E. B.: *Religion in Primitive Culture,* Harper & Row, Publishers, Incorporated, New York, 1958.

Weber, Max: *The Protestant Ethic and the Spirit of Capitalism,* trans. by T. Parsons, George Allen & Unwin, Ltd., London, 1930.

World Almanac, New York World-Telegram, New York, 1964.

Yinger, J. Milton: *Religion, Society, and the Individual,* The Macmillan Company, New York, 1957.

Young, K., and R. W. Mack (eds.): *Principles of Sociology,* 3d ed., American Book Company, New York, 1965.

social problems

Social problems arise out of the efforts of a society to achieve and maintain a particular system of social operations. The problems arise specifically with respect to the defined goals and objectives of the society as a whole. Two general sources of problems are:

1. *The behavior of individuals in ways which are interpreted as damaging to important social values.*
2. *The development of conflicting social operations and contradictory goals in the subsystems within the great culture.*

In the study of causes of social problems, it is important to recognize that there are no simple answers and that no single intellectual discipline can provide a full understanding of the factors involved. The fields of sociology, social psychology, anthropology, and, in a peripheral sense, medicine and economics make valuable contributions to the social problems area.

In seeking to understand the variables principally associated with social problems, we must appreciate two categories of factors. First are the factors involved in the disintegration of conflict situations. What is the process, the sequence, and the motivation implicit or explicit in the breakdown or evasion of the desired behavioral and normative standards? It is necessary not only to study the delinquent, the criminal, the alcoholic, and the psychotic. It is equally necessary to understand the behavior and achievements of the striver, the law-abiding citizen, the person for whom temptations to steal cannot be said to exist.

It is not within the purview of this section to catalog all the social problems which confront our society or even to analyze in depth all the major social problems we have. Rather, two representative kinds of problems have been selected for presentation. They are, respectively, mental illness and relationships among minority groups. In Unit 1, Dr. Donald Allen first defines what social problems are and then investigates the typology, incidence, and social consequences of various types of mental illness. In Unit 2, he points out specific aspects of racial and ethnic relations which continue to present enormously grave problems to our society.

mental illness as a social problem

DONALD E. ALLEN

1

Definitions

1 Horton defines a social problem as "a condition affecting a considerable number of people in ways considered undesirable about which it is felt something can be done through collective action." Juvenile delinquency fits (some/all) these criteria (Horton and Leslie, 1955, p. 4).

all

2 Merton defines social problems as "breakdowns or deviations in social behavior, involving a considerable number of people, . . . [and] widely regarded as immoral, illegal, or potentially destructive of some established institution." By this definition, juvenile delinquency and other forms of crime would constitute ________ ________ (Merton and Nisbet, 1961, p. 11).

social problems

3 Sociology is most briefly defined as the science of society. Social problems concern processes which impede the functioning or damage the structure of society. Social problems would be significant to the field of ________.

sociology

4 Nervous and mental diseases as social problems are of interest to all behavioral scientists—the sociologist, psychologist, social psychologist, and anthropologist. They also constitute a medical problem and are therefore of interest to the field of ________.

medicine

5 Within the field of medicine, the psychiatrist is particularly concerned with nervous and mental ________.

disorders (disease, etc.)

6 The most central values for each society are likely to form the core of major social problems. In an affluent society which stresses private property and a high standard of living, wrongful appropriation of ________ would constitute a basic social problem.

property

7 There is no official list of social problems, and sociologists differ about what to include. All include crime, delinquency, and mental illness as social problems. None now includes child labor because this problem has been resolved through legislation and social custom. Thus, _______ _______ vary over time and circumstances.

social problems

8 Social problems may be conceptualized from either structural or functional viewpoints. The institutions which make up organized society have fixed patterns of organization, statuses, values, and goals. These stable aspects of institutions exemplify the _______ of society.

structure

9 Processes which break down or disorganize these patterned arrangements of people impair the _______ of society.

structure

10 Elliott believed that structure is more basic to society than function, and stated that "social disorganization is a process by which the relationships binding persons together in groups are strained, loosened or broken. When patterns of interaction which hold the group together are impaired or disrupted, _______ _______ results" (Elliott and Merrill, 1961).

social disorganization

11 Homans (1950, p. 369) defines disintegration of the small group as a condition "marked by a decline in the number of activities . . . the frequency of interaction between members, and by a weakening of control over the behavior of individuals." In this context, disintegration is clearly similar to _______.

disorganization

12 When Homans talks about activities and interaction, and the control of behavior of individual members by a group, he is actually referring to what goes on in the group. This exemplifies the functional aspect of the group rather than the _______ aspect.

structural

13 A social institution is an organized framework for conserving or achieving social values and goals. The family is an organized framework of statuses which produces and acculturates new members into the society. The family is a social _______.

institution

14 The family may be weakened or disrupted by sexual behavior outside of marriage, by desertion and neglect, and by too easy divorce procedures. Family breakdown impairs the structure of society and therefore constitutes a _______ _______.

social problem

15 Public institutions are seriously menaced by white-collar crime. When dishonest officials embezzle funds, violate their trust, or manipulate corporate assets for purely personal advantage, they generate a serious social problem in the form of ________-________ ________.

white-collar crime

16 Society has the power to create institutional agencies to safeguard or maintain its organization. One group of institutions is maintained to extend social control over persons whose behavior otherwise would destroy or weaken the social matrix in which they operate. An example of such an institution would be a ________.

court (prison, mental hospital)

17 Social problems presuppose a value. Social values are concepts of what is good or what is conducive to the positive interests of ________.

society

18 Clinard (1963, p. 9) defines social values as the central goals of a culture or subculture. If juvenile delinquents organize a gang with fixed structure and defined organizational goals, it constitutes a ________ and would necessarily have social values.

subculture

19 Values sought by professional thieves, drug addicts, and other members of deviant subcultures represent short-term values which gratify the ________ but damage the larger society.

individual

20 Social problems, on the contrary, are stated with regard to long-term ________ which benefit or conserve the larger society.

values

21 The basic viewpoint for assessing social problems is not that of a subculture or a segment of society, but rather the viewpoint of the ________ ________.

whole society

22 Social problems are sometimes interpreted in antagonistic ways by different sectors of society. Slum clearance and urban renewal are favored by civic-minded citizens and by downtown merchants. They are often bitterly opposed by those who ________ from slums.

profit (gain)

23 Weinberg (1960, p. 17) rejects the static structural view of social disorganization and asserts the superiority of the functional view of social problems. Social problems persist as a natural outgrowth of ongoing social process in this ________ view.

functional

24 Social deviation consists of behavior at variance with or opposed to the norms and expectations of behavior prescribed for a social role. Patterned behavior within fairly well-defined limits is the definition for social ________.

role

25 Role regulation applies to everyone—to bankers, mothers, fathers, teachers, and children. Behavior such as embezzlement, adultery, homosexuality, or auto theft violates these roles in our culture and constitutes ________ ________.

social deviation

26 Patterned behavior in an ordered system of interaction constitutes the ongoing social process by which social institutions operate. This process requires that persons accept, master, and effectively perform the appropriate ________ ________.

social roles

27 Some persons are incapable of accepting the standard roles in society. Severely retarded persons cannot perform roles in conventional employment or occupation. Since they cannot ________ normally in society, retarded persons constitute a social problem.

participate (function)

28 The chronic alcoholic and the drug addict are similar to severely retarded persons (whose condition is involuntary), except that their incapacity appears to be at least partly ________.

voluntary

29 They are unable to accept the responsibility of a normal employment and occupation or can function only to a limited degree. Such persons also are unable fully to perform appropriate social ________.

roles

30 Ambiguous roles carry the seeds of a social problem. The ambiguous situation contains undetermined or inherently contradictory meanings. Some nineteen-year-old adolescents are still treated like children, but are expected to act like ________.

adults

31 They may be considered too old to be dependent on parents, if not in school, but not old enough to hold a "man's" job. Such a person is temporarily the victim of ________ roles.

ambiguous

Not necessarily, but it shows how complex analysis is.

32 The phenomena which are most accessible to observation, categorization, and analysis are the things people actually do in social situations. Barker and Wright (1954) found that it required nearly four hundred pages to describe one child's behavior for one day. Does this support the oft-heard argument that human behavior is too complex for scientific analysis? ______.

attitude

33 Attitudes represent a predisposition to act in a certain way with respect to a given situation. An ______ is inferred from the previous behavior or expressed beliefs of an individual.

behavior

34 Attitudes are based on beliefs, values, goals, and orientations to these goals. An antisocial attitude in a large number of persons will give rise to a social problem in countering the resultant antisocial ______.

attitudes

35 Those seeking to convert a criminal, a delinquent, or an alcoholic to socially positive behavior usually seek to modify his ______.

family

36 A process of individuation has been identified by early sociological theorists, such as Tönnies, Simmel, and Durkheim. The operation of the public market, the highly elaborate division of labor, and the growth of cities tend to break down the influence of the simple, permanent, primary group, such as the ______ or the neighborhood.

institutionalization (usually in a public jail)

37 The individual today has much freedom of movement. He can select his own activities and functions, independent of his family and neighbors. In colonial times, the deviant, broken-down, or withdrawn individual was taken care of in the family unless he was so violent as to require ______.

society

38 Today, the delinquent, the alcoholic, and the mentally unbalanced individuals are more likely to be considered the responsibility of ______ rather than of the family alone.

individual

39 Full individuation requires extensive training, social skills, flexibility, and an understanding of social process. If there is lack of capacity, or if the necessary training, skills, or understanding are impaired, the ______ is less likely to make his own interests compatible with those of the larger society.

40 Social process involves continuing change and readjustment. Change takes place at a fast tempo in the life cycle of the individual and at some slower rate in the society as a whole. The periods of infancy, childhood, adolescence, parenthood, full maturity, and retirement represent successive levels which require ________.

change

41 The larger society undergoes social changes which often invalidate previous social values. Thrift was once a social value manifested in saving money. In modern society the thrift concept is better served in the judicious investment of money. The concept of thrift has altered in the process of social ________.

change

42 Success in modern society requires rational investment in personal resources. The well-adjusted youth invests heavily in his own ________.

education (training)

43 The maladjusted youth who expends all his resources for immediate gratification is likely to fall into the category of juvenile ________.

delinquency

44 The automobile allows the worker to live 10 to 30 miles from his place of work, but creates incredible traffic congestion. The automobile has provided beneficial change but has also created new social ________.

problems

45 Social problems associated with the color line have altered, and some American Negroes have experienced some improvement in social and economic status as a result of ________ ________.

social change

46 Some parts of the culture lag behind others in the process of social change. Cultural traits involved in technology and the use of physical objects ________ rapidly.

change

47 Practice often lags several decades behind scientific discovery. Ogburn (1922) identified this difference as cultural ________.

lag

48 Local police forces often become handicapped when confronted with a nationally organized crime syndicate. In this instance, police organization shows ________ ________ compared with criminal organization.

cultural lag

49 Cultural lag is manifested in the segments and subordinate parts of society. Corporations required ________ time to adapt electronic computer techniques to their accounting, billing, and analysis procedures.

lag

subcultures

50 The sciences require time to adapt their theory to new concepts which modify accepted "laws." Cultural lag clearly affects various ________ of the great culture.

REVIEW: *Social problems occur on three levels: at those of the individual, the group, and the (sub)culture. They proliferate rapidly in times of social change and may be in part related to cultural lag. In former times, the local community handled social problems informally. In large modern countries they are handled formally in specialized institutions.*

Categories of Social Problems

relative

51 The identification and definition of social problems vary relative to social perspective within a society and according to cultural variation. Since social problems depend on variation in time, in culture, and by social perspective, they are ________ rather than absolute.

social problems

52 Social problems inhere in training and controlling individuals in economic productive processes. A change in technology will therefore produce a change in ________ ________.

changes

53 Since social problems relate to changing facets of a society, we cannot say that they are absolute. Rather, social problems are relative to many kinds of ________ in society.

group

54 Problem behavior involves rejection of, withdrawal from, or hostility to group norms. Cohen (1955) states that delinquent boys' groups join together in rejecting middle-class values. In this instance, problem behavior can be studied at the ________ level.

norms

55 Social problems always have basic reference to the norms of the great culture. The society's basic normative system is expressed in symbols which are inculcated in the members. Typically, deviants, delinquents, and criminals reject some basic ________ of the great culture.

kill

56 Owing to cultural lag, it is entirely possible that the normative system of the great culture may itself contain contradictory elements. The biblical Commandment, "Thou shalt not kill," is in conflict with a soldier's duty to ________ the enemy in wartime.

norms

57 The functioning of organized society requires an accepted set of norms or rules of behavior. However, no society can maintain full and universal compliance with its ________.

normlessness

58 Every society must endure some degree of normlessness by some of its members. Durkheim used the French term anomie to refer to the phenomenon of norm violation or ________.

anomic (normless)

59 If a society permitted all its norms to fall into disuse, Durkheim would refer to it as an ________ society.

humanity

60 Grave social problems arise when an entire culture is in conflict with more universal values. The Nazi government's crimes of genocide (the murdering of entire ethnic groups of people) were termed a crime against ________.

Negro

61 In the United States, the conflict between the ideals of democracy, freedom, and equal justice for all have been squarely denied by racial discrimination, whereby some white Americans forbid Americans of ________ extraction equal access to public facilities (Myrdal, 1944).

discrimination

62 There are many who assert that the much higher incidence of crime, delinquency, and mental derangement among Negroes is directly related to racial ________.

time (temporal)

63 Social problems vary drastically in regard to time; we can term this type of variation ________ relativity.

time

64 In 1900 in the United States, the sale and consumption of alcoholic beverages was a private matter. In 1930, the sale of such beverages violated Federal law. In 1966 nearly all states and most localities permitted the sale of alcoholic beverages. Formal changes in the law produced significant changes in this social problem over ________.

crime

65 Social problems vary by a kind of cultural relativity, as in the case of suicide in Japan and the United States. In Japan, suicide has been accepted from classical times as an honorable alternative to defeat or embarrassment. In the United States, attempted suicide is legally classified as a ________.

culture (society)

66 Legal pressure against gambling has been strong and there is vocal condemnation of gambling in the United States. In Germany and France, gambling is fully legal, and national lotteries are permitted. Gambling is not inherently a social problem except in terms of the ______.

abortion

67 Abortion is regarded differently in the United States and Japan. In the United States, ______ is illegal unless required for the health of the mother, and only on authority of a physician.

cultural relativity

68 Abortion is regarded as murder by many religious groups. However, in Japan, abortion clinics provide an abortion to any woman who wants one for a small fee. The differing attitudes toward abortion constitute an evidence of ______ ______.

delinquents

69 Juvenile delinquency shows a rising trend. About 2 percent of the child population between the ages of ten and seventeen are delinquent (Merton and Nisbet, 1961). From 80 to 90 percent of ______ are boys, typically convicted of malicious behavior or stealing.

suburban

70 There is a much higher reported rate of juvenile delinquency among working-class children than among middle-class children, and much higher rates in the poorer residential and slum areas of cities than in the wealthier ______ areas.

class

71 Cohen (1955) hypothesizes that delinquency primarily expresses a protest by working-class boys against middle-class morality. It appears that delinquency rates are related to social ______.

juvenile

72 Porterfield (1946, pp. 32–35) compared the delinquent acts of 337 Texas college students with the delinquent acts of a group of 2,049 delinquents appearing before a Fort Worth judge. He found that the incidence of delinquency and the seriousness of delinquent acts were about equal between the two groups. This suggests that delinquency may be quite widespread in the ______ population.

punished

73 Criminal law is enacted by a political authority, for specific offenses, and applies uniformly to all adults. Violation of criminal law is usually ______ by imprisonment or monetary fines or both.

The rate of serious crimes in the United States in 1964 reached 1,361 per 100,000 population. Since 1958, crime has increased six times faster than our population growth. About 92 percent of all crimes reported to the police involve no violence (Federal Bureau of Investigation, 1965, pp. 1–4).

There are about twenty times more men than women prisoners in Federal and state prisons in the United States (Pollak, 1950, pp. 44–56). This may be related to the fact that males have primary responsibility for procuring property in our society.

74 Criminal behavior is much more widespread than crime reports indicate. Wallerstein and Wyle (1947) randomly sampled the New York City area. Of 1,020 men and 678 women included, about 91 percent admitted having committed one or more crimes since reaching age sixteen. The sample included ministers, professors, scientists, and businessmen. We can conclude that _______ behavior may be found throughout our society.

criminal

75 Durkheim described three basic types of suicide: the egoistic, the anomic, and the altruistic. The suicide committed to save face, escape pain, or give vengeance on another exemplifies Durkheim's concept of _______ suicide.

egoistic

76 A suicide committed out of a sense of despair, futility, or boredom illustrates Durkheim's _______ _______ type.

anomic suicide

77 A suicide committed to save one's friends, serve one's country, or provide for one's widow could exemplify the _______ suicide.

altruistic

Table 25. Suicide Rates per 100,000 by Sex for 1933

Country	*Total*	*Male*	*Female*
Denmark	24.1	32.3	16.0
Japan	20.5	24.5	16.5
United States:			
White	10.8	17.2	4.6
Nonwhite	3.8	6.4	1.3
Spain	5.9	9.1	2.9
Eire	2.3	3.3	1.2

SOURCE: World Health Organization, "Mortality from Suicide," *Epidemiology and Vital Statistics Report*, IX, no. 4, Geneva, 1956, p. 250. Used by permission.

three

78 From Table 25, it appears that, in general, about ______ times as many suicides are committed by men as by women (World Health Organization, 1956, p. 250).

alcoholics

79 In 1956 there were about 68 million adult drinkers of alcoholic beverages and a residue of about 5 million confirmed drinkers, or alcoholics. About 8 percent of the men and 1.4 percent of the women over twenty years of age could be classified as ______.

suicide

80 According to Ivy (1959, p. 82), the death rate among America's 5 million alcoholics is 7 percent per annum. Life expectancy is about sixteen years from the onset of alcoholism and about fifty-one years from birth. Since alcoholism is at least partly voluntary, is self-inflicted, and hastens death, it is basically similar to ______ as a social problem.

drug addicts

81 Persons using habit-forming drugs finally enter a state of periodic or chronic intoxication harmful to themselves and to society. The characteristics include (*a*) an overpowering compulsion to obtain and take the drug; (*b*) a tendency to increase the dose; (c) a psychological and physical dependence on the effects of the drug. Persons manifesting these three characteristics are described as ______ ______ (United Nations Expert Committee on Drugs, 1950).

Table 26. Narcotic Addicts by Ethnic Origin

Ethnic origin	*Percentage*
Negro	60
Puerto Rican	7
Mexican American	5
Native white	27

SOURCE: U.S. Bureau of Narcotics, *Traffic in Opium and Other Dangerous Drugs,* Washington, D.C., 1959, p. 43.

Negroes

82 The Federal Bureau of Narcotics (1958, p. 43) has a register of 46,266 active narcotic addicts in the United States. Most of these narcotics addicts are ______.

twenty

83 Since the Negro population represents only one-tenth of the total population, yet has more than twice the percentage of the native white registered addicts (see Table 26), the Negro rate is more than ______ times the white rate.

Table 27. Arrests for Sex Offenses, United States, 1964

Offense	*No. of arrests*
Forcible rape	9,450
Prostitution	28,190
Other sex offenses	58,082
Total for sex offenses	95,722
Total for all offenses	4,582,974

SOURCE: Federal Bureau of Investigation, *Uniform Crime Reports for the United States, 1964,* 1965, p. 106.

2

84 Sex offenders accounted for about ______ percent of all arrests for major crimes in cities (see Table 27).

deviation (crime)

85 Alcoholism, drug addiction, suicide, delinquency, and sex deviation represent categories of ______ by individuals.

socialized

86 An understanding of individual deviations and of the social problems they constitute may logically be developed through an investigation of the process by which individuals are ______.

parts (subcultures)

87 The great culture is the total culture of a society. Although the great culture is conceived of as a whole, it is made up of a large number of component ______.

changes

88 In all modern industrial societies the component parts of the great culture are undergoing changes at varying rates and in divergent directions. Any equilibrium achieved among the parts of the culture will be upset by the varying kinds of ______.

problem

89 Any major change occurring within the great culture requires readjustment of some cultural elements and is likely to bring about a social ______.

social change

90 Understanding social problems arising from conflicts within the great culture requires analysis of the process of ______ ______.

Immigrants typically must accept unskilled labor with low wages and minimal job security. Therefore, problems associated with low rates of pay, low status, and substandard dwelling areas tend to make their adjustment more difficult.

slaves / citizens

91 Migration typically leads to problems of ethnic or racial relations. The American Negroes were originally transported to the United States involuntarily to provide labor under the system of slavery. With the forcible termination of the slavery system in the Civil War, they were in an ambivalent status. They were in practice neither ________ nor ________ in the Southern states.

unemployment

92 Unemployment complicates the adjustment problems of adolescents newly out of school and entering the labor market for the first time. Negro workmen are typically the last to be hired in good times and the first to be released in recessions. They typically suffer about ten times higher rates of ________ than white workers.

unemployment

93 Automation increases output, lowers costs, and improves quality control. Its long-run effects are to increase wealth and real income, but its short-run effects are to displace workers, to render some skills obsolete, and to create technological ________.

population

94 Overpopulation produces grave social problems. In an area where a million people could live comfortably, a billion people might find physical survival impossible. Poverty and economic strangulation may in time result from unlimited expansion of ________.

Egypt's population almost doubled in thirty-five years, reaching 20 million in 1962. Egypt supports 1,250 people per square mile of cultivated land, compared with 30 per square mile in the United States. About 90 percent of the Egyptians live directly from agriculture, and their standard of living is lower than that of the English peasant of the seventeenth century (Davis, 1961, p. 300).

overpopulation

95 Egypt's low standard of living is a direct result of ________.

Table 28. Birth and Death Rates, United States, 1964

Births	21.2 per 1,000 population per year
Deaths	9.4 per 1,000 population per year
Surplus	11.8 per 1,000 population per year

SOURCE: U.S. Department of Health, Education, and Welfare, *Vital Statistics Report, Annual Summary for the United States, 1964,* 1965, pp. 5–6.

1.2

96 From figures shown in Table 28, the rate of population increase is about _______ percent per year. This rate of increase will double the population in about fifty-nine years.

worse (greater)

97 World population passed the 3 billion level in 1962, and is increasing at a rate of 1.7 percent per year. This will double the world's population in forty years (Merton, 1961, p. 291). Any social problems which are aggravated by increasing population density will become much _______ with each passing decade.

REVIEW: *Social problems arise from strains and conflicts between individuals and social groups in violation of the norms of a society. Therefore social problems vary in extent and in impact with different societies and at different times in the same society. The American problem of race relations is a specific product of strains and conflicts in social adjustment arising from an earlier domestic institution of slavery. Suicide, although common to both Japan and the United States, constitutes a rather different social problem in the two cultures. Juvenile delinquency appears to be increasing in recent years in the United States. This would suggest that adolescents may be experiencing increasing strain in adjusting to the requirements of adult society. The rate of crime commission has similarly increased in recent years. Offenders are chiefly men, and offenses are primarily involved with property. Withdrawal patterns are manifested by individuals who become alcoholics or drug addicts. More general types of problems arise from the uncontrolled increase of population in countries where the means of subsistence are already overtaxed. Automation is an example of a problem arising directly as a result of technological change. All these problems require continuing adjustment and readjustment in each society.*

Mental Disorders

mental health

98 Mental health embraces the concept of full normal mental capacities, coupled with a well-adjusted, stable personality. Some persons shift smoothly into a series of socially operable roles consistent with their age and sex. Such persons exhibit good _______ _______.

99 Rennie and Srole (1955) estimate that only about 11 percent of the working class and about 19 percent of the middle class merit a rating of good mental health. At least 80 percent of our population falls short of this standard. Probably about 20 percent manifest varying degrees of mental ________.

illness

100 Mental illness may occur under two conditions. First, if there is demonstrable organic damage, as to the brain, which explains the illness, we may say that it has an ________ cause.

organic

101 Second, mental illness may occur with no demonstrable organic damages. If there is no organic cause for the illness, but only the inability to *function* normally, it must be classified as a ________ illness.

functional

102 If there is nothing organically wrong, the patient is usually diagnosed as having a ________ mental disorder.

functional

103 A precise description of symptoms is difficult, because mental illness often exhibits mixed symptoms. To bring some order to diagnosis, American workers in mental health fields have adopted a standard nomenclature of ________ for different mental illnesses.

symptoms

104 If a disease is characterized by a group of symptoms, the set of symptoms is called a syndrome. If all elements of the syndrome are manifested, then diagnosis is relatively ________.

certain (positive)

105 Individuals vary, however, in the way they manifest symptoms. If mental diseases were clearly marked by a specific and relatively invariable set of symptoms, positive identification of the ________ would be possible.

syndrome

106 Before the development of specific treatments, mental hospital wards were often like prisons. Violent patients were locked in padded cells, strapped to their beds, or trussed in a heavy canvas jacket with their arms strapped around the body. This procedure provided no treatment, but it did provide control over the patient's ________.

behavior

107 Insanity is a legal concept. It refers to persons legally declared to be of unsound mind by competent medical authority. Commitment to a mental hospital may be ordered by a judge. The patient is then in ________ custody.

legal

Table 29. Admissions to Public Mental Hospitals

	Patients in thousands			
	1960	*1961*	*1962*	*1963*
Admissions	235	253	267	285
Net live releases	191	216	227	247
Deaths	50	47	50	49
Resident patients (Dec. 31)	536	528	516	505

SOURCE: U.S. Department of Health, Education, and Welfare, *Health, Education and Welfare Indicators,* 1964, p. 7.

decreased

108 Admissions to public mental hospitals in the United States increased from 1960 to 1963 (see Table 29), but the number of resident patients _______.

discharges

109 If admissions increased but the resident population decreased, while the death rate remained the same, there would have to be an increase in _______.

29

110 The percentage of increase of patients discharged from 1960 to 1963 was about _______ percent.

control

111 The marked increase in discharges of mental patients might be related to the introduction of tranquilizing drugs from 1954, since the tranquilizers provided much improved _______ of patients (Joint Commission, 1961, p. 7).

mental illness

112 Strecker (1930) estimated that 75 percent of all patients visiting the general practitioner are emotionally disturbed and that 5 percent are psychotic (Weinberg, 1960). It appears that most of those who see physicians are likely to manifest _______ _______ along with organic illness.

psychosis

113 Of the categories shown in Table 30, _______ is the most prevalent reason for commitment.

114 In World War II, about 6 percent of all hospital admissions were diagnosed as psychoneurosis and psychosis. Symptoms tended to be rather intense, but of short duration, and they responded well to treatment. Usually these

Table 30. Commitment for Mental Illness, United States, 1949

Category	*No. committed*
Psychosis	100,000
Mentally deficient	1,400
Alcoholism	18,500
Drug addiction	2,000

SOURCE: U.S. Bureau of the Census, *Statistical Abstract of the United States,* 1954, p. 91.

cases were associated with definite and identifiable stresses and shocks. Along with psychosis, doctors now began to include ______ as a true mental illness.

psychoneurosis

115 Psychoses are disturbances with relatively more severe symptoms than those of ______. Both these conditions will be described more fully in a subsequent section.

psychoneurosis

116 Another type of disorder which has become a social problem in our society is mental deficiency. Mental deficiency is primarily indicated by a pronounced and continuing lack of ability to learn. A child who displays a continuing lack of ability to learn is ______ ______.

mentally deficient

117 Individuals who are unable to learn the general requirements of social living or the specific requirements of social or occupational roles also pose a ______ to the larger society.

problem

118 Hereditary mental retardation occurs because of defective genes. Most defective fetuses die in utero, and are miscarried (Elliott and Merrill, 1961, p. 273). If the defective fetus survives to be born, its survival is often accompanied by ______ ______.

mental retardation

119 Tredgold (1952) distinguishes four sources of mental deficiency which are not hereditary. These include (*a*) traumatic feeblemindedness due to accidental damage; (*b*) infectious deficiency from a disease affecting the nervous system; (*c*) degenerative deficiency from unknown causes; and (*d*) deprivative ______ from malnutrition.

deficiency

120 Tredgold (1952) estimated that about 1 percent of the total population is mentally deficient. In the United States, according to this estimate, there are about 2 million mental defectives, less than 8 percent of whom are in ________.

institutions

121 About 89 percent of all mental defectives are born to apparently normal parents. Since the majority of such cases arise among apparently normal parents, sterilizing the mentally retarded would have very (little/much) effect on such births.

little

122 Mental disorganization is a type of functional disorder. Persons who are born apparently normal and healthy, but who later develop aberrant mental functioning are said to be mentally ________.

disorganized

123 Diseases can be described in terms of their effects or their symptoms. They can be also described in terms of the etiology or causes. The preferred way to describe a disease is in terms of its ________.

etiology

124 The American Psychiatric Association and the American Medical Association have adopted a standard nomenclature for mental, or emotional, diseases and for physical diseases accompanied by mental ________.

disorder (disorganization, etc.)

125 For convenience, we shall discuss three broad categories of emotional disturbance. They include neurotic disorders, psychotic disorders, and brain syndromes. Of these three types, the category most likely to be accompanied by demonstrable organic damage to the nervous system is ________ ________.

brain syndromes

Psychoneurotic Disorders

126 It has been estimated (Strecker, 1930) that about one-fourth of the population is sufficiently afflicted with neurotic disorders to impair personal relations and job performance, but these ________ for the most part remain untreated. (See also Gurin, Veroff, and Feld, 1960; Malzberg, 1963.)

disorders (i.e., people with these disorders)

Neurotic reactions often appear to arise from a conflict of values and purposes, which leaves the victim unsure of himself. Some psychiatrists, e.g., Freud, interpret this as a basic conflict between "nature" and civilization.

conflict

127 Other authorities, such as Harry Stack Sullivan, Karen Horney, and Erich Fromm, regard such conflicts as arising within the culture. The male child is expected to compete and cooperate. He seeks personal freedom, but must accept discipline and regimentation. These are examples of intracultural _______ (Merton and Nisbet, 1961, p. 168).

insecurity

128 The neurotic is the victim of insecurity which may arise from lack of support from parents, withdrawal of parental love, or instability of the family. The neurotic suffers repeated frustration as a result of conflict and _______.

The neurotic's behavior can be classified according to several reactions:

1. *anxiety reactions*
2. *conversion reactions*
3. *phobic reactions*
4. *obsessive-compulsive reactions*
5. *hypochondriacal reactions*

These reactions may occur singly or in combination.

disorganized (upset, etc.)

129 The anxiety reaction in its milder chronic form may be characterized by restlessness, insomnia, lack of appetite, constipation, inability to concentrate, and irritability in interpersonal relations. The person may be explosive, forgetful, unfriendly, and relatively _______ in his personal life.

conversion

130 The anxiety of the neurotic may be converted to some other form of reaction. When an individual develops amnesia or one of the various forms of hysteria, we have an example of the _______ reaction.

amnesia

131 When anxiety is "converted" to amnesia, the patient suffers a partial loss of memory. The individual who disappears from his usual residence and forgets his name, address, phone number, other identification, family and relatives, and occupation is a victim of _______.

complete

132 Because the amnesia victim forgets selectively, his loss of memory is partial rather than _______.

133 On the other hand, the amnesia victim does not delude himself as to who he is. He does not invent another identity for himself. Instead, he tends to insist that he has no idea of his ________.

identity

134 Hysteria also involves a displacement of anxiety. For this reason, conversion reactions are sometimes referred to as dissociations. The neurotic who believes himself suddenly blind ________ himself from his anxiety.

dissociates

135 Hysteria can also manifest itself in general or limited functional paralysis. The afflicted person may be unable to move his limbs or his entire body. In this condition he also presumably escapes from his ________.

anxiety

136 As with the amnesic form of conversion, a person manifesting hysterical conversion attempts to escape from his anxiety by ________ it into an ailment which is socially recognized. The patient's conviction as to his condition is sincere.

converting

137 A phobia may be defined as an extreme and irrational fear of some object, situation, or place. Symptoms of the phobic reaction include excitement, nausea, aversion, and panic. The phobic reaction is an irrational ________ reaction.

fear

138 People suffering phobic reactions are presumed to project the fear implicit in neurotic anxiety onto some object or situation in the environment. The ________ permits the patient to focus and identify his underlying generalized fears and to make specific reactions to them.

phobia

139 Phobias often have a rational element of threat or danger connected with them. Thus, acrophobia, or the irrational fear of high places, can be connected to a ________ of falling.

fear

140 The phobic has experienced injury from falls in the past and has a justifiable basis for alarm. But the alarm which he projects is exaggerated beyond the reasonable dimensions of the danger, and the ________ manifests it to a more extreme degree than do normal persons in the same situation.

neurotic (phobic person)

141 An irrational, persistent dread of water, germs, animals, crowds, or other objects and events would illustrate the ________ reaction.

phobic

compulsive

142 Obsessive-compulsive reactions involve a constantly repeated pattern of thought or action which has no rational purpose or advantage proportionate to the duration of the action. Many kinds of behaviors may become subject to incessant repetition, and thus are ________.

obsessive (obsessional)

143 Obsessions relate to thought patterns, often connected closely with some kind of fear. The neurotic who is constantly preoccupied with the same thoughts exemplifies the ________ pattern.

hypochondriacs

144 The hypochondriacal neurotic is preoccupied with his health. Such a person tends to be a ready victim for the endless parade of nostrums and panaceas offered as patent medicines. People who make a lifelong habit of preoccupation with ill health are called ________.

neurotic

145 The neuroses constitute a comparatively mild form of mental illness, in which the more severe manifestations are usually temporary, although the basic ________ orientation is usually chronic.

REVIEW: *Mental illness need not be accompanied by observable organic damage. If there is no organic damage, mental illness is classed as a functional disorder. In recent years the treatment of mental disorders has improved markedly through use of the tranquilizing drugs, which provide better control of patients and improved effects of therapy. Mental deficiency is indicated where learning ability is below normal. The mentally retarded can benefit from intensive training. Neurotic disorders arise from variations in the anxiety reaction. Neurotic disorders are often identified with specific kinds of phobias, which are manifested in irrational and uncontrollable fears of objects, situations, or places. When the neurotic displaces his anxiety with an imaginary physical disability, he is manifesting a case of hysteria. Most neurotic disorders are sufficiently mild that they do not prevent social functioning, but they are difficult to treat and tend to be chronic.*

Psychotic Disorders, Psychopathy, and Brain Damage

psychotic

146 Psychiatrists and psychologists are not agreed on the relation between neurotic illnesses and the more severe psychotic illnesses. Neurotic behaviors may absorb the effects of anxiety and therefore protect the neurotic from the more severe form of ________ illness (Cameron, 1947, p. 277).

147 Neurotic illness usually does not lead to psychotic breakdown. The neurotic does not demonstrate disorientation, delusions, and extended severe depression, which may characterize the ________ patient.

psychotic

148 The so-called "psychopathic" person usually manifests normal health and intelligence. His distinguishing characteristic is that he demonstrates an indifferent attitude to the reactions, rights, and interests of other ________.

people

149 A shortsighted preoccupation with his own immediate gratification marks the ________ person.

psychopathic

150 The psychopath does not typically cooperate with others or support group values. Having little sense of responsibility to others, he often avoids employment and the discipline that goes with it. Arsonists and "confidence men" have often been diagnosed as ________.

psychopaths

151 The psychopath resists therapy and the efforts of others to assert influence over him. He takes a truculent pride in living for himself. The psychopath presents a difficult problem to ________.

society (others)

152 Psychosis is usually differentiated from neurosis in terms of the severity of symptoms, the disorientation of the psychotic, and the methods of treatment employed. Psychotic illness is typically incapacitating, and is much more difficult to ________.

treat

153 Psychotics who do have periods of violent behavior experience them at varying intervals, and are usually quiet otherwise. In general, the psychotic person is seriously ________.

ill (disturbed)

154 The psychotics manifesting purely functional disorders make up well over half of the institutionalized mental patients. Such patients show few, if any, organic symptoms which could account for their mental ________.

illness

155 About 45 percent of all mentally ill patients have symptoms of schizophrenia. The word means "split mind" or "split personality," but the cleavage characteristic is not much in evidence in the ________.

symptoms

156 This disease is predominantly an affliction of adults between the ages of fifteen and forty-five. Persons within these ages who display severe disorientation, incoherence, and unresponsiveness may be diagnosed as suffering from ________.

schizophrenia

Psychiatrists are not agreed as to whether schizophrenia is one illness or a family of illnesses. However, five schizophrenic conditions are identified: simple schizophrenia, hebephrenic type, catatonic type, paranoid type, and mixed schizophrenia.

symptoms

157 The fact that these are classed as a single disorder implies that there must be some common _______ for all subtypes (Coleman, 1960, p. 234).

withdrawn

158 A common attribute of all forms of schizophrenia is withdrawal. The patient becomes unresponsive to others and ceases to take interest in normal daily activities. He seems unaware of the people or objects of his environment and appears to drift and daydream constantly. He appears to have _______ from reality.

schizophrenia

159 The schizophrenic takes little interest in his appearance or condition or in food and people. He does not seem to follow the current situation. He has indifferent or very blunted emotional reactions. These are generally the characteristics of simple _______.

schizophrenia

160 Persons suffering from simple schizophrenia are not usually dangerous. They drift through time with their own private stream of disordered fantasy. They may demonstrate other forms of schizophrenia. There is no set progression between the different types of _______.

stuporous

161 A person diagnosed as a catatonic schizophrenic manifests symptoms of the simple schizophrenic, but in addition goes through irregular cycles of excited and stuporous behavior which appear meaningless and unrelated to the situation. Often the excited phase alternates with a _______ phase.

catatonic

162 In the excited phase, the _______ patient is hyperactive and dangerous. He may attack others, injure himself, or merely chatter in an animated way.

environment

163 In the stuporous phase, the catatonic patient is motionless and apathetic, staring into space with no change of expression. He may assume a statuesque pose for a number of hours. Stuporous patients sometimes must be fed through a tube. Catatonic stupor represents marked lack of responsiveness to the _______.

164 The catatonic also manifests a depressed state in which signs of melancholia appear. Periods of excessive hyperactivity, stupor, and/or melancholia are characteristic of the ______ form of schizophrenia.

catatonic

165 Patients diagnosed as suffering from hebephrenic schizophrenia demonstrate silly laughter. The schizophrenic who typically giggles and laughs irrationally demonstrates ______ symptoms.

hebephrenic

166 The paranoid schizophrenia is characterized by active delusions. Some paranoids believe that others are plotting to kill or harm them; others may adopt grandiose delusions (the so-called "Napoleonic complex"). The ______ is sometimes dangerous because he may try to avenge himself on someone he fancies as his enemy.

paranoid

167 A schizophrenic who believes himself to be God, a millionaire, or an emperor would be deluded about his identity and therefore would be demonstrating ______ symptoms.

paranoid

168 In many schizophrenic patients there is a rather wide variety of symptoms, which may include stuporous periods, hebephrenic periods, moments of depression, brief periods of excitement, periods of paranoid delusions, and periods of simple daydreaming. These may occur in any sequence or combination, and such a patient is classified as a schizophrenic reaction of ______ type.

mixed

169 Hollingshead and Redlich (1958, p. 227) point out that diagnostic subcategories of schizophrenia can be identified only in exceptional cases. They note that most ______ patients exhibit different symptoms. They would classify all schizophrenics as ______ types.

schizophrenic
mixed

170 The schizophrenic reaction may be transient. Typically this is the case with a reasonably well-adjusted person who has a ______ reaction to a sudden or very intense conflict.

schizophrenic
(psychotic)

171 Schizophrenic reactions which are deep-seated (e.g., manifesting withdrawal behavior from childhood) may be very unresponsive to treatment. Such patients may live in a mental hospital forty or fifty years and show little improvement. Severity is closely related to the ______ of symptoms.

duration

schizophrenic breakdown

172 Schizophrenics typically show a pattern of withdrawal and failure before their breakdown. They are unwilling to compete or to learn the ways of their peer group. Weinberg (1950) relates their breakdown to a loss of self-esteem. Failure in school, in business, or in marriage may induce a ________ ________.

Table 31. Schizophrenics without Schizophrenic Relatives

Social class	*Number*	*Percent*
I and II	25	84
III	64	70
IV	266	67
V	281	64

SOURCE: M. B. Clinard, *The Sociology of Deviant Behavior*, rev. ed., Holt, Rinehart and Winston, Inc., New York, 1963, p. 328. Used by permission.

relatives

173 There is much schizophrenia without any recognized incidence of it among relatives. We can infer from Table 31 that only about one-third of all schizophrenics have close ________ who are schizophrenics.

schizophrenic

174 Environmental factors seemingly associated with schizophrenia include a harsh, cold, overdemanding mother and a relatively noncommunicative father. These conditions do not necessarily bring about schizophrenia, but they may create a tendency or predisposition to ________ reactions.

predisposition
vulnerable

175 "In families where the infant does not receive affection and . . . the child . . . [has no] . . . security in his relation to those most significant to his care, vulnerable personalities may be generated" (Merton and Nisbet, 1961, p. 165). The combination of a genetic ________ plus a ________ personality creates a strong probability of schizophrenia.

withdrawal

176 Withdrawal and conflict are sometimes mentioned as etiological factors for schizophrenia since these conditions are typically associated with schizophrenic breakdown. However, the most constant symptom of the schizophrenic patient is his complete ________ from reality and from social interaction.

conflict
interaction

177 The milder cases of schizophrenic withdrawal are sometimes triggered by a sudden change of environment or by a particular failure, but the most chronic cases manifest a long history of refusal to accept ________, a refusal to compete, and very low levels of ________.

depressed

178 Another major group of emotional disorders consists of the manic, depressive, and manic-depressive psychoses. The manic-depressive usually goes through some cycle of hyperactive periods and _______ periods.

manic

179 When the patient is very active, he may become violent, attack others, or injure himself. These are examples of _______ symptoms.

depressive
suicide

180 Depressive periods are marked by a deep despondency and suicidal tendencies. A depressive period may last several days and may recur at more or less regular intervals. The greatest danger of the _______ period is that the patient may commit _______.

recover

181 The manic-depressive patient is oriented to reality; i.e., he "knows who he is." The prognosis is usually good, because typically, the rational capacity is not seriously impaired. Most manic-depressive patients can be expected to _______ within a few months.

involutional melancholia

182 One type of severe depression, termed "involutional melancholia," often accompanies glandular changes and the effects of menopause and functional life readjustments. Men from fifty to sixty and women from forty to fifty face adjustment problems during the years when the normal functions, values, and perspectives of life may have to be reorganized. Moodiness and depression to the point of mild disorientation and despondency are characteristic of _______ _______.

brain (body)

183 In addition to functional psychoses, organic psychoses mark a category of mental illness which is accompanied by some form of damage to the _______.

brain

184 This class of mental illness includes deluded, unbalanced, and disoriented behavior, with the presumption that _______ damage is at least contributory.

aged

185 Arteriosclerosis, or hardening of the arteries, often leads to senile dementia, or mental illness of the _______.

arteriosclerosis

186 Brain functioning is impaired because the arteries in the brain are affected. Damage to the brain tissue results. At present there is no effective way to arrest or reverse the process of _______.

187 Aged, senile people suffer a general decline in the efficiency of most body organs. Even in the absence of clear signs of arteriosclerosis, this aging process is often accompanied by some loss of ______ acuity.

mental

188 Dementia among the aged includes symptoms of forgetfulness, irrationality, paranoid suspicions of others, or melancholia. Suicidal tendencies are also present in senile ______.

dementia

189 Brain damage occurs from other causes. Prolonged periods of intoxication suffered by the chronic alcoholic in time damage the cerebral cortex. In some instances, alcoholic ______ represents mental illness which might have occurred from other causes.

psychosis

190 The chronic alcoholic may experience delusions and hallucinations of a nightmarish form as one symptom of alcoholic psychosis. Since violent trembling accompanies this delirium, it is called ______ tremens.

delirium

191 Prolonged intoxication from the use of alcohol or drugs may produce permanent damage to the ______ ______ and result in chronic mental disorder.

cerebral cortex

Psychotic disorders are usually much more severe than neurotic disturbances, but psychotic disorders have become much more amenable to treatment. In the functional psychotic disorders there is no observable damage to brain tissues. The most common form of functional psychosis is schizophrenia, which is characterized by lack of orientation, delusion, and general withdrawal from the social and physical environment. Manic-depressive psychosis is marked by extreme variations of mood and activity level, but there is usually no disorientation or delusion. Manic-depressive psychosis is most amenable to treatment. Of the many kinds of brain damage, that caused by arteriosclerosis, or hardening of the brain arteries, is the most prevalent. The resulting limitation of blood supply to the brain tissues results in irreversible damage. Prolonged intoxication with alcohol or drugs also may produce permanent damage to brain tissues and result in chronic mental disorder.

Incidence of Mental Illness in the United States

192 There were about 630,000 patients resident in 992 public and 498 private mental hospitals and centers in the United States in 1960. About 96 percent of these are in the large public ______ (U.S. Census, 1960, Inmates of Institutions, 12, 13).

hospitals

psychotic

193 Refer to Table 32. The largest general category of patients admitted to state and county hospitals in 1963 is classified as ______ disorders.

Table 32. First Admissions to State and County Mental Hospitals, United States, 1963 (262 of 284 hospitals)

Diagnosis	*Male*	*Female*	*Total*	*Percentage*
Acute brain syndromes, with	(3,568)	(1,157)	(4,725)	3.8
Alcohol intoxication	2,922	577	3,497	
Other	646	582	1,228	
Chronic brain syndromes, with	(17,709)	(14,325)	(32,034)	26.0
Alcohol intoxication	1,967	540	2,507	
Cerebral arteriosclerosis	8,831	7,310	16,141	
Senile brain disease	3,063	3,705	6,768	
Other	3,848	2,770	6,618	
Psychotic disorders	(14,860)	(18,384)	(33,244)	27.1
Involutional psychotic	1,194	2,696	3,890	
Manic-depressive reactions	676	972	1,648	
Psychotic-depressive reactions	808	1,528	2,336	
Schizophrenic reactions	11,618	12,845	24,463	
Other	564	343	907	
Psychoneurotic reactions	4,739	8,557	13,296	10.7
Personality disorders	(21,031)	(5,676)	(26,707)	21.6
Personality disturbance	5,702	2,887	8,589	
Antisocial reaction	1,808	363	2,171	
Alcoholism addiction	11,068	1,862	12,930	
Drug addiction	1,133	340	1,473	
Other	1,320	224	1,544	
Transient disturbance	2,185	1,674	3,859	3.1
Mental deficiency	2,186	1,311	3,497	2.8
Undiagnosed	2,367	1,635	4,002	3.2
Without mental disorder	1,508	360	1,868	1.5
Other	111	137	248	0.2
Total new admissions	70,264	53,216	123,480	100.0

SOURCE: U.S. Department of Health, Education, and Welfare, Public Health Service, *Patients in Mental Institutions, part* II, 1963, pp. 21–23.

schizophrenic

194 Within the main category of the psychotic disorders, almost 70 percent of the admissions are diagnosed as ______ reaction.

involutional

195 The second largest category within the psychotic disorders admissions is the ______ psychotic.

middle / females

196 The involutional reaction is manifested primarily by persons of ______ age, and predominantly by ______.

chronic brain

197 The second largest main category of admissions, comprising 26 percent of all admissions, is the ______ ______ syndromes.

cerebral arterio-sclerosis

198 Within the chronic brain syndrome category, the highest frequency of cases is that of ______ ______.

arteries

199 Arteriosclerosis means calcification or hardening of the ______.

aged

200 Cerebral arteriosclerosis most frequently affects ______ people.

Table 33. Movement of Patients in Mental Hospitals, 1963

	284 of 284 state and county hospitals	*366 of 578 general hospitals with psychiatric facilities*	*172 of 250 private hospitals*
On hospital books Jan. 1	657,813	8,689	14,617
Admissions	297,139	212,705	75,157
Released alive	233,746	166,233	73,429
Transferred to other hospitals	14,312	45,124	
Deaths	51,789	1,246	1,696
On hospital books Dec. 31	655,105	8,791	14,649

SOURCE: U.S. Department of Health, Education, and Welfare, Public Health Service, *Patients in Mental Institutions,* 1963, part II, p. 12, part III, pp. 9, 35.

more

201 General hospitals admitted (fewer/more) mental patients in 1960 than did the state and county mental hospitals in 1963 (see Table 33).

community

202 General hospitals were able to discharge about 75 percent of those admitted as mental patients to the ______.

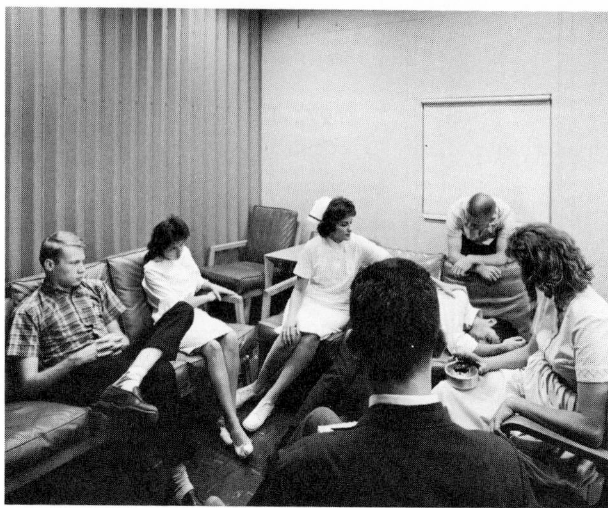

Withdrawal of a mental patient during group therapy. (*Wide World Photos*)

22

203 General hospitals discharged about ______ percent of their mental patient admissions to mental hospitals.

general

204 Private mental hospitals discharged only about one-third as many patients as did the ______ hospitals.

extended (prolonged)

205 About seven of every ten mentally ill patients admitted to mental hospitals may expect to be released with partial or full recovery (Kadish, 1965). If about 6 percent of those admitted die in the hospital, about 24 percent must be retained in the hospital for ______ care.

improvement

206 Prolonged hospitalization itself may have a negative effect on the patient. He may lose communication with family and friends. This may prolong his maladjustment indefinitely. Consequently, mental hospitals are beginning to adopt a more active policy of discharging patients, at least on a trial basis, if they demonstrate any ______.

Social Class, Ethnic Factors, and Mental Illness

class

207 A number of studies have shown a consistent relationship between social class and mental illness. In general, there is a much higher incidence of schizophrenia among the more impoverished elements of the working class and a greater incidence of neurosis in the middle ______.

six

208 Faris and Dunham (1939, p. 36) studied the distribution of the homes of all hospitalized psychotics in Chicago and found rates of 362 psychotics per 100,000 population in the center of the city, as compared with 65 per 100,000 population in the outer suburban residential zones. The poorer working-class resident has almost ______ times more likelihood of becoming psychotic.

center
suburbs

209 Schroeder (1940, p. 201–209) corroborated the Faris and Dunham data. He found a similar distribution of psychotic patients in St. Louis, Omaha, Kansas City, Milwaukee, and Cleveland. In each case the rates were highest near the ______ of the city and declined sharply in all directions toward the ______.

Table 34. Class Status and Distribution of Patients and Nonpatients in the Population

Social class		*Nonpatients*	*Patients*
I	(upper)	3.0%	1.0%
II	(upper middle)	8.4	7.0
III	(lower middle)	20.4	13.7
IV	(upper lower)	49.8	40.1
V	(lower lower)	18.4	38.2

SOURCE: A. B. Hollingshead and F. C. Redlich, *Social Class and Mental Illness,* John Wiley & Sons, Inc., New York, 1958, p. 199. Used by permission.

33 (1/3)

210 See Table 34. The upper class has about ______ percent of its proportionate share of the psychotic population.

45 (10/22)

211 The lower-middle class has about ______ percent of its proportionate share of the psychotic population.

85 (39/46)

212 The upper-lower class has about ______ percent of its proportionate share of the psychotic population.

250 (45/18)

213 The lower-lower class has about ______ percent of its proportionate share of the psychotic population.

inverse

214 It appears from Table 35 that there is an ______ relation between mental hospital admissions for men and the income and prestige level of their occupations.

Table 35. First Admissions per 100,000 of Psychotics by Occupation

Managers	19
Professionals	23
Personal Service Women	105
Unskilled Workers	202

SOURCE: R. Frumkin, "Occupation and the Major Mental Disorders," in A. M. Rose (ed.), *Mental Health and Mental Disorder,* W. W. Norton & Company, Inc., New York, 1955, p. 136. Used by permission.

schizophrenia

215 There is variation in the incidence of mental illness by ethnic groups. For example, in New York State, Negroes make up 45 percent of all schizophrenic patients, but make up 6.2 percent of the total population. Negroes have about seven times their proportionate share of ______ (Dept. of Mental Hygiene, 1952).

Table 36. Neurosis in Ethnic Groups, New York State

	A	B	A/B
Ethnic group	*Percent of total neurosis*	*Percent of total population*	*Ratio of incidence to total population*
Jewish people	44	16.7 (1937)	2.63
Negro people	11	6.2	1.77

SOURCE: M. L. Barron, *American Minorities,* Alfred A. Knopf, Inc., New York, 1958, p. 132. Used by permission.

two

216 The incidence of neurosis is more than ______ times greater for the two ethnic groups combined than it is for the general population (see Table 36).

Jewish

217 The highest incidence of neurosis in New York State is manifested by the ______ people.

families

218 It has been suggested elsewhere that intrafamily associations are related to mental illness. The relatively large difference in the incidence of neurosis between Jewish and Negro people in New York could be related to differences in associations within the ______ of the two groups.

Treatment of a mentally disturbed boy in a family therapy session. (*Wide World Photos*)

219 Odegard (1936) surveyed the incidence of psychosis among Norwegian immigrants in Minnesota and made a comparison with hospital admissions in Norway. His data showed only 59 admissions to mental hospitals in Norway for each 100 among Norwegian immigrants in Minnesota. The native Norwegians were better adjusted than were the Norwegian ________ group.

immigrant

220 Odegard's data also showed that the Norwegian immigrants to the United States had higher rates for schizophrenia, paresis, alcoholism, and senile dementia than those who remained in Norway. Possible explanations for the difference are (*a*) the immigrant group is not truly representative of native ________, (*b*) the new environment is more ________, (c) the immigrant group is now on a different ________ ________ level.

Norwegians
challenging (difficult)
social class

221 Private mental hospitals care for about 3 percent of all mental patients. They are typically upper-middle- and upper-class patients who can afford the heavy expenses of relatively prolonged ________ treatment.

private

222 Public hospitals average well over 2,000 patients each and tend to be overcrowded and understaffed (Merton and Nisbet, 1961). The average cost per patient per year is about $1,400 for minimal care at the custodial level. At this level, the patient receives no treatment, rarely sees a doctor, and therefore has little chance of ________.

recovery (improvement)

Occupational therapy. (*Wide World Photos*)

financially

223 If minimal care at the custodial level merely results in prolonging the period of hospitalization, it proves to be a very expensive mode of treatment, both socially and ______.

treatment

224 Stress on treatment and discharge of patients, coupled with tranquilizer drugs for patient control, has greatly increased the probability of success of ______.

Table 37. Effects of Hospitalization of Mental Patients Three Years after Admission

Effect	*1935*	*1950*
Released alive	55%	72%
Retained continuously	36	22
Dying in hospital	10	6

SOURCE: Department of Mental Hygiene, New York State, *Sixty-fourth Annual Report, 1952*, pp. 172–173.

schizophrenia

225 Analysis of cohorts, or groups of patients admitted at a particular time, shows that in 1935 about 55 percent were released within three years; in 1950 about 72 percent were released within three years. The improvement was made primarily in the treatment of ______ (Merton and Nisbet, 1961, p. 169).

released alive

226 Improvement in treatment is most emphatically demonstrated in the ______ ______ category.

REVIEW: *Social problems represent a logical by-product of social standards. Society requires organization, persons proficient in playing requisite roles in institutions, a technology, and a set of norms. Any social process or type of behavior which is generally interpreted as injurious or contrary to social standards may be defined as a social problem. Implicit in the definition of a social problem is the belief that some social action can ameliorate the situation.*

Social problems require identification, exploration, and some modifications of social structure and behavior. Often the absolute dimensions of the problem are determined as much by the criteria and interests implicit within the defining process as by the so-called "objective" aspects of the situation.

SUMMARY

Mental illness has been used to demonstrate one type of social problem area in reasonable detail. The data on mental illness apply almost exclusively to the United States population. The application of the concept on a cross-cultural basis was not attempted. Mental illness has become a problem of national concern. It is distributed through all levels of society, but consistently manifests a much higher incidence in the lower social strata. At the same time, the clinical understanding of etiological and even symptomatic factors leaves much to be desired. A large portion of the cases are either undiagnosed or only provisionally diagnosed on the basis of symptoms.

The theoretical basis for treating mental illness is as unsatisfactory as is the diagnostic basis. However, there has been a marked improvement in control of symptoms both among the neuroses and the psychoses, owing to the introduction of tranquilizing drugs. Improved control has permitted improved therapy in the group and community milieu (Rapoport, 1960). The proportion of mental patients recovering and achieving discharge from the hospital has increased dramatically in the past decade. Meanwhile, both Federal and local government agencies have endeavored to expand the research effort and the capacity of treatment facilities in hospitals, in out-patient clinics, and in special mental health clinics.

SELF-REVIEW QUIZ

1 Individuals who are unable or unwilling to meet the basic requirements of society often band together and generate social problems as more or less organized ________.

2 When some parts of a culture change faster than others, disparities of goals and functions arise due to ________ ________.

3 According to Cohen, the high incidence of delinquency among working-class boys is in part a protest against ________-________ values.

4 The rise in crime rates in the United States could be partly explained by the increased rate of social ________.

5 The problem of rapidly expanding population results from reduced death rates coupled with relatively higher ________.

6 Mental illness which is not caused by demonstrable organic symptoms is classed as a ________ disorder.

7 Treatment of mental illness has become steadily more effective because the patient's behavior is more effectively controlled through ________ drugs.

8 Mental deficiency is marked primarily by lack of ability to ________.

9 In neurosis, both anxiety reactions and conversion reactions appear to be grounded on an underlying ________.

10 A neurotic who irrationally focuses his fear on an object or situation suffers from a ________.

11 Lack of orientation, delusion, and generalized withdrawal are primary symptoms of ________.

12 Extreme variation of mood and activity level, without delusion or disorientation, is characteristic of ________-________ psychosis.

13 Arteriosclerosis limits the supply of blood and results in irreversible damage to the ________.

14 Although most patients suffering from psychotic disorders are not dangerous, there may be danger of aggressive behavior in the ________ state of schizophrenia.

15 The two largest categories of mental patients in United States mental hospitals are ________ ________ and ________ ________-________ ________.

16 Comparing social classes, the rate of schizophrenia appears to be highest in the ________-________ social class.

17 Mental illness is a social problem because it interferes with the performance of the ________ as a member of society.

REFERENCES

Barker, R., and H. Wright: *Midwest and Its Children,* Harper & Row, Publishers, Incorporated, New York, 1954.

Barron, M. L.: *American Minorities,* Alfred A. Knopf, Inc., New York, 1958.

Bogue, D.: *Population of the United States,* The Free Press of Glencoe, New York, 1959.

Bureau of Narcotics: *Traffic in Opium and Other Dangerous Drugs,* Washington, D.C., 1959.

———: *Prevention and Control of Narcotics Addiction,* Washington, D.C., 1962.

Cameron, N.: *Psychology of Behavior Disorders,* Houghton Mifflin Company, Boston, 1947.

Clinard, M. B.: *The Sociology of Deviant Behavior,* rev. ed., Holt, Rinehart and Winston, Inc., New York, 1963.

Cohen, A. K.: *Delinquent Boys,* The Free Press of Glencoe, New York, 1955.

Coleman, J. C.: *Personality Dynamics and Effective Behavior,* Scott, Foresman and Company, Chicago, 1960.

Davis, Kingsley: "World Population Crisis," in R. K. Merton and R. A. Nisbet (eds.), *Contemporary Social Problems: An Introduction to the Sociology of Deviant Behavior,* Harcourt, Brace & World, Inc., New York, 1961.

Department of Mental Hygiene, New York State: *Sixty-fourth Annual Report,* 1952.

Durkheim, Emile: *The Division of Labor in Society* (tr. from French, 2d ed., 1902, by G. Simpson), The Free Press of Glencoe, New York, 1933.

Durkheim, Emile: *Suicide, A Study in Sociology* (tr. from French by J. Spaulding and G. Simpson), The Free Press of Glencoe, New York, 1951.

Eaton, J. W., and R. J. Weil: *Culture and Mental Disorders,* The Free Press of Glencoe, New York, 1955.

Elliott, M. A., and F. E. Merrill: *Social Disorganization,* 4th ed., Harper & Row, Publishers, Incorporated, New York, 1961.

Faris, R., and H. Dunham: *Mental Disorders in Urban Areas,* The University of Chicago Press, Chicago, 1939.

Federal Bureau of Investigation: *Uniform Crime Reports for the United States, 1964,* 1965.

Fromm, Erich: *Escape from Freedom,* Rinehart & Company, Inc., New York, 1941.

Frumkin, R.: "Occupation and the Major Mental Disorders," in A. M. Rose (ed.), *Mental Health and Mental Disorder,* W. W. Norton & Company, Inc., New York, 1955.

Gurin, G., J. Veroff, and S. Feld: *Americans View Their Mental Health, A Nationwide Interview Survey,* Basic Books Inc., Publishers, New York, 1960.

Hollingshead, A. B., and F. C. Redlich: *Social Class and Mental Illness,* John Wiley & Sons, Inc., New York, 1958.

Homans, G. C.: *The Human Group,* Harcourt, Brace & World, Inc., New York, 1950.

Horney, Karen: *The Neurotic Personality of Our Time,* W. W. Norton & Company, Inc., New York, 1937.

Horton, R. B., and G. R. Leslie:

Sociology of Social Problems, Appleton-Century-Crofts, Inc., New York, 1955.

Ivy, Andrew C.: *Science Newsletter,* vol. 76, Aug. 8, 1959.

Joint Commission on Mental Illnes and Health: *Action for Mental Health,* Basic Books, Inc., Publishers, New York, 1961.

Kadish, Joseph: "Care of Mentally Ill Changing Rapidly," *U.S. Public Health Reports,* vol. 80, February, 1965.

Kramer, M., et al.: "A Historical Study of Disposition of First Admissions to a State Mental Hospital," U.S. Dept. of Health, Education, and Welfare, Public Health Monograph, no. 32, 1955.

Malzberg, B.: "Mental Disorders in The United States," in A. Deutsch and H. Fishman (eds.), *The Encyclopedia of Mental Health,* vol. 3, Franklin Watts, Inc., New York, 1963.

Merton, R. K., and R. A. Nisbet: *Contemporary Social Problems: An Introduction to the Sociology of Deviant Behavior,* Harcourt, Brace & World, Inc., New York, 1961.

Meyers, J. K., and B. H. Roberts: *Family and Class Dynamics in Mental Illness,* John Wiley & Sons, Inc., New York, 1959.

——— and L. Schaffer: "Social Stratification and Psychiatric Practice," *American Sociological Review,* vol. 19, June, 1954.

Myrdal, Gunnar, Richard Sterner, and Arnold Rose: *An American Dilemma,* Harper & Row, Publishers, Incorporated, New York, 1944.

Odegard, O.: "Emigration and Mental Health," *Mental Hygiene,* no. 259, October, 1936.

Ogburn, W. F.: *Social Change,* W. B. Huebsch, New York, 1922.

Pollak, O.: *The Criminality of Women,* University of Philadelphia Press, Philadelphia, 1950.

Porterfield, A. F.: *Youth in Trouble,* Leo Postman Foundation, 1946.

Rapoport, R. N.: *Community as a Doctor,* London, Thomas, 1960.

Rennie, T. A. C., and Leo Srole: "Urban Life and Mental Health," Paper presented to American Psychiatric Association, 1955.

Schroeder, C.: "Mental Disorders in Cities," *American Journal of Sociology,* no. 201, 1940.

Simmel, Georg: *The Sociology of Georg Simmel,* K. H. Wolf (tr. ed.), The Free Press of Glencoe, New York, 1950.

Strecker, E. A.: "Psychiatric Education," *Mental Hygiene,* 14: 797, 1930.

Sullivan, Harry S.: "The Interpersonal Theory of Psychiatry, H. S. Perry and M. L. Gawel (eds.), W. W. Norton & Company, Inc., New York, 1953.

Sutherland, E. H., and D. R. Cressy: *Principles of Criminology,* 6th ed., J. B. Lippincott Company, Philadelphia, 1960.

Thorpe, L. P.: *The Psychology of Mental Health,* 2d ed., The Ronald Press Company, New York, 1960.

Tönnies, Ferdinand: *Community and Society,* C. Loomis (tr. ed.), Harper & Row, Publishers, Incorporated, New York, 1963.

Tredgold, A. F.: *A Textbook of Mental Deficiency,* 8th ed., The Williams & Wilkins Company, Baltimore, 1952.

United Nations Expert Committee on Drugs Liable to Produce Intoxication: Reports 6, 7. World Health Organization Technical Report Series no. 21, New York, 1950.

U.S. Bureau of the Census: Inmates of Institutions, 1960.

U.S. Bureau of the Census: *Sta-*

tistical Abstract of the United States, 1954.

U.S. Department of Health, Edution, and Welfare, Public Health Service, *Patients in Mental Institutions,* parts I–III, 1963.

———: *Health, Education and Welfare Indicators,* December, 1964.

———: *Vital Statistics Report, Annual Summary for the United States, 1964,* July, 1965.

Wallerstein, J. S. and C. J. Wyle: "Our Law Abiding Lawbreakers," *Probation,* April, 1947.

Weinberg, S.: "A Sociological Analysis of a Schizophrenic Type," *American Sociological Review,* 600–610, October, 1950.

Weinberg, S.: *Social Problems in Our Time,* Prentice-Hall, Inc., Englewood Cliffs, N. J., 1960.

World Health Organization: "Mortality from Suicide," *Epidemiology and Vital Statistics. Report,* IX, no. 4 Geneva, 1956, p. 250.

racial and ethnic relations

DONALD E. ALLEN

2

When one racially or ethnically distinguishable population intrudes upon another, a problem of cultural adjustment is generated. When both groups survive the intrusion, economic processes, patterns of communication, and systems of social relations must be modified on some standardized basis to permit the continued functioning of the resultant society. If there is a difference between the degree of organization, technological resources, and power of the two groups, the weaker group is usually compelled to accept the less advantageous position in the new society until its members can overcome their disadvantages. It is the purpose of this unit to identify the social principles and processes involved in the resolution of the relationship between racially or ethnically distinguished populations. It should be noted that the process of intercultural blending and merging of ethnically and racially distinct peoples is a very ancient one. All modern ethnic groups are themselves the transitory product of a complex and little-known process of cultural and social assimilation. The different peoples and races have continued to mingle, intermarry, and amalgamate in all the areas of contact. In conjunction with the continuing process of social and cultural development, the mores, technology, language, and social norms have constantly undergone modification at varying rates.

Concepts and Principles

inherited

1 The term "race" refers to a large, statistical aggregate of people manifesting a group of biologically inherited visible traits (Rose, 1964). The French cannot be called a "race" in this sense since the French do not manifest visible traits which are ______.

several traits

2 Inherited visible traits include variation in pigmentation of skin, eyes, and hair, and minor variation in the form of eyelids, nose, ears, and lips. No one of these traits can provide a reliable indicator for racial classification. Racial classification can be applied only if ________ ________ are used.

statistical aggregates

3 Anthropologists have applied racial subgroupings to more than a hundred statistical aggregates of people. However there is general agreement only on three major racial groupings; the Caucasoid or white-brown group, the Mongoloid or brown-yellow group, and the Negroid or brown-black group. None of these racial groups is "pure" since the Caucasoid has mixed genetically with both the Mongoloid and Negroid groups, but they can be distinguished as ________ ________.

Caucasoid

4 An aggregate of people with skin varying from ruddy to dark brown, eyes varying from blue to black, hair varying from light yellow to black would probably be classified as ________.

Negroid

5 A chemical substance called melanin makes the skin appear dark. All normal people have some melanin in their skin, but those who have large amounts of this chemical plus relatively thicker lips, smaller ears, and black wavy hair would probably be classed as ________.

Mongoloid

6 An aggregate of people inheriting a tendency to bronze or yellowish skin, due to the presence of carotene, exhibiting folded eyelids and straight black hair, would probably be classed racially as ________.

cultural traits

7 An ethnic group is distinguished by specific cultural traits, such as a distinctive language, cultural system, or manner of living. The millions of German immigrants to the United States could be classified as an *ethnic group* because they had distinctive ________ ________.

ethnic group

8 Cultural traits are learned. If groups of immigrants learn and adopt the distinctive cultural traits of another society they can be assimilated into another ________ ________.

race

9 The characteristics denoting race, such as the form of facial features and skin pigmentation, are inherited. Therefore an individual cannot voluntarily change from one ________ to another.

race (racial classification)

10 An individual's racial characteristics will not interfere with his learning the cultural traits of an ethnic group. Therefore he can become assimilated into an ethnic group regardless of his ________.

miscegenated

11 If persons from two different races marry and have offspring, miscegenation is said to have occurred. In such a case the two races have been ________.

fallacious (false)

12 In an absolute sense, racial mixing has continued from the earliest times. In historic times, Negroid peoples continuously mixed with Caucasoid peoples through ancient Egypt, Ethiopia, Greece, and Rome, and with Mongoloid peoples in Europe, Central Asia, Southeast Asia, and Oceania. Caucasoid peoples mixed with Mongoloid in Central Asia, the Middle East, and Eastern Europe. In the absolute sense, the concept of racial purity is empirically ________.

mates

13 The spread of hereditary factors may also be illustrated in terms of geographic diffusion, which operated throughout prehistoric times. This occurred because some individuals typically took ________ from neighboring tribal groups.

Table 38. Individuals' Direct Ancestors, Assuming 25 Years per Generation

Generations	*Years*	*Direct ancestors*	*Generations*	*Years*	*Direct ancestors*
1	25	2	16	400	65,536
2	50	4	17	425	131,072
3	75	8	18	450	262,144
4	100	16	19	475	524,288
5	125	32	20	500	1,048,576
6	150	64	21	525	2,097,152
7	175	128	22	550	4,194,304
8	200	256	23	575	8,388,608
9	225	512	24	600	16,777,216
10	250	1,024	25	625	33,554,432
11	275	2,048	26	650	67,108,864
12	300	4,096	27	675	134,217,728
13	325	8,192	28	700	268,435,456
14	350	16,384	29	725	536,870,912
15	375	32,768	30	750	1,073,741,824

14 The world's human population is estimated to have increased to about 545 million by 1650 (Carr-Saunders, 1936). Table 38 indicates that each person had about 536 million direct ancestors going back ________-________ generations or ________ years.

twenty-nine
725

15 Since the number of one's direct ancestors in thirty generations exceeds the world's population 750 years ago, it appears that each person's direct ancestry tends to reach the limits of available ________ within 750 years.

population

16 If we assume an average distance of 20 miles between prehistoric tribal groups and an average of twenty-five years in the regenerative cycle, then hereditary elements can be transmitted a distance of 20 miles from the tribe of origin in twenty-five years, and at a distance of 100 miles in ________ generations or ________ years.

five / 125

17 If hereditary elements are transmitted 100 miles per 125 years, in 12,500 years or 500 generations, they travel ________ miles.

10,000

18 In prehistoric times, this process of lateral translation of hereditary elements was continuous. Every child receives some of his ________ ________ from points 10,000 miles distant from his birthplace, going back about 12,500 years in his ________.

hereditary elements
ancestry

19 In historical times, large-scale intercontinental migration had the effect of ________ the process of mixing and diffusing hereditary elements.

accelerating (increasing)

20 Processes involved in racial and ethnic relations can be explained in terms of a few social science principles. A concept which explains a category of relationships or events may be termed a ________.

principle

21 In this context, the concepts of mobility, social integration, cultural alternatives, rationalization, persistence of norms, and cultural lag will be employed as explanatory ________ in racial and ethnic relations.

principles

22 When a group of people moves out of its original cultural locus and intrudes into space occupied by another cultural group we may describe what has taken place in terms of movement in space, or spatial ________.

mobility (movement)

23 Migration by many members of a society generates a problem in racial or ethnic relations if the mobile element intrudes into territory occupied by another ______.

society

24 Men live in organized groups characterized by systematized patterns of social relationships. When ethnically differentiated groups become intruded, their association as individuals and as groups tends to become ______.

systematized

25 The principle of social integration underlies the process whereby individuals develop standard ways of ______ in specific kinds of situations.

acting (behaving)

26 If two newly conjoined ethnic groups begin a regular exchange of physical and manufactured objects on an understood value system, this indicates that a certain degree of ______ ______ has been achieved.

social integration

27 If members of two newly conjoined ethnic groups begin to provide specialized services, the development of occupational specialties contributes to the further ______ of the society.

integration

28 All human groups have organized methods and techniques for providing the basic requirements of social life. The conjunction of two ethnic groups allows a selection of alternatives for many of these techniques and methods. In the development of relations between two conjoined ethnic groups we may identify a principle of the ______ ______ ______ (Murdock, 1945).

selection of alternatives

29 Native Indians usually adopted the steel knife and abandoned the flint knife because the steel knife is more ______.

functional (serviceable, useful)

30 A white doctor extracting a projectile from a settler's anatomy would prefer the Indian method of anesthetizing the wound with crushed coca leaves to the white man's technique of biting on a bullet. Anesthetization makes the operation ______ to perform.

easier

31 In the process of selecting alternatives, man tends to prefer the more functional alternative. Thus, the merging of two ethnic groups will tend to produce a more efficient combined society than ______ ______ could produce separately.

either group

32 The alternative which is rejected tends to disappear, and the selected alternative tends to be employed universally in the whole ______.

society

33 Societies are supported by maintaining various shared values. Protection of life, the position of family members, private property, and the public interest represent important shared ______ in Western society.

values

34 Values are supported by norms. A social norm is defined as a rule or law regulating behavior within a society. Laws forbidding theft, murder, rape, and treason are examples of social ______.

norms

35 The process of selecting alternatives may be impeded by social norms or rules. Although norms and rules are modified over longer time periods, people tend to ______ rapid change in social norms over short periods of time (Sumner, 1906).

resist

36 People believe that the stability and security of their group depends upon the preservation of social norms. Norms, therefore, tend to be highly persistent. A principle which accounts for retardation in sharing and cultural integration between two conjoined ethnic groups is the ______ of social norms.

persistence

37 The mature member of an ethnic group often clings to the norms of his childhood group throughout his lifetime. The weakest point in the system for maintaining social norms is where they are transmitted to ______ ______ ______.

the new generation (the child)

38 The social process of changing values, norms, techniques, and behavior patterns can be considered together in the concept of social ______.

change

39 We would expect the rate of social change to be highest in places where a high frequency of social encounters occurs in conjunction with a large variety of social settings. These conditions are best fulfilled in modern society in ______ ______.

large cities

40 The frequency of social encounters and the variety of social settings are at a minimum in ______ areas.

rural

41 Summarizing the last two frames, it is apparent that social change, including adjustive changes between ethnic groups, is relatively rapid in _______ _______ and relatively slow in _______ _______.

urban areas
rural areas

42 Ogburn (1950) originated the concept of "cultural lag" to designate dislocations resulting from different rates of development in different parts of a culture. The differential rate of development in rural areas and urban areas of a particular culture illustrates Ogburn's principle of _______ _______.

cultural lag

43 Social action consists of the sharing of ideas, behaviors, methods, objects, and activities among persons. Sharing tends to generate similar or homogeneous understandings, attitudes, ideas, methods, and objects. In each society, shared activities produce a trend toward increased _______.

homogeneity (similarity)

44 As a society becomes more homogeneous, localized differences tend to _______.

diminish (disappear)

45 Humanity may be classified in three broad aggregates by combinations of superficial biological traits which may be referred to as _______.

races

46 Humanity may also be classified in several thousand smaller groups distinguished by major cultural differences which may be referred to as _______ groups.

ethnic

In summary, there are three major racial groups and several thousand distinct ethnic groups in the world. Biological characteristics designating the Negroid, Mongoloid, and Caucasoid groups are more universally diffused than are cultural traits designating ethnic groups. Social change is usually resisted over the short term, but new cultural traits are accepted and diffused over time.

Stages in the Cycle of Adjustment: Contact and Competition

47 Two intruded ethnic groups must complete a process of adjustment to attain a stable relationship. They must make selections among various cultural alternatives which will introduce changes for the new society. The series of changes constitutes a process of _______.

adjustment

48 For scientific analysis, it is necessary to identify regular stages in the process of adjustment. Park (1949) identifies a patterned sequence of (*a*) contact, (*b*) competition, (c) accommodation, and (*d*) assimilation in the adjustment of racial or ethnic relations. These four elements are irreversible, and therefore constitute ________ in the process of adjustment.

stages

49 Each of the four stages typically endures for a considerable period of time. The westward-moving frontier of European migrants generated contact with new tribes of North American Indians from 1607 to 1850 and later, a period of about ________ years.

250

50 The contact phase was immediately followed in the frontier zone by an equally prolonged period of resistance and intermittent "wars." This period constituted the second stage, or the ________ stage.

competition

51 Cultural traits are transmitted between generations. Adults, as cultural transmitters, preserve the previously learned cultural traits. They tend to reject new cultural alternatives. Thus adults tend to ________ the rate of cultural change.

retard (slow down)

52 The young, in the process of acquiring traits, can learn either the old traits or the new traits, if alternatives are available. The young may actually prefer the new traits; this tends to ________ ________ the rate of ________ ________.

speed up / cultural change

53 The amount of accommodation which can occur between two intruded ethnic groups is roughly proportional to the range of differences between the two cultures they represent. People from two European ethnic groups can adjust to each other within about two generations (forty years) because of the relatively small ________ ________ ________.

range of differences

54 The process of accommodation involves a mutual sharing of the preferred alternative ________.

traits

55 The more highly integrated systems of traits are more specialized, usually more efficient, and hence more likely to be preferred. The direction of accommodation is predominantly toward the ethnic group whose culture is more highly ________ and more ________.

integrated / efficient

traits

56 Assimilation represents the terminal stage of relations between two previously distinctive ethnic or racial groups. In this stage the sharing of preferred alternative cultural traits has produced full diffusion of the preferred traits and a virtually complete supersedence of the rejected cultural _______.

ethnic group

57 Since neither group can be distinguished by differences in cultural traits, they must now be recognized as a single _______ _______.

voluntary

58 Relations between intruded ethnic groups depend at first on the type of initial contact. From the intrusive population we may identify three types of *voluntary* intrusion and two types of *involuntary* intrusion. Invasion, colonization, and immigration are examples of _______ intrusion.

involuntary

59 The forcible movement of refugees or of individuals in slave status into another ethnic group constitutes an example of _______ intrusion.

outsiders (strangers, enemies)

60 The intrusive population and the host population initially view each other as _______.

mastery (dominance)

61 If the intrusive element is well organized and more powerful than the host element of population, the intrusive element is in a position to assert _______ over the host element.

upper (highest)

62 The intrusive element would then constitute the _______ stratum of the newly combined society.

lowest

63 If the intrusive element is unorganized and weak, arriving as immigrants or captives, it may either constitute or merge with the _______ stratum of society.

resistance (hostility)

64 In either case, the intrusive element becomes related to the host society on some institutionalized basis. Intergroup tension is reduced through a series of adjustments, but the tension usually produces some _______.

competition

65 The period of resistance and hostility fits into Park's typology of stages as _______.

preserve (retain)

66 Competition may arise regarding any of the cultural traits of the ethnic groups in contact. Examples include organization and control, work and productivity, religion, mores, and social relations. Each group seeks to _______ its own cultural traits at the expense of the other group.

successful

67 The most extreme forms of competition consist of attempts to exterminate or expel an opposing ethnic group. Such attempts are rarely ________.

preserve (retain)

68 The American Indian population north of the Rio Grande River was estimated at 850,000 in 1800 and 610,000 in 1950. Of some 300 Indian languages in use in this area in 1500, more than 150 were still in use in 1960 (McNickle, 1962). The American Indian has been able to ________ much of his culture.

segregated

69 Attempts to isolate or segregate an ethnic group also constitute a form of competition. Continued coercion by a dominant ethnic group may keep a weaker group separated or ________ from the larger society.

war (warfare)

70 If the subordinate ethnic group is capable of organized resistance, the coercing group may resort to sustained or intermittent ________ to gain control.

individuals

71 If the subordinate ethnic group is not capable of organized resistance, force, violence, and the threat of force may be imposed on isolated ________ of the subordinate group.

Table 39. Lynchings, Whites and Negroes, in the United States, 1882–1959, by Decades

	Whites	*Negroes*	
1882–1891	751	732	
1892–1901	381	1,124	
1902–1911	76	707	
1912–1921	50	553	
1922–1931	23	201	
1932–1941	10	95	
1942–1951	2	25	
1952–1959	1	4	
Total	1,294	3,441	Grand total 4,735

SOURCE: C. F. Marden and Gladys Meyer, *Minorities in American Society*, 2d ed., American Book Company, New York, 1962, p. 247. Used by permission.

equal (the same)

72 The number of Negro victims of lynching in the decade 1882–1891 appears to be approximately ________ to the number of white victims (see Table 39).

seven

73 The total white population at that time was about seven times greater than the Negro population. Therefore the rate of lynching was about ________ times greater for Negro people than for white people.

10

74 From Table 39, it can be seen that the incidence of lynching declined rapidly from 1900 to 1951, but throughout this period the ratio of Negro to white victims remained nearly constant at about ________ to 1.

Table 40. Offences Alleged in Lynchings in United States, 1882–1930

Offence	*Percentage*
Homicide	38
Assault	6
Rape	16
Attempted rape	7
Theft	7
Insults to whites	2
Miscellaneous*	24

* Miscellaneous includes refusal to pay a note, boastful remarks, and testifying against a white man.

SOURCE: Arthur F. Raper, *The Tragedy of Lynching*, The University of North Carolina Press, Chapel Hill, N.C., 1933, p. 36. Used by permission.

Myrdal writes: "It is the custom in the South to resort to violence and threats of violence against the life, personal security, property, and freedom of movement of Negroes. There is a wide variety of behavior, ranging from mild admonition to murder . . ." (Myrdal, Sterner, and Rose, 1944).

powerless (unable)

75 An oppressed racial or ethnic minority is usually ________ to resist.

strengthen (consolidate)

76 Armed uprisings by intruded subordinate groups in the United States, Brazil, and the Union of South Africa have been quickly suppressed. This only helps to ________ the position of the dominant racial or ethnic group.

resistance

77 Although the subordinate group is denied the use of forceful resistance, it may employ a long-term strategy of passive ________.

passive resistance

78 The economic boycott, organized use of legal remedies, peaceful assemblies, parades and demonstrations, and organized protest through dramatic, news, and artistic media are examples of ______ ______.

dissatisfaction

79 Negro Americans have never been satisfied with discriminatory treatment, invidious "racial" comparisons, denial of equal protection of the law, or denial of their right to equal participation in political and social institutions. Their recent exercise of massive nonviolent resistance has served to demonstrate their ______.

organized

80 The nonviolent resistance program had considerable success before it became ______ resistance.

Table 41. Negro American Interest in Nonviolent Actions for Equal Rights

Type of protest	*Have participated*	*Willing to participate*
March in demonstration	12%	51%
Picket a store	9	46
Take part in sit-in	8	49
Go to jail	4	47

SOURCE: William Brink and Louis Harris, *The Negro Revolution in America,* Simon and Schuster, Inc., New York, 1964, p. 67. Used by permission.

approve (support)

81 Some Southern white people have contended that most Negro Americans are satisfied with existing conditions and that the recent protest movement is only the work of a few malcontents. The data in Table 41, however, indicate that a large portion of the Negro American population strongly ______ the massive protest.

satyagraha

82 In the Union of South Africa, Mahatma Gandhi developed a mode of passive resistance termed "satyagraha." In the words of Gandhi, "The sight of suffering on the part of multitudes of people will melt the heart of the aggressor" (Kuper, 1957). The passive resistor who relied on his people's suffering to influence the oppressor would be employing Gandhi's principle of ______.

83 The African National Congress and the South African Indian Congress, in 1952, initiated passive resistance in the form of protests, demonstrations, and the deliberate violation of apartheid laws in the Union of South Africa. The insistence on segregation or "apartness" of white and nonwhite people is similar to racial ________ in the United States.

segregation

84 The only immediate effect of the 1952 passive resistance campaign in the Union of South Africa was that the white-controlled government further extended its legal system to exclude nonwhites from areas and activities desired by white peoples (Kuper, 1957). The white South Africans were extending their policy of ________.

apartheid

85 In India, over several decades, Gandhi's program of resistance had a tremendous effect. Gandhi contributed very significantly to the official repudiation of the caste system and to securing India's independence from British control through his program of ________ ________.

passive resistance
(satyagraha)

In review, three types of voluntary intrusion of one population into another's area are invasion, immigation, and colonization. Competition arises because both groups seek to preserve their own customs and cultures. A mild form of competition used by some subordinate groups is passive resistance.

Stages in the Cycle of Adjustment: Accommodation and Assimilation

86 A society operates through a system of reciprocal relationships, ordered on a normative basis, for fulfilling the economic requirements of its members. If two ethnic groups become permanently intruded, they must establish a new system of ________ ________ in a process of accommodation.

reciprocal relations

87 In establishing a new system of relations, each of the two groups must alter some of the old ways of thinking, communicating, and working to develop a common system. Altering old patterns of social behavior to adjust to a new social system is referred to as the process of ________.

accommodation

A racial relations committee. (*Wide World Photos*)

ethnic (racial)

88 Accommodation is essentially a search for a viable and orderly system of social relations by both groups. During the accommodation period each group retains its identity as an ________ group.

unintegrated (unadjusted)

89 Accommodation is a partial, step-at-a-time adjustment which removes some distinctions but retains other distinctions between the accommodating groups. Although some areas of social relations are adjusted into an integral system, other areas may remain ________.

steps (stages)

90 By definition, accommodation is gradual, takes place through time, and consists of a series of ________.

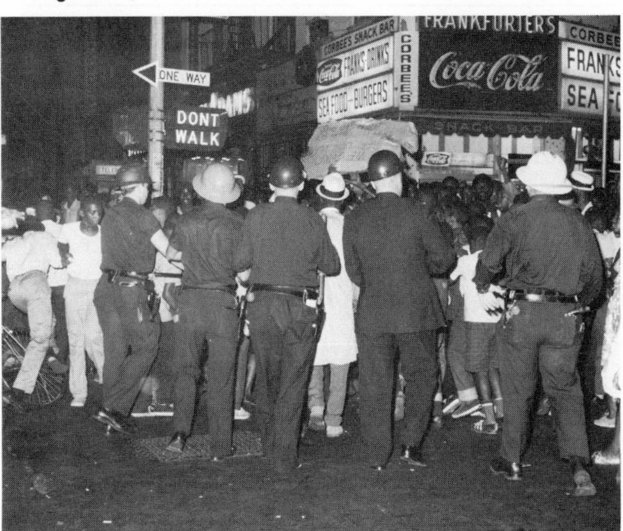

Controlling Negro crowds during civil rights disorders. (*Wide World Photos*)

91 Accommodation requires continuing alteration both in social behavior patterns and in the normative systems which maintain the regularity of social behavior. This implies that the social adjustment is not yet ______.

completed (ended)

92 Accommodation fails to satisfy the full need for efficient relations and simultaneously requires changes in traditional patterns. Therefore, accommodation is likely to produce ______ in both ethnic groups.

maladjustment (dissatisfaction)

93 As each step in the accommodative series comes to be accepted, it is regarded as a part of the ______ pattern of the society.

traditional

94 Though there is social friction in each step in the accommodative process, the trend of the series of steps is cumulative. The trend is to achieve a more and more complete ______ of the two groups into one society.

integration (fusion)

95 We may identify three levels of association in society. These are the economic, the institutional, and the personal levels of association. The least intimate of these levels of association is the ______ level.

economic

Table 42. Accommodation of Negro Americans in American Society

	Accommodation periods		
Type of association	*Slavery 1620–1865*	*Segregation 1865–1966*	*Equality (projected)*
Economic association:			
Productive type	Forced labor, agricultural	Labor, unskilled semiskilled	By skill and ability
Productivity level	Low	Limited	Equal
Consumption pattern	Subsistence	Poverty level	Normal range
Buying power	None	Limited	Equal
Institutional association:			
Religious participation	Limited	Limited	Equal
Educational participation	None	Limited	Equal
Political participation	None	Limited	Equal
Legal protection	None	Limited	Equal
Personal association:			
Social relations	None	Limited	Equal
Marital relations	None	None	Limited
Sexual relations	Illicit, white male, Negro female	Illicit, white male, Negro female	Limited

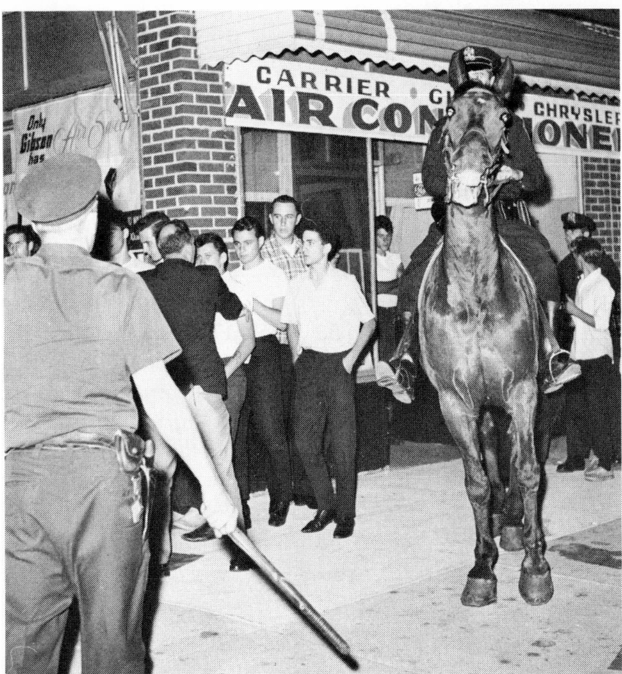

Controlling white groups during civil rights disorders. (*Wide World Photos*)

economic

96 The initial basis for accommodating Negroes into American society under slavery represents the _______ level of association (see Table 42).

religious

97 In the period 1865 to 1966, segregation operated to restrict the participation of Negroid Americans in educational, political, and legal institutions. The one area remaining open for the development of Negroid American leadership was in _______ institutions.

limit (reduce)

98 Restricting the Negro American's participation in public institutions would presumably _______ his efficiency elsewhere in the society.

productivity (success)

99 Restricting Negro children's participation in educational institutions would reduce their later _______ in the economic area.

equal

100 If the projection in Table 42 is correct, then the Negro American's participation in public institutions on a basis of equality will probably be associated with relatively _______ participation in the economic sphere.

101 The greatest resistance to full equality of association of Negro Americans with other Americans occurs in ________ association.

personal

102 Projecting the tempo of change in the two centuries of slavery and the century of segregation, it could be estimated that the Negro American will achieve general equality on the economic and institutional levels during the next few ________.

decades

103 In 1517 Bartholomé de Las Casas, a priest, proposed to Charles V of Spain that African Negroes be substituted for the enslaved Indians, who were fast reaching extinction under forced agricultural labor in the West Indies. Las Casas argued that the ________ were stronger and more able to survive (Berry, 1951).

Negroes

104 The African Negro was brought to the Americas because he was ________ as an agricultural worker.

stronger (more able)

105 In the Americas of the colonial period, Negroes, whites, and Indians alike were held in bondage. The Indians could withdraw, and the whites could secure the protection of the laws. Only the Negro was unable to escape the increasingly severe laws which bound him in ________.

slavery

106 Miscegenation, or racial mixing, became *general* after the arrival of the first Negroes in the American Colonies in 1619. Maryland laws of 1664 and 1691 recognized the problem of status for offspring resulting from the ________ of white and black in marriage.

miscegenation

107 The Southern states wanted to increase the number of those subject to slavery, and color emerged as the token of slave status. By fiat of the state legislatures, slave status resulted from any trace of ________ (Handlin, 1957).

color (Negro ancestry)

108 The United States 1960 Census of Population classifies as Negroes all persons of Negro and mixed Negro and white descent, and persons of mixed American Indian and Negro descent, unless the Indian ancestry very definitely predominates or unless the individual is regarded as an Indian in the community (U.S. Bureau of the Census, 1961). The effect of this definition is to ________ the number included in the Negro population.

extend (maximize)

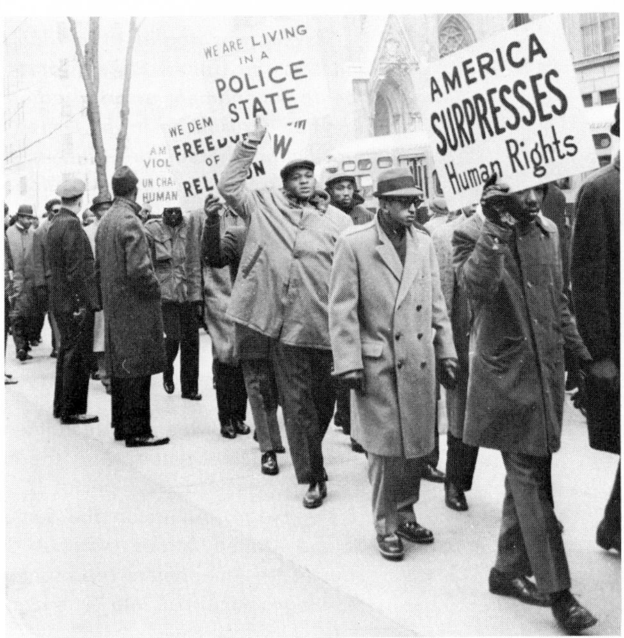

A demonstration for civil rights. (*Wide World Photos*)

109 Slavery rested solely upon force. As Walter puts it, "Brutality was common on large plantations, and the typical overseer preferred physical force to incentives as a method of governing slaves" (Walter, 1964; Myrdal, Sterner, and Rose, 1944). Under these conditions the slave had no civil rights and received no effective protection from the ________.

law (government)

110 In the Dred Scott decision of 1875, United States Supreme Court Chief Justice Roger Taney declared "A Negro has no rights which a white man is bound to respect" (Marden and Meyer, 1962). Within context, this dictum rested upon the Negro's status as property under the system of ________.

slavery

111 Taken out of context, the Taney dictum deprives one category of persons of all rights and relieves another category of persons from all responsibility solely upon a basis of ________.

color (race)

112 The *de facto* status of Negro slaves became a *de jure* status by the Supreme Court's decision in the Dred Scott case. In other words, what had generally been practiced in fact now had the recognition of ________.

law

Slavery was abolished in 1865 by the Thirteenth Amenc ment to the United States Constitution. In 1868, the Fou teenth Amendment asserted equality of rights: "All perso born or naturalized in the United States and subject to tl jurisdiction thereof are citizens of the United States a of the State wherein they reside. No State shall make enforce any law which shall abridge the privileges or in munities of citizens of the United States; nor shall an State deprive any person of life, liberty, or property without due process of law, nor deny to any person within its jurisdiction the equal protection of the laws" (Art. XIV, par. 1).

113 The Fourteenth Amendment did not constitute an attempt to accommodate to the Negro American, because it did not accord any special ________. Rather, it granted to the Negro American the same status as other citizens of the United States, without distinction. Therefore the Fourteenth Amendment represented a legal act to ________ the Negro American into American society.

status (privilege)

assimilate

114 In various parts of the United States, particularly in the South, those regarding themselves as white used various methods to ________ full citizenship and the equal protection of the laws from those they classed as Negroes.

deny (withhold)

115 Systematic exclusion of Negro Americans from "white" schools, public facilities, and public accommodations constituted a general pattern of ________.

segregation

116 Discrimination consists of special selection, favorable for white, unfavorable for Negro, in providing opportunities for employment, voter registration, jury duty, public service, police protection, and the administration of justice (Mendelson, 1962). Segregating public institutions on the basis of race is a special case of ________.

discrimination

117 The United States Supreme Court in *Plessy v. Ferguson,* 1896, asserted that segregated railroad accommodations were legal if they were substantially equal. Thus, segregation, like slavery, became ________ by decision of the Supreme Court.

legal

118 The existing practice of racially segregated schools, as in Washington, D.C., provided the precedent for that Court decision (Humphrey, 1964). Since this kind of accommodation between the races was imposed by white people, it clearly sought to maintain the ________ status of the Negro.

segregated (inferior)

119 Men order processes through rational or quasi-rational belief systems. A belief system may be indicated by adding the suffix "ism" to a root word. Thus, a belief system resting on the assumption of racial superiority or racial inferiority would be called ______.

racism

120 The racist assumes that race determines mental abilities. Putnam (1961, p. 25) attributes Negro successes in intelligence tests to "mulattoes whose successes are largely proportionate to the admixture of white genes." This implies that the Negro cannot equal the white man's intelligence, owing to the limitations of his ______.

race (heredity)

121 Putnam (p. 27) also links cultural traits to inherited racial differences: "A group taken out of the cultural environment of their own race and brought up in that of another . . . become parasites upon the culture of the second race . . . and too many of them, too freely integrated must in the long run lower the ______ of the second race."

culture

122 In the past three centuries there has been much more extensive integration of white and Negro races in the United States than in Europe. According to the racist argument, the culture of ______ ______ ______ should be distinctly inferior to that of ______ as evidenced in terms of education, science, and productivity.

the United States
Europe

Benedict (1959, p. 98) notes that racism includes the dogma that the hope of civilization depends on eliminating some races and keeping others pure. Putnam (1961) states that "complete integration of these races, particularly in the heavy black belts of the South can result only in the parasitic deterioration of the white culture, with or without genocide. The sin of Cain would pale by comparison." *(Emphasis supplied.)*

123 This quotation suggests that genocide is preferable to complete integration of the races, and fits Benedict's definition of ______.

racism

124 There is no evidence that civilization has ever been retarded by the mingling of peoples or races. In fact, civil standards, civil manners, and civil rights have all developed where ______ of different peoples and races occurred.

mingling

125 Exploring the reverse of the racist argument, one can contend that segregation retards civilization. The most segregated and most isolated peoples would be the most distinct from others, genetically and culturally. At the same time the most segregated and isolated peoples would be least affected by ________.

civilization

126 If segregation produces cultural retardation, we would expect the poorest cultural and economic development in areas maintaining the greatest degree of ________.

segregation

United States Army intelligence tests administered to hundreds of thousands of inductees in World War I were classified by race. The medians (midscores, a type of average) for Northern whites and Southern Negroes are shown in Table 43.

Table 43. Army Intelligence Test Medians

Southern whites		*Northern Negroes*	
Mississippi	41.25	New York	45.02
Kentucky	41.50	Illinois	47.35
Arkansas	41.55	Ohio	49.50

SOURCE: Otto Klineberg, *Race Differences*, Harper & Row, Publishers, Incorporated, New York, 1936, p. 182. Used by permission.

127 According to the data in Table 43, the ________ ________ were inferior in intelligence scores to the Northern Negroes.

Southern whites

No scientific data support innate differences in intelligence based on race (Berelson and Steiner, 1964, p. 495). But the school systems in the Northern states were demonstrably superior to those of the Southern states—in terms of length of school year, level of teacher qualification, expenditure per pupil, and number of years of schooling achieved by pupils.

128 The superior Negro performance could better be attributed to the superiority of ________ in the Northern schools than to superiority of race.

education (schooling)

Table 44. Comparison of Negro and White Intelligence Scores (arranged by age of subjects)

Source	Negro and white subjects	Actual Negro overlap of white average	Required Negro overlap for equality	Ratio of Negroes to whites above white average (col. 3/col. 4)
Pasamanick*	300 Negro and white children at 40 weeks	49.4%	50%	99%
	300 Negro and white children at 3 years	44	50	88
Rhoads, 1945	3-year-old children, Philadelphia	30	50	60
Brown, 1944	Kindergarten children in Minneapolis	31	50	62
Tanser, 1939	Chatham, Ontario, Canada, grade school children	17	50	34
Bruce, 1940	Poor 9–10-year-olds, rural Virginia	18	50	36
McGurk, 1953	High school seniors, upper socioeconomic quartile:			
	Cultural test	24	50	48
	Noncultural test	19	50	38
	Lower socioeconomic quartile:			
	Cultural test	55	50	110
	Noncultural test	29	50	58
Shuey, 1942	College freshmen, New York City	18	50	36
U.S. Army, 1918	Inductees in World War I	27	50	54

* The Pasamanick data are presented in the following form:

Category	I.Q. at age: 40 weeks	3 years
White	105.4	111.2
Negro	104.5	98.9

SOURCE: Frank McGurk, "A Scientist's Report on Race Differences," in H. H. Humphrey (ed.), *School Desegregation Documents and Commentaries,* Thomas Y. Crowell Company, New York, 1964, pp. 247–253; Benjamin Pasamanick and Hilda Knoblock, "Race, Complications of Pregnancy, and Neuropsychiatric Disorders," *Social Problems,* 5:266–275, 1958. Used by permission.

forty weeks
99 percent

129 Table 44 shows that the group of Negroes most closely equal to the whites is the Negro group aged _______ _______, where the ratio is _______.

forty weeks

130 In Table 44, the only Negro group achieving a ratio of approximately 99 percent of the white children scoring above the white average are Negro children aged _______ _______.

60

131 Comparing Negro and white children from three to five years of age, the data suggest that the proportion of above-white-average Negro children to above-white-average white children is about _______ percent.

35

132 Among grade school children the ratio of Negro children to white children scoring above the white average intelligence score declines to about ______ percent.

decreases

133 In reviewing the results in frames 129 and 130, as regards variation in age up to about age twelve and variation in performance on intelligence tests, we can see that as age increases, Negro performance ______.

higher

134 After the children reach later adolescence (age seventeen to twenty-five), the proportion of above-white-average Negro children to above-white-average white children appears to be (higher/lower) than it was during the preadolescent grade school period.

social environment

135 Poorer performance of Negro children on intelligence tests could be associated primarily with either hereditary or environmental factors. If Negro children are about equal to white children in infancy, but are progressively lower after ten years' exposure to the social environment, the major factor producing the difference is probably ______ ______.

socioeconomic

136 Investigators seeking to compare intelligence scores for Negro and white children attempt to match the comparison groups on as many socioeconomic factors as possible. Income, quality of home, father's occupation, parents' education, and the family situation are examples of ______ factors.

matched

137 If groups of Negro and white children are precisely matched on income, education, quality of home, and father's occupation, and yet show a difference in average intelligence test scores, the differences in performance cannot be attributed to the factors in which the two groups are ______.

discrimination

138 Segregation, exclusion, and rejection, as forms of racial discrimination, may have considerable effect on the motivation and attitudes of Negro children in schooling and in testing. They would not affect white children. Therefore, groups of Negro and white children cannot be matched on racial ______.

environment

139 To prove that hereditary factors and not environmental factors explain differences between the intelligence test scores of Negroes and whites would require isolation of a specific intelligence factor which could be shown to vary regularly with variations of hereditary factors from one generation to another, but which was unaffected by changes in ________.

heredity (genes)

140 To date, biologists associate genes only with specific structural and chemical characteristics of organs. They do not associate genes with the generalized functioning of complexes of organs, as with respiration, circulation of blood, or mental performance. As yet there is no satisfactory evidence for associating performance on intelligence tests with ________.

Osage Indian children, benefiting from high living standards derived from oil income, met national standards on performance and language tests, although Indian children in general score below Negro children on intelligence tests. A sample of 3,000 white, east Tennessee mountain children showed a median intelligence quotient gain from 82 to 93 over children in the same geographic region from 1930 to 1940, as a result of rapid improvements in the schools (Pettigrew, 1964).

social environment

141 The differences in performance on intelligence tests in those cases is associated with changes in the ________ ________.

Southern-born Negro boys moving to New York City manifest the average intelligence scores shown in Table 45 when grouped according to years of residence in New York.

9
23

142 From Table 45, it can be seen that the Southern-born Negro boys' average intelligence score increased ________ points after six years' residence in New York and ________ points after twelve years' residence in New York.

Table 45. Intelligence Scores by Years' Residence in New York

Years in New York	*Average intelligence score*
1–2	64
3–4	67
5–6	73
7–8	83
9–11	85
12	87

SOURCE: Otto Klineberg, *Negro Intelligence and Selective Migration,* Columbia University Press, New York, 1935, p. 271. Used by permission.

about equal

143 A close comparison of average test standings between Philadelphia-born and Southern-born Negro ninth graders who entered Philadelphia schools in grade 1A (see Table 46) shows that the two groups are ________ ________.

1 point

144 The greatest difference between these two groups on any test is ________ ________.

intelligence / numbers
reasoning / paper form test

145 Comparing Southern-born Philadelphia Negro ninth graders entering Philadelphia schools in Grade 1A with those entering six years later in Grade 7A disclosed a difference of 6 points in ________; 9 points in ________; 5 points in ________; and 8 points on ________ ________ ________.

years

146 In all four tests, the level of performance varied directly with the number of ________ spent in Philadelphia schools.

Table 46. Intelligence Scores of Ninth-grade Negro Children in Philadelphia

Where born	*Entered Phila. sch.*	*Intelligence quotient*	*Number skills*	*Reasoning*	*Minnesota paper form test*
Philadelphia	Kindergarten	97	72	38	33
Philadelphia	1A	94	67	34	30
South	1A	93	68	35	29
South	3A	89	62	29	23
South	5A	90	62	29	25
South	7A	87	59	30	21

SOURCE: Everett S. Lee, "Negro Intelligence and Selective Migration: A Philadelphia Test of the Klineberg Hypothesis," *American Sociological Review,* 16:227, 1951. Adapted.

An entire first-grade class of twenty-six Negro children and their parents received special indoctrination. Then the children received seven months of intensive training designed to expand their interests and improve reading readiness. Three similar first-grade classes in the same school, receiving no special training, were used as controls. Average scores on the reading-readiness test were (Brazziel and Terrell, 1962):

First grade class	*Centile on national scale*
Experimental class	50
Control class A	16
Control class B	14
Control class C	13

50
equal to

147 The national centile scale has 100 ranks; the midrank or average on the national centile scale is ______. Therefore the experimental first-grade class of Negro children was ______ ______ the national average for first-grade children.

children / parents
children

148 Two environmental factors were associated with the Negro first graders' dramatic improvement in reading readiness. These environmental factors include (*a*) special indoctrination of the ______ and their ______; and (*b*) intensive training of the ______ in the special reading program.

In the judicial review preceding the school desegregation decision, the Supreme Court recognized that segregated schools injure minority-group children and usurp their rights. Leading social scientists attested that "segregation produces feelings of inferiority and humiliation . . ."; "that minority group children often react with a defeatist attitude and a lowering of ambition . . ."; and that they "tend to be hypersensitive and anxious about relations with the larger society" (Brown v. Board of Education).

improve (better)

149 This testimony would be substantiated if, after a period of genuinely integrated schooling, minority-group children were to ______ their school performance relative to that of white children.

School administrators representing twelve desegregated communities testified to the Civil Rights Commission in 1959 on the effect of desegregation on academic standards. All twelve reported that desegregation had produced no lowering of academic standards. Louisville, Kentucky, St. Louis, Missouri, and Washington, D.C., reported very substantial improvements in Negro children's performance and some improvement in white children's performance (Pettigrew, 1964).

segregation in schools

150 The removal of segregation in schools produced improved performance by minority-group children. This tends to substantiate the social scientists' testimony and the Supreme Court's finding that _______ _______ _______ is injurious to minority-group children.

achievement

151 Relating achievement to ethnicity, Rosen (1959) states that "Negroes often train children relatively early on self reliance, but there is little stress on achievement training." Negroes in the lowest of five social classes produced the lowest average achievement scores of five ethnic groups. This would be expected if segregation tends to depress _______ in Negroes.

minority groups

152 Negro writers reflect minority reactions to discrimination. Baldwin (1961) describes the black man's relation to the whole white world as unutterably painful. Johnson (1948) expressed shame that his race should suffer the indignities of mob violence. These reactions agree with the social scientists' assertion that segregation of _______ _______ produces anxiety and tension.

Table 47. Four Types of Reaction to Discrimination by Members of Minority Groups

	Accepts inferior status	*Rejects inferior status*
Accepts segregated role	1. Submission	3. Avoidance
Rejects segregated role	2. Withdrawal	4. Integration

SOURCE: Adapted from Peter I. Rose, *They and We: Racial and Ethnic Relations in the United States,* Random House, Inc., New York, 1964, p. 131. Adapted by permission.

153 Minority-group members can accept both segregation and inferior status, or they can reject both, or they can accept one and reject the other. The "Uncle Tom" type of Negro accepted segregation, readily cooperated with all whites, including those who forbade him to vote or to complain. In Table 47, the "Uncle Tom" type of Negro falls in category ______.

1 (submission)

154 Some fair-skinned Negroes reject segregation, but acknowledge the inferior status of Negroes. Each year several thousand such people abondon their Negro racial identification, and pass over into the white group. These people belong in category ______.

2 (withdrawal)

155 Many well-educated and successful Negroes do not feel inferior to white people, but avoid contacts with them as much as possible in social, economic, and occupational activities. Such people accept ______ but reject ______ ______.

segregation / inferior status

156 The Black Muslim movement rejects the white culture's political and religious basis. "Muslims do not vote . . . they resist induction into the military service . . . and they categorically reject Christianity . . ." (Essien-Udom, 1962, p. 27). The Muslims, calling themselves the "elect of God," are obliged to pursue a righteous life which would justify their special status. The Black Muslim group belongs in category ______ of Table 47.

3 (avoidance)

157 The American ideal requires equal rights, human dignity, and personal development to the limit of one's capacities. The Negro American who accepts these ideals would reject both segregation and inferior status and would be classified in category ______.

4 (integration)

12
12

158 In Part A of Table 48, ______ percent of the Negro respondents were unemployed, and ______ percent reflected dissatisfaction with their unemployed status.

159 From the figures in Part A, Table 48, it appears that virtually all the Negro respondents in skilled, white-collar, professional, business, or civil service positions were satisfied with their ______ status.

job

160 The attitude of all unemployed Negro respondents to their unemployed status was one of ______.

dissatisfaction

Table 48. What Negro Americans Want

A. Negro attitudes on employment	*Jobs held*	*Jobs qualified for, wanted*	*Satisfied**	*Dissatisfied**
Unemployed	12%	0%	0%	12%
Unskilled labor	31	9	9	22
Domestic service	17	6	6	11
Skilled labor	10	29	10	
White collar	10	14	10	
Retired on pension	7	9	7	
Professional	5	10	5	
Business executive	4	18	4	
Civil service	4	5	4	
	100%	100%	55%	45%

B. Negro opinion on integrated employment	*Total*	*Non-South*	*South*
Prefer mixed group	76%	84%	68%
Prefer mostly Negroes	11	6	17
Not sure	13	10	15

C. Negro opinion on integrated housing	*Total*	*Non-South*	*South*
Prefer mixed neighborhood	64%	75%	55%
Prefer all-Negro neighborhood	20	11	27
Not sure	16	14	18

* Figures inferred from first two columns by unit author, Donald E. Allen.

SOURCE: William Brink and Louis Harris, *The Negro Revolution in America,* Simon and Schuster, Inc., New York, 1964, pp. 156–158. Used by permission.

48
33

69

161 Negro respondents in unskilled labor plus domestic service totaled _______ percent. Negro respondents dissatisfied with these job levels totaled _______ percent. The ratio of dissatisfaction among unskilled laborers and domestic service workers combined was 33/48. Approximately _______ percent were dissatisfied.

integration

162 Analysis of the Negro attitudes on integrated employment and integrated housing (see parts B and C, Table 48) demonstrates a strong preference for _______ in both employment and housing.

employment / housing

163 Myrdal, Sterner, and Rose (1944, p. 61) predicted that Negro Americans would have a higher degree of interest in economic equality than in social equality. Comparing parts B and C of Table 48, we find that there are about 12 percent more total Negro preferences for integrated ________ than for integrated ________, which confirms the prediction.

North / South

164 A clear majority of Negro Americans in all areas of the United States desire equality and integration in employment and in housing, but the majority is larger in the ________ than in the ________.

integration
equality

165 Relating the data in Table 48 to the categories of response to discrimination in Table 47, we can clearly see that only a small proportion of Negro Americans enter the withdrawal or avoidance categories. About 70 percent nationwide, and 60 percent in the South, reject both segregation and inferior status. They seek ________ into American society and ________ to other Americans.

In summary, accommodation tends to preserve differences between racial and ethnic groups. Economic exchange and minority-group associations represent different levels of accommodation. Conversely, racism breeds segregation and discrimination, both of which are strongly rejected by the group against whom they are practiced.

racial / ethnic

166 Assimilation may be defined as a process whereby an intrusive ethnic or racial group achieves complete and indiscriminate participation and membership in society without regard to ________ or ________ identification (see Berry, 1951; Allport, 1958).

acculturation

167 Assimilation is a process which takes place in two steps, acculturation and full membership. First, the intrusive group must learn and accept the general culture of the host society, including its attitudes, ideas, beliefs, values, and language. Internalizing the culture of a society is called ________.

participation (membership)

168 The second step of assimilation is the achievement of full and indiscriminate ________ in the host society.

169 Social forces which drive groups toward assimilation are particularly strong in the modern achievement-oriented society. In the United States, for example, there is great stress on personal ________.

achievement

170 Communication with members of the host society in daily travel, shopping, and performance at the place of employment makes it essential for the intrusive group members to gain fluency in using the ________ of the host society.

language

171 Urban society is dynamic, mobile, and impersonal. Its effective functioning requires uniform standards and equal treatment. Rural society is relatively more static and nonmobile. Social relations and status are on a personal basis. Assimilation would therefore tend to be rapid in ________ areas and relatively retarded in ________ areas.

urban / rural

172 American society is based on technological efficiency. Nearly 22,000 occupational specialties must be integrated into a great variety of productive and service enterprises. Selecting workers and specialists on the basis of ethnic or racial antecedents rather than on objective standards of training and ability seriously reduces ________.

efficiency

173 Hitler regarded the Jews as a "polluted race" and sought to eliminate them. His program drove out Jewish scientists such as Albert Einstein, Lise Meitner, and Max Planck, who did much to give atomic weapons to the United States in World War II. Hitler deprived Germany of valuable specialized services because he classed people by ________ rather than by abilities.

"race"

174 In modern urban societies where objective and impersonal standards are applied in rewarding the individual, the most able and the most willing are selected for training, employment, and advancement. Such a system provides an intrusive ethnic or racial group opportunities for ________ into the occupational structure of the society.

assimilation

175 High social mobility facilitates assimilation. Easy vertical (social class) mobility and horizontal (geographic) mobility help all members of society reach their maximum potential. High ________ also accelerates assimilation.

mobility

176 War brings about rapid changes in a society. Millions of people move geographically. Quick advancement is accorded to the able, and rigid systems of production and property control are often destroyed or reorganized and remanned. The effect is to permit rapid ________ of minority groups.

assimilation

177 Migration produces changes in status for minority groups. The massive movement of the United States population from rural to urban areas is fully shared by Negro Americans. In 1910, 73 percent of Negro Americans were dispersed in rural areas. By 1960, 73 percent of Negro Americans were in the urban areas. (Brink and Harris, 1964). Improved education and job opportunities in the city tend to raise the Negroes' ________.

status

The nation's fifteen metropolitan areas of more than one million population have received the greatest concentration of Negro Americans. In 1960, six cities had over 25 percent Negro population. Chicago and New York were anticipating 33 percent Negro population by 1970, and Washington, D.C., already had over 50 percent Negro population in 1960 (Grodzins, 1962, p. 87).

178 Heavy urban concentrations are able to assert effective political power. Negroes in the cities discussed above have achieved assimilation as American citizens because of their ________ ________.

political power

179 Rapid technological change results in realignment of jobs. It increases specialization and special education requirements. It increases productivity and real income. It increases social mobility, and therefore, in the long term, tends to ________ assimilation of ethnic or racial groups.

hasten (accelerate)

180 From 1820 to 1960 about 42 million people migrated to the United States from more than two dozen European countries. More than 30 million of them spoke languages other than English. These immigrants and their descendants were or will be ________ into the American society in two to four generations.

assimilated

181 Negroid peoples constituted about 20 percent of the United States population in 1820, but only about 9 percent in 1920, owing to the influx of ________ ________ from Europe. In 1960, the Negro population constituted slightly over 10 percent of the total.

white immigrants

182 In institutional and personal relations, the assimilation of Negro Americans has been considerably retarded by discriminatory legislation which has maintained a fairly rigid ________ of Negroes from the rest of society.

segregation

assimilation

183 Negroes, supported by some other Americans, have successfully waged a series of legal battles over the past fifty years to achieve equal recognition as citizens with regard to voting, police protection, jury duty, education, and government service. These successes have gradually provided more complete ______ in political functions.

institutional

184 According to Table 49, more than 90 percent of white people with previous social contact, and more than 75 percent of the whole white American population, and nearly half of the white American population and nearly half of the white Southerners are willing to share on a nondiscriminatory basis with Negro Americans in ______ areas.

Table 49. White Feeling about Contact with Negroes

A. *Institutional areas*	*Previous social contact group*	*Nationwide*	*South*
Would object to:			
Working next to Negro on job	8%	17%	31%
Eating lunch next to Negro	4	20	50
Sitting next to Negro on bus	5	20	47
Sitting next to Negro at movie	6	23	54
Own child at school with Negroes	9	23	55
Using same restroom as Negroes	9	24	56
B. *Personal areas*			
Would object to:			
Trying on clothing that Negro tried before	16	32	57
Own child bringing Negro friend home to supper	16	41	76
Negroes as next-door neighbors	26	51	74
Close friend or relative marrying Negro	70	84	91
Own teen-age daughter dating Negro	80	90	97

SOURCE: Adapted from William Brink and Louis Harris, *The Negro Revolution in America*, Simon and Schuster, Inc., New York, 1964, p. 148. Used by permission.

neighbors

185 Nationwide, about 49 percent of white Americans would not object to Negroes as ______. According to Table 48, 64 percent of Negroes would prefer interracial neighborhoods (Brink and Harris, 1964).

Negro

186 Of white people with previous social contact with Negroes 74 percent would not object to ______ neighbors (Table 49).

interracial

187 These data support two inferences regarding interracial relations. First, a slight majority of the American people would accept ______ housing.

increase

188 Second, after more people experienced interracial housing, the percentage of those willing to accept it would probably ______.

White respondents in integrated and segregated units in a housing project were asked whether the Negro people in the project were pretty much the same as white people or different. (See Table 50).

Table 50. Housewives Who Hold Negroes in the Project in Different Degrees of Esteem

Degree of esteem	*Integrated projects* Koaltown	Sacktown	*Segregated projects* Bakerville	Frankville
Respect Negroes as equal	72%	79%	43%	39%
Feel Negroes are inferior	11	13	37	35
Neutral	17	8	20	26

SOURCE: M. Deutsch and M. E. Collins, *Interracial Housing: A Psychological Evaluation of a Social Experiment*, University of Minnesota Press, Minneapolis, 1951, p. 82.

support

189 These data tend to ______ the second inference, frame 188.

White soldiers in World War II indicated their attitudes toward having Negro platoons in their military organizations in combat.

Table 51. Attitude of White Soldiers toward Association with Negro Soldiers

Extent of army contact with Negroes	*Dislike very much*	*Good idea*
No colored platoons in white companies	62%	18%
Men in same division as colored troops	24	50
Men in same regiment as colored troops	20	66
Men in a company with a Negro platoon	7	64

SOURCE: Samuel A. Stouffer, *The American Soldier*, Princeton University Press, Princeton, N.J., 1949, vol. I, p. 594.

favorable

190 Companies contained about 200 men, and regiments about 2,000. Divisions contained about 20,000 men. Stouffer's (1949) figures show that as white American soldiers associated more closely with Negro American soldiers the white soldiers' attitudes became much more ________.

daughter-dating

191 According to Table 49, in the most personal areas there is general unwillingness to accept ________-________.

amalgamated

192 Amalgamation refers to a biological mixing of hereditary characteristics. Races are distinguished by biological characteristics. As racial groups interbreed, the two racial groups become ________.

Racial mixing progresses generation by generation by powers of 2 and by powers of the reciprocal of 2. An individual has 2 parents, 4 grandparents, 8 great-grandparents, 16-great-great-grandparents, and so on:

Powers, or generations	1	2	3	4	5	6	7	8	9	10
Expansion of 2	2	4	8	16	32	64	128	256	512	1,024
Reduction of 1/2	1/2	1/4	1/8	1/16	1/32	1/64	1/128	1/256	1/512	1/1,024

white

193 If one white male should have two children by one Negro female, and they and their descendants marry unmixed Negroes and reproduce their numbers through ten generations, the tenth generation would include 1,024 mixed individuals, each carrying 1/1,024 ________ ancestry.

2½

194 If 5 percent of all Negro children received half white ancestry through white fathers the white ancestry in each Negro generation would equal ________ percent.

40

195 If such a substitution of white ancestry were repeated regularly for sixteen generations in the Negro population, the total amount of white ancestry diffused through the Negro population would be 16×2.5 or ________ percent.

Table 52 arranges average measurements of characteristic Negroid features to determine how well they agree with claimed white ancestry, based on the characteristics of Negro respondents and their knowledge of their parents and grandparents. White people are characterized by narrower nostrils, thinner lips, greater seated height, and lighter skin color.

Table 52. The Negro-White Amalgamation

Genealogical class	N	*Percent*	N	*Nostril width, mm*	*Lip thickness, mm*	*Seated height, cm*	*Color index*
No known white	439	28.3	109	43.4	23.9	87.3	75.5
More Negro than white	490	31.7	129	41.3	22.5	88.1	68.3
About same Negro & white	393	25.2	95	39.9	22.0	88.0	62.1
More white than Negro	229	14.8	30	37.5	18.8	89.1	48.7
Total	1,551	100.0	363				

SOURCE: Adapted from Melville J. Herskovits, *The American Negro: A Study in Racial Crossing*, Indiana University Press, Bloomington, Ind., 1964.

no known

196 According to the data, the Negro group with the widest nostrils, the thickest lips, the shortest seated height and the darkest skin color index claimed ________ ________ white ancestry.

40

197 According to Table 52, respondents claiming either equal Negro and white ancestry plus those claiming more white than Negro ancestry total ________ percent.

72

198 About ________ percent of Herskovits's respondents claimed some known white ancestry.

narrowest
thinnest / lightest

199 The group claiming more white than Negro ancestry demonstrated measurable evidence in support of this claim: of the four groups, those claiming to know of more white than Negro ancestry had the ________ nostrils, the ________ lips, and the ________ skin color index.

white

200 Racial mixing started soon after 1620 when the first Negro women arrived in the American Colonies. Lighter Negro women tended to be preferred in racial mixing. By 1750, Negroes of only 1/32 Negro ancestry resulted, and these became difficult to distinguish from whites. By 1800, hundreds of persons with very small fractions of Negro ancestry could easily have passed over into the ________ population.

256,000

201 If by 1800, 1,000 very light, unrecognizable Negroes had passed over into the white population, their descendants would have completed eight generations by 1960. If the population remained stable, their descendants in eight generations would number ______ by 1960.

4,096,000

202 With natural increase, the population doubled each forty years. Thus the population generated in frame 201 would be doubled an additional four times, yielding a total of ______ descendants after 160 years.

A sample of 346 Negro families of mixed ancestry included 10 percent who had one or more members who had assumed white racial identity and had married white. Assuming that about 4 percent of all Negro families have such members, Burma (1946) estimated that about 2,500 very light Negroes pass into the white population each year.

amalgamated

203 The American Negro and white populations are slowly being ______ into a single population (Burma, 1946).

To summarize, increased mobility promotes racial and ethnic assimilation. Adaptation and diffusion of cultural alternatives tend to be retarded by older people and in rural areas. Segregation, according to Park (1949), represents a form of accommodation. There is no incontrovertible evidence that intelligence test scores are determined by race or heredity; rather, differences between racial groups imply environmental determination. Urbanization tends to accelerate assimilation. In America, amalgamation of the white and Negro races over 300 years has produced a Negro population with 20 to 40 percent white ancestry, and seems to be promoting gradual assimilation of the Negro race by the white race in this country.

SUMMARY

Racial or ethnic relations arise when one distinctive ethnic or racial population becomes intruded into another. The intrusion may occur through a massive military conquest and occupation or through a massive immigration of integrated ethnic groups. It may also occur by the volun-

tary or involuntary immigration of individuals. Initial contact brings an exploratory phase as the two kinds of peoples begin to learn how to communicate with each other. A competitive period may follow in which armed conflict occurs. In some cases the weaker population is destroyed, partially destroyed, or expelled. Usually, however, a period of at least partial accommodation follows.

Accommodation is manifested initially in economic areas. These areas include technology, productive processes, specialized labor, and trade. As the two populations develop a shared value system and a common culture in the economic areas, the next stage of accommodation arises in the institutional areas. The minority population gradually becomes incorporated into the religious, educational, and political institutions of the host culture. The third stage of accommodation is in the personal areas where the two populations lose their distinctive qualities and begin to associate as social equals on an individual basis. After accommodation has become general through all three levels of association, the economic, the institutional, and the personal, full assimilation of the peoples may take place. When this stage is reached, the two original populations become merged in one common culture. The original ethnic or racial groups are no longer distinguishable for any social purpose, although individuals will continue to exercise and apply their personal preferences.

The process of accommodation is much accelerated by conditions which increase mobility either geographically or in the various social classes of occupation and income. In recent decades the rapid pace of urbanization, coupled with intra- and international migration, has accelerated the accommodative process in the United States. The rapid conversion of productive processes and the rapid rise in the volume and variety of production has placed a heavy stress on youth and on education. These factors have also accelerated social mobility and the accommodative processes. The accommodative processes, like other major social changes, have occurred so rapidly that the more tradition-oriented of the older generations tend to see themselves discomfited and their values discredited. War and military preparation have also added to the pressures of mobility and to the need for accommodation and change. The result is that accommodative changes which might have extended over hundreds of years in an agrarian society may be compressed into a few decades in a rapidly changing urban society. The trend of the accommodative changes is toward greater functional efficiency for the society as a whole.

SELF-REVIEW QUIZ

1 Population intrusion through military conquest and occupation, massive immigration, or integrated ethnic groups gives rise to ________ ________.

2 When immigration gives rise to population intrusion, at least two phases ordinarily are undergone prior to accommodation. They are the ________ and the ________.

3 From 1902 to 1941, the number of Negro lynchings in the United States was roughly ________ times greater than for whites in each ten-year period.
   a. fifty
   b. twenty
   c. ten
   d. five

4 The initial basis for accommodating Negroes into American society under slavery represents the ________ level of association.
   a. institutional
   b. economic
   c. personal

5 Systematic exclusion of one group by another from public facilities and accommodations represents ________. Special selection in providing opportunities for employment, voter registration, and administration of justice represents ________.

6 Klineberg's data about intelligence tests administered during World War I showed that:
   a. Northern Negroes scored higher than Northern whites.
   b. Southern Negroes scored higher than Northern whites.
   c. Northern Negroes scored higher than Southern whites.
   d. Southern whites scored higher than Northern whites.

7 Data in this unit about racial differences on intelligence tests suggest that ________ is the most important variable in accounting for such differences.
   a. heredity
   b. occupation
   c. prestige
   d. education

8 Brink and Harris, in *The Negro Revolution in America,* point out that most Negroes:
   a. prefer to live in all-Negro neighborhoods
   b. prefer to live in mixed neighborhoods
   c. prefer to work mostly with Negroes
   d. prefer to work mostly under whites

9 When a minority group achieves indiscriminate participation and membership in society without regard to ethnic or

racial identification, the process of ________ has been achieved.

10 Acculturation and full membership represent the two major steps in the ________ of one group into another.

11 Deutsch and Collins's study of integrated-segregated housing demonstrates that between 72 and 79 percent of whites in the ________ housing projects respected Negroes as their equals.

12 Burma's study of Negro families of mixed ancestry suggests that about ________ Negroes pass into the United States white population each year.

a. 500
b. 1,000
c. 2,500
d. 5,000

REFERENCES

Allport, Gordon W.: *The Nature of Prejudice* (abridged), Doubleday & Company, Inc., Garden City, N.Y., 1958.

Baldwin, James: *Nobody Knows My Name,* Dell Publishing Co., Inc., New York, 1961.

Benedict, Ruth: *Race: Science and Politics,* The Viking Press, New York, 1959.

Berelson, Bernard, and Gary Steiner: *Human Behavior: An Inventory of Scientific Findings,* Harcourt, Brace & World, Inc., New York, 1964.

Berry, Brewton: *Racial and Ethnic Relations,* Houghton Mifflin Company, Boston, 1951.

Brazziel, William, and Mary Terrell: "Experiment in Development of Readiness in a Culturally Disadvantaged Group of First Grade Negro Children," *Journal of Negro Education,* 31:1–7, Winter, 1962.

Brink, William, and Louis Harris: *The Negro Revolution in America,* Simon and Schuster, Inc., New York, 1964.

Burma, John H.: "The Measurement of Negro Passing," *American Journal of Sociology,* 52:18–22, July, 1946.

Carr-Saunders, A. M.: *World Population,* Clarendon Press, Oxford, 1936.

Deutsch, M., and M. E. Collins: *Interracial Housing: A Psychological Evaluation of a Social Experiment,* University of Minnesota Press, Minneapolis, 1951.

Essien-Udom, E. N.: *Black Nationalism: A Search for an Identity in America,* Dell Publishing Co., Inc., New York, 1962.

Gendell, Murray L., and Hans L. Zetterberg: *A Sociological Almanac of the United States,* 2d ed., Charles Scribner's Sons, New York, 1964.

Grodzins, Morton: "The Metropolitan Area as a Racial Problem," in Earl Raab (ed.), *American Race Relations Today,* Doubleday & Company, Inc., Garden City, N.Y., 1962.

Handlin, Oscar: *Race and Nationality in American Life,* Doubleday & Company, Inc., Garden City, N.Y., 1957.

Herskovits, Melville J.: *The American Negro: A Study in Racial Crossing,* Indiana University Press, Bloomington, Ind., 1964.

Humphrey, Hubert H. (ed.):

School Desegregation Documents and Commentaries, Thomas Y. Crowell Company, New York, 1964.

Johnson, James W.: *Autobiography of an Ex-colored Man,* New American Library of World Literature, Inc., New York, 1948.

Klineberg, Otto: *Negro Intelligence and Selective Migration,* Columbia University Press, New York, 1935.

———: *Race Differences,* Harper & Row, Publishers, Incorporated, New York, 1936.

Kuper, Leo: *Passive Resistance in South Africa,* Yale University Press, New Haven, Conn., 1957.

Lee, Everett S.: "Negro Intelligence and Selective Migration: A Philadelphia Test of the Klineberg Hypothesis," *American Sociological Review,* 16:227–233, 1951.

McGurk, Frank: "A Scientist's Report on Race Differences," in H. H. Humphrey (ed.), *School Desegregation Documents and Commentaries,* Thomas Y. Crowell Company, New York, 1964.

McNickle, D'Arey: *The Indian Tribes of the United States,* Oxford University Press, Fair Lawn, N.J., 1962.

Marden, C. F., and Gladys Meyer: *Minorities in American Society,* 2d ed., American Book Company, New York, 1962.

Mendelson, Wallace: *Discrimination,* Prentice-Hall, Inc., Englewood Cliffs, N.J., 1962.

Montagu, M. F. A.: "Intelligence of Northern Negroes and Southern Whites in the First World War," *American Journal of Psychology,* 58:161–188, 1945.

Murdock, George P.: "The Common Denominator of Cultures," in R. Lincoln (ed.), *The Science of Man in the World Crisis,* Columbia University Press, New York, 1945.

Myrdal, Gunnar, Richard Sterner, and Arnold Rose: *An American Dilemma,* Harper & Row, Publishers, Incorporated, New York, 1944.

Ogburn, W. F.: *Social Change,* The Viking Press, Inc., New York, 1950.

Park, Robert E.: *Race and Culture,* The Free Press of Glencoe, New York, 1949.

Pasamanick, Benjamin, and Hilda Knoblock: "Race, Complications of Pregnancy, and Neuropsychiatric Disorder," *Social Problems,* 5:266–278, Winter, 1958.

Pettigrew, Thomas F.: *A Profile of the Negro American,* D. Van Nostrand Company, Inc., Princeton, N.J., 1964.

Putnam, Carleton: *Race and Reason,* Public Affairs Press, Washington, D.C., 1961.

Raper, Arthur F.: *The Tragedy of Lynching,* The University of North Carolina Press, Chapel Hill, N.C., 1933.

Rose, Peter I.: *They and We: Racial and Ethnic Relations in the United States,* Random House, Inc., New York, 1964.

Rosen, Bernard C.: "Race, Ethnicity, and the Achievement Syndrome," *American Sociological Review,* 24:47–60, 1959.

Stouffer, Samuel A.: *The American Soldier,* Princeton University Press, Princeton, N.J., 1949, vol. I.

Sumner, William G.: *Folkways,* Ginn and Company, Boston, 1906.

U.S. Bureau of the Census: *Census of Population: 1960, Supplementary Reports,* P.C. (S1)–10, Sept. 7, 1961.

U.S. Supreme Court: *Brown v. Board of Education,* 347, U.S. 483, 1954.

U.S. Supreme Court: *Plessy v. Ferguson,* 163, U.S. 537, 1896.

Walter, E. V.: "Violence and the Process of Terror," *American Sociological Review,* 29:248, 1964.

appendix

human learning: processes shared with subhuman species

VERNON H. EDMONDS

This special unit has been added to the program because it contains concepts and data particularly relevant to Unit 1, Part 2. It was not included in the major context of the book, however, because many readers will not need to rely on the information contained herein for an understanding of social learning.

It is well to be acquainted with some of the theoretical statements about learning which have been derived from the study of subhuman animals. Certainly, some learning processes are essentially the same for subhuman animals and Homo sapiens. This was emphasized in the presentation of principles of classical (Pavlovian) conditioning and operant (instrumental) conditioning given in the companion volume to this one (Part 3, Human Behavior, *McGraw-Hill Book Company, 1965). It is reaffirmed in this section. Here Guthrie's association theory (viz., contiguity learning), Thorndike's effect theory (much like operant conditioning), and the theory of insightful learning are discussed in terms of their adequacy to explain learning processes common to most mammals.*

In addition, this section presents the inadequacies of these theories for explaining certain forms of complex human behavior. Particularly, the acquisition and communication of complex symbols and language forms is discussed in some detail.

Therefore, this unit is recommended for readers not familiar with the companion volume and for those desiring a deeper penetration of the problems of human learning. The reader is warned that the ideas presented here are not simple or easy to grasp. They are significant, however, and the sophisticated student certainly should be familiar with them.

Much controversy still rages over the number of "irreducible" types of learning. Some maintain there is only one. Others maintain there are two, three, and even five. No attempt is made to settle such a difficult issue; however, three generic types of learning are given fairly intensive treatment. Whether these three generic types can accurately and meaningfully be subsumed under fewer headings or should be further analyzed and expanded may be open to question, but there should be no question that understanding some of their basic differences is a logically sound starting point.

Controversy also rages over whether there are genuine, as contrasted with apparent, differences in the learning processes of different species of animals. This should not be confused with the issue concerning whether some animals, man included, learn certain types of behavior that other animals do not and cannot learn. As we know and recognize these types of behavior, there can hardly be any question that some animals do not and cannot learn types of behavior that are readily learned by other species of animals. The question of species differences in types of learning processes is much more difficult and is not stressed in this section. Rather the emphasis is upon processes and behaviors common to both man and some of the subhuman species.

The types of learning dealt with here are (1) contiguity-type learning, which is also commonly referred to as "classical conditioning," "respondent conditioning," or simply, "conditioning"; (2) effect-type learning, which is also commonly referred to as "instrumental conditioning," "instrumental learning," "trial-and-error learning," "problem solving," and "operant conditioning"; and (3) instrumental insight, usually referred to as "insightful learning." An attempt is made to indicate the general types of human behavior that are accurately and meaningfully subsumable under each of these three types of learning.

Contiguity Learning

Box 1. Contiguity Learning

In a pioneer study Pavlov (1927) found that in the absence of previous learning a dog would salivate when food powder was placed in its mouth. A buzzer or a tick of a metronome would, of course, not elicit the salivation response upon first presentation. The procedure involved sounding a buzzer or starting a metronome and then introducing food into the dog's mouth. After several such sequences the dogs would salivate to the buzzer or metronome presented alone.

In an experiment by Miller, Murphy, and Mirsky (1955) a monkey's position in a dominance hierarchy was markedly altered by subjecting other monkeys in the group to electric shock while the monkey whose position was changed was in view. The "monkey in view," designated as "No. 53," rose from ninth place in a group of ten to third place. Presumably the fear reaction to the electric shock was transferred to monkey No. 53 after one or more pairings of shock and monkey No. 53. It is also significant that some monkeys that were not exposed to the shock treatment became subordinate to monkey No. 53 when placed in the group after the other monkeys had been conditioned.

Razran (1949), using a procedure very similar to Pavlov's, presented a number of words to human subjects just before having them eat candy. The candy initially elicited salivation. The words, of course, did not. After several such sequential presentations the human subjects were salivating to the words alone. Subsequent to these sequential presentations, the salivating response was also elicited by words that sounded like those used in the word-candy sequence (homophones) and to words that meant the same thing but sounded differently (synonyms).

It is well known that an electric shock will produce an increase in the electrical conductivity of the skin. Cook (1937) using human subjects presented a green light immediately before shocking his subjects. After several such sequences the subjects responded with a marked increase in electrical conductivity of the skin when the green light alone was presented. An increase in electrical conductivity of the skin is commonly accepted as an indicator of emotional response. In this case it very probably indicated the presence of fear or anxiety.

Buzzers and metronome ticks prior to the sequence presentations. Monkey No. 53 prior to simultaneous presentation of Monkey No. 53 and shock to other monkeys. Words prior to sequence presentations. Green light prior to sequence presentations.

1 If a "neutral stimulus" is defined as "a stimulus that does not elicit a given response at a given point in time in the history of an organism,"[1] then the neutral stimuli in each of the experiments described in Box 1 are, respectively, +++++.

[1] Terms to be defined and defining terms are placed in quotation marks for the sake of clarity. No one is being quoted unless a reference is given with respect to the quotation.

food powder in the mouth, electric shock, eating candy, electric shock

2 An "adequate stimulus" is, by definition, "a stimulus that elicits a given response at some given point in time of an organism's history." The adequate stimuli in each of the above experiments are, respectively, +++++.

3 An adequate stimulus may be either an unconditioned stimulus or a conditioned stimulus. An "unconditioned stimulus" is, by definition, "a stimulus that elicits a given response in an organism in the absence of any previous experience with that stimulus." All of the adequate stimuli described in Box 1 are ________ stimuli.

unconditioned

Buzzers and metronome ticks *after* the sequence presentations. Monkey No. 53 *after* the shock plus monkey No. 53 presentations. Words *after* the word-candy sequence presentations. Green light *after* the green light-shock sequence presentations.

4 A "conditioned stimulus" is one that "elicits a learned response." That is, it elicits a given response only after some prior learning experience with it. Conditioned stimuli in the Box 1 examples are, respectively, +++++.

5 The only reason for using "adequate stimulus" instead of "unconditioned stimulus" in describing this type of learning is that much learning of this type does not involve an unconditioned stimulus. Pavlov, for example, trained dogs to salivate to a light after they had learned to salivate to a buzzer by presenting the light just before the buzzer was to sound. The buzzer in this case is an adequate stimulus, but it is not an ________ ________.

unconditioned stimulus

6 To give another example of neutral-stimulus–conditioned-stimulus learning, value-laden adjectives, such as domineering, stingy, generous, and kind, have been used to condition emotional reactions to nationality groups. In this case the value-laden adjectives are the ________ ________ since they were presented second in the sequence and were already eliciting learned emotional reactions of a pleasant or unpleasant nature.

conditioned stimuli

time

7 "Contiguity" means "closeness." The type of closeness illustrated in these examples is that of (time/space). Contiguity learning is essentially a process of *partial stimulus substitution*. It is obvious that a green light does not become a complete stimulus substitute for an electric shock. Look at the diagram below and designate that part of the response to shock for which the green light is a substitute.

anxiety

$S \longrightarrow S \longrightarrow R$
green light — shock — pain and anxiety
(dashed arrow from green light to pain and anxiety)

salivation

8 It is also obvious that words are not complete substitutes for candy. But words can, and did, substitute for candy with respect to the partial response of ______ in the Razran study (see Box 1).

There are several ways of diagraming this basic learning process of partial stimulus substitution. Two fairly common ways are depicted below.[2]

1. $S_n \longrightarrow ?$
   $S_a \longrightarrow R$
2. $S_n \rightarrow S_a \rightarrow R$

2 (the second way)

9 Which of the two ways of diagraming more clearly indicates the temporal sequence of the two generic types of stimuli? ______.

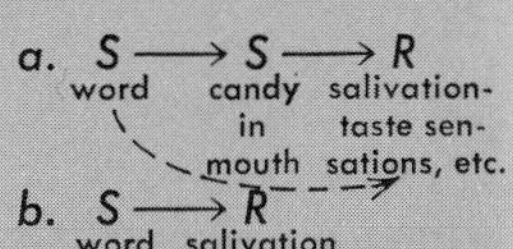

10 The buzzer conditioning performed by Pavlov can thus be diagramed as follows:

a. $S \longrightarrow S \longrightarrow R$
buzzer — food powder in mouth — salivation-taste sensations, etc.

b. $S \longrightarrow R$
buzzer — salivation

Now diagram Razran's word conditioning in a similar way.

11 The general proposition which explains learning of this type is the "contiguity hypothesis."[3] Birch and Bitter-

[2] In these diagrams S_n refers to a neutral stimulus with respect to R, and S_a refers to an adequate stimulus with respect to R.

[3] The generalization is, perhaps, more frequently called "the law of contiguity." It makes little or no difference which term is used. The "hypothesis" designation is preferred because it does not imply complete certainty concerning the accuracy of the generalization.

man (1951) phrase it this way: "When two stimuli are presented contiguously, the first acquires some of the functional properties of the second." From this statement it should be clear that there are two independent variables in this type of learning. One of these independent variables is the temporal ________ of the two relevant stimuli (see frame 7). The other is the sequence, or ________, of their occurrence.

contiguity
order

12 If a stimulus that does not elicit a given response is followed closely in time by a stimulus that elicits the response a number of times, then the first stimulus will become a partial substitute for the second. This is the ________ hypothesis.

contiguity

13 In this type of learning there are two independent variables. What are they? +++++.

a. The order of occurrence. Apparently S_n must precede or occur simultaneously with S_a (Deese, 1958).
b. The temporal contiguity of occurrence. Apparently partial stimulus substitution is maximized when S_a follows S_n by about one-half second (Deese, 1958).

Emotional Learning

14 The next basic question that needs to be answered is, What types of human behavior are learned in this fashion? From the illustrations used does it appear that some learned glandular responses are acquired in this fashion? ________.

Yes[4]

Some simple involuntary muscle responses, such as those involved in erection of body hair, pupil contraction, and

[4] It has been demonstrated many times with respect to salivation and sweating of palms and forehead. It is such sweating that produces the increase in electrical conductivity of the skin referred to in Box 1.

blinking of the eyes, are also susceptible to this type of learning.

unconditioned stimuli

15 One very widespread hypothesis is that emotions are learned in keeping with the contiguity hypothesis. The more specific form of this hypothesis entails specifying that emotions become attached to stimuli by a very specific conditioned reflex process identical to that of learning to salivate to particular stimuli. If this specific hypothesis is true then one would expect to find ________ ________ that would, in the absence of previous experience with such stimuli, elicit each type of emotional response.

unconditioned stimuli

16 Physical pain seems to elicit a fear response in the absence of any previous exposure to the pain (Miller, 1951). It thus seems that pain-producing stimuli are ________ ________ for the fear response.

No, not in a very strict sense of this term.[5]

17 Watson (1919) reported that sudden loss of support and loud, sudden noises would elicit fear in young children upon the first occurrence of these events. But there is a problem here. A child who is being played with by being tossed in the air is not frightened by a sudden loss of support. Neither is one normally frightened by a sudden, loud noise if he anticipates it and knows it is harmless, as, for example, in playing with firecrackers. Are these stimuli, then, unconditioned stimuli with respect to the fear response? ________.

They are all sudden and unanticipated and, in the context of their occurrence, they are strange.

18 Chimpanzees can be frightened if a skeleton is suddenly jangled in their cage.[6] Monkeys can be frightened by a sudden introduction of bizarre "creatures" in their pen (Harlow, 1955). And anyone knows that a simple leaf from a tree can be a frightening stimulus if it suddenly and unexpectedly flutters in front of one's face. What is common to all these apparently unlearned conditions of fear? +++++.

strangeness

19 It should be noted that all these stimuli, with the possible exception of those which are physically painful, do not inherently elicit fear but do so only as a function of the manner in which they occur. That is, they elicit fear under conditions of suddenness and ________.

[5] At least they are not the specific and invariant antecedents of fear in the way that electric shock is a strict and invariant antecedent of increased sweating as measured by increased electrical conductivity of the skin surface. The same difference applies with respect to the specific and invariant food-powder–salivation sequence.

[6] Actually they could rather certainly be frightened by jangling anything in their cages. The skeleton is used, perhaps, to help frighten the experimenter.

strange[7]

20 Hebb and Thompson (1954) have shown that adult chimpanzees are predictably frightened by either a clay model of a chimpanzee head or a motionless (anesthetized) chimpanzee. These stimuli, as presented, were neither sudden nor intense, but they were ______.

fear

21 Virtually any object or event will naturally elicit ______ if its occurrence is extremely strange, sudden, and intense.

No

22 To repeat, the evidence is rather substantial that any stimulus will elicit fear if it is presented just right (Miller, 1951). Will any stimulus elicit salivation if it is presented just right? ______.

unconditioned stimuli

23 There appear to be several basic differences between emotional learning and simple conditioned reflex learning. One difference, for example, between learning to salivate to a buzzer and learning to fear an object is that, with the possible exception of physically painful stimuli, there are no ______ ______, as such, that elicit fear.

manner

24 Second, the conditioning of glandular and simple muscle reflexes does not appear to be contingent upon the manner in which the unconditioned stimuli occur, whether, for example, they are sudden or strange, whereas for emotional conditioning the occurrence of the response is largely determined by the ______ of occurrence of the eliciting stimuli.

Love is a basic human emotion. What are the unconditioned stimuli, if any, for this emotion? Harlow (1955), proceeding with dummy surrogate mothers, reports that baby monkeys spend more time close to terry cloth "mothers" than they do with wire "mothers" even though the latter have been their source of food (milk in this case). He also reports that baby monkeys when frightened regularly run to and cling to the terry cloth "mothers" in preference to the wire "mothers."

[7] It is, of course, possible that disembodied heads and motionless bodies would continue to elicit fear in chimpanzees after frequent and prolonged exposure to them. If so then the hypothesis that unlearned stimuli for fear must be strange, sudden, or intense would have to be rejected. So far as the author knows, such a test has not been conducted.

a. the amount of time spent in close proximity to an object
b. running to and clinging to an object when frightened

25 The two indicators of "love" in Harlow's study are +++++.

26 Harlow maintains that "contact comfort" is a major unlearned condition for the love response. Do his data confirm[8] this hypothesis? ________.

Yes

27 Harlow has also found that baby monkeys reared in isolation from people and other monkeys for the first several months of life do not engage in mutual grooming and embracing when they are subsequently placed in an enclosure with other monkeys. As adults such monkeys are "loners" who want little or no contact with other monkeys. Does this additional datum confirm Harlow's "contact comfort" hypothesis? ________.

Yes[9]

28 Back to the original question, Are there unconditional stimuli for the love response? ________.

No[10]

[8] "Confirm" is used to refer to "a logical relationship between hypothesis and fact in which the fact indicates that the hypothesis is true." "Disconfirm" is used to refer to "a logical relationship between hypothesis and fact in which the fact indicates that the hypothesis is false." Notice that no mention is made of "proof." When a fact is said to "confirm" or "disconfirm" a hypothesis, no other meaning is intended than that the fact *to some extent* increases or decreases the level of confidence one can justifiably have concerning the truth of the hypothesis.

[9] It also suggests another hypothesis, namely, that love, or liking, for others must be established during the first few months of life if it is ever to be established. That this is true of Rhesus monkeys can hardly be questioned. Whether it is true of humans is open to question. There is some very indirect evidence that for humans the crucial period is at least much longer and may not even exist. It is also virtually impossible to rear children even in approximate isolation from other people because even with the best medical and nutritional attention they will either die or become agitated or depressed idiots. See R. S. Spitz, "The Role of Ecological Factors in Emotional Development in Infancy," *Child Development,* 20:145–155, 1949.

[10] Not in the sense that there are unconditioned stimuli for salivation, eye blinks, palm sweating, etc. What Harlow's experiments seem to show is that even the existence of a bona fide love response is contingent upon a prolonged and pleasant contact with other bodies. This may be true of people as well as monkeys; however, the critical period is probably longer and may be absent.

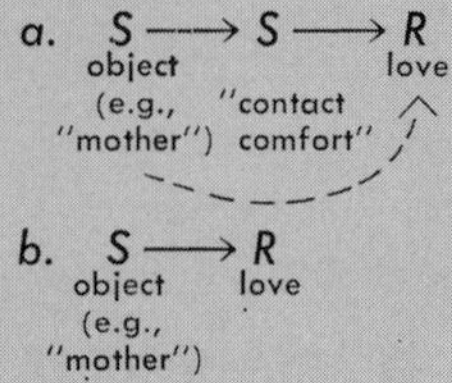

29 Although learning to love someone or something does not appear to be a specific conditioned reflex, it is nonetheless plausible that it is learned in accordance with the contiguity hypothesis. Using contact comfort as the hypothetical adequate stimulus, diagram the process as if it were learned by the contiguity process (refer to frames 7 to 10 for help).

No

30 Anger or hostility is another basic emotion. What unconditioned stimulus or stimuli, if any, will elicit it? Watson (1919) reported that restricting a child's movements was an "unconditioned stimulus" for the "rage response." Of course, there are many situations in which a person can restrict a child's movements and not elicit a rage response. Is, then, restriction of movement an unconditioned stimulus for hostility in the same way that food-in-the-mouth is an unconditioned stimulus for salivation? ________.

frustration

31 Berkowitz (1962), after surveying an immense amount of theory and research, concludes that ". . . frustrations produce an emotional state, *anger,* which heightens the probability of occurrence of drive-specific behaviors, namely aggression." In this theory, ________ is the cause of hostility.

probable

32 Aggression is a (probable/certain) effect of hostility.

No

33 Is frustration a specific, objectively designatable, stimulus like food-in-the-mouth or electric shock? ________.

drives (needs, etc.)

34 Frustration is not a specific stimulus, but rather a relationship between the organism and the environment in which the satisfaction of more or less intense ________ is blocked.

is not

35 Thus, although one may learn to hate an object, or at least feel anger toward it, if that object occurs contiguously with frustration, the learning (is/is not) a matter of a specific stimulus substitution.

contiguity

36 It is apparent from studies of hostility that people often have hostile feelings toward individuals, groups, and objects that could not have been temporally contiguous with frustration. It would even appear that some are not even conceptually present under frustrating conditions. Thus it appears that the ________ hypothesis is inadequate as a complete explanation of how people learn to make hostile responses.

emotional

37 Dewey and Humber (1951) reason that if emotions are learned in exactly the same manner as simple conditioned physiological reflexes, then an acquired stimulus setting off an emotional response should cease to set it off after repeated presentation. They say that such is not the case (see Box 2). If one accepts their "if-then" assumption and the accuracy of their generalization, then ______ responses are not learned in precisely the same way that simple physiological reflexes, such as salivation, are learned.

Box 2. Are Acquired Emotions Conditioned Reflexes?

On one point we find it necessary to diverge from the interpretation as given by Mowrer on the nature of the conditioned response. He takes the position that "It now seems preferable to apply the term 'conditioning' to that type of learning whereby emotional (visceral and vascular) responses are acquired." And again, "But it is also apparent that the law of effect is not adequate to account for the process whereby these secondary drives are themselves acquired: and it is for this latter process, exclusively, that the term 'conditioning' should be reserved." Thus Mowrer's position is that any learning in which association is an adequate explanation of learning is conditioning. This appears to the present writers to be a questionable decision, and for the following reasons: Any scientific concept should, if it is to serve its function of unambiguous communication well, be applied to as homogeneous a category of data as possible. The conditioned response on the one hand and all other types of associational learning on the autonomic nervous system level on the other appear to be so disparate that it is illogical to apply a single concept to both processes. *Evidence of this disparate nature of the two is found in one of the widely accepted tests of the conditioned response (a test, incidentally, which gains in validity with the acceptance of the basic Mowrer thesis), that of experimental extinction. If the response is conditioned, continued presentation of the conditioned stimulus, without reinforcement by accompanying it with the unconditioned stimulus, will result in the extinction or disappearance of the conditioned response. This test rules out the associational learning of emotion as described by Mowrer. Continued presentation of a hated, feared, or loved object or situation will not, other things remaining equal, result in the extinction of the emotional response.* In the true conditioned response or reflex, there is an original response. In the true conditioned response or reflex, there is an original pairing of specific stimulus and specific response, whereas in the *associational emotional learning the original relationship is a neutral one, and becomes emotionally related only because of the peculiar situation under which the association is made. So, because we believe the disparate nature of the two processes of conditioning and association-emotional learning to be real, we find it impossible to justify employing a single concept to distinguish both.*

* Richard Dewey and W. J. Humber, *The Development of Human Behavior,* The Macmillan Company, New York, 1951, pp. 133–134. (Emphasis supplied.)

38 One problem with this argument lies in the inaccuracy of the generalization that emotional responses cannot be extinguished by repeated presentations of the conditioned stimulus in the absence of the "unconditioned stimulus." Jones (1924*a*), for example, extinguished a fear response of a child to a rabbit by bringing a rabbit nearer and nearer to him on successive occasions while the child was eating. Jones (1924*b*) reports a number of other successful attempts to eliminate fear in children by this procedure. Thus the emotional state of fear, at least, seems to be susceptible to ________ by repeatedly presenting the conditioned fear stimulus in the absence of any unconditioned stimulus for fear.

extinction

39 To the central question, Are emotions learned in accordance with the contiguity hypothesis? the best answer we can give at this time is (yes/perhaps/no).

perhaps

Some fears appear to be learned in this fashion (see Box 1). This, of course, does not rule out the possibility that some are not acquired in this fashion. "Sheer contiguity," for example, seems to be at best a partial and dubious explanation for some intense and permanent phobias.

40 None of the emotional reactions is apparently ________ initially by a specific external-to-the-organism stimulus, as are salivation, pupil contraction, etc.

elicited (produced, etc.)

41 Even a painful stimulation which seems to elicit fear in the absence of previous experience is defined in terms of the organism's reaction to it, rather than in terms of its intrinsic properties apart from the ________.

organism

some

42 Contiguity learning, but not a *specific stimulus substitution* learning, seems to be at least a *partial explanation for* (some/none) of the learned emotions.

hostile

43 Contiguity learning, however, seems particularly inadequate as a *complete explanation* of how people develop ______ feelings toward other things, other people, and toward even themselves.

none

44 Furthermore, ______ of the emotional responses seem to be initially elicited by some very definite and specific stimulus, as are certain simple muscular and glandular reflexes. (See Box 2 for a somewhat parallel critique of the "conditioned reflex" theory of emotional learning.)

REVIEW: *The position taken here can be summarized as follows: (1) The unlearned conditions of emotional responses are not specific objective stimuli per se. (2) Once an emotional reaction is occurring, contiguous neutral stimuli will in some cases acquire the capacity for arousing the emotional reaction in future situations in which the original condition for the emotional reaction is absent. That is, some emotional learning, perhaps especially that of young children and animals, is acquired in a manner that is in keeping with the contiguity hypothesis. (3) Some emotional learning, perhaps especially that of adult humans, probably occurs in the absence of contiguity of neutral stimuli and the unlearned conditions of emotional response. In short, some emotional learning is associational. Some isn't. None is due to a specific, external-to-the-organism stimulus substitution.*

Box 3. Effect (Feedback) Learning

In some pioneer experiments on learning, Thorndike (1911) placed hungry cats in boxes in which a door could be opened by pulling a string. Food was placed close to, but outside, the boxes. The cats would typically meow and thrash around until they accidentally pulled the string and escaped to "food and freedom." As the number of such occasions increased, the cats slowly but surely spent less and less time in the boxes prior to pulling the string. If the experiments were kept up long enough, the cats would immediately pull the string with little or no waste motion.

Sheffield, Wulff, and Backer (1951) placed male rats reared in isolation from females in a maze. A female rat in heat was at the end of each maze. The rats that ran the maze were allowed to copulate with the female rats but were withdrawn prior to ejaculation. These "naïve" male rats gradually learned to run the maze with decreasing errors and in a decreasing amount of time until they ran it without errors in a minimum of time.

Wolf et al. (1964) trained a child to wear eyeglasses, which he had previously refused to wear, by making certain highly desired portions of his meals contingent upon wearing the eyeglasses. Time spent with glasses on was further increased by making going for walks contingent upon wearing eyeglasses.

Two patients in a mental hospital would not eat unless fed, at least part of the time, by nurses. The nurses were instructed to "accidentally" spill food on the patients while feeding them. After a number of such "treatments," the patients began to feed themselves and continued to feed themselves after the nurses failed to continue to "accidentally" spill food on them (Ayllon and Michael, 1959).

Verplanck (1955) controlled the rate of expression of opinion by having experimenters (1) agree with the expressed opinion, (2) repeat the expressed opinion, (3) disagree with the expressed opinion, and (4) make no response at all to the expressed opinion. The rate of expression of opinion increased markedly when the experimenter either agreed with the subjects or repeated their expressed opinion. The rate of expression of opinion declined markedly when the experimenter either disagreed with them or failed to make any response.

Effect Learning

action[11]

45 Whatever definition one uses of "learning," it always entails some change of behavior in a given situation. The behavior that undergoes change in each of the illustrations in Box 3 is most accurately labeled (emotion/cognition/action/visceral reaction).

d (either *a* or *b*)[12]

46 In each case some kind of action is followed closely in time by:

a. reward
b. punishment
c. a neutral state of affairs, i.e., neither reward nor punishment
d. either *a* or *b*

[11] Of course other changes may be, and in some cases probably are, involved but changes in action are always involved.

[12] A "neutral state of affairs" is possibly a correct label for the absence of any response on the part of the experimenters in the Verplanck study. However, "punishment" is probably a more correct label, since no response to one's expression of opinion is generally reported as producing an unpleasant feeling.

a. "Food and freedom" in the Thorndike study.
b. Copulation in the Sheffield, Wulff and Backer study.
c. Certain foods and going for walks in the Wolf study.
d. Agreement with subject and repeating subject's expressed opinion in the Verplanck study.

47 What rewards are present in each of the studies? +++++.

a. Spilling food on subjects in the Aylion and Michael study.
b. Disagreeing with subject or making no response to subject's expression of opinion in the Verplanck study.

48 What "punishments" are present in the studies? +++++.

They are rewarding.[13]

49 What is the common property of all the events that increase the probability of the action recurring in a future similar situation? ________ ________ ________.

[13] Thorndike said they were "satisfying states of affairs." Olds ("Pleasure Centers in the Brain," *Scientific American*, 195:105–116, 1956), when writing for nonbehavioristic readers, stipulates "pleasure" as the common property of things that increase the probability of recurrence of an action. Deese (*The Psychology of Learning*, 2d ed., McGraw-Hill Book Company, New York, 1958, p. 33) very appropriately says: "Although it does not sound very enlightening to say that reinforcing stimuli are things that animals like, this common-sense definition contains the germ of some of our most important theoretical ideas about reinforcement." There are a number of alternative hypotheses as to the common denominator of the events that increase the frequency (probability) of response recurrence. The more interested and advanced reader will probably find chap. 12, "Current Developments: Reinforcement and Drive," and more particularly, the subsection entitled "Needs, Drives, and Incentives" in Hilgard's *Theories of Learning* (2d ed., Appleton-Century-Crofts, Inc., New York, 1956) interesting and revealing with respect to this question. Since it is impossible to deal adequately with all the contrary and contradictory interpretations concerning the common denominator of reinforcing events, we shall leave the controversy to the learning theorists and use the somewhat primitive commonsense notion of reward.

They are punishments.[14]

50 What is the common property of those events that decrease the probability of the recurrence of an action in a future similar situation? ________ ________ ________.

have not

51 The more common tendency in descriptions and interpretations of learning processes is to ignore the question pertaining to the common properties of events that increase or decrease the frequency of recurrence of actions.[15] In such discourse the objective concept of "reinforcement" is used. If we say that, in the studies cited, food and escape from confinement, copulation, going for walks, agreeing with expressed opinion, etc., are "reinforcers" we (have/have not) stipulated what these things have in common beyond the effect of increasing the recurrence rate of the actions which preceded them.

frequency (rate, probability)

52 As the term is used by such writers "reinforcement" refers to anything that increases the ________ of responding in a given situation.

is no

53 If we ask the question, "What is common to all things that increase the frequency of responding in a given situation? then reinforcement (is/is no) answer to the question.

common

54 Reinforcement is no answer to this question because it simply labels the effect of these diverse things without specifying what they have in ________.

increases

55 Skinner (1938) states the basic generalization of this type of learning as follows: "If the occurrence of an operant[16] is followed by presentation of a reinforcing stimulus, the strength is increased." A "reinforcing stimulus," by definition, is a stimulus that ________ the frequency of responding.

[14] A neutral consequence, i.e., one that is neither rewarding nor punishing seems to have the same effect. There are, however, no definite neutral feedbacks (consequences) in the illustrations used here.

[15] See, for example, L. F. Malpass, "Principles of Learning," in L. F. Malpass (ed.), *Human Behavior*, McGraw-Hill Book Company, New York, 1965.

[16] For our purposes "operant" can be equated with action, i.e., movement of parts of the body.

If the occurrence of an operant is followed by presentation of a stimulus that increases the frequency of responding, the frequency of responding is increased.[17]

56 By "strength" Skinner means "frequency of responding." Substitute these definitions for the terms "reinforcing stimulus" and "strength" in Skinner's statement and restate it. +++++.

reward

57 From the illustrations it would seem that any action followed closely in time by ______, or what Thorndike called "a satisfying state of affairs," increases in frequency of occurrence in future similar situations.

punishment

58 Conversely, it would seem that any action followed closely in time by ______, or what Thorndike (1911) called "an annoying state of affairs," decreases in frequency of occurrence in future similar situations.

closeness (contiguity)

59 There are two independent variables in this type of learning. One is the type of "feedback" with respect to the action. The other is the ______ in time that the feedback follows the action.

a. reward—increase
b. punishment—decrease[18]
c. neither reward nor punishment—decrease

60 What effect do (*a*) reward, (*b*) punishment, and (c) neither reward nor punishment (types of feedback) have upon the future frequency of occurrence of the action which precedes them? +++++.

As stated earlier, the time that elapses between the occurrence of an action and the occurrence of the reward or punishment is an independent variable in this type of

[17] This, of course, is a good way of saying absolutely nothing, and illustrates well the complete circularity of a generalization in which "reinforcement" is used to refer to the common property of reinforcing events. It consists of discovering a name rather than naming a discovery.

[18] Perhaps "temporary decrease" would be a more adequate label for the effect of punishment, since a number of studies have shown that once punishment was withdrawn, frequency of responding increased sharply, then decreased, so that the total number of responses made prior to extinction were about the same for punished and nonpunished groups. Other studies, however, show a prolonged, and probably permanent, inhibition of the response. Although it is a basic issue, we shall not attempt to determine why the decrease in responding is temporary in some cases and permanent in others. The end result is the same in both cases—a decrease in frequency of responding.

learning. It is virtually impossible, for example, to train a rat to do something if the reward is delayed for over thirty seconds. The contiguity-of-effect requirement probably applies to all animals and preverbal children.

follow

61 For animals and preverbal children the relevant effects must ______ the action closely in time.

This learning process has been diagramed in a number of ways. Mowrer (1950), at one time, diagramed it like this:

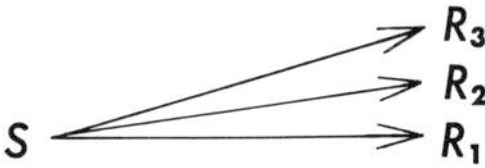

Another way of diagraming this type of learning is indicated below:

action

62 The *a* after the *R* indicates that the type of response involved is an ______, i.e., a contraction of skeletal muscles involved in motion and locomotion.

reward, punishment, or "nothing" (neutral state of affairs)

63 The *r,p,n* subscript of *S* refers to the differential types of feedback, namely, +++++.

64 This is intended to convey the idea that the frequency of occurrence of the response is determined by its stimulus consequences in terms of reward, punishment, or a neutral state of affairs. Referring to Box 3, substitute the specific action and rewarding stimulus involved in the first given experiment.

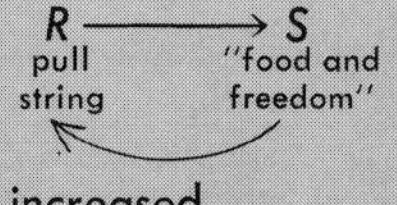

increased

65 Food and freedom, of course, ______ the probability that the string would be pulled when the cat was placed in the same or a similar box in the future.

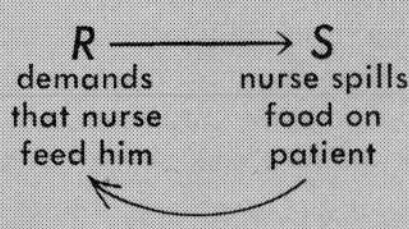

66 Make similarly specific substitutions for the fourth experiment referred to in Box 3.

decreased

67 In this case, of course, the "accidental" spilling of food on the patient substantially ______ the probability that the patient would continue to demand that the nurse feed him.

REVIEW: *In general, then, action followed closely in time by:*

1. *reward increases in frequency*
2. *punishment decreases in frequency*
3. *"nothing" decreases in frequency*

In the future we shall refer to this generalization as the "effect hypothesis." It is similar to Thorndike's "law of effect." "Effect" is a useful designating term here because the controlling events follow the response rather than precede it, as is the case in contiguity learning.

In order to avoid any reference to nonobservable events, some people talk about the "empirical law of effect" by which they mean that food consumption to an animal deprived of food will reinforce actions that precede its consumption, water consumption to an animal deprived of water will reinforce action that precedes water consumption, etc. Sheffield (1958, p. 365) appropriately comments upon this type of usage as follows: "As currently used, effect is defined as anything which strengthens instrumental responses. We can collect a list of such events and get a workable statement of the law of effect as follows: 'If a response occurs contiguously with a neutral stimulus pattern it will become connected to that pattern if it is followed by one of the things in this list.' However, this workable law gives only a circular description of the operations producing 'effect' . . . it leaves us up in the air about the outcome of an untried event. It also makes the law of effect exceptionless and untestable."

does

68 When we reflect upon the observable classes of reinforcing events, such as food, water, copulation, escaping from confinement, repeating a person's expressions, etc., it is apparent that one (does/does not) end up with an open-ended "etc." type of statement which refers to "one of the things on this list."

common

69 The empirical law of effect, therefore, has the property of not specifying what reinforcing events have in ________.

circular

70 If we say that reinforcing events have the common property of strengthening instrumental responses, we are being completely ________ in the same way that Skinner's law of conditioning is completely circular (see frames 53–56).[19]

[19] To the author's knowledge there is only one "empirical law of effect" that is neither open-ended nor circular. If interested, see David Premack, "Toward Empirical Behavior Laws: I. Positive Reinforcement," *Psychological Review*, 66:219–233, 1959.

Effect versus Contiguity Learning

Our next major question is, What human behavior is learned in this effect (feedback) fashion? This is still an open question, but the evidence is extensive and rather consistent in indicating that any action is subject to modification in terms of rewarding or punishing effects.

71 There are many learning theorists who maintain that all learning is of the contiguity type. There are also many who maintain that all learning is of the effect type. The interesting thing is that proponents of each position can, to their own satisfaction, interpret all experiments as confirming, or at least being consistent with, their hypothesis. Behavior learned in accordance with the effect hypothesis is very much in dispute; however, there is a fair level of consensus that ________, at least, is learned in this fashion.

action

72 It may be that contiguity- and effect-type learning are basically, though covertly, the same type of process. But, as we know them, there are a number of more or less basic differences. First, effect-type learning involves response modification and substitution, whereas contiguity-type learning involves partial ________ substitution.

stimulus

73 For example, in Thorndike's experiments, the responses of the cats in cages gradually changed in that new responses were ________ for older ones and in that the string-pulling response was progressively ________ into a smooth efficient response.

substituted
modified

74 On the other hand, the salivation response to food-in-the-mouth is not replaced by another response. Neither is the salivation response ________ to any significant extent by its consequences.

modified

75 Second, the controlling events in contiguity-type learning *precede* the response, whereas in effect-type learning the controlling events ________ the response.

follow

76 The term "effect" refers to this basic difference between contiguity- and effect-type learning, namely, that +++++.

the controlling events in contiguity-type learning precede the response, whereas in effect-type learning the controlling events follow the response

no

77 Third, an event that strengthens an action in effect-type learning will strengthen almost all, and perhaps all, other actions, whereas in contiguity-type learning an event that strengthens a response will typically strengthen (all/no) other response.

will not

78 For example, food consumption following a bar press will strengthen not only the bar-pressing response but also successful choices in a maze, string pulling, and probably any action whatever. On the other hand, electric shock will strengthen the response of fear to a green light but it (will/will not) strengthen any other kind of emotional reaction to the green light.

obviously[20]

79 There are other differences, but these will suffice to show that the two types of learning referred to here are not (obviously/possibly) the same thing in disguise.

Instrumental Insight

effect

80 Thus far, learning has been treated either as an automatic partial stimulus substitution (contiguity learning) or as a rather blind trial-and-error sort of thing (________ learning.)

a cognitive understanding of relationships

81 Every student knows, of course, that much of the material he learns while attending school is not learned *purely* and *simply* in either of these ways. Some of the things a student learns are "insightful" in the sense that the learning involves a cognitive understanding of relationships. "Insight," in this sense, refers to +++++.

One type of relationship that is frequently and suddenly understood is that of a means-end nature. When one suddenly understands a means-end, or causal, relationship, instrumental insight is said to occur.

instrumental insight

82 Thus, if one readily understands in the absence of trial and error that turning an airplane rudder to the right will make the airplane turn right then ________ ________ is involved.

[20] It is possible that they are the same thing in disguise, but this is a very complex, difficult, and controversial issue which goes well beyond the purpose of this section.

instrumental

83 In this section we shall deal with understanding means-end relationships. In other words, we shall study _______ insight.

A widely paraphrased illustration is given by Hilgard (1956, p. 236), who assisted Yerkes with some instrumental insight studies of chimpanzees: "The problem set the animal was to obtain a banana from a long hollow box, open at both ends. The box, essentially a rectangular tube, was firmly fastened to the floor of a large cage. The banana was inserted through a trap door in the middle of the box under the watchful eye of the animal, then the trap door was securely padlocked. The chimpanzee, after a number of unsuccessful efforts to obtain the banana by direct attack—reaching in either end of the tube with hands and feet, attempting to lift the tube from the floor—seemed to give up temporarily. . . . This extraneous behavior took the form of playful cavorting. In this mood the animal incorporated into her play the hoe handle which was standing in the corner of the room, climbing it, and throwing it. Once the handle fell with its end near the open tunnel. The chimpanzee stopped her play, became calm, looked reflective, and, for the first time in her history used the pole as a tool to push the banana out of the far end of the tube."

Deese (1958, p. 277), in commenting upon this experiment, says, "How can this behavior be explained away as an example of instrumental conditioning? Indeed it is difficult to do so. The ape appeared to see very readily the relationship between the box and the stick. This, by no stretch of the imagination, is similar to the rat's perceiving the relation between pressing the lever and obtaining food in the Skinner box."

effect

84 By "instrumental conditioning" Deese means _______ learning as we have used the term.

effect (instrumental)

85 A rat learning to press a lever after a number of lever-press–food sequences exhibits _______-type learning.

insight

86 If Deese's appraisal is correct then the chimpanzee's learning exemplifies instrumental _______ rather than a blind trial-and-error type of effect learning.

insight

87 This example indicates that interruption of movement followed by an efficient solution to a means-end problem is an indicator of instrumental _______.

single

88 Yerkes (1943) reports that once the chimp used the stick there was no lost time or motion in future exposures to the same problem. In other words, here is a case in which error rate or time spent prior to solution fell to a minimum after a single occurrence of the effective response. Another indicator of insight is repetition of an efficient solution to a problem after a ______ occurrence of the efficient solution.

One type of task frequently posed for chimpanzees uses food, usually bananas, that is suspended from the ceiling of their cage. Several boxes are placed in the cage so that by stacking one box upon another the chimpanzee can climb the boxes and reach the food. Chimps vary a great deal in the length of time it takes them to "see" the means-end relationship when they are initially confronted with the problem; however, if a chimp is allowed to observe another chimp stack the boxes and get the food, the observing chimp will normally solve the problem immediately when given the opportunity.

before

89 The observing chimp's solution to the problem occurs (before/after) he makes an overt response to the problem.

instrumental insight

90 Learning how to do something by observing another do it is another indicator of ______ ______.

Kohler (1925) placed his most intelligent chimpanzee in a cage where there were two sticks. One stick would fit securely into the socket of the other. Some food was placed far enough away from the edge of the cage that it could be obtained only by fitting the two sticks together and raking it in. The solution came suddently after the chimp had given up direct methods and begun to play with the sticks. Not only was there no waste time or motion in the future when the chimp had the sticks, but if they were not present he would go "in search" of them and upon finding them would immediately put them together and get the food.

instrumental insight

91 Detour behavior in which the animal does not try to obtain a goal directly but rather proceeds by indirect but effective means is another indicator of ______ ______.

REVIEW: *There are other important indicators of instrumental insight, but, by way of summary, instrumental insight is indicated by:*

1. *interruption of movement followed by an efficient solution to the problem*
2. *repetition of the efficient solution after a single occurrence*
3. *learning a solution to a problem by observing another perform the correct solution*
4. *detour behavior in which an animal makes no attempt to obtain a goal directly, but rather goes in search of the effective means*

does not

92 Although the references of effect-type learning and instrumental insight learning refer to qualitatively distinct processes it (does/does not) follow that any given instance of instrumental learning will involve either blind trial-and-error or insight, but not both.

Undoubtedly much of the instrumental learning of primates involve mixtures of these two types. Most instrumental learning in primates is, perhaps, somewhere in between pure blind trial and error, on one hand, and pure insight, on the other.

Deese (1958, p. 277) maintains that insight learning is clearly not the same thing as effect-type learning, but questions any need for formulating one or more new learning principles to account for insight learning: "Such a need diminishes further when it becomes apparent that there is a more or less continuous gradation between trial-and-error solution and solution by insight. Furthermore, some observations indicate that a background of simple instrumental learning is necessary for the occurrences of insight."

Yes

93 Does the Harlow and Harlow (1949) study, summarized in Figure 16, give some support to Deese's hypothesis that insight is based upon a "background of simple instrumental learning?" ________.

trial / error

94 The Harlow and Harlow study shows that instrumental insight is greatly facilitated by a background of uninsightful ________- and-________ learning.

Figure 16. Instrumental insight in monkeys. In drawing (**a**) a monkey is confronted with two different objects. Under one of them is always a raisin or a peanut. In drawing (**b**) the monkey has learned consistently to pick the same object. In drawing (**c**) the monkey has learned consistently to choose one object which differs from two others. In drawings (**d**) and (**e**) the monkey has learned a much more complicated process: In drawing (**d**) it learned that when the board is of a certain color it must choose the object that is odd in shape; in drawing (**e**) it learned that when the board is of another color it must choose the object that is odd in color. In all these problems the monkey first learned to solve the problem by trial and error. Later it solved them immediately by understanding. SOURCE: H. F. Harlow and M. K. Harlow, "Learning to Think," *Scientific American,* 181: 37, 1949. Used by permission.

no

95 The position that instrumental insight is merely the end result of previous trial-and-error learning is a common one. If this position is true then there should be (no/marked) differences between species with respect to the probability of insightful solutions to problems with which they are equally familiar.

disconfirms

96 But, of course, there *are* marked species differences with respect to the probability of insightful solutions to problems with which they are equally familiar. This empirical generalization ________ the hypothesis that previous instrumental conditioning is the *sole* determinant of insightful solutions.

insightful

97 People are vastly more capable of insightful solutions than chimpanzees. Chimpanzees are much more capable of insightful solutions than monkeys (Yerkes, 1943). Monkeys are much more capable of insightful solutions than rats. One can go on, but it is apparent that a high positive correlation exists between the aggregate intelligence of different animal species and the frequency of ________ solutions to instrumental problems.

greater

98 Correspondingly, the more elaborate the development of the brain, especially the cortex, the ________ the probability that the animal will be able to "see," i.e., imagine, the means-end solution to a problem.

should not

99 Likewise, if previous trial-and-error learning is the only factor determining the probability of insightful learning, then insightful solutions (should/should not) occur when animals are known to be confronted with a problem for the first time.

correct

100 Yerkes (1943) is convinced that many of the problems set for the chimpanzees in his study were completely new to them. Presumably, the only previous learning involved in the solutions of some of the problems was that of learning how to move parts of the body in a coordinated fashion. Since many of the chimps had been reared under supervision since birth, it is very likely that Yerkes' conviction is (correct/incorrect/open to serious question).

disconfirmation

101 If Yerkes' judgment is correct, then the instrumental conditioning hypothesis, when considered as the sole explanation of instrumental insight, is given further ________.

intelligence

102 When one imagines the probability of an insightful solution to a problem that is equally new to a goldfish, on one hand, and to a person, on the other, it should be obvious that insightful solutions are to a very great extent contingent upon differences with respect to (intelligence/previous trial and error).

At least two types of variables are involved in determining the occurrence of instrumental insight. One of these is structural, consisting more specifically of the proportionate volume and complexity of the cortex of the brain. The other is the amount of previous trial-and-error learning in situations similar to the one encountered in the insightful solution.

is not

103 The spatial arrangement of things in the environment is also an important type of variation determining the occurrence of insight (Yerkes, 1943; Hilgard, 1956). Personality factors having nothing to do with previous experience with the problem also have a marked effect upon insightful learning in people (Krech, Crutchfield, and Ballachey, 1962). There should be no question that insight (is/is not) solely the end product of simple instrumental (effect-type) learning.

would not[21]

104 Even *if* instrumental insight were contingent upon previous trial-and-error learning this (would/would not) indicate that insight is trial-and-error learning in disguise.

REVIEW: *The "man on the street" has always differentiated between rather blind trial-and-error learning, such as learning to walk or roller-skate, and insightful learning, such as some of the responses a person makes when confronted with rowing a boat for the first time. Many psychologists have maintained, and still do, that the differences are only apparent. Many others try to "explain it away" by maintaining that insight is only the end product of previous simple trial-and-error learning.*

For an assessment of the impact of reports of insightful learning in animals upon the learning theorists of the time *see Box 4.*

[21] The reader's existence is undoubtedly contingent upon the prior existence of his father, but this hardly "means" that he is his father in disguise.

Box 4. The Significance of Insightful Learning

Hilgard* has commented upon the effects of the early experiments concerning insightful learning in animals upon learning theory when learning theory was "in the grips of a confident but sterile behaviorism" as follows:

It is hard to see at this distance why such a common sense and familiar notion as insight in learning should have created such a stir. But at the time Watsonian behaviorism had, in fact, won support for a fairly "hard-boiled" view of learning, according to which the organism was played upon by the pushes and pulls of environment and reacted in ways essentially stupid. Lloyd Morgan's canon, which had seriously undercut the attributing of higher mental processes to animals, had fairly well succeeded via behaviorism in excising them from men also. Therefore, the return to a more balanced view, represented by the insight experiments, gave new hope to teachers and others who saw thinking and understanding returning to respectability. Insight was not a new discovery—it was a return to a conception laymen had never abandoned. Nobody uninfluenced by peculiar doctrines would ever have denied insight as a fact. . . .

Animal psychologists like Yerkes, who had never espoused behaviorism, welcomed the new movement as a natural development. Yerkes himself had done experiments on insightful learning . . . and the intelligence demonstrated by Kohler's apes did not surprise him. Curiously enough, insightful learning in subhuman animals was less threatening to theorists than learning by understanding in man, chiefly because it was still the rather rare and unusual behavior among animals. Rats still learned mazes, it was thought, without insight. So the animal experimenters added insight experiments to their list and continued both old and new experiments. But if the insight doctrine were to be accepted in human learning, the field would be wide open for destroying all the familiar laws of learning as they applied to man. It is not surprising that those who were at the time concerned more largely with human learning . . . should all have been cool to the insight concept.

* E. R. Hilgard, *Theories of Learning*, Appleton-Century-Crofts, Inc., New York, 1956, pp. 224–225.

Responding to Symbolic Stimuli

conditioned stimulus

105 "Sign," as the term is used here, refers to "any stimulus that partially substitutes for another stimulus."[22] This sounds very much like the definition of a ________ ________ (see frames 4–6 and Fig. 16).

[22] It is assumed that no stimulus can completely substitute for another.

106 In Pavlov's experiments with dogs, the buzzer becomes a ______ of food-in-the-mouth. (See Box 1.)

sign

107 In Razran's study of salivation, words become ______ of candy or, perhaps better, eating candy.

signs

108 In Cook's experiment a green light becomes a sign of ______ ______.

electric shock

109 Some signs, however, are probably not conditioned stimuli in the strict sense of this term. For example, a swastika may elicit many of the same responses as the word "Fascism," but it is at least doubtful that the swastika regularly occurred shortly *before* the word "Fascism," in keeping with the classical model of contiguity learning. All conditioned stimuli are signs, but some ______ are probably not conditioned stimuli.

signs

110 Signs may be either natural or arbitrary. Signs are natural if the stimuli occur contiguously in nature. Which of the following sign-significate pairs are natural?

a. lightning-thunder
b. thumbs down-disapproval
c. cross-Christianity
d. rabbit track-rabbit

a and *d*

111 "Arbitrary signs" are "signs that are not correlated in nature with the things they represent." Which of the sign-significate pairs in the previous frame are arbitrary? ______.

b and *c*

112 A buzzer for Pavlov's conditioned dogs was an ______ ______ of food-in-the-mouth.

arbitrary sign

113 In Cook's experiment a green light was an ______ ______ of electric shock.

arbitrary sign

114 If "symbols" are defined as "arbitrary signs" then both human and infrahuman animals learn to respond to ______.

symbols

115 It should be noted, however, that, although subhuman animals readily respond to symbols, they have never been known to create them. They do, of course, possess more or less complex forms of communication through the use of ______ signs, such as growls, screeches, baring of teeth, etc.

natural

concepts

116 A "concept" is defined here as "an awareness of something that is absent from the sensory environment." The reader at this moment cannot see the state of Florida, but there is, presumably, some awareness of what is entailed by the term, "Florida." Likewise the White House can be readily imagined without looking at it. These are examples of ______.

No[23]

117 Can one be certain that the monkeys in the Harlow study (Fig. 16) are making conceptual responses to board colors? ______.

conceptual

118 The chimpanzee's solution to the banana-in-the-box problem would indicate that some rudimentary form of ______ behavior occurred in that there appeared to be some kind of imagining of the effect of running the hoe handle through one end of the box.

sensory (physical)

119 Likewise the chimpanzee's activity described as "going in search" of the sticks that could be stuck together appears to involve at least some rudimentary conceptual behavior in the sense that there was apparently an awareness of something not present in the ______ environment.

conceptual

120 There is, however, no substantial evidence that subprimate animals make ______ responses to symbols although it is apparent that they make emotional, visceral, and active responses to symbols.

Instrumental Language

use

121 "Language," as the term is used here, refers to "an articulation of symbols in such a way as to form words and sentences." Mowrer (1960) reports that a couple in Missouri taught their parakeet, "Blueboy," to recite the first two stanzas of "Mary had a little lamb." It is obvious that Blueboy has learned to (understand/use) language.

would

122 If Blueboy understood what he was saying he (would/would not) be able to carry on a coherent conversation with someone.

birds

123 Certain species of birds are the only subhuman animals that learn to use language, although a chimpanzee was once taught to say a couple of poorly pronounced words (Mowrer, 1960; Hayes, 1951). The use of language is, therefore, limited to people and certain species of ______.

[23] The question as to whether the monkeys are thinking, i.e., conceptualizing, is a difficult one, but it is possible that the monkeys are responding to the sensory change with respect to color without any definite awareness, as such, of "odd shape" or "odd color."

understand

124 Since, however, no parakeet, or other talking bird, has ever been known to carry on a coherent conversation with anyone, it is apparent that they do not _______ the conceptual references of such language.

contiguity

125 There are no known unconditioned stimuli for verbal responses. Hence, learning to speak, in either parakeet or child, is not a clear and simple case of _______-type learning.

effect

126 It is also virtually impossible to teach a bird to talk by just waiting until he says something and then rewarding him. This indicates that learning to talk is not a pure and simple case of _______-type learning.

Your answer should roughly parallel Mowrer's: "In order for a bird to learn to make a particular word sound, that sound has first to be heard, repeatedly, in a pleasant agreeable context" (Mowrer, 1960, p. 73).

127 Mowrer (1960), after making an extensive study of talking birds, emerged with the following empirical generalizations: (*a*) A bird will usually say a word sooner or later if the word is frequently repeated by the trainer while the bird is eating or drinking. (*b*) Frequent repetition of the word by the experimenter will not in itself result in the bird saying the word. What conclusion would you make from these data? +++++.

contiguity

128 Presumably the words become partial stimulus substitutes for eating and drinking in the sense that they take on some of the rewarding characteristics of these activities. In this respect, at least, instrumental language learning first involves _______ learning.

The words have probably become pleasant sounds because they have occurred frequently and contiguously with such pleasant experiences as eating and drinking.

129 Birds, like their young human counterparts, are reported to repeat words rather frequently after they first occur. Assuming that repetition of such words is not naturally rewarding, why is this so? +++++.

effect (feedback)

130 Once the bird begins to talk, the pronunciation of the word and the frequency of its occurrence can be controlled by prompt provision of rewards. The bird's progress is typically slow and continuous. This third phase of instrumental language learning in birds is apparently a rather pure case of _______-type learning.

mouths

131 It is often said that men frequently use words to bring things into their mind. The birds, in this third phase of instrumental language learning, use words to bring things (food or water) into their ______.

different

132 Although human language learning obviously involves much more than the language learning of birds, there is little reason to suppose that the initial instrumental language learning of children is basically ______ from that of the birds.

SUMMARY

In this section we have stressed learning processes and learning behaviors that are common to both human and subhuman species. To concentrate solely upon the processes and behaviors that are supposed to be distinctively human not only involves making speculative assumptions in most cases but leaves a big gap in one's understanding of human learning.

Contiguity learning is essentially a process of partial stimulus substitution. There are at least two independent variables—the order in which the stimuli occur and the temporal contiguity of their occurrence. If stimulus N is to become a partial substitute for stimulus A, then stimulus N must either precede or occur simultaneously with stimulus A. Maximum stimulus substitution occurs when stimulus N precedes stimulus A by about one-half second. In other words, the closer any two stimuli occur in time, up to 0.5 of a second, the greater the probability that the first will become a partial substitute for the second. This proposition is referred to as the "contiguity hypothesis."

The acquisition of glandular responses seems to occur in this fashion. The acquisition of simple smooth muscle reflexes also appears to take place in keeping with the contiguity hypothesis, but the data in regard to these responses are not particularly conclusive. "Autistic thinking," i.e., reflection by free association, is at least to a great extent learned in this fashion; however, directed and rational thought can hardly be a product of this process. If emotions were learned purely and simply in keeping with the contiguity hypothesis it would be an extremely significant process for understanding human behavior; however, it is very doubtful that such is the case—especially where the emotions of anger and love are concerned. It seems that the most accurate conclusion one can draw at the present time is that much emotional learning is in keeping with the contiguity hypothesis but that such learning is not simply a matter of specific stimulus substitution. Anger and love, particularly, seem to be naturally aroused not by specific stimuli but by more complex relations between the person and the environment in which the person's needs are either blocked or satisfied.

Effect learning is essentially a modification or substitution of responses as a result of the rewarding or punishing consequences of such responses. In general, responses followed closely in time by reward increase in frequency, whereas responses followed closely in time by either punishment or nothing of consequence decrease in frequency. This proposition is referred to as the "effect hypothesis." Actions are rather definitely acquired and modified in keeping with the effect hypothesis. Thoughts and emotions appear not to be, but this position is still open to some question.

Insightful learning of the instrumental type is common in man and the apes. It is present in attenuated form in some of the lower mammals. It is undoubtedly facilitated by previous trial-and-error learning. Insightful solutions, however, are clearly not solely the end products of simple trial-and-error learning. This conclusion is supported by the marked species differences, the insightful solutions to completely new problems, and the personality determinants of insightful solutions to problems that are equally familiar to different human subjects.

Acquiring various responses to symbols is common to both human and subhuman animals, but subhuman animals, in contrast to man, do not create symbols and, except in the somewhat artificial situations of animal training and experimentation, they rarely, if ever, learn to respond to them.

Both man and the talking birds learn to use language; however, it is apparent that birds develop no conceptual understanding of propositional language. The instrumental language learning of birds, and presumably the instrumental language learning of young children, appears to be a three-phase process. In the first phase, words occur contiguously with rewarding events. In the second phase, words, after their first emission, are frequently repeated, presumably because they have acquired secondary reward value during the first phase. In the third phase, word pronunciation and frequency are controlled by rewarding and punishing consequences.

SELF–REVIEW QUIZ

1 In insightful learning the solution occurs:
   a. imaginatively prior to its overt occurrence
   b. after varying amounts of trial and error
   c. only if there is enough intelligence to permit it to occur
   d. without any previous experience with the problem

2 No subhuman species has ever been known to:
   a. respond to symbolic stimuli
   b. create a symbolic environment
   c. use language
   d. communicate by use of complex signs

3 If stimulus N is to become a partial substitute for stimulus A then:
   a. A must occur shortly before N.
   b. A must occur shortly after N.
   c. A and N must occur at exactly the same time or A and N must occur contiguously with respect to time.

4 Frustration is always, or at least nearly always, followed by some degree of
   a. anger
   b. aggression
   c. both of these
   d. neither of these

5 Given the "fact" that baby monkeys love terry cloth "mothers" who have not been sources of food more than they love wire "mothers" who have been sources of food, one can:
   a. conclude that contact comfort is the primary unlearned condition of love in human babies
   b. tentatively conclude that satisfaction of biological drives is not an important source of love for primates
   c. tentatively conclude that pleasant body contact is an important source of love for primates
   d. only conclude that infant monkeys had rather lie on terry cloth than wire

6 The effect hypothesis is most adequate as an explanation of how people learn to
   a. talk
   b. walk
   c. fear social disapproval
   d. assume the role of parent

7 Which of the following are indicators of instrumental insight?
   a. permanent loss of errors after a single solution
   b. efficient solution to a problem after observing another engage in the correct sequence of responses

c. gradual and permanent loss of errors

d. interruption of effort followed by an efficient solution

ANSWER: *b, c, d; a, b, d; a, c, d;* or *a, b, c.*

8 Which statement is true?

a. Symbolic environments do not exist for animals.

b. Animals do not communicate by arbitrary signs.

c. Human and subhuman responses to language differ most with respect to emotional reactions.

d. The main difference between people and animals is that people possess a will of their own, whereas animals do not.

9 Fear is naturally aroused by:

a. certain specific stimuli such as a loud noise or sudden loss of support

b. stimuli that reach a certain level of strangeness, suddenness, or intensity

c. repulsive objects, such as snakes, scales, etc.

d. ambiguous stimuli

10 The fact that man and some of the more intelligent animals can solve some unfamiliar, instrumental problems in the absence of trial and error indicates that:

a. An understanding of the means-end relationship precedes active effort in such cases.

b. Such organisms are capable of abstract logical reasoning.

c. They have a long history of trial and error with respect to components of the instrumental problem.

d. There are no fundamental differences between people and some of the more intelligent animals.

11 The word "effect" in the term "effect hypothesis" calls attention to one of the basic properties of the type of learning referred to, namely, that:

a. The controlling events follow the response.

b. The controlling events precede the response.

c. The organism's action always has some effect upon the environment.

d. The controlling stimuli must follow each other closely in time.

12 Effect-type learning differs from contiguity-type learning in that in effect-type learning:

a. The controlling events follow the response.

b. An event that strengthens a response will strengthen almost any other response.

c. Repetition usually leads to insight.

d. The response made to a stimulus is often modified or replaced though the stimulus itself is not associated with any other environmental stimuli.

ANSWER: *a; a, b; a, b, d;* or *a, b, c, d.*

13 The effect hypothesis is most adequate as an explanation of how people learn to:

a. skate

b. engage in scientific research

c. fear social disapproval

d. think logically

14 The acquisition of emotional responses differs from the acquisition of glandular responses in that, in the acquisition of emotional responses:

a. The response is made to a complex relationship between the organism and its environment.

b. The responses are more subject to deliberate control.

c. The adequate-neutral stimulus sequence is reversed.

d. The response is determined primarily by the objective properties of the stimuli.

15 If one is willing to extrapolate from monkey to man then the Harlow and Harlow study indicates that children love other people because they:

a. feel good

b. look good

c. first love them

d. are sources of gratification of basic survival needs, such as hunger, thirst, warmth

16 Differences between emotional learning and glandular-reflex learning are most obvious when one compares learning to:

a. salivate to a buzzer with learning to hate Negroes

b. ski with learning to cry

c. salivate to a buzzer with learning to fear a green light

d. control stimulation with learning to control anger

Multiple Choice. After the hypothesis there are numbered sets of data. Answer according to the following key:

a. The datum confirms the hypothesis.

b. The datum disconfirms the hypothesis.

c. The datum is unrelated to the hypothesis.

Hypothesis: Insightful learning requires no new explanation since it is merely the end product of simple trial-and-error learning.

17 With previous experience with a problem held constant, there are marked species differences with respect to the probability that an insightful solution will occur.

18 Insightful solutions of problems occur in chimpanzees who have been reared in isolation from the problems or components of the problems to which they are exposed.

19 When intelligence and previous experience with a problem are held constant, human subjects vary greatly in their ability to arrive at insightful solutions. Such variations, moreover, are significantly correlated with certain personality traits, such as dogmatism.

20 Ability to solve logical or instrumental problems insightfully varies markedly from one individual to another in any school subject.

REFERENCES

Adkins, D. C., and S. B. Lyerly: "Factor Analysis of Reasoning Tests," Adjutant General's Office, PRS Report no. 848, 1951.

Ayllon, T., and J. Michael: "The Psychiatric Nurse as a Behavioral Engineer," *Journal of Experimental Analysis of Behavior*, 2:323–334, 1959.

Bair, D. M.: "Laboratory Control of Thumbsucking by Withdrawal and Reinforcement," *Journal of Experimental Analysis of Behavior*, 5:525–528, 1962.

Berkowitz, Leonard: *Aggression: A Social Psychological Analysis*, McGraw-Hill Book Company, New York, 1962.

Birch, H. G., and M. E. Bitterman: "Sensory Integration and Cognitive Theory," *Psychological Review*, 58:355–361, 1951.

Cook, S. W., and R. E. Harris: "The Verbal Conditioning of the Galvanic Skin Reflex," *Journal of Experimental Psychology*, 21:202–210, 1937.

Deese, James: *The Psychology of Learning*, 2d ed., McGraw-Hill Book Company, New York, 1958.

Dewey, Richard, and W. J. Humber: *The Development of Human Behavior*, The Macmillan Company, New York, 1951.

Harlow, H. F.: "Love in Infant Monkeys," *Scientific American*, 192:68–74, May, 1955.

Harlow, H. F., and M. K. Harlow: "Learning to Think," *Scientific American*, 181:36–39, February, 1949.

Hayes, Catherine: *The Ape in Our House*, Harper & Row, Publishers, Incorporated, New York, 1951.

Hebb, D. O. and W. R. Thompson: "The Social Significance of Animal Studies," in Gardner Lindzey (ed.), *Handbook of Social Psychology*, vol. 1, Addison-Wesley Publishing Company, Inc., Cambridge, Mass., 1954.

Hilgard, E. R.: *Theories of Learning*, 2d ed., Appleton-Century-Crofts, Inc., New York, 1956.

Hilgard, E. R., and D. G. Marquis: *Conditioning and Learning*, revised by G. A. Kimble, Appleton-Century-Crofts, Inc., New York, 1961.

Hovland, C. I., and R. R. Sears: "Minor Studies of Aggression: VI. Correlation of Lynchings with Economic Indices," *Journal of Psychology*, 9:301–310, 1940.

Jones, M. C.: "A Laboratory Study of Fear: The Case of Peter," *Pedagogical Seminar and Journal of Genetic Psychology*, 31:308–315, 1924*a*.

Jones, M. C.: "The Elimination of Children's Fears," *Journal of Experimental Psychology*, 7:383–390, 1924*b*.

Kohler, Wolfgang: *The Mentality of Apes*, Harcourt, Brace & World, Inc., New York, 1925.

Krech, David, R. S. Crutchfield, and E. L. Ballachey: *Individual in Society*, McGraw-Hill Book Company, New York, 1962.

Lambert, William W.: "Stimulus-Response Contiguity and Reinforcement Theory in Social Psychology," Gardner Lindzey (ed.), *Handbook of So-*

cial Psychology, Addison-Wesley Publishing Company, Inc., Cambridge, Mass., 1954.

Lawson, R., and M. H. Marx: "Frustration: Theory and Experiment," *Genetic Psychology Monographs,* 57:393–464, 1958.

McClelland, D. C., and F. S. Apicella: "A Functional Classification of Verbal Reactions to Experimentally Induced Failure," *Journal of Abnormal and Social Psychology,* 40:376–390, 1945.

Miller, N. E.: "Learning Drives and Rewards," in S. S. Stevens (ed.), *Handbook of Experimental Psychology,* John Wiley & Sons, Inc., New York, 1951.

Miller, N. E., and R. Bugelski: "Minor Studies of Aggression: II. The Influence of Frustrations Imposed by the Ingroup on Attitudes Expressed toward Outgroups," *Journal of Psychology,* 25:437–442, 1943.

Miller, R. E., J. V. Murphy, and I. A. Mirsky: "The Modification of Social Dominance in a Group of Monkeys by Interanimal Conditioning," *Journal of Comparative and Physiological Psychology,* 48: 392–396, 1955.

Mowrer, O. H.: *Learning Theory and Personality Dynamics,* The Ronald Press Company, New York, 1950.

Mowrer, O. H.: *Learning Theory and the Symbolic Processes,* John Wiley & Sons, Inc., New York, 1960.

Olds, James: "Pleasure Centers in the Brain," *Scientific American,* 195:105–116, October, 1956.

Pavlov, I. P.: *Conditioned Reflexes,* Oxford University Press, Fair Lawn, N. J., 1927.

Premack, David: "Toward Empirical Behavior Laws: I. Positive Reinforcement," *Psychological Review,* 66:219–233, 1959.

Razran, G.: "Stimulus Generalization of Conditioned Responses," *Psychological Bulletin,* 46:337–365, 1949.

Sheffield, D.: "The Contiguity Principle in Learning Theory," *Psychological Review,* 58: 362–367, 1958.

Sheffield, D., J. J. Wulff, and R. Backer: "Reward Value of Copulation without Sex Drive Reduction," *Journal of Comparative and Physiological Psychology,* 43:3–8, 1951.

Skinner, B. F.: *The Behavior of Organisms,*Appleton-Century-Crofts, Inc., New York, 1938.

Solomon, R. I., and L. C. Wynne: "Avoidance Conditioning in Normal Dogs and in Dogs Deprived of Normal Autonomic Functioning," *American Psychologist,* 5:264, 1950.

Solomon, R. I., and L. C. Wynne: "Traumatic Avoidance Learning: The Principles of Anxiety Conservation and Partial Irreversibility," *Psychological Review,* 61:353–385, 1954.

Spitz, R. S.: "The Role of Ecological Factors in Emotional Development in Infancy," *Child Development,* 20:145–155, 1949.

Thorndike, E. L.: *Animal Intelligence,* The Macmillan Company, New York, 1911.

Verplanck, W. S.: "The Control of the Content of Conversation: Reinforcement of Statements of Opinion," *Journal of Abnormal and Social Psychology,* 51:668–676, 1955.

Watson, J. B.: *Psychology from the Standpoint of a Behaviorist,* J. B. Lippincott Company, Philadelphia, 1919.

Wolf, M. M., T. Risley, and H. Mees: "Application of Operant Conditioning Procedures to the Behavior Problems of an Autistic Child," *Behavior Research Therapy,* 1:304–312, 1964.

Yerkes, R. M.: *Chimpanzees,* Yale University Press, New Haven, Conn., 1943.

Answers to Self-review Quizzes

Part I, Unit 1

1 natural / social
2 *d*
3 society
4 symbol
5 religion
6 *b*
7 *b*
8 *a*
9 Yes, but he would not survive as we know him.
10 the ideological, sociological, and attitudinal components
11 cultures
12 physical environment
13 (*a*) Universals
(*b*) Specialties
(*c*) Alternatives

Part I, Unit 2

1 *b*
2 *d*
3 e
4 c
5 *b*
6 c
7 *b*
8 *b*
9 *a*
10 c
11 *d*
12 *d*
13 c
14 *d*
15 *d*
16 *d*

Part I, Unit 3

1 *d*
2 c
3 *d*
4 *a*
5 e
6 *b*
7 *b*
8 disconfirm
9 lower and higher
10 c
11 directly and inversely
12 caste and class
13 more
14 *a*

Part II, Unit 1

1 *a*
2 *a*
3 *d*
4 *b*
5 *a*
6 *a*
7 *a*
8 c and *d*
9 c
10 *b*
11 *d*
12 c
13 *a*, *b*, c, and *d*

Part II, Unit 2

1 incentive manipulation; persuasion
2 nonlegal
3 imprisonment, fines, death
4 c
5 *a*
6 *b*
7 *d*
8 c
9 *a*
10 *b*
11 e
12 negative
13 white-collar
14 *d*
15 compliance

Part III, Unit 1

1 structure
2 conjugal union
3 family
4 orientation
5 procreation
6 maturation
7 twenty-five
8 controlling
9 subsystem
10 structure
11 incest taboo
12 spouse

13 protogenerational
14 neogenerational
15 monogamy
16 extended
17 nuclear

Part III, Unit 2

1 functions
2 roles
3 repertoire
4 (*a*) regeneration
(*b*) domicile
(*c*) socialization
(*d*) control
(*e*) social integration
5 children
adulthood
6 parent
7 home
8 continuous functions
9 mother
10 end state
11 achievement function
12 education
13 married
14 society

Part III, Unit 3

1 e
2 *b*
3 *b*
4 *d*
5 *b*
6 c
7 *b*
8 *a*
9 *d*
10 *a*

Part III, Unit 4

1 *b*
2 *a*
3 c
4 c
5 *d*
6 c
7 *a*
8 *d*
9 *a*

Part III, Unit 5

1 emotional and sets of beliefs
2 goals
3 symbolic
4 totemism
5 theistic
6 death, suffering, and frustration
7 moral
8 integrated
9 voluntary
10 polity (organization)
11 evangelism and religious education
12 denomination
13 profits / interest
14 democratic
15 religious
16 63
17 the church

Part IV, Unit 1

1 groups
2 cultural lag
3 middle-class
4 change
5 birthrates
6 functional
7 tranquilizing
8 learn
9 fear
10 phobia
11 schizophrenia
12 manic-depressive
13 brain
14 paranoid
15 psychotic disturbance and chronic brain syndrome
16 lower-lower
17 individual

Part IV, Unit 2

1 ethnic (racial) relations
2 exploratory, competitive, partial accommodation (any two)
3 *b*
4 *b*
5 segregation / discrimination
6 c
7 *d*
8 *b*
9 assimilation
10 assimilation
11 integrated
12 c

Appendix

1 *a*
2 *b*

3 *b*
4 *a*
5 *c*
6 *a*
7 *a, b, d*
8 *b*
9 *b*
10 *a*
11 *a*
12 *a, b, d*
13 *a*
14 *a*
15 *a*
16 *a*
17 *b*
18 *b*
19 *b*
20 *c*

NAME INDEX

SUBJECT INDEX